On the Job

On the Job

A History of American Work Uniforms

Heather Akou

BLOOMSBURY VISUAL ARTS
LONDON • NEW YORK • OXFORD • NEW DELHI • SYDNEY

BLOOMSBURY VISUAL ARTS
Bloomsbury Publishing Plc, 50 Bedford Square, London, WC1B 3DP, UK
Bloomsbury Publishing Inc, 1359 Broadway, New York, NY 10018, USA
Bloomsbury Publishing Ireland, 29 Earlsfort Terrace, Dublin 2, D02 AY28, Ireland

BLOOMSBURY, BLOOMSBURY VISUAL ARTS and the Diana logo are trademarks
of Bloomsbury Publishing Plc

First published in Great Britain 2024
Paperback edition published 2025

Cover design by Adriana Brioso
Cover image © GraphicaArtis/Getty Images

A catalogue record for this book is available from the British Library.

A catalog record for this book is available from the Library of Congress.

ISBN: HB: 978-1-3503-4938-4
PB: 978-1-3503-4942-1
ePDF: 978-1-3503-4939-1
eBook: 978-1-3503-4940-7

Typeset by RefineCatch Limited, Bungay, Suffolk

For product safety related questions contact productsafety@bloomsbury.com.

To find out more about our authors and books visit www.bloomsbury.com
and sign up for our newsletters.

To my father, Michael Wall

Contents

Preface

I grew up in a small, working-class town in northern Wisconsin. For most of my childhood, my father worked in a factory that made tires for cars, trucks, and tractors. Although he had earned a college degree in chemistry, he never used it. At the time, working in a factory was a good job for a married man with children. When I was a freshman in high school the factory closed, and all the workers, including my father, lost their jobs. That was not unusual in the 1980s and 1990s, when so many US manufacturers were moving their factories to Mexico or China.

As I considered what I wanted to do with my own life, I was keenly aware that my family and community regarded some jobs as "good" and some not so good. Working in a factory was good because it paid well. Working as a cashier at a fast-food restaurant was not good because it paid minimum wage. (Ironically, I had a birthday party at Burger King when I was five years old; my family ate there all the time.) Working as a teacher or an accountant—like my father's sisters—was good because the jobs were stable and required an education. The same was true for my father's brother, who held a highly skilled job as a computer programmer. None of them wore uniforms to work. My father—who had served in the US Army and learned Chinese so he could work as a translator and avoid being sent into combat in Vietnam—was highly skeptical of authority figures and uniforms. Some of that skepticism rubbed off on me.

The first time I wore a uniform for work was during college. I took a summer job at an amusement park that I had visited as a child, thinking it would be an easy and fun way to earn money. The basic uniform was simple: steel-blue shorts, a button-down shirt (white with blue and red pinstripes), and a gray plastic nametag. Footwear and clothing for cold weather were not provided. Sunglasses were allowed, but hats were not. Rain suits were available for purchase at the park's office, but only uniform rain gear was allowed (nothing from home). For almost two months I worked out in the park, ushering guests on and off the rides. I quit when there was a tornado warning one night and our supervisors evacuated the guests but not the workers; it was clearly not a place where the management cared about my health and safety.

Behind the offices there was a locker room where workers could change clothes since it was forbidden to wear your uniform outside of work. There were bins for dirty uniforms and a place where you could claim up to four sets of clean uniforms at a time. My goal was always to get the men's uniform instead of the women's uniform. I doubted that the guests noticed any differences, but the men's shorts were longer and the shirts did not have puffed sleeves. Being an unusually tall woman at nearly 6 ft (182 cm), the women's uniforms were just not big enough for me. I could squeeze into the largest size available, but the shorts felt inappropriately short. The shirts were so tight around my chest that they prevented me from crossing my arms in front of my body. The men's uniforms were more comfortable, but I wasn't supposed to have them since I was clearly a woman. I wish I had photographs of that uniform and the people I worked with. Digital cameras and smartphones did not exist back then.

After college, I held somewhat more creative jobs. I worked at an art gallery, building custom frames for displaying paintings, prints, and photographs. I worked as a weaver for an entrepreneur who designed custom rugs and upholstery fabrics. In graduate school, I worked as a student advisor, a research assistant, and later as an instructor. My employers had expectations for how I should dress, but none of them required uniforms.

Still, as an emerging historian of fashion and dress from a working-class background who lived in a working-class neighborhood in Saint Paul, Minnesota, I couldn't help but notice how the workers around me were dressing—the postal carriers, the clerks at the grocery store, the nurses coming home from their shifts, and the police writing parking tickets. It wasn't until much later that I realized how the visual landscape of my childhood and early adulthood was mostly absent from the academic literature on fashion. I thought I wasn't interested in American fashion, but in hindsight I just couldn't relate to it. I flipped through the magazines and watched the films and music videos, but I could never afford to look like those women. I wasn't even that interested in trying. I was too tall, too athletic, and eventually a bit too fat. I could go shopping, but a lot of clothes didn't fit. Most of the people around me were not into fashion either.

For the first decade of my career, my research focused on African (mostly Somali) dress and contemporary Islamic fashion. While I still publish in those areas from time to time, that background has allowed me to approach American Studies and the history of dress in the US in novel ways. I am not fazed when fashion collections (or even museums in general) do not have the kinds of objects I wish to study. I had to build my own collection of Islamic fashion; it was equally exciting to build my own collection of historic and contemporary work uniforms, which are pictured throughout this book. I hope this volume will inspire more scholarship about work uniforms and—just as importantly—more collecting in museums, so working-class histories can be better understood through material culture.

Acknowledgments

My publisher and I gratefully acknowledge all third-party copyright holders who granted permission to reproduce images in this book.

This project was generously supported by a fellowship from the Indiana University (IU) Presidential Arts and Humanities Program, Bloomington, Indiana, which gave me a course release and allowed me to invite Dr. Jane Tynan to campus for a wonderful series of discussions about how military combat uniforms compare to work uniforms. The university also allowed me to take a semester-long sabbatical during a critical time in the process of writing this book.

I have been fortunate to be surrounded by scholars who are interested in primary sources and material culture. In particular, I would like to thank my faculty colleagues and students in the MA in Curatorship program, Eric Sandweiss, Diane Reilly, Jason Jackson, Liliana Rocha, Emily Zarse, and others who have greatly enriched my thinking about primary source research. While I was director of the Sage Collection at IU—a position I held from 2017 to 2021—the librarians at IU Archives invited me to give a presentation about engaging with fashion objects for a workshop on using primary sources in the classroom. One of those workshops connected me with Marco Arnaudo, a professor of Italian Studies who asked me to show his students some historic military uniforms from the Sage Collection, one of the many inspirations that led to this project on work uniforms. My students in the fashion design program at IU (in courses on fashion theory and "autobiographies of dress and the body") were another influence as they graciously shared their personal experiences with school and work uniforms.

As I collected historic and contemporary examples of work uniforms and learned more about them through a wide variety of primary and secondary sources, I was fortunate to have friends and family members who let me share my enthusiasm and think out loud, especially Theresa Winge, Heather Bradshaw, Hayley Scruggs, Beth Samuelson, Deborah Reichmann, and my teenagers, Jamilah and Khaliq Akou, who never rolled their eyes and even said, "that's cool," on occasion. In some cases, I was able to communicate with people who sold me uniforms on eBay (not my only source for collecting, but one of them);

they were excited to help with my project and to know their vintage items were going to a good home.

During the process of writing, I presented segments of my work to colleagues at the Popular Culture Association, Costume Society of America, Dress and Body Association, and a pandemic-themed online conference hosted by Liuda Aliabieva, the editor of *Russian Fashion Theory*. Their interest in my research kept me going through the isolation of the pandemic. In June 2022, I gave an interview for the podcast, *Chasing Leviathan*, which renewed my thinking about "shame" as a component of prison uniforms and some work uniforms. My participation in the IU Presidential Arts and Humanities fellowship program also gave me valuable opportunities to think out loud about my work with distinguished peers and guests. I would particularly like to thank Edward Dallis-Comentale and Jason Kelly for their outstanding leadership.

Every effort has been made to trace copyright holders and to obtain their permission for the use of copyrighted material. However, if I have inadvertently overlooked any individual or organization, the publishers will be pleased, if notified of any omissions, to make the necessary arrangements at the first opportunity.

Abbreviations

AFL-CIO	American Federation of Labor and Congress of Industrial Organizations
BSCP	Brotherhood of Sleeping Car Porters
CBM	Church of Body Modification
CDC	Centers for Disease Control and Prevention
CFDA	Council of Fashion Designers of America
EEOC	Equal Employment Opportunity Commission
FLSA	Fair Labor Standards Act
GAO	Government Accountability Office
JBIUA	Journeyman Barbers International Union of America
NALC	National Association of Letter Carriers
NAUMD	Network Association of Uniform Manufacturers & Distributors
NPS	National Park Service
OSHA	Occupational Safety and Health Administration
PPE	Personal Protective Equipment
QSR	Quick Service Restaurant
USACE	US Army Corps of Engineers
WAAC	Women's Army Auxiliary Corps (US Army)
WAVES	Women Accepted for Volunteer Emergency Service (US Navy)

Note on Citations

In this book, I've included two major types of digital sources:

1. Digital publications, government documents, and some media with a date and format that is unlikely to change, e.g.:

   Derek Thompson, "Workism is Making Americans Miserable," The Atlantic, February 24, 2019, at: https://www.theatlantic.com/ideas/archive/2019/02/religion-workism-making-americans-miserable/583441/.
   Malca Chall and Joyce A. Henderson, "A Maid with the Pullman Company, 1926–1931," interview by Frances Mary Albrier, University of California, 1979, at: https://oac.cdlib.org/view?docId=hb696nb3ht;NAAN=13030&doc.view=frames&chunk.id=div00046&toc.depth=1&toc.id=div00046&brand=oac4.

2. Commercial media where there is no release date and the material could be reformatted or disappear without warning, e.g.:

   Angela Brown, "Why Uniforms Work: The Psychology of Uniforms," Ask a House Cleaner, February 21, 2021, https://askahousecleaner.com/why-uniforms-work/.

In the first category, the date listed in the citation is the date of publication or the date provided by the copyright holder. I have not provided an additional access date. In the second category, the date listed in the citation is the date I accessed the source.

As much as possible, I have given sources in the second category stable links by submitting them to the Wayback Machine at Archive.org. These URLs are listed in the Notes after the original source. For example, the following is a link to a stable version of "Why Uniforms Work":

   https://web.archive.org/web/20230804124833/https://askahousecleaner.com/why-uniforms-work/

Please note the "web.archive.org" designation at the beginning of the URL.

1

Introduction

Why Uniforms?

While the coronavirus has changed the way many workers do their job—whether in person or from home—it hasn't significantly reshaped the culture of work for a majority of employed adults.[1]

Pew Research Center, December 2020

For better or worse, work is one of the defining features of American culture. In 2019, a staff writer for *The Atlantic* described work as a kind of religion for many Americans, "based on the belief that work is not only necessary to economic production, but also the centerpiece of one's identity and life's purpose."[2] Even compared to other countries in the Global North—where farming is highly mechanized and most people work in other industries such as construction, education, and healthcare—Americans spend extraordinary amounts of their lives training for work, seeking work, performing work, and recovering from work. As a deeply rooted American citizen, I can say from first-hand experience that work organizes most American lives and colors many of our non-work decisions: where to live, when and where to eat, when to sleep and wake up, when and where to start a family, etc. Americans ask their young children, "What do you want to be when you grow up?" Teenagers are pushed hard to get serious—not about their relationships or pleasures in life—but about choosing and working towards a career.

American society is also known for emphasizing individualism.[3] Of course, there are variations on this, because the US is such a large and diverse country. There are some cultures (particularly among immigrants and the working class) that have a more communitarian attitude, whether by necessity or intentional choice.[4] However, the media—television, films, magazines, and social media—is oriented towards individualism because advertisers expect consumers to make decisions based on their individual needs and preferences. The fashion industry is deeply enmeshed in this individualistic approach to decision-making and consumption. To a certain extent, this is understandable. If I buy a pair of denim jeans, I am probably buying them to wear for myself, not for everyone in my family to wear collectively. I wear them for practical reasons (to stay warm and avoid breaking laws against public nudity), but my purchase also says something about my individual tastes and preferences. The cut reflects my physical fitness and body image. The brand (expressed through the style and/or logo) says something about my location and social position. Wearing jeans instead of a skirt sends a signal about my gender identity, my age, my activities for the day, and perhaps my religious beliefs. Jeans are not just a piece of clothing, but an entire package of visual and cultural symbolism.[5]

Some individuals develop a consistent "uniform" for themselves and even use that word to describe it. One famous example is Steve Jobs, who wore the same style of dress every day for years: a black turtleneck sweater that Issey Miyake designed specifically for him,[6] medium-blue Levi's jeans, and gray New Balance sneakers. Elizabeth Holmes—founder of the (now dissolved) medical technology corporation, Theranos, adopted a very similar uniform to invite comparisons with Steve Jobs and to "present an image of restrained, cool intelligence."[7] It is important to note that these were individual choices; nobody forced Jobs and Holmes to wear any particular clothing. Conformity and similarity alone do not define work uniforms.

Compared to fashion, work uniforms are notable for disrupting individual expression and bringing visibility to power dynamics. Steve Jobs wanted his executives to wear the same Issey Miyake sweater, but he abandoned the idea when they resisted.[8] Anybody who has ever worn a uniform for school or work or to serve in the military can easily imagine the reasons why Apple executives refused to go along with Jobs' plan. Uniforms are often unattractive and uncomfortable. Designed for "average" bodies, they fit poorly on people with any kind of difference like large muscles, broad shoulders, a thick waist, or unusually short legs. A true uniform is not optional. Wearing something else requires asking for permission, which may or may not be granted. This lack of authority is humiliating. Even if a required uniform fits, it might not be a color, texture, or style that is fashionable, warm enough (or cool enough), or suitable to the individual wearer's personality. For example, if I'm the kind of person who always wears dresses, I might resent—or refuse to take—a job that would force me to wear pants.

Over time, uniforms send a message to the wearer that "your needs and desires do not matter, the company comes first." People who make decisions about work uniforms receive an inverse message: "Your desires are important, and you are entitled to make decisions that impact other adults." These messages can become deeply ingrained when they are sustained over years, decades, or even generations. Both are dangerous when taken to extremes. Workers can enter a state of learned helplessness,[9] no longer believing that they deserve better or have the necessary authority to make their own decisions. Executives can become grossly over-confident about the appropriateness and finality of their decisions, punishing individuals for wanting other options. Uniforms make hierarchies visible, but they also serve to maintain them; it can become difficult for the managing class to imagine workers as peers when they don't look like peers.

Uniforms in the Body of Literature

Because uniforms play such a central role in these power dynamics, there are anecdotes about them scattered throughout the academic literature, particularly in labor history, cultural studies, sociology, and gender studies. They also appear in books written by journalists and workers. For example, *Hand to Mouth: Living in Bootstrap America* by Linda Tirado (about Tirado's adult life as a wife, mother, and worker in the food service industry), has notes about work uniforms and how a lack of dental insurance led to years of pain and embarrassment over her appearance.[10] It includes a forward by Barbara Ehrenreich, an investigative journalist who worked at a series of minimum-wage jobs as a waitress, housekeeper, nursing-home aide, and Walmart cashier in order to write, *Nickel and Dimed: On (Not) Getting by in America*.[11] It is strikingly rare, however, for this literature (whether academic or journalistic) to include any photographs of uniforms or detailed descriptions based on first-hand observations, which are essential for establishing how they look and feel (aesthetics) and how they change over time. For example, *Uniforms and Nonuniforms*—a groundbreaking book about the definition and purposes of uniforms, published by sociologist Nathan Joseph in 1986[12]—does not contain any images. *Uniforms: Why We Are What We Wear*, published by historian Paul Fussell in 2002,[13] offers a feast of personal, literary, and historical stories about uniforms, but the only images are line drawings on the cover. The materiality of uniforms is not the focus of the book.

The first academic book focusing on uniforms that did include images was *Uniforms Exposed: From Conformity to Transgression* published in 2005 by

Jennifer Craik,[14] a scholar in cultural studies who frequently writes about fashion. Notably, the longest case in the book's section on work uniforms is about flight attendants—a glamorous career with uniforms designed by some of the biggest names in fashion design, like Mary Quant and Georgio Armani.[15]

In most cases, however, the men and women who design work uniforms never become famous. In 1998, a journalist for *Forbes* interviewed Stan Herman, who was best known for his influential role as President of the Council of Fashion Designers of America (CFDA).[16] Musing over his career, he recalled how his first job as a freelance designer was to create new uniforms for car rental agents at Avis. "I thought, 'Uniforms? Am I crazy? Gas station attendants wear uniforms," [...] "Then I saw that Bill Blass and Valentino were doing airlines—that gave some real cachet to it."[17] Herman designed uniforms for well-known corporations including FedEx, McDonald's, TWA, JetBlue, and Sandals Resorts, but was virtually unknown to the public. Bill Blass—along with most other designers of uniforms for flight attendants such as Halston, Edith Head, Oleg Cassini, and Ralph Lauren[18]—were chosen to design the uniforms because they were already famous; however iconic or well conceived, their uniform designs did not *make* them famous. Changes in uniforms over time could be viewed in a very broad sense as fashion,[19] but fashion designers are rarely the driving force behind them.

Uniform: Clothing and Discipline in the Modern World, edited by Jane Tynan and Lisa Godson (2019) also includes photographs. It has two chapters about dress in the workplace—one about white-collar business suits in London and one about redesigned uniforms for flight attendants at Qantas[20] (Australia's flagship airline). To date, however, no academic book has focused entirely on work uniforms outside of the military[21] or nursing.[22] A few have explored school uniforms,[23] sports uniforms,[24] and religious dress[25] (a topic that overlaps with work and school uniforms). Distinguishing between these different categories of uniforms is important because the function(s) they serve can vary so dramatically. For example, military uniforms distinguish soldiers from non-soldiers and direct the use of lethal violence.[26] They also convey messages about hierarchy, nationalism, and the deeds of individual soldiers. The dress uniform shown in Figure 1.1, for instance, has a variety of patches and service ribbons that give knowledgeable viewers information about the wearer's service during the Second World War.

School uniforms are rarely hierarchical and say little about the individuals who wear them, but still reflect and shape the ideology of the institution. Athletic uniforms—which are typically worn with pride and are used to build "team

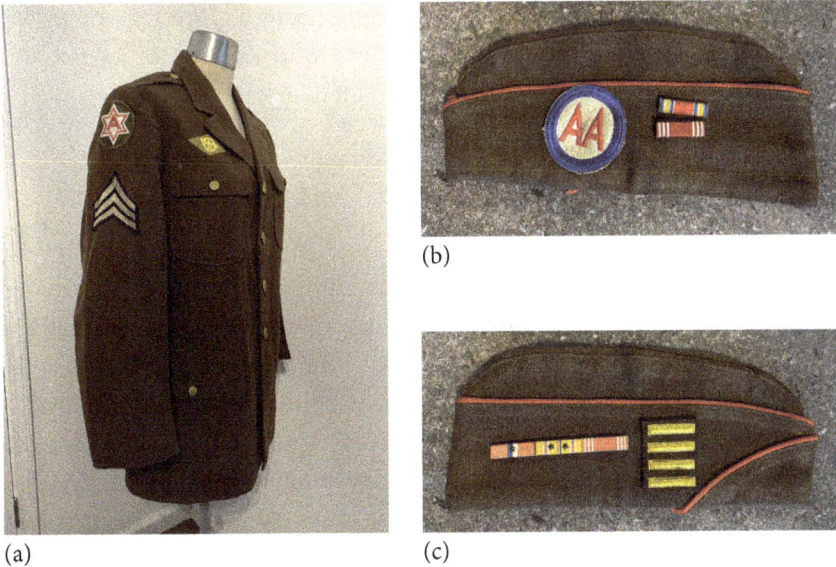

Figure 1.1(a–c) US Army dress uniform for a veteran of the Second World War, 1941–5, with insignia indicating his division (6th Infantry), rank (Sergeant), and honorable discharge status; (b) insignia on the garrison cap indicates his function (Anti-Aircraft), with ribbon bars for "Good Conduct" and "Allied Victory"; as well as (c) his place of service (the Philippines) and length of service (24 months). Author's research collection.

spirit"—are also highly functional. The helmets worn by elite cyclists make them more aerodynamic;[27] they look similar because the technology works, not to enforce social conformity. High-tech polyurethane swimsuits were banned from being worn as uniforms in international competitions for giving teams with more access to the technology an unfair advantage.[28] Athletes work extremely hard for places on elite teams, so being able to wear the uniform can be an exciting privilege, even though (like military or school uniforms) the individual has little input on the style.

Occupational uniforms serve a wide variety of purposes. In the United States, police uniforms are similar to military uniforms in both style and function.[29] Target, a major retailer with stores in all 50 states, refers to its employees as "team members" and uses uniform dress (khaki or denim bottoms, red shirts, and white name tags with the Target logo)[30] to build team unity, even though most jobs within the stores require few (or no) qualifications and are not very prestigious. In a country where there is no universal healthcare, little time for vacation, and no guaranteed access to paid leave, most working- and middle-class Americans spend tremendous amounts of time at work, feeling pressured to "give 110%" and to behave as if they were playing on a sports team or serving in a military unit. There is enormous pressure to make jobs that are not very meaningful or rewarding seem more important than they are.

Uniformity and the Limits of Fashion Theory

When looking at uniforms holistically, it can be difficult to draw a line between uniforms and costumes[31] or between other types of dress where people cultivate a similar appearance for aesthetic and/or cultural reasons. For instance, in the US it is common at large weddings to have multiple bridesmaids all wearing the same dress. Sociologist Nathan Joseph explored this topic at length in *Uniforms and Nonuniforms*, making a distinction between uniforms and uniformity.[32] A good example of occupational uniformity is the white-collar business suit, which typically includes long pants and a matching jacket, a plain-colored button-down shirt, a necktie, and polished leather shoes. Although corporate dress codes in the US are no longer as strict as they were before "business casual" became a trend,[33] many white-collar workers—especially men—still voluntarily wear this style of dress.[34] Small deviations, like wearing a brightly colored shirt or a pair of athletic shoes instead of leather dress shoes, can be acceptable in some cases (like a professional athlete giving a press conference). Depending on the wearer's social position and/or personality, long-term refusal/failure to follow the rules might be viewed negatively (as a sign of incivility or lacking seriousness), neutrally (as an individual quirk), or even positively (as a sign of creativity). There may or may not be any penalty for the white-collar worker.

For blue-collar workers[35] who deviate from written dress codes and uniforms, the penalty can be much more immediate and severe, ranging from warnings to termination of employment. In 2020, for example, two workers at a grocery store in Arkansas were repeatedly disciplined and then fired for refusing to wear a new style of uniform apron.[36] The case rose to public attention only because the Equal Employment Opportunity Commission (EEOC) filed a lawsuit on behalf of the workers alleging discrimination on the basis of religion, leading to a six-figure settlement. Since labor unions are generally weak in the US and most non-managerial jobs are held "at will," the threat of termination is a constant hum in the background. In an article outlining the history and meaning of at-will employment, legal scholar Clyde Summers observed how distinctive and common this legal principle is in the US compared to other developed countries:

The assumption is that the employee is only a supplier of labor who has no legal interest or stake in the enterprise other than the right to be paid for labor performed. The employer, as owner of the enterprise, is legally endowed with the sole right to determine all matters concerning the operation of the enterprise [in effect having a] divine right to rule the working lives of its subject employees.[37]

Employers can fire workers for any reason as long as there is no pattern of discrimination that can be proven in a court of law—an action that workers rarely pursue, since lawsuits cost time and money and can make other employers reluctant to hire them. This includes the right for adults (employers) to tell other adults (workers) how to dress—a level of coercive control that many people would consider abusive in personal relationships outside of work.[38]

This dynamic presents a real dilemma for theorizing about occupational uniforms as a type of fashion. They change over time, but the people who wear them have little choice in the matter. Most fashion theories do not apply in circumstances where individual choice is lacking. A cashier at McDonald's cannot simply choose to dress like the manager. A flight attendant cannot choose to dress like a pilot. Employers typically want to make different roles visually distinctive and reinforce hierarchies, not blur the lines between them. In this context, one of the most popular theories to explain how and why fashion changes known as "trickle down" theory (proposed by Thorstein Veblen[39] and further developed by Georg Simmel[40]) has little usefulness because there is no opportunity for employees (the lower class) to imitate their employers (the upper class). Without free choice, the alternative theories of "trickle-across" and "bubble-up"[41] also do not make much sense. Few managers choose to dress like their employees.[42]

Another common explanation for fashion change is "adoption theory" based on the work of sociologist Everett M. Rogers.[43] More complicated than trickle-down theory, it categorizes individuals based on how quickly or slowly they adopt specific new ideas, technologies, and/or styles and places them on a bell curve: innovators and early adopters, followed by the early and late majority (the masses), and finally laggards. Widely used by scholars in business and the social sciences, within fashion studies this body of research focuses heavily on the innovators and early adopters who are most likely to design and/or purchase new styles of clothing.[44] As summarized by fashion historian Marilyn DeLong, individuals adopt new fashions because they perceive them as having "some relative advantage" such as "a new fabric technology or simply being consistent with self-concept or what one's friends are wearing."[45] In a 1992 meta-analysis of fashion studies research informed by adoption theory, Dorothy Behling found consensus that early adopters are typically young, unmarried, "have a relatively high income and occupational level," and are (unsurprisingly) interested in fashion. They also "tend to be gregarious or social, conforming, and competitive."[46] The bedrock assumptions of this research are that individuals are consumers and make choices about what to wear, even if their choices are constrained by factors such as availability, affordability, trends in aesthetics, and social loyalties.[47]

While scholars in some disciplines such as public health and environmental studies have given more attention to the late majority and laggards—since their main concerns are why some people resist new ideas and how to encourage more widespread adoption—little is known about these categories with regards to fashion adoption. In 2017, Jane Workman and Seung-Hee Lee proposed using just four categories to study fashion consumers (change agents, early adopters, late adopters, and reluctant adopters), noting that, "One of the most glaring gaps in research is how little is known about later adopting consumer groups. About all that can be said is that they differ from earlier adopting groups."[48] Although they described research to address this gap as "important," to date they have focused only on consumers who buy past-season merchandise from discount stores—not people who resist consumerism[49] or who lack opportunities to make choices, such as workers in jobs that require uniforms.

Much recent theorizing about fashion seems almost impossible to connect to uniforms. In *Adorned in Dreams*, Elizabeth Wilson argued that "in modern western societies no clothes are outside fashion,"[50] yet she also defined fashion as "an aesthetic vehicle for experiments in taste and a political means of expression for dissidence, rebellion, and social reform."[51] While the most glamorous uniforms might resonate stylistically with freely chosen fashionable clothing, there is nothing rebellious about them; most businesses are not trying to disrupt the status quo.[52] In the second edition of *The Fashioned Body*, Joanne Entwistle made an effort to reconnect the individual with the social by seeking to understand the "*desire* to be 'in fashion' that promotes consumption"[53] (recognizing contradictory impulses towards choice and conformity). In his introduction to the revised edition of *Fashion Theory: A Reader* (a massive, 800-page volume) Malcolm Barnard mused about the challenges of trying to define fashion:

> Even at first glance, the apparently simple question 'What is fashion?' is not an easy one to answer. Fashion is either one of the crowning achievements of western civilisation or it is incontrovertible evidence of consumer culture's witless obsession with the trivial and the unreal. It is either creative to the point

of being an 'art', enabling individuals and cultures to express their inner feelings and personalities, or it is exploitive to the point of criminality, forcing people to work and spend more than is healthy for them or society.[54]

Ironically, while this quote mentions work, it assumes that individuals work to gain opportunities for fashion consumption. It does not consider how they dress while working.

Occupational uniforms are not "art" and do not give the people who wear them much freedom to express "inner feelings and personalities." Uniforms are clearly "dress," defined by Joanne Eicher as "any system of body modifications and supplements" that makes visible some dimensions of the wearer's identity such as "age, gender, occupation, religion, community, and ethnicity."[55] It is far less clear whether work uniforms could be viewed as a type of "fashion." The workers who wear them have little choice, but there is not a total absence of choice in the system. Uniforms are a lucrative business, yet consumption happens in ways that are often very different from the consumption of clothing designed for personal use.

Although it is not well known among fashion scholars today, one theory of fashion that has some resonance with occupational uniforms is the concept of "collective selection." In the 1930s, sociologist Herbert Blumer studied the women's fashion industry in Paris and developed the term collective selection to describe how designers and buyers (even when operating in total secrecy) tend to arrive at similar conclusions about the latest trends:[56]

> There were three lines of preoccupation from which [fashion designers] derived their ideas. One was to pour over old plates of former fashions and depictions of costumes of far-off peoples. A second was too brood and reflect over current and recent styles. The third, and most important was to develop an intimate familiarity with the most recent expressions of modernity as these were to be seen in such areas as the fine arts, recent literature, political debates and happenings, and discourse in the sophisticated world.[57]

Compared to fashion designers, uniform designers are inspired by different types of materials, ideas, and constraints (patents, new technologies, feedback from business owners, the offerings of competitors, etc.), but the concept of "collective selection" is still useful for understanding how standards for aesthetics are developed and how they change over time, even when the people who wear them lack choice. Blumer was careful to describe fashion as a phenomenon that occurs in "diverse areas of human group life"[58] and not something limited to clothing.

The term "anti-fashion" might seem like a better fit for uniforms—a concept describing circumstances where individuals and/or groups reject fashion systems. Ted Polhemus and Lynn Procter developed the term in the 1970s to describe styles of dress among urban subcultures (such as Punks) that deliberately reject capitalist consumption and mainstream fashion trends.[59] This concept has gained some traction among scholars who study religious dress and slow fashion.[60] However, anti-fashion as a whole is just as difficult to define as fashion. Philosopher Nickolas Pappas has described anti-fashion as existing "among other ways of dressing, including fashion, uniforms, and traditional costume. These all recognize one another, not to the point of anti-fashion's *passing* for a fashion but enough so that it is one thing you can do, among others, to present your body in public."[61] Work uniforms are somewhat intertwined with fashion— they involve consumption, change, and presentation of the human body—but they are not quite the same as fashion or even anti-fashion.

As explored in this book, some of the conditions of work uniforms that distinguish them from fashion are the following:

1. It typically takes years or even decades (not weeks or months) for significant changes in work uniforms to occur.
2. Changes in uniforms are driven by employment laws (external) and norms within specific industries (internal), not by the media (external) or needs for self-expression (internal). Durability and/or safety are primary concerns.
3. The people and companies that design work uniforms are usually unknown to the public and operate outside of the major fashion hubs (i.e., New York).
4. Businesses that design, manufacture and/or sell uniforms typically persist for much longer than fashion businesses, often for decades.
5. People who wear occupational uniforms have very little individual choice about their style of dress while they are on the job.
6. Most uniforms are mass-produced, so reproducibility is highly valued. In (increasingly rare) cases when they are not, they are designed to resemble uniforms worn elsewhere by the same type of worker. Artistry and unique presentations are not highly valued.

Some of these conditions may or may not apply to other types of uniforms, such as school and military uniforms. There may also be variations in other countries. Fashion historian Nicolas Cambridge has argued that Japanese fashion designers are much more interested in the sartorial traditions of workers and work uniforms than European fashion designers,[62] but are they known for designing actual work uniforms? Are any uniform designers household names in Japan? In this respect, it is unclear to me whether Japan is any different from the US (or Europe).

Standardization in the Late Nineteenth Century

In the early nineteenth century most Americans owned very little clothing, which was made either at home or by a professional tailor or dressmaker. That began to change with new technologies such as the tape measure,[63] sewing machine,[64] and paper sewing patterns,[65] which allowed for much more rapid production of clothing in a range of standardized sizes. This is now known as mass manufacturing or ready-to-wear,[66] which is how most (but not all) work uniforms are made in the twenty-first century.

The US Army began issuing standardized regulations for uniforms during the War of 1812,[67] however the Civil War (1861–5) helped kick mass manufacturing into high gear. In April 1861, Brooks Brothers—a manufacturer of both tailored and ready-to-wear garments in New York City—was issued a contract to produce 12,000 uniforms for the Union Army. The company's struggle with such a large order led to accusations that it was taking advantage of the situation (and taxpayer dollars) by deliberating producing "shoddy" goods:[68]

> UNFIT FOR USE—The uniforms furnished to the United Turner Rifles [20th New York Infantry Regiment] from the Quartermaster's Department, were found to be utterly unfit for the war. The buttons were too weak for service, and badly placed, the cloth of wretched quality and diverse colors, and the sewing poorly done. The cloaks only were retained, all the rest of the uniforms were promptly sent back to the contractors by order of the Colonel.[69]

Despite the negative press, Brooks Brothers (and many other companies that supplied ready-to-wear during the Civil War) thrived on the steady income from government contracts. This kind of history sets the business of uniforms apart from the business of fashion and helps to explain why many companies that design and manufacture uniforms have been able to stay in business for decades. Brooks Brothers is better known today for its business attire and for hiring fashion designer Zac Posen,[70] but supplied uniforms to the US military until the late 1940s.[71]

In 1898, a columnist for the *Boston Daily Globe* wrote an editorial marveling over how uniforms were becoming a common part of the city's aesthetic landscape:

[Now] the brave firemen rival the police in the distinctiveness of their uniform. Nobody can mistake them when they appear in their buttons and caps, any more than one can fail to distinguish a letter carrier. Perhaps you never stopped to think how many thousands of citizens are uniformed in these branches alone of public service—the fire, the police and the postal. [...]

In the hotels, for example, you know the bell boy by his uniform, and you discover the porter by his uniform, and you do not have to look twice for the bartender even if he has stepped in front of the bar for a moment, for he has his apron uniform, too. And then the chambermaids and the female servants about the house wear each their distinctive dress. And the chef in the kitchen is easily distinguished by his cap and other accessories, and the waiters generally have their coats and badges to designate them.[72]

Most of the uniforms described in the editorial were for men (and to a lesser extent children),[73] simply because they held most of the paying jobs outside of the home.

One of the first mass-produced uniforms for women was designed by Theresa Dell Angelica, a German dressmaker from Milwaukee. In 1884, Theresa married Cherubino Dell Angelica, an Italian immigrant who was working as a chef on railroad dining cars. Her design for a chef's jacket was so well received that the couple moved west from Chicago to St. Louis and began manufacturing clothing in their home under the name "Gents Furnishing."[74] After Cherubino's tragic death in a shipwreck in 1898, Theresa renamed the business "T.D. Angelica" and grew it into a major supplier of hospitality uniforms and linens.[75]

In the late 1880s, the couple was hired to supply uniforms for a chain of restaurants that Fred Harvey was establishing along the Atchison, Topeka, and Santa Fe railway line.[76] His goal was not just to serve food, but to provide train passengers with high-quality dining experiences, recruiting white, middle-class women (mostly from the Midwest) to serve as waitresses. These women became known as Harvey Girls and their uniforms were integral to the branding of the Harvey House restaurants:

The appearance of the Harvey Girls mirrored the appearance of the Harvey Houses: clean, businesslike, and efficient, with little or no personal variation from person to person or place to place. Their uniform, hair, and makeup codes were outlined in detail by Fred Harvey. Harvey must have been acutely aware of the opportunity for public criticism of single women away from home, and so he dressed the Harvey Girls in outfits befitting a nun: plain, starched, black-and-white skirts, bibs, and aprons; and high-collared shirts, with black shoes, black stockings, and hairnets. The uniform was first introduced in 1883 and changed little over the next fifty years. Skirts, even in the 1920s, when styles shortened, were precisely eight inches from the floor. Harvey Girls wore no jewelry and could not chew gum or wear any makeup.[77]

The comparison to nuns was somewhat apt based on the colors of the uniform and how the young waitresses were cloistered in dormitories during their off-work hours (Figure 1.2). However, the silhouette and construction of the uniform was not unfashionable in the late 1800s.

This uniform was immortalized in a musical comedy by MGM, *The Harvey Girls* (1946), starring Judy Garland as a virtuous young waitress and Angela Lansbury as a burlesque dancer in a nearby hotel. While Lansbury's costume was exaggerated for comedic effect with excessive ruffles and feathers, both outfits had the "Gibson Girl" silhouette: high collars, long sleeves with puffed shoulders and long skirts, with a slim waist to emphasize the wearer's chest.[78] Over the next few decades, the silhouette of fashionable women's dress changed dramatically (for reasons that had little to do with waitresses), but the Harvey Girl uniform—an icon of the Harvey House brand—barely changed. It simply disappeared when the last restaurant closed in 1955.

Property of National Screen Service Corp. Licensed for display only in connection with the exhibition of this picture at your theatre. Must be returned immediately thereafter.   "THE HARVEY GIRLS," An M-G-M Picture   Copyright 1945, Loew's Inc. Permission granted for newspaper and magazine reproduction. Made in U.S.A.   45/445

Figure 1.2 Angela Lansbury (left) and Judy Garland (center) in *The Harvey Girls* (MGM, 1946). Photograph by Metro-Goldwyn-Meyer via Getty Images.

Purpose and Outline of this Book

My aim in this book is to lay a foundation for the study of occupational uniforms and to explore a variety of reasons why they do and do not change. While they sometimes look like mainstream fashions, work uniforms are generally not designed, selected, or worn for the same reasons. My purpose for focusing on the US is not just because work uniforms are so integral to American material culture, but because uniforms can vary significantly from one country to another, even within the same occupation. In *Uniforms Exposed*, for example, Jennifer Craik remarked that butchers wear "distinctive navy and white striped aprons" but did not specify that this look is limited to the UK and some Commonwealth countries like Australia.[79] American butchers wear a different style of uniform: a long, white jacket that buttons down the front, similar to jackets worn by barbers, doctors, and dentists (Figure 1.3). When they wear aprons, they are usually long

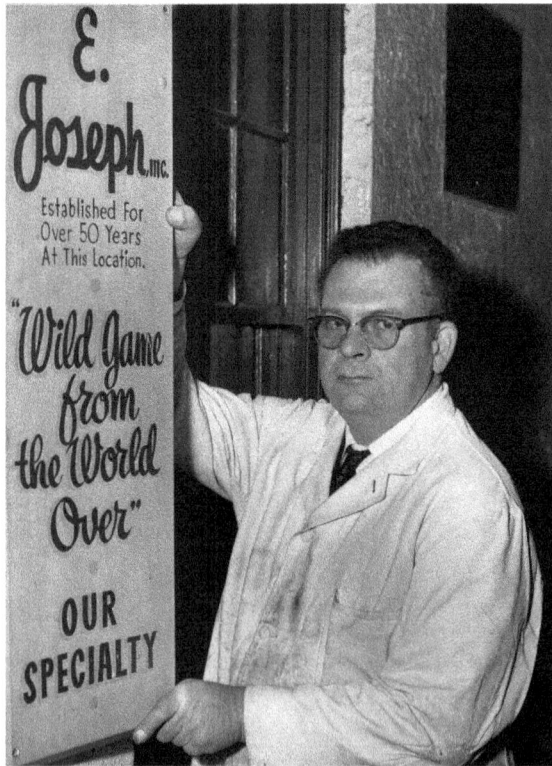

Figure 1.3 New York City butcher, Milton Joseph, Jr., in 1957. Photograph by Herman Hiller for the *World Telegram & Sun* (New York), Library of Congress, Prints and Photographs Division, LC-DIG-ppmsca-12740.

(extending from chest to knees) with thin straps at the neck and waist and solid-colored fabrics (most commonly green, blue, red, or brown). The color of the apron is not as important as the white color of the jacket.

I decided to avoid writing about military uniforms—partly because the subject is large and has already (somewhat) been studied—but also because serving in the military is more of a lifestyle than a job. Whether designed by the state or by groups of rebels,[80] combat uniforms are intended to erase individual identities as much as possible so soldiers can be remade in the image of the team—a team that is necessary for their survival.[81] For similar reasons, I decided not to include uniforms worn by religious authorities, like Catholic vestments. I also decided to leave uniforms that are largely hidden from the public (such as the disposable coveralls worn by meat packers) out of this book, but there is undoubtedly much that could be written. Blue jeans were invented to meet the needs of gold miners in California,[82] not to excite fashion consumers.

Instead, this book focuses on uniforms worn within "service industries." These jobs can be skilled or unskilled,[83] high-paying or low-paying, middle class or working class, physically demanding, and/or emotionally demanding,[84] but they all involve significant social interactions with customers. These interactions are mediated by the symbolic messages in uniforms, which impact the customer's perception of the business and by extension, the brand. *Encyclopaedia Britannica* defines the "service industry" as

> that part of the economy that creates services rather than tangible objects. Economists divide all economic activity into two broad categories, goods and services. Goods-producing industries are agriculture, mining, manufacturing, and construction; each of them creates some kind of tangible object. Service industries include everything else: banking, communications, wholesale and retail trade, all professional services such as engineering, computer software development, and medicine, nonprofit economic activity, all consumer services, and all government services, including defense and administration of justice.[85]

Some service-industry workers produce finished goods (such as baristas who turn coffee, milk, ice, and syrups into elaborate drinks), but manufacturing is not the focus of the job. Currently, more than 130 million workers in the US hold "service-providing" jobs.[86]

This book also focuses on the twentieth and early twenty-first century, when the mass manufacturing of clothing was already well established in the US. It includes case studies on uniforms for men and women (which is critical for understanding how uniforms have shaped norms for gender expression), historic and contemporary occupations, and both well-known and lesser-known job titles. I decided to write about meter maids rather than the police because the job title was short-lived, but also because the uniforms highlight struggles over the employment of women in a male-dominated industry.

While there are some people who still work as "doormen," they have some of the most archaic and elaborate work uniforms. Nurses, on the other hand, work in a much more common occupation; their practical uniforms have changed several times over the last century. Maids, gas station attendants, and fast-food workers have largely been left out of the academic literature on dress and fashion, but millions of people have worn these uniforms—reflecting and shaping the dynamics of race, gender, and social class in US society. It would take an encyclopedia series to cover the entire range of occupational uniforms, so by necessity this book is just a sample.

Although I considered several different ways to organize my data, I ultimately decided to split this book into chapters based on the types of employers. The advantage of this organization is that it highlights how different industries—and different workplaces—have internal logics of their own that determine how uniforms are selected and change over time. Bars do not work like hospitals and vice versa; they rarely compare themselves to one another.

The next chapter, "Taking Cues from Royalty: Maids, Porters, and Doormen," explores the intimate environments of upper-class households and home-like settings. Work uniforms worn in these settings originated from long-standing European conventions (such as livery and the master-servant relationship), making visual distinctions between employers and workers and highlighting the employer's wealth and good taste. These uniforms are not completely divorced from fashion but have been some of the slowest changing.

Chapter Three, "Working for Mom and Pop: Barbers, Attendants, and Waitresses," focuses on small, often family-run, businesses. With few employees, entrepreneurs could (and still can) produce their own uniforms, but many buy or rent them from uniform suppliers. While sales have shifted from catalogues to websites, uniform manufacturers have long been pressed to satisfy two competing needs: to stand out with pleasing designs, but also to produce standardized uniforms that fit the existing expectations of small business owners and their customers.

Chapter Four, "Contagion, Caring, and Qualifications: Uniforms in the Healthcare Industry," focuses on a very complex set of jobs including nurses and doctors, aides, candy stripers, pharmacists, dentists, veterinarians, and medical office staff. Medical uniforms have been tweaked and transformed many times over the last century as employers have responded to changes in fashion, advances in technology, and the needs of their highly trained workers, but have also influenced popular culture and occasionally fashion. Although some employers provide (and even launder) uniforms for medical workers, most retailers in the twenty-first century who still sell uniforms directly to the public specialize in the healthcare industry,[87] supplied by a growing array of small and large uniform manufacturers.

Chapter Five, "Government Work: Postal Carriers, Meter Maids, and Park Rangers," focuses on a very different set of jobs where workers use uniforms to represent a local, state, or national government. With rare exceptions (such as dress uniforms worn by some high-ranking administrators), their uniforms are typically quite plain and give workers little control over their appearance, although unionization is common among government workers and has given them some collective input into how their uniforms are designed, paid for, and worn. This chapter includes a discussion about the influence of military uniforms on mainstream fashion and on the uniforms of non-military government workers.

Chapter Six, "Corporate Branding: Receptionists, Bankers, and Baristas" focuses on large-scale private employers. In contrast to mom-and-pop businesses, the people who make decisions about uniforms for corporate employees do not work directly with them. Managers give feedback on uniforms—which are sometimes redesigned based on complaints or to make the jobs seem more appealing to potential applicants—however, uniforms are chosen primarily to fit the company's brand and to make the workers an extension of that brand. With examples from the hospitality, banking, and food service industries, this chapter illustrates how workers play a significant role in creating the "experience" for customers. It also delves into "fashion trends," which sometimes work in favor of corporations and sometimes do not.

Chapter Seven, "Adult Entertainment: Sexualized and Embodied Uniforms," ventures into jobs in theaters, casinos, sports bars, and "breastaurants" where uniforms put the bodies of men and women on display for visual consumption. This is a very American set of occupations (and uniforms) that have not translated well to other countries. Hooters' attempt to expand into the UK was soured by protestors.[88] Chippendales, established in 1979, developed an iconic uniform that flirts with the look of an upper-class servant: a white collar and cuffs with a black bowtie, but worn without a shirt. Importantly, workers' bodies in these industries are regulated just like clothing and should be viewed as part of the uniform.

In the last chapter, "Conclusion: Envisioning the Future," I consider legal challenges to uniforms and dress codes (particularly among government and corporate employees), the impact of political activism on work uniforms and dress codes, and how the COVID-19 pandemic of 2020–3 has created demands for protective equipment outside of the healthcare industry. Reflecting on the previous chapters, I also consider what conditions make uniforms attractive or acceptable to employees and what conditions limit or prevent the use of uniforms.

Taking Cues from Royalty

Maids, Porters, and Doormen

As I scoured archives, image databases, and auction websites for examples of work uniforms, I was often struck by this question: is it a uniform if the employer only has one employee? To what extent is similarity necessary to recognize an item of dress as a uniform? Published in 1929, a popular guide on *The Art of Cooking and Serving* opened with a chapter about "The Servantless House," observing that only the truly wealthy could afford more than one maid.[1]

This chapter focuses on people paid to work in the households and homelike settings (train cars, hotels, apartment buildings, etc.) of the wealthiest Americans. In doing so, it brings two important considerations to the fore. First, even if there is only one employee in a particular workplace, there may be others dressed the same way doing the same work in other places. It is impossible to know whether the outfit worn by the woman in Figure 2.1 was made by hand or mass manufactured, however the shape of the dress and the relatively dark color (designed to contrast with the white apron and cuffs) was the standard for domestic servants. Being able to afford a maid is a sign of household wealth, but only if visitors can easily identify the worker as a servant (and not, say, as a friend or member of the family).

Second, uniforms are about power and not just similarity. Deciding how another adult should dress without their input—and requiring that style as a condition of employment—is a dominating behavior by an employer. In the introduction to *Maid in the U.S.A.*, sociologist Mary Romero recalled visiting a colleague in El Paso, Texas who had hired a teenage girl from Mexico to work as a live-in servant:

> Although Juanita was the same age as my colleague's oldest daughter and but a few years older than his two sons, she was [...] assumed to have different wants and needs. I witnessed the following revealing exchange. Juanita was poor. She had not brought toiletries with her from Mexico. Since she had not yet been

paid, she had to depend on her employer for necessities. Yet instead of offering her a small advance in her pay so she could purchase the items herself and giving her a ride to the nearby supermarket to select her own toiletries, the employer handled Juanita's request for toothbrush, toothpaste, shampoo, soap, and the like in the following manner. In the presence of all the family and the house guest, he made a list of the things she needed. Much teasing and joking accompanied the encounter. The employer shopped for her and purchased only generic brand items, which were a far cry from the brand-name products that filled the bathroom of his sixteen-year-old daughter. Juanita looked at the toothpaste, shampoo, and soap with confusion; she may never have seen generic products before, but she obviously knew that a distinction had been made.[2]

Romero's colleague may have felt that he was being helpful or generous, but in the process of openly discussing Juanita's grooming habits and then buying products without her presence or input (and making it impossible for her to use other products, at least in the beginning) he was exercising power over her appearance.

Figure 2.1 "Negro Domestic Servant" in Atlanta, Georgia, 1939. Photograph by Marion Post Wolcott for the US Farm Security Administration, Library of Congress, Prints and Photographs Division, LC-USF34-051738-D.

Terms for this type of worker have changed over the last century. In the early 1900s, women who worked in upper-class households were called maids, nursemaids, cooks, and/or laundresses, depending on their specific duties. In the 1920s and 1930s, the preferred term became domestic servant or just "domestic." By the 1970s, these workers had become known as cleaners and housekeepers, terms that are also used in the hospitality industry.

Although the title of "porter" has largely disappeared, it originally referred to men who served middle- and upper-class travelers. Doormen are greatly reduced in number, but still exist in some exclusive hotels and apartment buildings, particularly in New York City. It is important to note that most of the workers in this chapter have been—and continue to be—immigrants and people of color, which has reinforced differences in power and social class in workplaces and in American society as a whole.

Uniforms for Maids

In 1901, *The Washington Post* published an editorial reputed to be from the Baroness von Rauch, sister-in-law of the late Prince Albert of Prussia (1809–1872).[3] The column gives upper-class women advice about hiring and managing young, working-class women as servants. While insisting that uniforms are unnecessary, it details a lengthy series of requirements for ensuring "cleanliness, comfort, nicety, and propriety":

> A girl's morning dress should be invariably of wash goods; for afternoon and evening wear, light wash dresses or black dresses of a smooth pattern, set off by a white collar and ditto cuffs [removable for laundering], are most appropriate. Some mistresses insist that their girls wear black afternoons and evenings, believing it is 'good form' and nothing else permissible, but it's really en regle only where dresses are furnished. Black being a very expensive color, a girl can't keep herself presentable unless she has several changes, hence it is customary in the best houses to either present the girls with the desired dresses or make them an allowance for the purpose.
>
> The dresses the girl wears in the house should have a close-fitting waist. Blouses or shirt waists are not to be tolerated, as they are apt to become loose and slip the girdle during work. Every self-respecting girl should have plenty of white aprons, as they give the appearance of cleanliness even, if for some reason or other, the servant isn't exactly tidy at a given moment. Strangers coming to a house are apt to judge its resources and social standing by the person who tends to the door. Still very few families can afford a girl for that work only.[4]

The column goes on to describe how household workers should be trained to serve meals, handle emergencies, and most importantly, reflect well on their employers during their interactions with guests, whether answering the door or pouring a drink. In *Theory of the Leisure Class*, Veblen described the dress of upper-class women as reflecting the wealth of their fathers and husbands (conspicuous consumption).[5] While the uniforms of maids were not designed to be showy or expensive, they were designed to be recognizable.

One of the wealthiest residents of Saint Paul, Minnesota, in the early 1900s was James J. Hill, chief executive of the Great Northern Railway (which Hill greatly expanded). At the time his mansion was completed in 1891, it was the largest and most expensive house in the state of Minnesota, with ample room for his large family plus numerous live-in servants.[6] As recorded in the 1900 US Census, eight of his nine children were still living at home (ranging in age from 15 to 30), but there were also nine servants living in the residence:[7]

Lizzie Shefchick, 28	Cook
Annette Anderson, 27	Housemaid
Katherana Hanson, 34	Housemaid
Amanda Swanson, 38	Waitress
Ida Chelburg, 30	Laundress
John Lennon, 24	Coachman
Frank Pliska, 29	Houseman
William Desmond, 22	Gardener
John Valene, 22	Coachman

Behind the main house, an additional coachman, William Gill, was living with his wife Helen in a separate building. None of the other servants were married; all of them were first- or second-generation immigrants from Europe (Scandinavia, Germany, Ireland, Scotland). A photograph of some of the servants (Figure 2.2) shows them wearing uniforms.

The two women standing in the back were wearing identical dark-colored dresses with white aprons, which covered the lower body and part of the chest. The colors and silhouette were very similar to the Harvey Girl uniforms; however, the Hill servants were also wearing "mobcaps," a style of head covering worn by the aristocracy and their maids in Europe in the eighteenth century.[8] One of the caps worn by Celia Tauer, second cook at the Hill house from 1909 to 1911, is now held by the Minnesota Historical Society (#2001.52.2). It is a flat circle of cloth with an embroidered edge and eyelets around the perimeter. To wear the

Figure 2.2 "Servants at the James J. Hill Residence, 240 Summit, St. Paul," *c.* 1910. Minnesota Historical Society, GT2.54 p9.

cap, the eyelets would have been threaded with a ribbon to cinch the cloth into a concave, hat-like shape. Dark ribbons are visible in the photograph.

The two women sitting in front were dressed nearly identically, but different from the women in the back. Was it their day off? Did they perform different work? Without written documentation about their positions, it is no longer possible to tell if the white dresses were also uniforms. Their similarity is the only thing to suggest that they were.

In 1896, a Jewish immigrant from Russia, Henry A. Dix,[9] opened a small factory in southern New Jersey to manufacture house dresses (also known in that area as wrappers), a simple style of clothing popular among working- and middle-class housewives. After his son, Mark, made a sale to Wanamaker's, a massive department store in Philadelphia, the company expanded rapidly.[10] In 1907, they leased a twelve-story building in New York City with 65,000 square feet of space[11] while maintaining three other factories in New Jersey.[12]

A biography written by Mark Dix gives fascinating insights into the company's history and early-twentieth-century innovations in the mass-manufacturing of clothing:

Ready-to-wear garments in those days were not trade-marked—except perhaps those of famous French houses—and it must have seemed presumptuous for an unknown manufacturer of Millville, New Jersey, to attach his own name to the cheapest of all garments. But I stood my ground [with Wanamaker's]. Pride and care and skill were being put into the Dix wrappers and our name would be there to identify them. Any store could cut the name out or leave it in, but no garment would be shipped without that little label, and none has been in the thirty-two years since then.[13]

Under the label "Dix-Make," the company also began producing uniforms for nurses, but it was difficult at first to sell them in stores. "The stores would not spend money to advertise, and whenever they did, they found it did not pay, for the response was very small. Either nurses had no time to read advertisements, or else they did not think it was possible to get the right sort of uniforms ready-to-wear."[14] Ultimately, Dix & Sons, Co. found more success by advertising in trade publications such as *Hospital World* and *RN: A Journal for Nurses*. When the company branched out into uniforms for maids, newspapers proved to be more useful for reaching their intended target: wealthy women with household servants.

In November 1922, Kaufman-Straus, a major department store in Louisville, Kentucky, took out a full-page advertisement in *The Courier-Journal* to suggest merchandise that wealthy shoppers might be interested in for Christmas presents, including furs, jewelry, fine china, and toys.[15] In the middle of the page, a section on "Maid's Uniforms, Aprons and Caps" advised,

> It is just as important to be careful of gifts of this character as in any other kind of Christmas remembrance. And so a specialized department on the Fourth Floor makes a feature of Uniforms, Aprons and Caps of the better kinds. The uniforms are from the famous house of Dix, which means that they are correctly fashioned and have all the little niceties of detail in their workmanship and finish.
>
> Dix-Make Maids' Uniforms in regulation style. Either of blue chambray, blue striped material, or black percale. Priced $4.00
>
> Dix-Make Maids' Uniforms of white linen. Splendidly designed and to be relied upon for lasting service. Priced $5.00

Employers would have viewed this kind of gift as bonus pay in lieu of cash. While it saved money for the workers (who would not have to buy their own uniforms), it also reduced self-expression through their choice of clothing.

Dix & Sons limited their palette of colors to white, indigo, gray, and black to ensure that their uniforms would be colorfast in the laundry.[16] By the 1930s, their competitors were clearly using a range of chemical dyes. In *The Washington Post*, Margaret Wallace counseled,

> The housewife who wishes to have her maid present a good appearance at any hour of the day will provide work uniforms for the morning and neat black ones with white aprons and caps for later in the day. Morning uniforms of green or blue or tan wash material can be had at very reasonable rates and caps and aprons also cost very little.[17]

In Los Angeles, another columnist suggested that upper-class households should stop dressing their maids "like a French comedy" and experiment with new colors and materials:

> A fundamental is that the parlor maid, the housemaid and the waitress are all dressed alike. The color depends upon the decorations of the home and the taste of its mistress. Emily Post suggests harmonizing the uniforms with the color scheme of the dining room. For instance, in a room done in blues and yellows the maids wore blue taffeta with aprons, collars and cuffs of plain, butter-colored organdie. Think of the attractive costumes possible to evolve when this idea is carried out![18]

In a wonderful example of conspicuous consumption (displaying wealth through a proxy, albeit a maid instead of a wife), an advertisement on the same page told potential customers: "Your Own Good Taste is Reflected in Your MAID'S UNIFORMS."

As the construction and silhouette of women's fashion changed radically in the 1920s, maids' uniforms did too. In 1922, *The Philadelphia Inquirer* ran a feature about unemployed actresses and chorus girls who hoped to find work as domestic servants. While speculating that employers were concerned about their skills, lack of dedication to the job, and how they might seduce husbands, the article featured a photograph of a dancer for the Ziegfeld Follies, Blanche Mehaffey (Figure 2.3), wearing the latest fashion in maids' uniforms.[19]

Compared to uniforms worn by maids at the turn of the century (Figure 2.2), the sleeves and hemline are much shorter, the neckline is lower, the apron is heavily embellished, and it has wide straps instead of a bib that covers the chest. The mobcap has been replaced with a frilly rectangle of cloth tied to the wearer's forehead with a wide piece of ribbon, more like a head band than a cap. A decade later, Emily Post advised that, "Head trimmings [are] never seen in smart houses any more. But when a woman who is otherwise valuable does her hair badly, something has to be chosen to make her head look small and trim."[20] The maid could not be allowed to look wild or unmanaged in her choice of hairstyle.

Figure 2.3 Feature on the feasibility of hiring unemployed actresses and chorus girls as household servants, 1922. *The Philadelphia Enquirer*, 1.

As immigration rates were curtailed in the early 1900s and white, working-class women gained new opportunities to work outside of the home—as factory workers, "beauty workers," secretaries, telephone operators, and shop girls in retail stores—there was also a shift in the demographics of household servants, coinciding with the Great Migration of Blacks from the South to northern cities like Chicago, Cleveland, Baltimore, and Philadelphia. Professor of American Studies and Women's Studies, Phyllis Palmer, has observed that this transition was accompanied by changes in how domestic servants were hired and compensated:

> Throughout this period, workers sought to transform domestic service from a norm of full-time resident service to a job with limited hours and clearly defined tasks, which was most easily gained through day work. The spectrum of domestic work included full-time living out, part-time and casual hire. All these forms coexisted during the twenty-five years from 1920 to 1945.[21]

Since black women had few other opportunities for paid employment, it was not uncommon for them to spend years or even decades working as domestic servants. Young, unmarried women who accepted live-in positions to save money often found them lonely and culturally isolating since they could not participate in the communities where their white employers lived.[22] Servants who were older and married also needed time to spend with their families and to manage their own households.[23]

Nationwide, there were waves of agitation for better working conditions and fair pay. In 1933, Loren Miller, a journalist for the black-owned newspaper, *California Eagle*, argued that if "club women" (members of social and philanthropic organizations) would expand their attention to the working conditions of domestic servants, real progress might be made:

> I see by the papers that "horrified" club women are registering considerable indignation over the exploitation of women and children in city and national sweat shops. These excited ladies have just learned that it is profitable and popular to force these "wage" earners to work for 12 to 16 hours per day for the munificent sums ranging from one to four dollars a week.
>
> Intelligent men and women have known these things for years and the bridge playing club ladies might have learned them long ago had they taken the trouble to read the hated radical papers which have been busy shouting these truths for decades. Or these same club ladies may take to the radical press and learn that the miserable exploitation of white women and children is as nothing compared to the merciless grinding down of Negro women and children in other sweat shops or on the peon farms of the south. And if it is too much (I suspect that it is) to expect our Los Angeles club ladies to look at the national scene I suggest that they take up the matter of the conditions, hours and wages of Los Angeles domestic servants many of whom are Negroes.[24]

When the Fair Standards Labor Act (FLSA) was passed in 1938—setting a nationwide standard for minimum wages and maximum hours—domestic servants were deliberately excluded from the law; they would not be included until 1974.[25]

In the 1940s, uniforms for maids were still being updated to keep pace with fashion. For example, an illustration in *The Wilkes-Barre Record* (Figure 2.4), can be recognized as a uniform only because of the text and the brand name (Dix).[26] The model is not wearing a cap or apron; the knee-length hemline, exaggerated shoulders, and rolled hairstyle were fashionable during that period. What is also striking is that the model is clearly a white woman—typical for employers of maids in Pennsylvania in 1941, but not for the maids themselves.

Figure 2.4 Advertisement for maids' uniforms sold by Isaac Long department store, June 9, 1941. *The Wilkes-Barre Record* (Wilkes-Barre, Pennsylvania), 10.

Although upper-class households were still hiring domestic servants in the 1950s, 1960s, and 1970s, the Civil Rights movement and second-wave feminist movement made the practice less socially acceptable. Department stores gradually stopped running ads for uniforms. In popular media, the most common look for a maid became a stereotype: a gray or black dress with a knee-length hemline and short sleeves, a white apron, and a white collar and cuffs. Examples include Rosie the Robot in the futuristic cartoon, *The Jetsons* (1962–3); Hazel Burke, played by Shirley Booth on *Hazel* (1961–6); Rosario Salazar, played by Shelley Morrison on *Will & Grace* (1998–2006); Marisa Ventura, played by Jennifer Lopez on *Maid in Manhattan* (2002); and Dorota Kishlovsky, played by Zuzanna Szadkowski on *Gossip Girl* (2007–12).

The Jeffersons (1975–85), a pioneering comedy featuring a wealthy black couple with a black maid (Florence Johnston, played by Marla Gibbs), living in a high-rise apartment on the Upper East Side of New York City, was more egalitarian.[27] In an episode titled "Florence's Union," a black maid named Millie, comes to the Jefferson's door wearing a black dress with a white apron, collar, and mobcap in order to talk with Florence, who is trying to convince her to join a union that the maids in the building are forming. At first, they try to keep it a secret from Mrs. Jefferson, who is supportive when they finally reveal the reason for Millie's visit:

> **Mrs. Jefferson**   Well, I used to be a maid myself, and believe me, Millie, I know exactly where you're at.
>
> **Millie**   So do I, but how do I get a ticket out of here?
>
> **Florence**   Well, joining the union would be a good start.
>
> **Mrs. Jefferson**   Boy did I have a mean boss. And you know what made me the maddest? Every time I'd start to talk, she'd say, "You people never know when to keep your mouths shut."
>
> **Florence**   Well, why didn't you quit?
>
> **Mrs. Jefferson**   Couldn't afford to. But I did call her names under my breath and made faces behind her back.

When Mr. Jefferson comes home and realizes that Millie works for the (white) owner of the building, he eyes her up and down and says, "I should have known … you got a lot more class than the rest of the maids in the building."

Florence rarely wore any kind of recognizable uniform. One of her outfits, now held by the Smithsonian National Museum of African American History and Culture, is a wrapped house dress made of brown, cotton gingham (Figure 2.5), designed by Betsey Potter specifically for the show. It does not have a manufacturing label.

In the 1980s, new corporations like Merry Maids, ServiceMaster, and Cleaning Authority (along with many smaller businesses run by entrepreneurs)

Figure 2.5 Typical house dress worn by actress Marla Gibbs in her role as Florence Johnston on *The Jeffersons*, 1975–1978. Collection of the Smithsonian National Museum of African American History and Culture, #2013.145.3ab.

began hiring people to work as house cleaners and then sending them out to clients—serving as intermediaries between employers and workers. The most common styles of corporate uniforms have become T-shirts and polo shirts, a subject that I return to in Chapter 6 on corporate work uniforms.

Theoretically, small businesses could choose any practical style of dress for cleaning, but often choose items that resemble corporate uniforms to meet the expectations of clients. Angela Brown, a long-time house cleaner who now runs a training business called Savvy Cleaner,[28] offers advice about uniforms in her podcast, "Ask a House Cleaner":

> Every single time you show up [at a client's house], if you look consistent, your clients think, "Oh, I'm getting the same quality job," and then they recommend that to their friends and their neighbors. But if you show up every time looking different, unconsciously the customer says, "Wait a second... something's different today. I don't know what it is." And they start looking at your work. And you get lots of callbacks because the customer can't figure out what it is, but something's different today.[29]

"Callbacks" (returning to fix real or perceived problems with the work) are best avoided since they do not generate new income. Uniforms also make workers look interchangeable:

> Let's say you have a house cleaner that's a main house cleaner for every house; if that person calls out sick or they have a family emergency, and you have to send someone else in... guess what? You're sending in someone that *looks just like them*. They're wearing the same uniform; they got their hair pulled back in the same bun [...] the customer expects they have the same quality of service.

On the YouTube version of the podcast, a viewer with her own cleaning business responded in the comments: "I am a team of one but because I have a uniform most clients always assume I have more cleaners working for me."[30]

Uniforms for Porters

In the United States in the early 1900s, trains were widely used for long-distance travel. Upper-class passengers paid to ride in Pullman cars, where they could eat fine cuisine, have drinks with their fellow passengers, and sleep in private quarters. Instead of getting off the train at major cities and switching to new lines, they would remain on board as the Pullman cars were decoupled and reattached to different trains.

After the Civil War, the inventor of the Pullman system, George Pullman, staffed the cars by hiring black men who had been freed from slavery to work as porters. His decision to create a racial caste system persisted after his death in 1897: only black men could work as porters, and they could never work (officially) as conductors:[31]

> [George Pullman] hired more Negroes than any businessman in America, giving them a monopoly on the profession of Pullman porter and a chance to enter the cherished middle class. He did it not out of sentimentality, of which he had none, but because it made business sense. They came cheap, and men used to slave labor could be compelled to do whatever work they were asked, for as many hours as told.[32]

At its height in 1925, the company employed 12,000 porters and 28,000 conductors. On some of the longest and most upscale lines, the company also hired a small number of black women to work as maids; their main tasks were to give manicures, to help female passengers with the washrooms, and to provide childcare as needed.[33]

The job of the porters was very grueling. They greeted passengers and helped them on and off the train, carried their luggage, mopped the floors, changed the linens on the beds, shined the passengers' shoes while they were sleeping, alerted them to stops, served meals, and attended to any other needs they might have during their journey. Begrudgingly, they were allowed four hours of sleep per shift. Under threat of being fired, they could only use blue blankets and blue mattresses that were designated for porters, which were placed in the most marginal locations on the train such as smoking rooms and washrooms.[34]

Even so, it was one of the few types of paid employment that black men could get, and one of the most prestigious since it allowed them to see what the country was like beyond their local communities. When porters were hired, they were required to buy their own uniforms from the Marshall Field's department store in Chicago,[35] which was owned by one of the major shareholders of the Pullman Company. In 1915, the cost was $17.75 for a white uniform (worn in the summer and during meal service) and $18.75 for a dark blue uniform (worn in the winter and for other duties such as cleaning).[36] At the time, a porter's salary was only eight dollars per week, so recruiters were forced to consider whether applicants had enough savings to accept the job. Despite the expense, many porters were proud to wear their uniforms (Figure 2.6):

> To whites, the porter represented service and luxury; to blacks, he represented status and mobility, both physical and social. One porter [phrased] it in this way:

"I used to wave at the white-suited porters when the train ran through, and I left South Carolina to get one of those jobs. Neckties were mandatory, and you have to understand, blacks were *elated* to get out of denims." Denims were field clothes, work clothes that reminded the men of slavery; the clean, crisp uniforms of the Pullman porters were seen as genuine status symbols, a major advance.[37]

The uniforms were undoubtedly sold in a narrow range of sizes, because the criteria for hiring porters were very specific: "porters should be of a certain age (not younger than twenty-five, nor older than forty), height (tall enough to reach the upper berths, which meant at least five-foot-seven, but under six-foot-one so they could clear the car door), and weight (slim enough to slip through the narrow corridors)."[38] The style was simple: a single-breasted jacket with a high collar and four metal buttons stamped with PULLMAN,[39] a matching vest, a

Figure 2.6 Pullman porter in a blue uniform and coat, 1943. Photograph by Jack Delano for the US Farm Security Administration, Library of Congress Prints & Photographs Division, LC-DIG-fsa-8d24965.

white button-down shirt, a necktie, coordinating pants, leather shoes, and a regulation cap. During hot weather and for especially dirty chores, the porters were allowed to remove their coats and jackets, exposing the vest, necktie, and button-down shirt.

Instructions for uniforms were included in the company's policy manual, *Car Service Rules of the Operating Department of Pullman's Palace Car Company*:

> **102. Uniform.**—The full uniform must be constantly worn while on duty, and until passengers have left the car, and no deviation from the prescribed pattern or material will be permitted. *It will not be worn off duty*, and it must be kept in a neat and tidy condition, paying strict attention to linen and neckwear.
> (2.) *Coats.*—The coat should be worn buttoned, and the outside breast pocket will be used for handkerchief only.
> (3.) *Jackets.*—Porters and waiters must wear their jackets buttoned, and while attending to buffet or janitor duties. In buffet cars the jacket worn in handling berths must not be worn while serving meals, nor will torn or dirty jackets be worn at any time.
> (4.) *Caps* will be laid aside whenever jackets are worn.
> (5.) *Slippers* may be worn only after passengers have retired.[40]

As the policy demanded, a photograph of a porter serving coffee or tea to passengers (Figure 2.7) shows him wearing a white jacket without a cap.

In 1917, an article in *The Day Book*, a free newspaper for workers in Chicago, described the cap as costing an additional $1.50.[41] One example, now held by the Smithsonian (2012.46.75.2) was manufactured by J. Apfelbaum and Co. in Chicago. All of the caps were the same color and shape, regardless of the season. They were made of black cloth and leather, with a flat top, short visor, and a length of metallic cord strung between two metal buttons.

An etiquette columnist, Amy Vanderbilt—who was a distant cousin of railroad magnate Cornelius Vanderbilt—quoted a letter that she had received from an "executive of the Chicago, Rock Island and Pacific Railroad Co." explaining how readers could tell the difference between ordinary train conductors and Pullman train conductors:

> It is easy to understand how anyone not knowing railroad operations could be confused when they see two gentlemen in blue and brass going through a train together. . . The way you distinguish one conductor from the other is in the badge across the front of the uniform cap. One says 'Pullman Conductor' and the other usually has the insignia of the railroad, in color, and the word "Conductor."[42]

Figure 2.7 Pullman porter working in a dining car in a white uniform, 1935. Photograph by Frank Willming for Pullman Palace Car Co., Pullman Palace Car Company Collection, Archives Center, National Museum of American History, Smithsonian Institution, AC0181-0000002.

Conductors were also distinguished from porters by the color of the cord on their caps: gold-colored for conductors and silver-colored for porters. Since porters could not advance in the ranks, their uniforms had no other symbols of hierarchy such as stripes or epaulets.

The shape of the cap was fairly standard across railroad companies, distinguishing the porters and conductors from other uniformed professionals

+⚹ *IF IT'S A CAP WE MAKE IT* ✥⚹+

Style No. 100
Railway Cap
Silk band and sides. Black leather top with two rows
of ventilated black braid.

Figure 2.8 Generic "railway cap" sold by Los Angeles Cap Company, *c.* early 1900s. *Uniform Caps*, 11, undated sales brochure in author's research collection.

who worked around the train stations such as the police, chauffeurs, bell boys, and delivery men. The Los Angeles Cap Company, for example, offered a "railway cap" that could be customized for different clients (Figure 2.8) with various trims, badges, and embroidery.

The Pullman uniform changed very little over time. Uniforms worn by porters at the turn of the twentieth century[43] were identical to uniforms in the 1940s (Figure 2.6). Although they were serving upper-class passengers—doing work that was very similar to household servants—there was no need for their uniforms to reflect the tastes and whims of the passengers; they were part of the Pullman brand identity. In 1930, a columnist for the *California Eagle*, a black-owned newspaper in Los Angeles, complained about how the company was reprimanding—and sometimes refusing to pay—any porter who arrived at the downtown office to collect his paycheck in a uniform that was not perfect:

> when he arrives from a hard trip, tired and anxious to get home, [he must] discard his uniform and pack it in his handbag, then put it back on when he arrives at the Seventh St. office. In packing it in his bag it naturally becomes

wrinkled which fact causes the porter to be reprimanded by Asst. Supt. Taylor who generally supervises the inspections.

If by chance Mr. Taylor happens to be out of town, and the inspection is in charge of porter Instructor Eldridge, a few wrinkles might be overlooked, as he was a porter for twenty years and knows what conditions they must work under, and how they have to cram their uniforms in a handbag, but Mr. Taylor expects them to be without a wrinkle regardless of conditions.[44]

The porters were forced to either take their uniforms home and press them or have them pressed (which took extra time) or take them to tailors and have them pressed for 50 to 75 cents[45] (added expense on a meager paycheck). In contrast, conductors had their uniforms inspected at the train station and were given lockers to keep them neatly stored.

Organizing into unions as the Brotherhood of Sleeping Car Porters (BSCP)[46] and the National Brotherhood of Dining Car Employees,[47] porters fought hard for better pay and better working conditions, actions now viewed as important precursors to the Civil Rights movement. In 1942, porters from Detroit sought a resolution to confront Pullman's management about "the question of monthly uniform inspection on pay days."[48] However, it was not until 1951, that the Pullman Company officially recognized the BSCP as a union, authorized to represent porters, maids, attendants, and bus boys.[49]

By the 1940s, the number of train passengers was declining throughout the United States, due to the rapid expansion of automobile travel, competition from buses (such as Greyhound, which was founded in Hibbing, Minnesota in 1914), and the increasing safety and comfort of commercial flights.[50] On January 1, 1969, the Pullman Company went out of business.[51]

At large, metropolitan train stations—such Grand Central Station in New York City and Union Depot in St. Paul, Minnesota—the title of "porter" persisted for some time as a reference to men who helped arriving and departing passengers with their luggage. They wore the same clothing as train porters but were better known as "red caps" because of the distinctive color of their head coverings. This is the origin of the term "skycap," referring to people who transport luggage for passengers at airports.[52]

Uniforms for Doormen

In the 1940s and 1950s, when apartment buildings in New York advertised for doormen, the term "porter" was sometimes included. For example, on May 19,

1943, the *Brooklyn Daily Eagle* published nine help-wanted advertisements for
doormen:

> DOORMAN, days; porter, white; 6-story elevator; reliable; room for porter;
> $80 month; advancement. Inquire Supt., 150 Crown St., Apt, A-1.

> DOORMAN, SWITCHBOARD OPERATOR—PERMANENT;
> CONGENIAL SURROUNDINGS. COLOR, AGE NO BAR. 769 ST.
> MARK'S AVE.

> DOORMAN-PORTER $80 per month, plus room and shower. See
> Superintendent, 745 Lincoln Place, near Nostrand Ave., Brooklyn.

> DOORMAN-PORTER (2), middle-age, new apartment house, good pay,
> room. MAnsfield 6-6763 or superintendent, 601 E. 19th St.

> DOORMAN-PORTER – $75 PER MONTH, PLUS ROOM. SEE
> SUPERINTENDENT, 10 MAPLE ST., BROOKLYN.

> DOORMAN-PORTER, $90. APPLY SUPERINTENDENT 120 OCEAN
> PARKWAY.

> DOORMAN FOR APARTMENT HOUSE WANTED. BROOKLYN,
> PHONE BUCKMINSTER. 7-1114.

> DOORMAN – WHITE, SOBER; $85 MONTH AND ROOM. APPLY
> AFTER 5 P.M., SUPERINTENDENT, 275 LINDEN BLVD.[53]

Like maids, some (but not all) doormen lived in the buildings they served.
Like porters, their duties typically included opening the door, greeting residents,
passing vital information along, and carrying packages upstairs. Living in an
expensive apartment building and paying extra for the building to employ a
doorman was—and continues to be—a symbol of upper-class luxury.

While the term "doorman" is now sometimes used in other settings (for
example, in nightclubs, doorman is a synonym for "bouncer") this chapter refers
specifically to doormen employed by upper-class apartment buildings and
luxury hotels—a job title that originated with aristocratic households in Europe.[54]
To understand why doormen have had some of the most archaic and heavily
ornamented occupational uniforms in the United States, it is necessary to delve
into the concept of "livery."

The *Oxford English Dictionary* gives many examples of how livery has been
used as a noun, but one cluster of definitions is specifically about clothing:

11a. The distinctive dress worn by the liverymen of a Guild or City of London livery company; (also) an item of this dress.

11b. More generally: the distinctive dress or uniform provided for and worn by an official, retainer, or employee (in early use esp. a single item such as a collar, hood, or gown, but more generally a suit of clothes or uniform) [...] typically distinguished by colour and design; the dress, uniform or insignia (e.g. *king's livery, riding livery*), by which a family, etc., may be identified.[55]

A book by historian Maria Hayward, *Rich Apparel: Clothing and the Law in Henry VIII's England*, gives examples of how livery was used by English nobility in the fifteenth and sixteenth century. Since the Crown did not have a standing army at that time, "the king or his commanders would look to their own households to provide the initial core of their force and they would usually issue them with some form of livery to identify them. This could either be of the king's livery colours (green and white) or a white coat with a red cross."[56] Although it was not mass-produced, this clothing was clearly a type of uniform with the same colors and insignia worn by different members of the same household. In times of peace, it distinguished the men as royal or noble servants; in times of war, it marked them as soldiers. With this dual purpose, the clothing acquired a symbolism of intimidation and political power. Queen Elizabeth I and King James II both limited the numbers of liveried servants that nobles could bring to court in order to minimize the visual threat to their own power.[57]

By the eighteenth century, contracts for male household servants typically included one set of livery per year.[58] Only men could work as doormen, since one of the responsibilities was to secure the household from external threats. Female servants, in contrast, were sometimes given secondhand clothing as gifts, but were typically expected to make or buy inexpensive versions of fashionable dress.[59] They were not issued livery because their main tasks were sewing, washing, cooking, and serving meals, not to look intimidating or to use force.

In 1871, The Gilsey—a fashionable hotel for upper-class travelers in New York City—adopted uniforms for its staff. "The Gilsey's urbane manager, Colonel James H. Breslin, created a mild furor when he decided to put his staff in livery. Newspapers noted that the 'boys' didn't much care for the gold braid and buttons. But, within the year, practically all fashionable New York hotels had liveried attendants."[60] Photographs of doormen from the early twentieth century, now available at the Library of Congress, were taken at the entrances to upscale hotels in Washington, DC: the Willard,[61] the Mayflower,[62] the Wardman,[63] the Lafayette,[64] the Prohatan,[65] and the Shovehan. (In 2021, only the Willard and Mayflower were still operating.)

Figure 2.9 shows a doorman at the Shovehan taking his hat off in deference to a guest who is arriving by car. His uniform consists of a long jacket with a row of metal buttons and metallic stripes on the sleeves (similar to military uniforms), matching pants, white gloves, and a cap with metallic trim. Like a police cap, it has a small visor and tapers outward, so the top of the hat is slightly wider than the wearer's head.

In 1938, one issue of *The New Yorker* (Figure 2.10) featured an illustration of a doorman fastidiously handing a single leaf to a street sweeper. While the size of his jacket is exaggerated for comedic effect, the shape of the hat and the other components of the uniform (the cap, white gloves, and stripes on the sleeves) were accurate for doormen in the early twentieth century.

During his extensive study of residential doormen in New York City, sociologist Peter Bearman found that one of their main functions was to provide

Figure 2.9 Doorman at the Shovehan Hotel in Washington, D.C., 1921. Unknown photographer for National Photo Company, Library of Congress Prints and Photographs Division, #LC-DIG-npcc-05432.

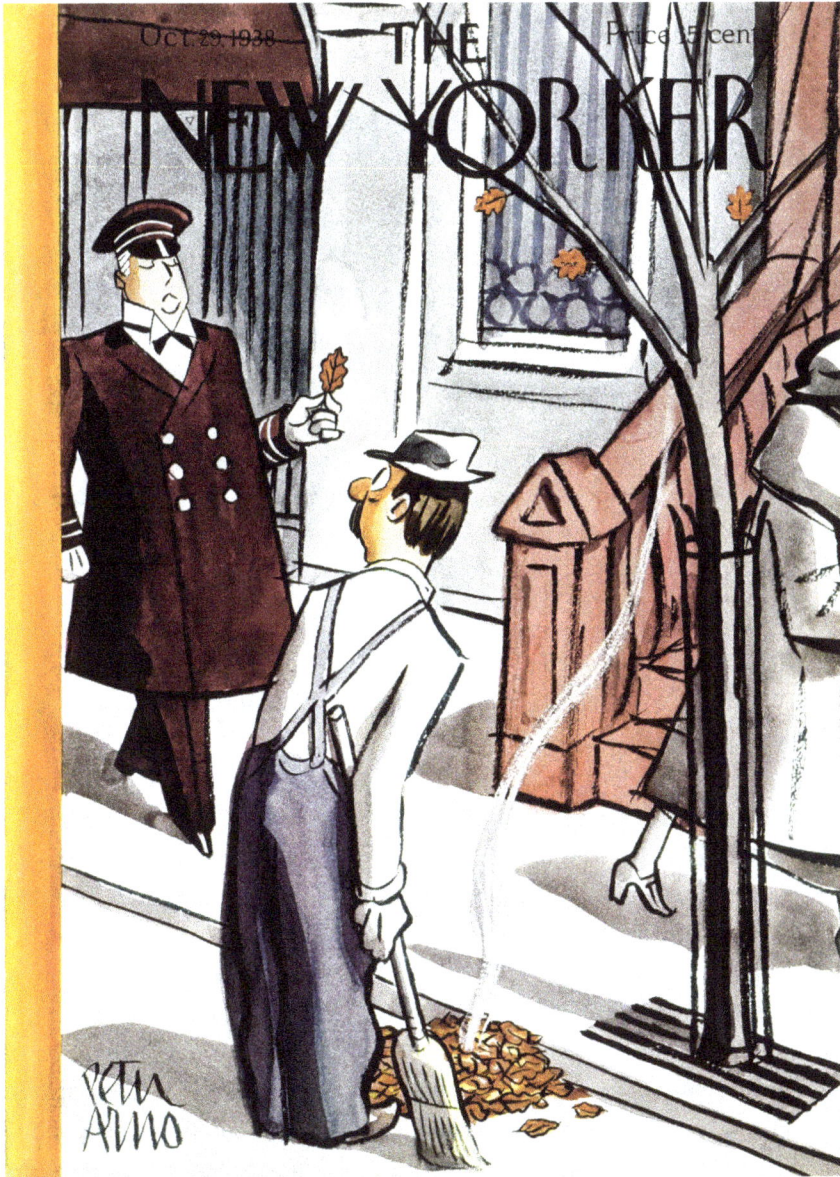

Figure 2.10 Doorman in uniform handing a single leaf to a street sweeper, October 29, 1938. Illustration by Peter Arno for the cover of *The New Yorker*. Estate of Peter Arno.

a sense of security by wearing uniforms and managing the appearance of the front of the building:

> In neighborhoods with doormen, the interior of the building is projected onto the street. This projection domesticates the area immediately in front of the

building, insulating it from uncertainty. Doormen are a critical element in this projection. First, by standing at the door (whether inside or outside), they project the interior onto the street. Second, doormen clean the area in front of their building. While it is obvious that neighborhoods with doormen are cleaner than those in other areas of the city—one can assess this simply by looking—it is the management of trash by doormen (and also the city) that makes these neighborhoods cleaner.[66]

Responding to Bearman's book in an editorial for the *New York Times*, a resident who "grew up in a doorman building" suggested that guards and cameras could replace the security function of doormen, but not their social function:

> [Opening doors] is almost purely ceremonial, and while it may smack of servility, can a tenant be blamed for taking pleasure in this show of respect, and the familiar greeting and smile that accompanies it? Anyone can open a door; only a doorman can make it mean something.[67]

In *The Doorman*, a children's book dedicated "in memory of our beloved doorman, John," the doorman is depicted as a friendly, well-organized, middle-aged black man. In one illustration, where John is drinking a cup of coffee before his shift begins, he is seated at a table wearing a white, button-down shirt, gray suspenders, and a dark blue necktie, with his uniform jacket hanging neatly behind him. In the rest of the book, he is shown in his full uniform; a dark blue, single-breasted jacket with brass buttons and gold trim on the sleeves and lapels, matching pants with a gold stripe down the side of each leg, and a cap with two rows of braided gold.[68]

In "cooperative" or condominium buildings where the tenants are owners, the uniforms for doormen reflect their collective taste and can vary from one building to the next. In 1963, a *New York Times* columnist observed, "in rental apartment houses, where the management staffs the building, and the emphasis is on keeping employees happy, elaborate uniforms are out. But in cooperative buildings, where tenant-owners can more easily dictate their wishes, elaborate uniforms are sometimes specified."[69] Fifteen years later, a columnist bemoaned that uniforms and standards for wearing them were disappearing. "Many old, established buildings and some of the new 'luxury' high rises still have their doormen in wing collars and tails—but mostly for winter. In the summer, even on Park Avenue, doormen can be spotted in shirtsleeves, which was unheard of not long ago."[70] Her upset was premature. In 2010, the *New York Times* ran a full-page feature on "The Latest (or Not) in Doorman Fashion." As revealed in interviews with doormen and building managers, some were maintaining their classic styles from the turn of the twentieth century. Others had adopted "modern" uniforms based on white-collar business attire:

BUILDING: 410-57 Corporation
LOCATION: 410 East 57th Street
These uniforms are expensive and classic, and the doormen wear white gloves, all the time. Each pair lasts about a week before it is sent to the laundry, and after three washings, the gloves are turned into rags for the cleaning staff. The building address is imprinted in gold on the peaked labels of the double-breasted jacket, and a stripe of gold piping runs down the side of the trousers.

BUILDING: 505 Greenwich Condominium
LOCATION: 505 Greenwich Street, SoHo
This is the building that started a downtown trend: uniforms for doormen that don't look like uniforms. [...] Seeking a modern look for a modern building, management opted for business suits over white shirts. [...] Hats or gloves? Please, no. The building's logo, 505 Greenwich, is embossed on the jacket lapels in an unobtrusive shade of maroon.[71]

Whether contemporary uniforms for doormen are based on livery or business suits, they remain some of the most elaborate, expensive, and deeply conservative of all work uniforms.

In 2013, Doug Weinstein, director of operations for a high-end property management company in New York City described how doorman uniforms are typically selected:

The managing agent will provide samples from numerous uniform companies. There are some buildings that want to have a very fancy uniform and then there are other buildings that want to get away from that and go very simple, let's say blazer and turtleneck, more toward the look of a boutique hotel rather than the standard epaulets with braids and scrawling writing on them.[72]

Some tenant boards (but not all) ask their doormen to model samples and give feedback on their proposals. While theoretically free to choose anything, the boards want their doormen to look like doormen—to share visual similarities with other doormen. This is accomplished by using catalogues and seeking input from professional property managers.

Outside of New York City, there seems to be more variation. For example, in Atlanta, when the Ten Pryor Building (also known as the Thornton Building) was constructed in the early 1930s, it was considered ultra-modern in comparison to other commercial buildings in the area.[73] The doormen wore innovative caps

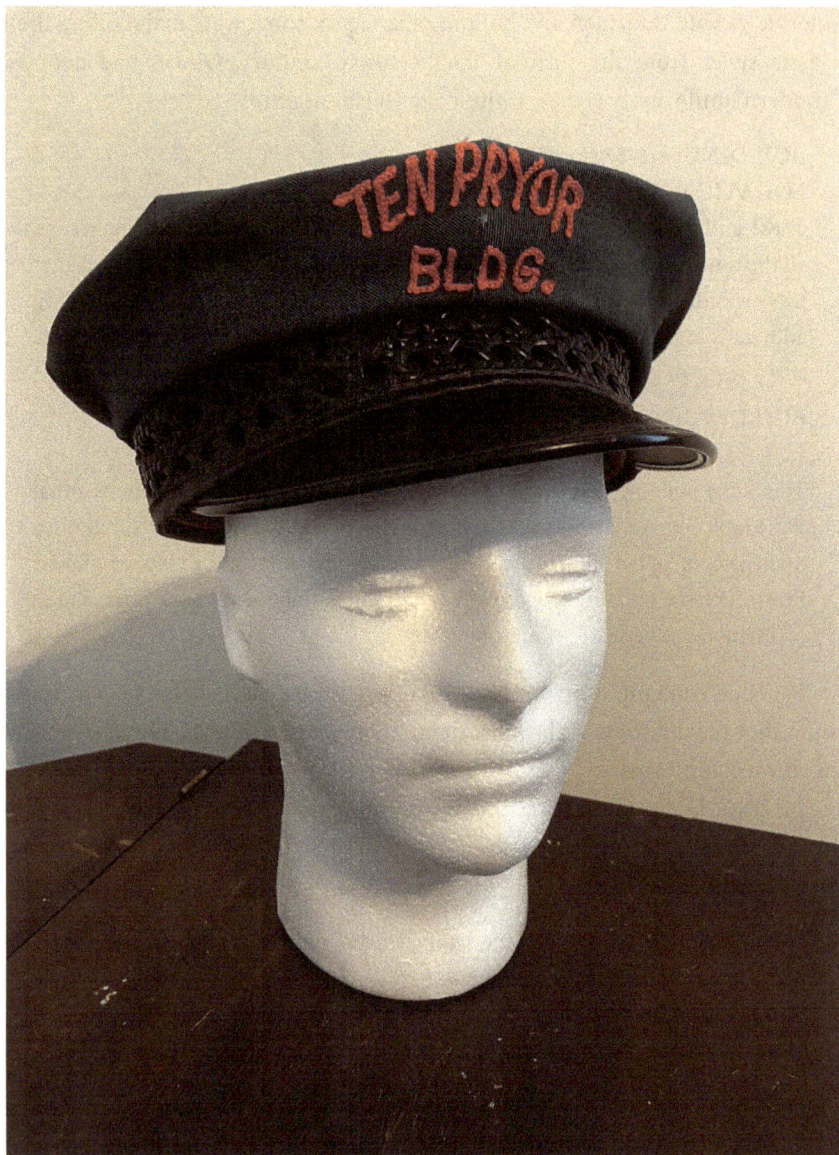

Figure 2.11 Cap for a doorman at the Ten Pryor building in Atlanta, Georgia, mid-twentieth century. Author's research collection.

with caning around the band for ventilation and two pieces of cloth that could be detached for cleaning: a white, cotton liner and a green canvas cover with the building's name embroidered in red (Figure 2.11).

In Cincinnati, Ohio, another innovative building, the Terrace Hilton Hotel, was built in 1948. *Architectural Digest* has observed that "It's sky lobby—a revolutionary idea—sat on the eighth floor, above a department store. It was the first hotel to have elevators without operators in them, and it even had sofas that would convert to beds at the push of a button."[74] It also had the city's only revolving restaurant,[75] a mural by Joan Miró (his first commission in the United States)[76] and a lounge known as the Kasbah. Postcards that were sold (or perhaps given) to guests described the inspiration for the lounge:

> The KASBAH Cocktail Lounge is patterned after the original Moroccan Kasbah. Twinkling stars and tropical plants create a romantic outdoor setting. Colorful murals, Moroccan canapes and cocktails, and Abdullah, at the entrance extending a warm welcome to our guests, further enhance the exotic atmosphere.[77]

"Abdullah the doorman" wore a uniform consisting of black pants and black leather shoes with a long white jacket. The jacket was embellished with gold patterns and accented with a red-and-white striped sash (Figure 2.12). He also wore a red-and-white turban—the finishing touch for a uniform that was an Orientalist fantasy. The hotel's location high above the street eliminated the need for the doorman to serve as security, which allowed for a less militaristic look. It is likely that other regional styles for doormen uniforms could be identified by doing research in local and state historical museums.

Figure 2.12 Detail of a postcard showing a doorman at the Kasbah Cocktail Lounge within the Terrace Hilton Hotel in Cincinnati, Ohio, *c.* 1965. Author's research collection.

Conclusion

This chapter has focused on maids, porters, and doormen, but more could undoubtedly be said about other categories of workers such as butlers, coachmen, chauffeurs, bell boys, gardeners, bodyguards, personal assistants, governesses, and nannies. In Los Angeles, some high-rises now employ "residential concierges" as a perk to attract and retain wealthy tenants:

> Though they don't wear the bulky overcoats, funky hat and white gloves that doormen do—besides, in L.A., who would really want to?—and the job description differs somewhat, the basic concept is the same: Concierges put a friendly, familiar face among the sometimes mean streets surrounding a high-rise apartment or loft. Want to get from downtown L.A. to the beach without a car? Need tickets to Cirque du Soleil? How about a hot tip for meeting people? The concierge has the answer or can get it for you.[78]

The question posed in this article, "Who would really want to [wear a doorman uniform]?" is intriguing; it demonstrates a level of practicality and empathy for the experience of being a doorman. The residential concierge is expected to have knowledge and social connections, allowing him (or her) to solve problems for tenants—not to be an anonymous servant.

In upper-class households, the social gap between employer and employee is wide. The next chapter turns to settings where this is not the case—small "mom and pop" employers.

Working for Mom and Pop

Barbers, Attendants, and Waitresses

In the United States, small shops, restaurants, and entertainment venues (such as theaters) are commonly referred to as "mom-and-pop" businesses. They have a single location—or at most, a handful of locations—and are run by their owners, who are middle class (not upper class) and work directly with their employees. The owner(s) are not necessarily highly trained, although they can be. The key is that they know every aspect of the business and are involved in its day-to-day operations. In contrast, larger businesses—known as corporations, chain stores, big-box stores, and "formula businesses"[1]—have many locations and owners who are disengaged from ground-level decisions, a topic that I return to in Chapter 6.

Definitions of "small business" vary. The US Small Business Administration—which defines whether a business is small for the purposes of taxation, loans, and grants—has created standards in the past based on the number of employees and annual gross income.[2] Currently, it uses a more complex formula based on percentages within specific industries. In the category of "Food Service and Drinking Places,"[3] for example, almost all establishments are small, so very small needs to be distinguished from normal small. In 2018, there were 492,791 businesses in the food service industry employing more than 12 million people. 180,341 (36.6%) had fewer than five employees (very small); only 0.4 percent (corporate chains) had more than 500.[4]

Many small business owners do not have the means and/or desire to grow their business. An article posted by the US Bureau of Labor Statistics notes,

Small firms are often younger (indeed, they are sometimes recent startups), more likely to be in rural areas, and more apt to be in industries with lower economies of scale, such as services. Small firms can represent a life stage before economies of scale are reached (or hoped-for future growth is attained), or they can be a stable anchor in the marketplace.[5]

Franchises—establishments where individuals pay larger corporations for the right to use their trademarks and business practices[6]—exist in a gray area between small and large. The owner takes the financial risk of running the business and is heavily involved in day-to-day operations but receives ongoing support from the corporation. This method of starting a business took off quickly in the United States after the Second World War.[7] This chapter includes some early franchises (gas stations and chain movie theaters), only because their uniforms were still selected in much the same way as smaller businesses.

Uniforms for Barbers

The profession of barber is a very old one. Historically in England, barber-surgeons were the first medical professionals. On March 22, 1800, the titles were split by decree of King George III; moving forward, only surgeons would be allowed to perform surgery, while barbers would be limited to shaving and styling hair.[8] In the US, the same split occurred.[9] While there have been a variety of terms for professionals—typically, but not always women—who cut and style women's hair (beauty operator, hairdresser, cosmetologist, etc.) "barber" is still the dominant term for professionals who cut and style men's hair.

In his book, *Cutting Along the Color Line*, historian Quincy Mills explored the complex interactions between shop owners, barbers, and customers that occur in barber shops:

> Barber shops are locations of economic exchange, but they are also spaces that facilitate public discourse. As businesses, barber shops operate as private spaces where grooming services are rendered. Yet, interactions between barbers and customers allow for public conversations between acquaintances and strangers. To consider the barber shop a commercial space means that we must take full account of the peculiar labor relations between owners and staff. Owners and employed barbers engage each other over 'independent labor' issues such as booth rent, percentages, professionalism, and opening and closing times. Also, barbers and patrons form intimate commercial relationships based on trust. Patrons do not switch barbers often, unless forced to because of extended travel or a move to a new city.[10]

Many individual barbers rent space within barber shops, blending the advantages of being an entrepreneur with some of the dynamics of being an employee, such as an expectation that the barber will adhere to standard procedures and dress codes. Segregation within neighborhoods, discriminatory licensing requirements,[11] and genetic differences in the textures of hair have led many barbers to specialize in particular ethnic and/or racial groups. As Mills noted, "Blacks did not patronize black barber shops solely because they were shut out of white shops. Rather, they patronized black shops because they knew the barbers valued them as customers and understood black culture enough to produce their desired hairstyles."[12]

Like the job title, uniforms for barbers have changed very little since the early 1900s. In 1928, the Associated Master Barbers of America, a trade group now known as the American Barber Association,[13] issued a revised manual for members about the history of the profession and best practices. It advised, "Barbers should be uniformed in white, but many use only a white coat, still the white trousers and shirt or white trousers and jacket gives a much nicer appearance. The uniform in the high-class shop should be changed daily."[14] While the book contains many illustrations, it shows only two options for a "regulation barber uniform" (Figure 3.1).

A catalogue produced by Angelica Jacket Co. in 1962 shows a pair of strikingly similar uniforms designed for "professional men" (Figure 3.2). In both

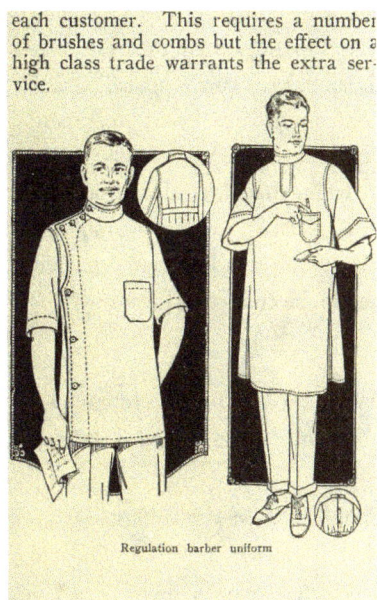

Figure 3.1 "Regulation barber uniform" in the *Standardized Barber's Manual*, 1928. Chicago: Associated Master Barbers of America, 25.

Figure 3.2 Illustration of two "professional" uniforms, 1962. *Angelica Washable Service Uniforms*, catalogue by Angelica Jacket Co. of St. Louis, Missouri, 21.

illustrations, the man on the left is wearing a light-colored (probably white) smock that buttons up the right side of the body and across the right shoulder. It has a high collar with one button and is slightly longer than a typical business suit, ending at the wearer's upper thighs instead of the hips. It has short sleeves that end just above the elbow. The only difference in the 1962 version is the addition of two pockets at hip level. The man on the right is wearing a tunic with a high collar and a placket (resembling a necktie) that hides a short row of buttons at the upper chest. Both garments have a single breast pocket that opens at the top. The length of both versions is the same, but the 1962 version has a waistband (or possibly, a separate apron) that makes it fit more closely to the body.

In 1932, two Jewish inventors in Chicago, Isadore Goldman and Jacob Cohen, patented their design for a "barber's coat" that had three important differences: it was a single-breasted jacket (with hidden buttons), it had a lower neckline (revealing the wearer's necktie and button-down shirt), and most importantly—the subject of the patent—it had pockets that opened at the side and could be partially detached for cleaning (Figure 3.3). The application noted,

> [It] has been found that during hair cutting operations small particles or lengths of hair find their way into [welt or patch pockets that open from the top] and gradually accumulate therein. When the coats, smocks or gowns are soiled and are sent to a laundry or clean coat service company, it is necessary to employ additional help for the purpose of removing or cleaning out the hair which has accumulated in the garment pockets. Even by turning the pockets inside out and thoroughly brushing the same, it has been found almost impossible to remove all of the short hair clippings so that after the garments are laundered and delivered for further use, hair clippings may still be found in the creases and seams within the pockets.[15]

The inventors argued that it was unsanitary for the clippings to remain, since they could "carry disease germs" that might be transmitted from one customer to the next.

It does not appear that this invention caught on. In the 1950s, Barco—a manufacturer based in Los Angeles (now better known for its medical and food-service uniforms)—launched a line of Mr. Barco uniforms for "doctors, dentists, barbers, and other professional men."[16] Made of Dacron polyester, an easy-care synthetic material that had recently been introduced into the ready-to-wear clothing market,[17] the jackets were produced in a variety of colors

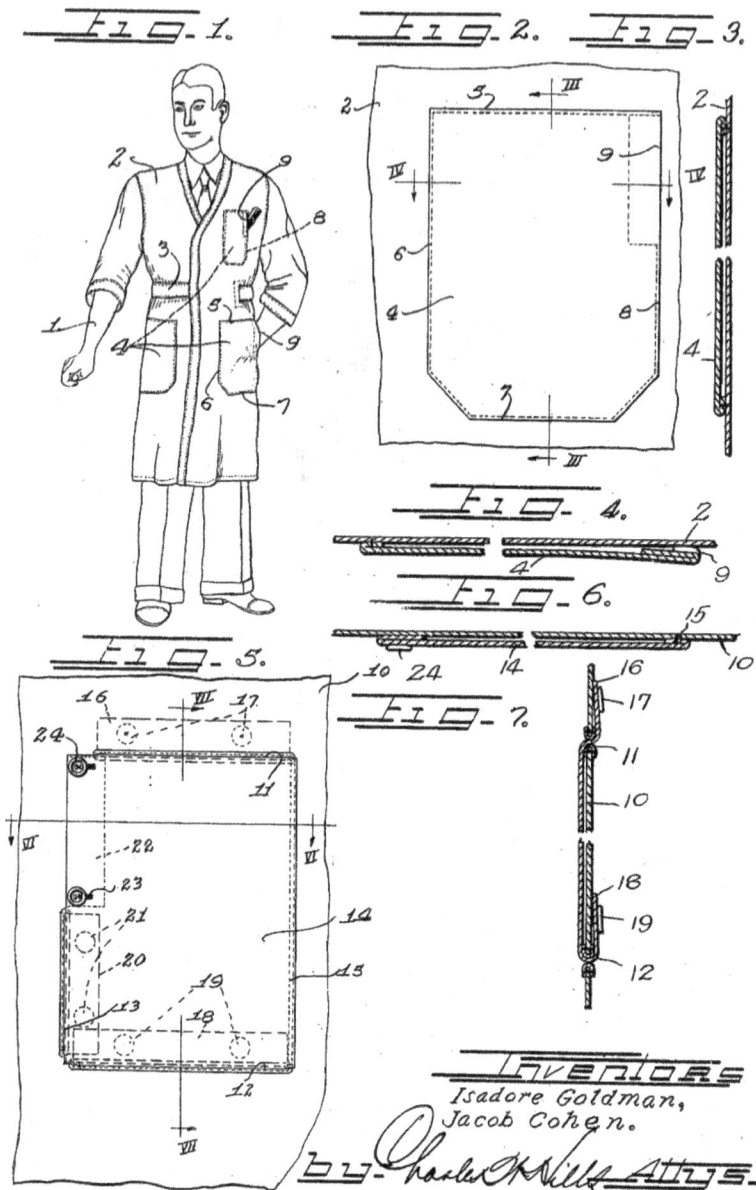

Figure 3.3 Illustration for a "barber's coat" with pockets that open at the side, invented by Isadore Goldman and Jacob Cohen, US Patent 1,878,275, 1932.

Figure 3.4 Mr. Barco jacket for "professional men" made of Dacron polyester, *c.* 1970. Author's research collection.

with zippers instead of button closures and pockets that opened at the top (Figure 3.4).

Simple patch pockets are easier (and less expensive) to manufacture than detachable pockets. Some states, however, forbid barbers from putting tools in their pockets. A typical example is the state of Louisiana:

§119. Sterilization

E. The sterilization of all tools and instruments shall be accomplished after use on each customer and before tools and instruments are re-used. No tools shall be left exposed on work stand, but shall be cleaned and placed in a sterilizing cabinet with approved disinfectant when not in use. *Combs and brushes shall not be kept in pockets of barber uniform.*[18] (Emphasis added)

If barbers cannot use their pockets to hold any tools that come into contact with clients, then the accumulation of tiny hair clippings in the pockets is not a significant health concern.

Minnesota was the first state (in 1897) that passed a law requiring barbers to be licensed. Local members of the Journeyman Barbers International Union of America (JBIUA) supported the bill, hoping that it would lead to better pay and working conditions.[19] After the law was passed, the union held a banquet to celebrate, with speeches by the governor, the mayors of St. Paul and Minneapolis, several judges, and union officials.[20] Today, every state has laws that regulate barbers and barber shops.[21] Because the laws vary,[22] a barber who moves from one state to another might not automatically qualify for a license.

In the twenty-first century, nearly half of all states in the US (22 out of 50) still regulate the uniforms, clothing, and/or appearance of licensed barbers. Many of the laws are succinct:

> While serving a client, a practitioner shall wear clean outer clothing.[23]
> The operator shall wear clean uniforms or clean clothes at all times.[24]
> Barbers in barber shops must be clean and neatly dressed.[25]
> All licensees shall wear shoes and clothing.[26]

New York has more extensive regulations for all "appearance enhancement" services, focusing on health and safety for both operators and customers. For barbers, it stipulates, "Any clothing worn by licensed individuals shall be clean and pose no health or safety hazard to the client or to the operator while attending a client."[27] Texas has the longest statement:

> Licensees shall wear clean top and bottom outer garments and footwear while performing services authorized under the Act. Outer garments include tee shirts, blouses, sweaters, dresses, smocks, pants, jeans, shorts, and other similar clothing and does not include lingerie or see-through fabric.[28]

Curiously, the Texas law is not limited to physical health and safety but makes a statement about modesty and by extension, morality.

Like nurses, doctors, dentists, and veterinarians (a topic I return to in the next chapter), many states require barbers to attend a training program that has been certified by the state. These programs can have dress codes that are more stringent and extensive than regulations for working barbers. For example, when residents of Mississippi apply for examination to become a barber or barber instructor, they must follow a very specific set of guidelines:

Rule 1.6 Application for Examination

a.   Students' attire for examination

1.   Students testing for Barber examination are to be dressed in a clean, professional smock, clean pants or skirt, well kept clean, closed toe shoes and maintain a high standard of personal hygiene and personal appearance.

2.   Students testing for Instructor examination may wear shirts and ties and/or professional smocks along with dress slacks or skirt, well kept, clean, closed toe shoes and maintain a high standard of personal hygiene and personal appearance.

3.   All pants/skirts must be worn on waistline. Skirts/dresses must be knee length. *No Blue Denim Jeans or Shorts allowed.* (Original emphasis)

Missouri requires barbers to maintain their clothing in "neat and clean condition at all times," but demands that students wear "washable uniforms."[29] Delaware does not regulate clothing for licensed barbers but requires that their apprentices receive 3,000 hours of training including 125 hours on the topic of "professional image" (Figure 3.5).[30]

As these laws have evolved, the barber uniform has become somewhat optional. Uniforms are an easy way—but not the only way—to convince

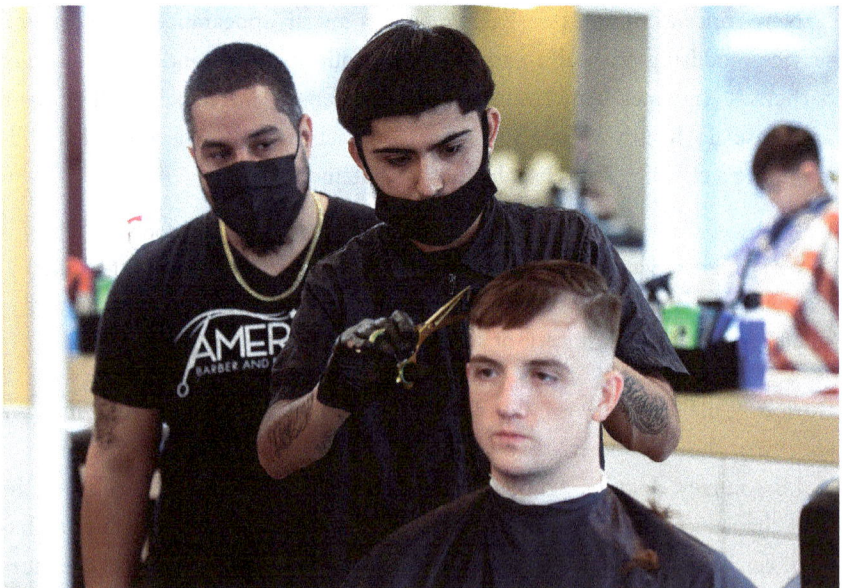

Figure 3.5 Student at American Barber and Beauty Academy in Reading, Pennsylvania with his instructor looking on from behind, June 15, 2021. Photograph by Ben Hasty / MediaNews Group / Reading Eagle via Getty Images.

inspectors that barbers are maintaining neat and clean facilities. LIC Salon Apparel, a contemporary manufacturer for "salon and spa wear" based in New York, offers a selection of uniform vests, jackets, and smocks for hair stylists and barbers, but invites business owners to customize them:

> All our clothing is manufactured with impeccable workmanship and tailored with fit and comfort in mind. We always invite you to build your own robe or uniform and customize it with your logo. We offer both screenprinting and embroidery for any [of] the garments you choose.[31]

Cutting and styling hair is a creative profession, however the long-standing patchwork of laws in the US that regulates barbers has limited the creativity of their uniforms.

Uniforms for Theater Attendants

Like barbers, attendants play a role in public health and safety. In the late 1800s, a series of deadly fires in packed theaters led governments around the world to enact new building codes. In 1892, the city of London began requiring theaters to install fire-resistant stage curtains made of "wire gauze, corrugated iron, or woven asbestos."[32] Since many fires started on stage (from gaslights, special effects, or from poorly designed electrical wiring), the idea was to shield the audience and prevent the fire from spreading to the rest of the building.

When the Iroquois Theatre opened in Chicago on November 27, 1903, it was described as a "spacious," "magnificent," and "modern fireproof" building.[33] Although the city had adopted stringent new building codes after the Great Chicago Fire of 1871,[34] it was struggling to enforce them.[35] When the stage at the Iroquois caught on fire during a matinee performance attended mostly by women and children, the asbestos curtain malfunctioned; in fifteen minutes, nearly 600 people were killed by the smoke, stampeding, and intense heat of the fire.[36]

Eddie Foy, an experienced actor who had been cast in one of the main roles, was in his dressing room when the fire began. Realizing that something was very wrong, he rushed to the stage. In his own words,

> Everything was excitement. Everybody was running from the stage. My [six-year-old] son, Bryan, stood in the first entrance to the stage and my first thought naturally was to get him out. They would not let me go out over the

footlights, so I picked up the boy and gave him to a man and told him to rush the boy out into the alley.

I then rushed out to the footlights and called out to the audience, 'Keep very quiet. It is all right. Don't get excited and don't stampede. It is all right.'

I then shouted an order into the flies [rigging for the aerialist performers], 'Drop the curtain,' and called out to the leader of the orchestra to 'play an overture.' Some of the musicians had left, but those that remained began to play. The leader sat there, white as a ghost, but beating his baton into the air.

As the music started I shouted out to the audience, 'Go out slowly. Leave the theater slowly.' The audience had not yet become panic stricken, and as I shouted to them they applauded me. The next minute the whole stage seemed to be afire, and what wood there was began to crackle with a sound like a series of explosions.[37]

Thanks to Foy's quick thinking, all of the performers (including the musicians) and most people who had been seated on the main floor made it out of the theater alive. Those who were in the balconies or had purchased tickets for "standing room only" were not as fortunate.

A few months later, an article in *The Sanitarian*, a national magazine focused on public health and safety, considered what additional laws and/or policies might be necessary for theaters. Noting that the science of fireproofing was still very new, the author argued:

As a matter of fact, the construction of a theater bears very little relation to the loss of life which results in a conflagration. The danger comes partly from the fire spreading rapidly, more to liability of suffocation from smoke and gases, but most of all to the unreasoning, blind panic which is so apt to seize a crowd when threatened with danger. [...] *Our theaters must not be merely fireproof but also panic-proof.*[38] (Emphasis added)

In 1916, Balaban & Katz Theatre Corporation, based in Chicago, began opening a series of grand movie theaters. The new technology was thrilling, glamorous, and more affordable than going to see live performances. Having learned from tragedies like the fire at the Iroquois, managers hired dozens of staff members to seat guests and enforce safety regulation:

The centerpiece of the special Balaban & Katz service was the corps of ushers. They guided patrons through the maze of halls and foyers, assisted the elderly and small children, and handled any emergencies that might arise in a crowd of four thousand in the auditorium and four thousand waiting for the next show. A picture palace had twenty to forty ushers and doorkeepers in attendance for all shows. Indeed, there was a regular changing of the guard throughout the day.

Balaban & Katz recruited its corps from male college students, dressed them in red uniforms with white gloves and yellow epaulets, and demanded they be obediently polite even to the rudest of patrons.[39]

Some of these standards are still in place today. For example, a training handbook for the Arsht Center in Miami, Florida—a theater that seats up to 2,400 guests for ballet, opera, and musical performances—gives attendants (known as "front of house ushers") detailed policies to follow regarding their appearance and behavior with guests. The dress code allows for some personal choice but includes three uniform items provided by the theater: a gray vest, a dark red floppy bowtie or necktie, and a name tag.[40]

> **Gentlemen** will be required to wear black slacks (no denim fabric), white long-sleeve dress shirt with collar, black socks & closed black rubber soled shoes (no trainers). **Ladies** will be required to wear black slacks (no leggings, capris, denim fabric) or skirt (knee length or longer) white long sleeve shirt or blouse with shirt collar, black socks & completely closed black rubber soled shoes (back & front i.e. no mules/slides/sandals & no trainers). Please note that black or neutral colored stockings must be worn if wearing a skirt. Shirts or blouses must be tucked in.
>
> Clothing should be neat & clean at all times. Each Usher will wear an Arsht Center vest, as well as a name tag. Vests will be provided to Ushers at the beginning of each shift, & are to be returned at the end of the shift. Each Usher will bring a flashlight (LED lights are prohibited), plus a pen/pencil to make notes during the pre-performance briefing.[41]

Much like flight attendants, ushers handle a variety of situations that might cause guests to panic such as fires, earthquakes, severe weather, medical crises, and violence. They must be easy to recognize as authority figures who can give orders in the event of an emergency, but they are also part of the guest experience. Acting as representatives of the theater, they are responsible for making guests feel welcomed and cared for.

The balance between these two functions is delicate; too much authority can seem uncaring, but too little makes it difficult for the staff to be recognized and obeyed during an emergency. Photographs of ushers from the mid-twentieth century reveal a range of uniforms. For example, a photograph taken in 1949 at the Paramount Theater in Atlanta, Georgia (Figure 3.6), which operated from 1920 to 1960,[42] shows different uniforms for different ranks and/or functions of workers within the theater.

Figure 3.6 Uniformed staff at the Paramount Theater in Atlanta, Georgia, 1949. Unknown photographer, Cinema Treasures, at: http://cinematreasures.org/photos/7094.

While some uniforms for theater attendants resembled the suits worn by hotel doormen and bell hops, a popular style for male ushers was the "Eton jacket," developed in England as a style of dress for young, upper-class boys attending elite private schools.[43] The 1962 catalogue for Angelica Jacket Co. had a range of Etons in different colors. Options included contrasting collars, piping on the lapels and sleeves, matching vests and cummerbunds, and detachable epaulets made of black, blue, gold, or maroon braid (Figure 3.7). Eton jackets in the 1988 Angelica catalogue were more streamlined and low-cost, but the upscale designs featured novelty fabrics, black piping, and gold-embroidered epaulets and cuffs, emphasizing new technologies (i.e., polyester) and "European" styling.

> For elegance and the utmost in good taste, choose Angelica's exclusively developed rectangular weave blends of 65% polyester and 35% cotton. Dramatic contrasting check Etons feature Italian lapels and sleeve piping in solid black. Light weight, wrinkle resistant, extremely durable, and comfortable.[44]

Figure 3.7 Design options for "Eton" uniform jackets, 1962. *Angelica Washable Service Uniforms*, catalogue by Angelica Jacket Co. of St. Louis, Missouri, 5.

Uniforms for "usherettes" (Figure 3.8)—a term for female ushers that is no longer in use—could vary even more than male uniforms, making it difficult to tell if existing garments were worn by theater attendants, waitresses, grocery clerks, or shop girls. For example, a 1939 patent for a woman's "uniform dress" (Figure 3.9) shows a garment that can be unbuttoned, turned inside out, and worn just as easily in reverse. In 1962, Angelica described the dress as providing "Two clean fronts with each laundering." It is unclear what occupation(s) it was intended for since nothing specific is suggested in the catalogue.[45]

Over time, the uniforms for theater attendants have become less elaborate and more unisex, often just pants, a button-down shirt, and a vest instead of a vest-jacket combination. In most movie theaters—which have been financially strained by television, home video devices, streaming services,[46] and more recently, the COVID-19 pandemic[47]—guests are now expected to seat themselves and the number of attendants is minimal. The aisles are marked with rows of tiny lights, exit signs are permanently lit, and pre-recorded announcements tell guests what to do in the event of an emergency.

Figure 3.8 Usherettes lined up for uniform inspection at the Roxy Theater in New York City, 1945. Photograph by A.I. Ravenna for the *World-Telegram* & *Sun* (New York), Library of Congress Prints and Photographs Division, LC-USZ62-121691.

Uniforms for Gas Station Attendants

Like movie theaters, gas stations (also known as filling stations) were a new phenomenon in the early twentieth century. In 1904, there were fewer than 60,000 motorized vehicles in the US. Drivers kept barrels of gasoline in barns and garages,[48] which—like kerosene used for lamps—could be purchased from grocery and hardware stores.[49] In 1907, a petroleum distributor in Seattle invented a crude pump using a repurposed hot-water storage tank with a gauge at the bottom[50] and began siphoning gas directly into vehicles. "The story goes that John L. Mclean, local manager for Standard Oil (now Chevron), witnessed impatient motorists waiting to buy 5-gallon cans of gasoline. He was inspired to figure out a better way to dispense the fuel using a piece of garden hose attached to a 30-gallon tank."[51]

By 1920, there were 15,000 gas stations scattered around the country.[52] Many were attached to grocery stores or had small "convenience stores" where

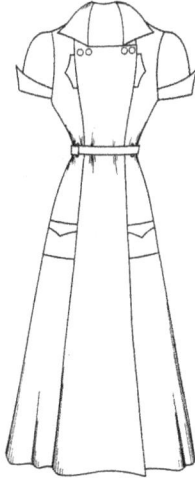 

FIG.1. FIG.2.

INVENTOR
VIOLA A. LEVY
BY
ATTORNEY

Figure 3.9 Illustration for a reversible "uniform dress" invented by Viola Levy, US Patent 115,117, 1939.

motorists could buy motor oil, parts to repair their vehicles, and simple meals,[53] but it was a hazardous business. In a book for collectors of petroliana,[54] author, Tim Steil, reflected:

> [The smell of gasoline is] pungent as freshly ground coffee, and full of danger and romance. Even a faint whiff is enough to make the heart race. For most people, it is the most dangerous substance they handle on a regular basis. A fraction of a gallon can poison you with its fumes, or explode into a deadly fireball.[55]

Although many gas stations were "owned and operated by individuals,"[56] their businesses were somewhat dependent on the brand names of major petroleum companies such as Standard Oil, Texaco, Gulf Oil, and Esso. As safety improved and some stations began allowing customers to pump gas under minimal supervision, many attendants "viewed self-service as a threat [to their jobs], and they received considerable support from local fire marshals."[57] In the 1940s and 1950s, many states established bans on self-service that were not lifted until the 1970s.[58]

Since the most important product at gas stations (gasoline) was essentially the same at every location, branding—through uniforms, architecture, signs, and packaging—was key to gaining attention and loyalty. Companies quickly developed distinctive colors and logos. In 1932, Unitog—a small uniform business based in Kansas City, Missouri—landed a contract with Continental Oil Company (Conoco) to design and offer basic uniforms to franchises. A history of Unitog notes that in the beginning, "Brookfield's offerings were remarkably small, consisting of just three items: a one-piece coverall, a grease coat for service station attendants, and a cap."[59]

As Unitog grew (in part due to a major government contract to produce coveralls for soldiers during the Second World War),[60] it developed lines of uniforms for other petroleum companies, repair shops, and automobile dealers. A 1954 mail-in order form for Esso gas stations illustrates how the company was selling uniforms and how much its design options had expanded. Unitog offered ten different products in a range of sizes: coveralls, a "lube coat," a button-down shirt with full-length sleeves, a sport shirt with elbow-length sleeves, pants, a cap (with matching covers for different seasons), a bowtie, a belt with a no-scratch buckle, a "melton jacket" for winter (made of wool), and an "Eisenhower jacket" modeled after a popular style of military uniform developed at the request of General Eisenhower during the Second World War.

The form advertised a discount: "1/4 the cost of your approved Esso-stripe uniforms will be paid for by Esso Standard Oil Co."[61] This money did not pass through the hands of the gas station owners, who were simply instructed to deduct the cost on the order form. Figure 3.10 shows one of the uniforms: striped coveralls with solid-blue cuffs and lapels, two large pockets and the Esso logo on the chest (a white oval with Esso embroidered in red); a white undershirt, black shoes, and a doorman style cap with the Esso logo.

The proprietary fabrics (designed just for Esso) were described as "Blue and White Esso Stripe" and "Electric Blue." Since the owners of the gas stations were paying 75 percent of the cost, they had to be persuaded of the value. A short letter from the company's president notes,

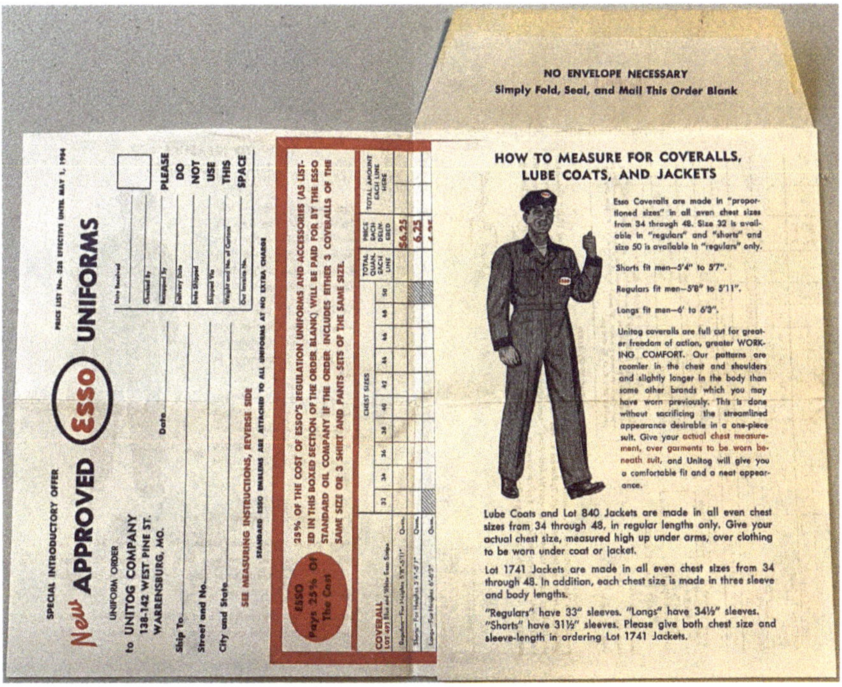

Figure 3.10 Mail-in order form for uniforms designed by Unitog for Esso gas stations, 1954. Author's research collection.

Regulation Esso uniforms are made by Unitog from Esso's exclusive vat yarn-dyed 'Esso 1953' blue-and-white pinstripe uniform material. Tailored to the latest Esso improved style and refinement specifications, plus Unitog's own famous 'proportioned sizes' and improved construction features, these are among the finest service station uniforms ever produced, and will 'pay out long before they wear out.' Unitog's pledge to you is 'the best in quality—the best in service,' now and in the years to come.[62] (Original quotation marks)

It is telling that this message was directed to "the Esso man"; there were no uniform options for women. Another Unitog brochure from 1970 shows a male gas station attendant handing a card to a female driver (Figure 3.11). He is wearing a very different style of uniform compared to the 1954 version: a light blue sport shirt with a dark blue "rally stripe" and the Gulf logo, dark blue pants with a black belt, and a dark blue baseball cap[63] with orange and white rally stripes.

The brochure is much larger and includes many new options: a hard hat (called a "flight cap"), a soft version of a railroad cap, a garrison cap (based on

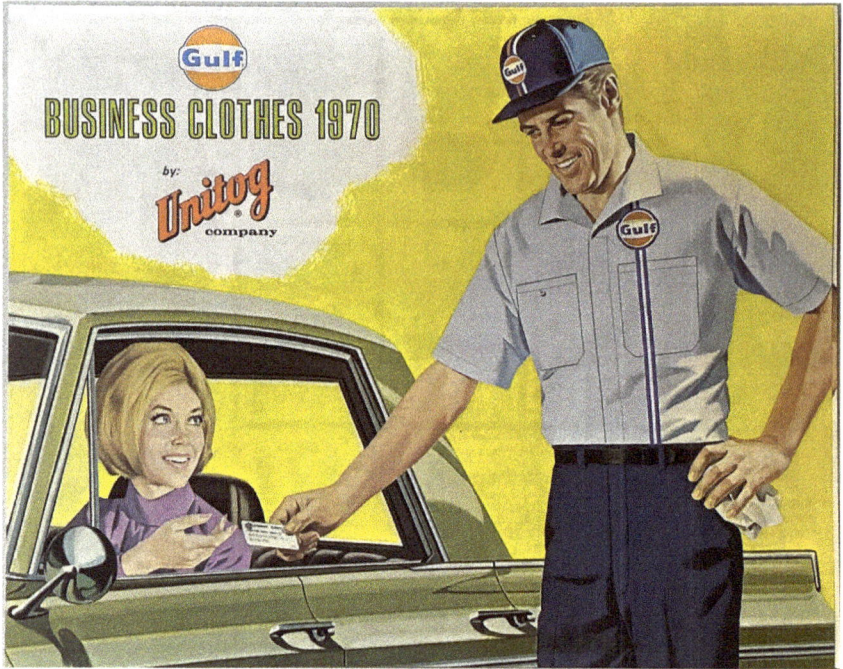

Figure 3.11 Mail-in order form for uniforms designed by Unitog for Gulf gas stations, 1970. Author's research collection.

military caps), a "fur trooper cap" and "polar coat" for very cold weather, a raincoat and rainsuit, sales blazer, thermal underwear, work gloves, and even knit "Gulf socks" in navy blue to match the uniform (Figure 3.12).

The 1970 brochure did not offer a discount for uniforms. The least expensive item (75 cents) was the clip-on bowtie; the most expensive was the sales blazer ($27.95, equivalent to more than $100 in 2021). In faint print, buyers were informed that invoices of more than $40 would receive "200 Great Race points" for every $10 ordered. This may have been a promotional tie-in to the 1965 film, *The Great Race*, a slapstick comedy about an epic automobile race that received several Academy Award nominations.[64]

In an article about the expansion of gas stations in Italy after the Second World War, historian Elisabetta Bini has observed that the marketing and business practices promoted by American companies such as Esso were highly gendered:

From the late 1940s on, Esso increasingly defined gas station work as a male job. While many gas stations continued to be run as family businesses and thus to

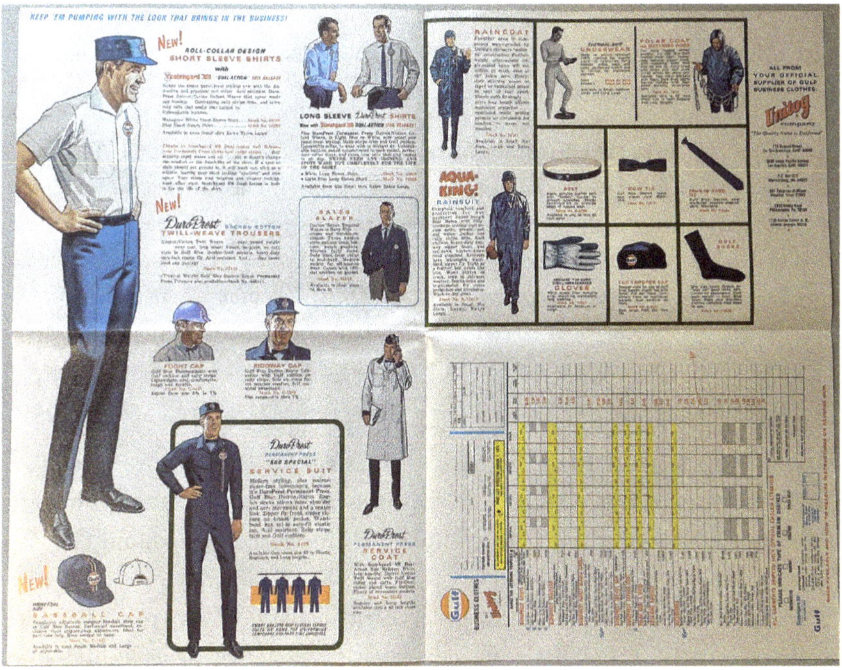

Figure 3.12 Inside of fold-out order form designed by Unitog for Gulf gas stations, 1970. Author's research collection.

include wives and daughters, along with brothers, nephews, and brothers-in-law, gas station management was only assigned to men, and Esso training was only offered to them. Until the second half of the 1960s, drivers were mostly men, and the gas station attendants (*benzinai*), who repaired and serviced their cars, thus needed to show their expertise over machines and bond with their mostly male clients over the appeal of new cars.[65]

Esso also encouraged attendants to wear "a clean and proper uniform," to shave daily, and to practice smiling in front of a mirror[66] to become more self-aware of their appearance and how they were engaging with customers.

Uniforms for Waitresses

As the job of gas station attendant was becoming entrenched as a masculine occupation, the job of waiter/ess was becoming increasingly feminine. In the introduction to *Dishing It Out*, labor historian Dorothy Cobble noted that between 1900 and 1970, the number of men and women employed to serve in restaurants grew ten-fold from 100,000 to 1,000,000, but the proportion of jobs held by men fell from two-thirds to just 8 percent:[67]

> Waitressing reveals the deeply gendered expectations surrounding the world of work. In the theater of eating out, the waitress plays multiple parts, each reflecting a female role. To fulfill the emotional and fantasy needs of the male customer, she quickly learns the all-too-common scripts: scolding wife, doting mother, sexy mistress, or sweet, admiring daughter. Other customers, typically female, demand obsequious and excessive service—to compensate, perhaps, for the status denied them in other encounters. For once, they are not the servers but the ones being served.[68]

Unlike gas stations, the products sold in restaurants—meals—were (and still are) highly varied, appealing to regional tastes and different needs and budgets. Expectations among customers can vary tremendously, even within the same establishment.

In the early 1900s, there was little visual distinction between maids and waitresses. In 1920, Frances Donovan—a writer now viewed as an untrained sociologist in the style of the Chicago School[69]—took a series of jobs as a waitress in order to understand the daily lives of working-class women. When she was hired by an agency that supplied waitresses for catered events, she noticed how many of her coworkers had developed their own uniforms. These were not true uniforms designed and/or mandated by an employer, but clothing that they knew would meet the expectations of wealthy clients and help them get paid work:

> On the Fourth of July, Hilda had an order from East Meadows [an exclusive golf club] for thirty girls to work 'extra' at three dollars per day. I was one of the number chosen; so I arranged to meet one of the others who had been at East Meadows on Decoration Day [Memorial Day, in late May]. I wore the black uniform of the waitress with white collar and cuffs. Molly was late in meeting me and I stood for a long time waiting for her. When she came, two other girls who knew her but whom I did not know, joined us.
>
> Molly did not introduce us . . . One of the girls said: 'I knew this lady was goin' out there the minute I seen her,' and she meant me. Always after that I carried my black [shirt]waist and white collars and cuffs in a small handbag just as the other girls did and wore a white [shirt]waist.[70]

In the 1920s, the typical full-time waitress "worked six days a week from seven in the morning until eight at night with a three-hour break between shifts in the

Figure 3.13 *The Waitress* by Isaac Soyer (1902–1981), *c.* 1934–1939. Smithsonian American Art Museum, Washington, DC / Art Resource, New York, 1975.83.111.

afternoon."[71] Pay decreased and hours increased during the economic depression of the 1930s, then improved in the 1940s with a shortage of male workers, changes in labor laws, and unionization among waitresses. However, many employers kept paychecks low by fining waitresses for minor mistakes and charging them for the cost of broken plates and stolen silverware.

In the 1930s, a Russian artist living in New York City sketched a waitress wearing a uniform that was remarkably similar to a maid's uniform (Figure 3.13): a dark dress with short sleeves and a low V-shaped neckline, a white collar and cuffs, a white apron, and a frilly white cap. It is not clear whether a pinafore-style apron (Figure 3.14), designed by Shane Company in the late 1930s or 1940s,[72] was intended for maids, nurses, waitresses, home use, or perhaps all the above. It is much larger than the apron shown in Figure 3.13 and would have covered the wearer's chest and most of her lower body, protecting her clothing from spills. It buttons up the back and has two large patch pockets at hip level.

Figure 3.14 Cotton pinafore-style apron made by Shane Company (1936–74) in Evansville, Indiana, *c.* 1940. Author's research collection.

By the 1940s, employers and waitresses had several options for acquiring uniforms. One affordable (but time-consuming) option was to construct them by hand, which was still common among working-class and rural households.[73] For example, a journal for rural families in the state of Pennsylvania, *Pennsylvania Farmer*,[74] had a pattern department based in New York City that designed and sold clothing patterns for home use. A catalogue from the early 1940s (Figure 3.15) had a patriotic cover featuring women dressed in various work uniforms (nurse, factory worker, etc.). The last four pages of the catalogue featured clothing patterns for "very essential service," "the assembly line," and "the home front."

Figure 3.15 Cover for a catalogue of sewing patterns sold by *Pennsylvania Farmer*, early 1940s. Author's research collection.

A4512—Work Uniform. Make this of stout denim, and no grease or grime can touch you. It fits closely at ankles. Sizes 14 to 20. *Department of Agriculture design.

A4437—Frock. This button-front is perfect for home or factory... even office wear. Size 34 to 48. Size 36, 3 yards 39-inch.

A4507—Apron. (Utility pockets for tools or recipes.) Sizes small (32-34), medium (36-38), large (40-42). Small, 3 1/8 yards 35-in.

A4462—Coat. Smartly fitted; designed with an eye to the military. Use a firm twill or herringbone mixture with velveteen collar. Sizes 11 to 17, 12 to 20.[75]

Another option was to buy uniforms ready-made from a department store. For example, in December 1948, Penney's department store in Klamath Falls, Oregon advertised clothing for men, women, and children as possible Christmas gifts in the local newspaper (Figure 3.16), including uniforms for waitresses.

A third option was to buy the uniforms directly from a uniform manufacturer. As the restaurant industry expanded dramatically in the mid-twentieth century (by embracing families and the post-war baby boom[76]) so did the range of colors and style options for waitresses. In 1962, Angelica touted the advantages of busying professionally designed uniforms:

> HERE, the best creative talents of the trade are at work for YOU! The practical beauty, the high degree of workmanship, and the unequalled excellence of each Angelica garment are the results of long, diligent research.
>
> An interesting drama is behind the launching of each number of the Angelica line. Not only do talented stylists actually invade America's fashion centers for new ideas and trends, but also buyers of materials scan markets for the finest fabrics, trimmings, braids and buttons, that will give the utmost in service . . .

CHILDREN'S 1-PC. SLEEPERS	**COTTON BLOUSES**
1⁴⁹ Children's one-piece cotton knit sleepers. Don't take it for granted—make sure they're good and warm. Attached feet and knit cuffs. Sizes 3 to 6.	Women's short sleeve cotton plaid blouses. Beautifully made and washable, too! Gay colored plaids in sizes 32-38. **1**⁹⁸
INFANTS' TRAINING PANTS	**WOMEN'S DENIM JEANS**
39ᶜ Infants' training pants made of either cotton or rayon material. Well made for long serviceable wear! Select now! Sizes 1-4.	Women's blue denim jeans. Western cut for snug fit. Side fastener. Double stitched and riveted at points of strain. Durable 8-oz. material. Sizes 12 to 20. **2**⁴⁹
GIRLS' FLANNEL PAJAMAS	**WAITRESS UNIFORM**
2⁹⁸ Girls' cotton flannel pajamas. Just what she needs these cold winter nights. Sizes 8-16.	Smartly tailored waitress uniforms for that working girl. They're made the way you like them. Snap front and slide fastener fronts. Sizes 10-44. **3**⁴⁹

Figure 3.16 Advertisement by Penney's department store for childrens' and women's clothing, including waitress uniforms, December 9, 1948. *Herald and News* (Klamath Falls, Oregon), 5.

In thrilling sessions behind closed doors at Angelica headquarters all this information is brought together, thoroughly digested and presented to the organization for final suggestions. Then and there, the styles that will make history are born . . .[77]

Waitresses were featured on the front cover and filled approximately one-third of the sixty-page catalogue. The "talented stylists" working for Angelica were never acknowledged by name.

Most of the designs had the same silhouette: a knee-length dress with puff sleeves and a built-in collar, a short apron (with a matching or contrasting pattern), black or brown pumps, and a matching, decorative cap. Some of the most unique were described as "costume dresses" for a Spanish, French, or Dutch-themed restaurant (Figure 3.17).

Figure 3.17 "Costume Dresses" for European-themed restaurants, 1962. *Angelica Washable Service Uniforms*, catalogue by Angelica Jacket Co. of St. Louis, Missouri, 30.

8054—Dress of Blue Broadcloth, trimmed with White Lawn. The unusual apron with its unique port-hole pockets becomes a definite part of the dress design by buttoning on with Blue Pearl buttons. Dress opens to below waistline. Two reinforced skirt pockets. Arm shields.[78]

The caps and headbands were sold separately, but were made of cloth (net, muslin, organdy, or lawn) in various colors. Some had ruffles, recalling historic uniforms for waitresses and maids, but others were starched and very simple with colorful trim for decoration. Industrial Uniform Co.[79] sold disposable caps for waitresses, soda jerks, chefs, and other restaurant workers that had similar shapes, but were made of white paper (Figure 3.18).

Verging on theater costumes, these fanciful uniforms and accessories may have helped to generate excitement and brand loyalty among people who could afford to eat in restaurants, but the cost was frequently passed along to the workers. "Until the late 1950s, most restaurants either required waitresses to pay for their uniforms or to rent them from the employer... Costs mounted if one worked for a whimsical employer who adopted every new uniform fashion or frequently changed dining-room supervisors."[80]

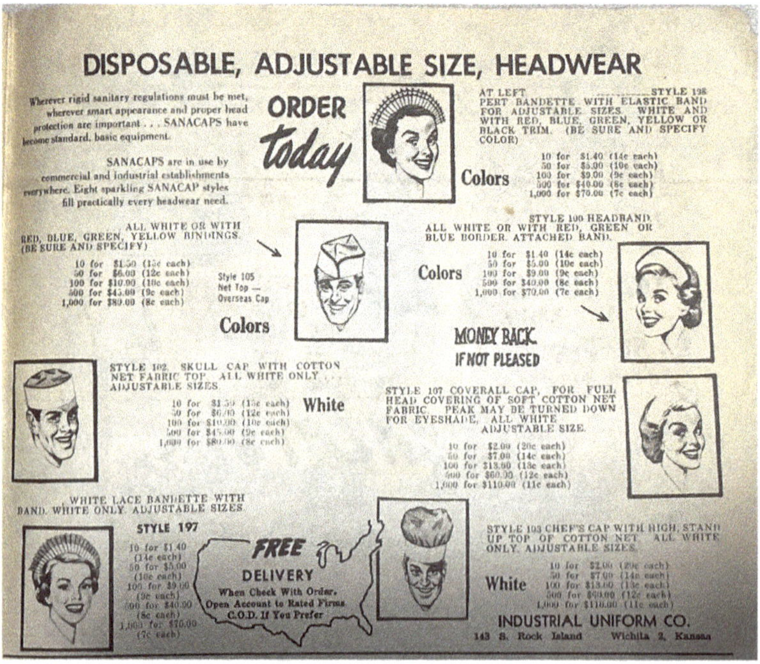

Figure 3.18 Undated catalogue from Industrial Uniform Co. in Wichita, Kansas, showing disposable paper caps for restaurant staff, c. 1950s. Author's research collection.

The shift to mass manufactured clothing for women after the Second World War also limited options for sizes. Sewing at home required skill, but it allowed women who were particularly tall and/or large to customize their uniforms. It is important to observe the very limited diversity of models shown as waitresses in the uniform catalogues: white, young, slim, and very feminine. The visual rhetoric is that old, pregnant, non-white, "stout" and non-conforming women[81] need not apply. Only one page in the 1962 Angelica catalogue shows a uniform for women with pants (Figure 3.19), an item of dress that was strongly associated with men until the 1970s. The blue-and-white outfit on the far right in Figure 3.19—still feminine with a tiny waist and exaggerated chest—is described in the catalogue as a "sailor boy" look.[82]

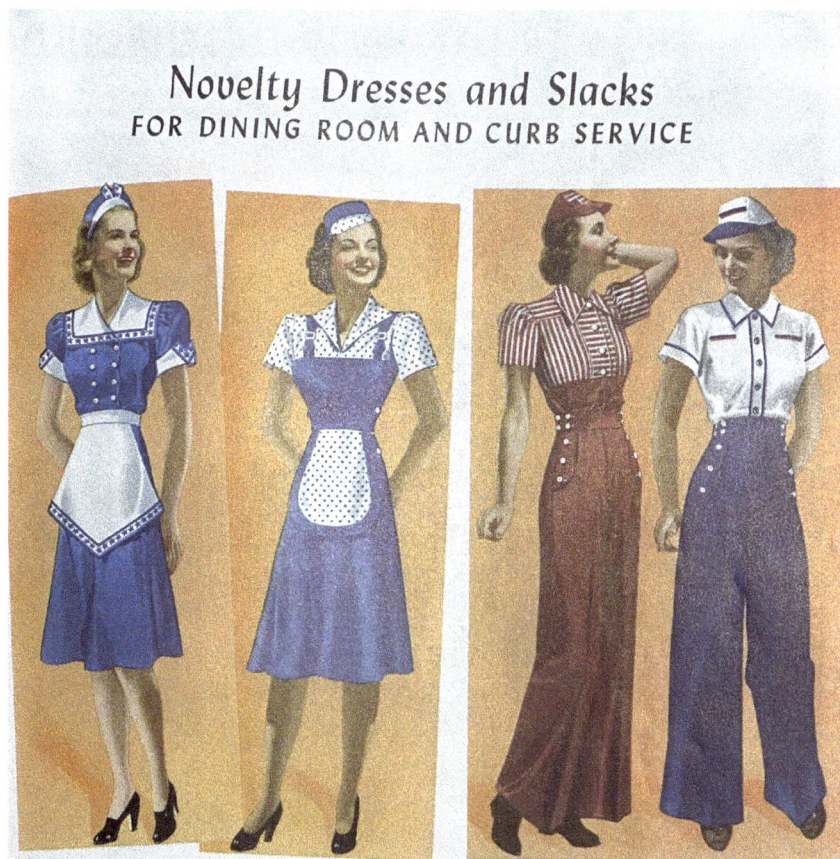

Figure 3.19 "Novelty Dresses and Slacks," 1962. *Angelica Washable Service Uniforms*, catalogue by Angelica Jacket Co. of St. Louis, Missouri, 39.

In the second half of the twentieth century, the waitresses' aprons and caps—
aesthetic links to the uniforms worn by maids and nurses—slowly disappeared.
The Angelica catalogue for 1988 featured three waitresses on the cover
(Figure 3.20), but the model in the center was not wearing an apron or a cap;
the ruffle on her chest was the only decorative element. Her outfit would

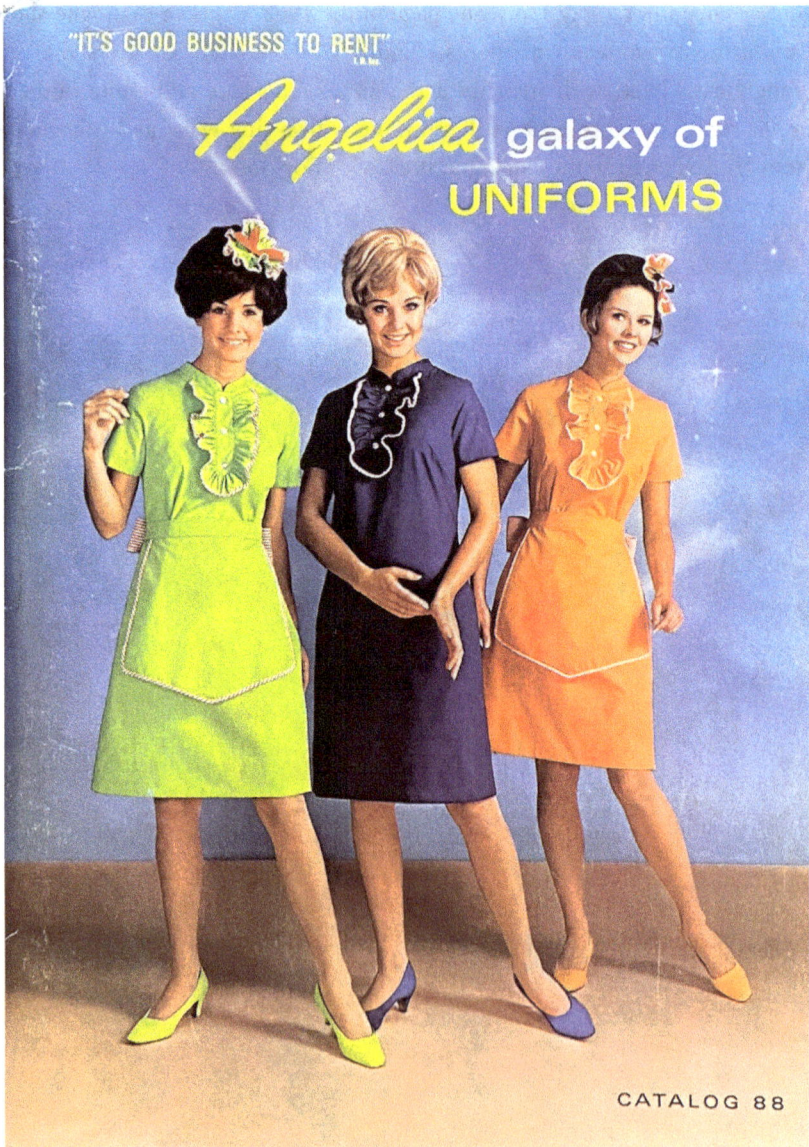

Figure 3.20 Catalogue cover featuring three waitress uniforms, 1988. *Angelica
Galaxy of Uniforms*, Angelica Uniform Co. of St. Louis, Missouri.

have been just as appropriate for working in an office as for working in a restaurant.

Despite changes in the styles of uniforms, the attitudes of employers and customers towards waitresses barely changed. In the 1980s, anthropologist Greta Foff Paules conducted research at a suburban restaurant in New Jersey that served mostly families; the waitresses (all women) included teen mothers, childless young women, mothers, and grandmothers well into their sixties. Some were experienced, full-time waitresses, while others were part-time workers picking up extra shifts.[83] Regardless of their age or depth of experience, they were commonly treated like household servants:

> [The waitress] is directed to wear a uniform that recalls the housemaid's dress and is prohibited from eating, drinking, and resting in public view. She is constrained to address as *sir* or *ma'am* those who are in turn encouraged to address her by first name, and she is placed in the symbolically demeaning position of receiving the greater part of her income in the form of tips conferred as gifts by strangers.[84]

More than two decades later, sociologist Emma Dowling made similar observations in her autoethnographic account of working as a waitress:

> You can depend on me. I am unflappable and will pander to your every wish, however obscure or absurd. Not that I would even ever let you know what I really thought of you; of course, I am always completely honest and sincere though. I don't just smile, I have a whole array of affects that I can call upon to produce your authentic, personal, and tailored experience, all in line with the training manual that teaches me how to be myself and think outside of the box. 'I'm sorry madam, say again? You would like the roast beef without potatoes because it's for your dog? Well, yes of course."[85]

These examples highlight a key difference between fashion and uniforms. Fashion is expected to change rapidly; those who set the fashion (or at least keep pace with fashion) are rewarded by positive social interactions. With uniforms, there is little reward—at least for the wearer—when the style changes quickly. The cost of the uniform not only reduces the worker's take-home pay, but turns her into an anonymous servant, regardless of whether the style is fashionable or not.

Conclusion

Uniforms can lead employers, employees, and customers to behave in ways that they might not otherwise behave. Sometimes, the effect is positive. A trusted barber is like a trusted medical professional—clean, well-trained, and with good advice. A theater attendant in a professional uniform commands respect, making the experience enjoyable and ensuring everyone's safety. Some workers in these environments take genuine pride in their uniforms.

Unfortunately, "mom and pop" businesses can also operate like dysfunctional families, stereotyping work by gender, exploiting the dynamics of power, and fostering deeply unhealthy interactions that ripple out into the larger society. In the US, these conditions—especially in the hospitality and food service industries—are reinforced by state and federal laws. In 1938, when the federal government established minimum wages under the Fair Labor Standards Act, an exception was made for "tipped employees" like waitresses who regularly receive part of their income from customers. Since 1991, employers have been allowed to pay tipped workers as little as $2.13 per hour; for everyone else, the minimum wage is $7.25 per hour. A fact sheet from the US Department of Labor states:

> Tipped employees are those who customarily and regularly receive more than $30 per month in tips. Tips are the property of the employee. The employer is prohibited from using an employee's tips for any reason other than as a credit against its minimum wage obligation to the employee.[86]

Waitresses may or may not earn more than that, depending on the generosity of customers, the cost of meals (since tips are calculated based on a percentage of the bill), and how busy or slow the restaurant is during a given shift. Many waitresses are underpaid because their employers steal their tips and/or fail to ensure that all their workers earn at least $7.25 per hour. As noted by the Economic Policy Institute in Washington, DC:

> Research indicates that having a separate, lower minimum wage for tipped workers perpetuates racial and gender inequities, and results in worse economic outcomes for tipped workers. Forcing service workers to rely on tips for their wages creates tremendous instability in income flows, making it more difficult to budget or absorb financial shocks. Furthermore, research has also shown that the practice of tipping is often discriminatory, with white service workers receiving larger tips than black service workers for the same quality of service.[87]

As women and minorities living in some of the worst economic conditions, these workers are often unable to confront their employers, who break the law with few consequences.

Today, large corporations often hire designers (or corporate uniform suppliers) to create new uniforms, however the standardized looks of many professions were developed and refined by designers who were entrepreneurs or who worked for the uniform manufacturers. They rarely worked directly for the businesses that required the uniforms or for the workers who would wear them. Sales were made mostly through department stores, catalogues, and order forms. In the mid-1900s, Angelica, Crest, Shane Company, and Barco were all selling uniforms for restaurant workers. Why should a manager choose one supplier over another? Manufacturers tried to stand out by offering innovative fabrics, low prices, and options for customization, but the choices of managers were driven by more immediate and practical concerns: they needed fresh designs to generate excitement in a competitive industry, and customers needed visual cues so they could recognize different types of workers (i.e., chefs vs. waitresses). Unless there was a shortage of workers, there was little need for designers and managers to consider the desires of workers.

4

Contagion, Caring, and Qualifications

Uniforms in the Healthcare Industry

Over the last century, medical uniforms have changed dramatically—not just for doctors and nurses, who are rare examples of middle- and upper-class workers wearing uniforms—but also for other types of staff employed in the healthcare industry such as laboratory technicians, office and cleaning staff, pharmacists, veterinarians, and dentists. Healthcare workers are licensed (like barbers) and need recognizable authority to ensure safety (like theater attendants), but they are also exposed to highly contagious diseases and use uniforms to protect themselves and their patients. These items are now known as "personal protective equipment" (PPE).

In Europe, the first non-religious uniform for nurses was developed in 1836 at a training school for women to work as doctors' assistants, established by Pastor Theodor Fliedner and his wife, Friedericke, in what is now the city of Düsseldorf, Germany. This institution predated the work of Florence Nightingale, who is more widely credited with developing the profession of nursing.[1] In an article about the earliest history of nurses' uniforms, Irene Scheussler Poplin argued that "attire was a matter of vital importance" in early-nineteenth-century Prussia:

> Without uniforms signaling respectability in a very class-structured, rigidly controlled, authoritarian society, nursing could not have succeeded. Respectable women could not have overcome the loathsome reputation associated with the 'derelicts' hired to do hospital nursing. As it was, nurses not only became recognizable by their dress, but their uniform clothing came to symbolize caring, professional competence, and, above all, unquestionable moral character.[2]

Uniforms were important not just for working nurses, but for convincing young women and their families that nursing was an important and socially acceptable occupation to pursue. In contrast to barbershops, theaters, and restaurants (where there is rarely a shortage of labor), the supply of nurses and other medical professionals has always been limited.

Professionalization and Cleanliness, 1870–1920

In North America, the first schools for nurses were established in the 1870s.[3] Museum curator, Christina Bates, has argued that the first uniform for nurses in the United States was established at Bellevue Hospital School in New York City,[4] which became one of the most prestigious nursing programs in North America. In its first year of operation, students had been allowed to wear the clothing of their choice. To convince them to wear uniforms, the school

> granted Euphemia Van Rensselaer—one of the students with a distinctive family name, social position, and personal beauty—a two-day leave of absence from Bellevue. She returned in a uniform, apron, and cap that had been made especially for her. Her tailored uniform consisted of a long blue seersucker dress with white apron, collar and cuffs, and a white cap. Within a week every nurse was wearing the uniform, which eventually became the mark of a Bellevue nurse. A pin designed by Tiffany and Company in 1880 also distinguished the graduates of Bellevue.[5]

Nurses' caps and pins became emblems of their qualifications and the schools where they were educated. The basic silhouette of the nurse's uniform—an ankle-length dress with long sleeves, a collar and cuffs, a cap, and an apron—was also widely adopted. An 1878 illustration (Figure 4.1) shows a nurse in the children's ward at Bellevue Hospital wearing a long, dark-colored dress, a light-colored apron that covers only the lower half of her body, and a frilly collar and cuffs. Her cap is gathered in the middle and has a frilled brim like a mobcap; however, the crown is stiff and stands several inches high. A history of Mount Sinai Hospital in New York City describes how the earliest uniforms were heavily starched:

> The dress was long sleeved and ankle length in blue-and-white stripes. The dress was covered with a full white apron, and both dress and apron were stiffly starched. The uniform was completed by high-top black oxford shoes, black cotton stockings, and an organdy cap. The uniform was not necessarily designed for comfort but to provide a suitably conservative appearance.[6]

Within a few years, the hospital adopted a 'blue Scotch plaid design' for the students' dresses to distinguish them from fully fledged nurses.[7] Other

CHILDREN'S WARD, BELLEVUE HOSPITAL.

HM July 78

let more of the shine in from the roof, and
on one of the upper stories there is a large
solarium, where the radiance of summer is
almost perpetual. We ascend by an elevator of more capacity than that of a fashionable hotel—an elevator of varnished maple,
which is the wood used throughout the
building, and alighting from that vehicle

Figure 4.1 Engraving of a nurse in the children's ward at Bellevue Hospital, 1878.
Originally published in *Harper's Magazine*, New York Public Library Digital
Collections, The Miriam and Ira D. Wallach Division of Art, Prints and Photographs,
at: https://digitalcollections.nypl.org/items/510d47e0-d391-a3d9-e040-e00a18064a99.

institutions with fewer resources did not require such uniformity. For example, a photograph taken in 1900 of nurse graduates from Livingstone College (a historically black college in North Carolina) shows them wearing identical caps, but with dresses, aprons, and neckwear in a variety of fabrics (Figure 4.2).

Male surgeons—who were much more free to pursue professional occupations, but were still preoccupied in the late 1800s with distinguishing themselves from barber-surgeons—were accustomed to operating while wearing their second-best professional clothing from their own wardrobes.[8] Some (but not all) wore butcher aprons to protect against stains. The adoption of uniforms among doctors lagged several decades behind the nurses, even in the same hospitals (Figure 4.3).

By the turn of the century, surgeons were beginning to realize the importance of washing their hands and sterilizing materials to prevent infections. The new standard became to wear a white "operating gown," which completely covered the wearer's clothing and fit closely around the neck and wrists. Surgeons also began to wear rubber gloves, face masks, and cloth caps to cover their hair. "Scrub suits"[9] consisting of simple white pants and white button-down shirts were introduced to replace street clothing in operating rooms (Figure 4.4).[10]

Nurse Training Class 1900, in E. T. I. School.   Some of these Nurses have seen service and given the highest satisfaction.   Their service is in constant demand.

Figure 4.2 Graduating class of nurses from Livingstone College in North Carolina, 1900. Unknown photographer, Schomburg Center for Research in Black Culture, New York Public Library Digital Collections, at: https://digitalcollections.nypl.org/items/510d47e4-4fea-a3d9-e040-300a18064a00.

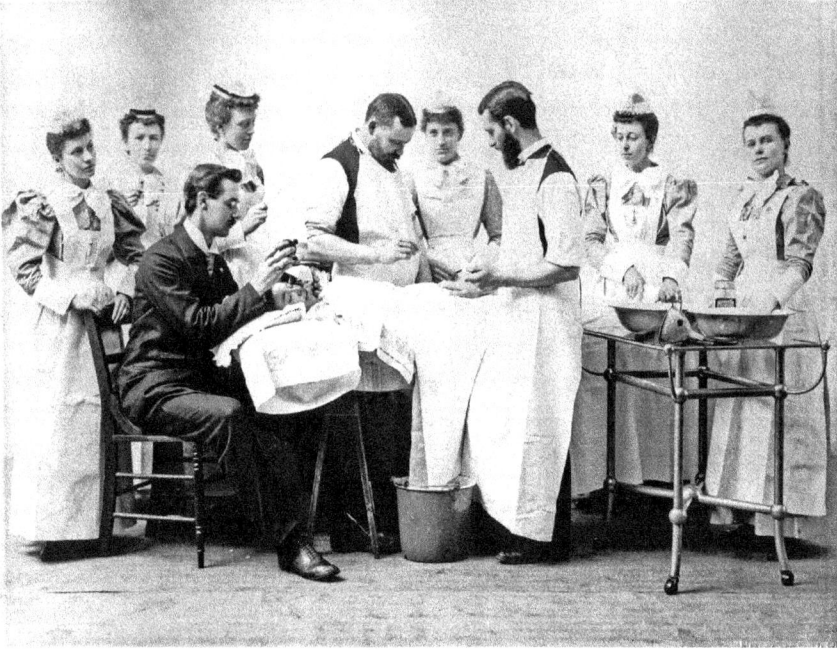

Figure 4.3 Operating room in Cleveland, Ohio, 1880. Photograph by Universal History Archive / Universal Images Group via Getty Images.

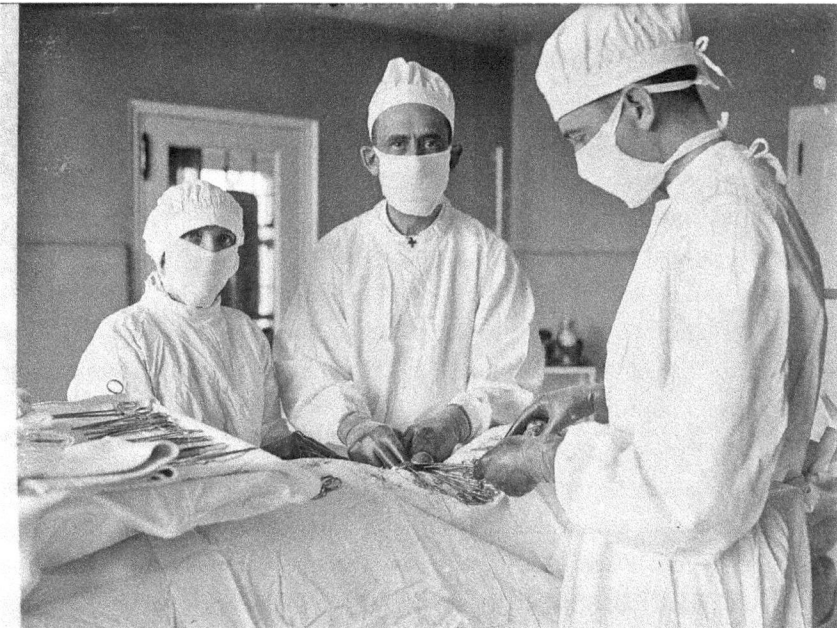

Figure 4.4 Surgical team wearing operating gowns, caps, and masks made of white cloth, 1922. Photograph by National Photo Company, Library of Congress Prints and Photographs Division, LC-DIG-npcc-23065.

As symbols of cleanliness and modern progress, hospitals began to paint their operating rooms white and to furnish them with white curtains, drapes, and towels. In 1914, a doctor at St. Luke's Hospital in San Francisco published an article in the *California State Journal of Medicine* arguing that black and green were more effective colors for surgery, since white was too blinding for surgeons trying to peer into the dark crevices of their patients' bodies. As an experiment, he convinced his employer to paint one operating room "spinach green" as the visual opposite to the color of blood.[11] The change was such a success that the hospital adopted green tiled walls, dark flooring, and black uniforms for all operating rooms. As the green color spread to other parts of the country (even for masks and operating gowns), it became better known as "surgical green" or "hospital green."[12]

Prestige, Branding, and Fashion, 1920–70

After the First World War (1914–18), fashions for women changed dramatically as they abandoned corsets, padding, and layers of undergarments for more natural silhouettes, shorter hemlines, and shorter sleeves. Mass production was not as widespread as it was for men's clothing, but it was gradually gaining acceptance even among middle- and upper-class women.[13] When Henry Dix & Sons advertised in *Hospital Management* in the 1920s, the company emphasized the ease of laundering, cost-effectiveness, and "smartness" of its mass-produced uniforms (Figure 4.5).

Elaborate nurse's caps persisted long into the twentieth century,[14] however the trend was to wear simpler caps with characteristic "wing" shapes on the sides[15] that could be flattened for easier laundering and ironing. One of the earliest examples (Figure 4.6) was patented in 1927 by Aline Mullinix, who worked as a nurse at Indianapolis City Hospital.[16] Over time, the caps also transitioned from covering the top of the head to sitting on the back of the wearer's head like a decorative accessory.

Under pressure to regulate hospitals more like businesses and to achieve financial stability, administrators turned to uniforms as a tool for better management of staff and to achieve a more favorable impression among patients who could afford to pay for their own healthcare. In an article for the *American Journal of Nursing* published in 1920, a nurse administrator in Peoria, Illinois argued that hospitals were essential for public health, but they could not afford to continue operating as if they were charities:

Figure 4.5 Advertisement for Dix-Make uniforms, 1920. *Hospital Management*, 9 (4): 77.

The hospital is, then, not only a public benefactor, it is one of the community's soundest business institutions and should be conducted as such. Many of our small hospitals are staggering under inadequate endowments and are bound by traditional ideals of rendering service to the sick without sufficient remuneration; consequently, their buildings are inadequate, with insufficient equipment, and good service is impossible, because funds are not available.[17]

In the period between the end of First World War and the beginning of the Second World War, nursing was one of the highest-paying, most stable, and most socially acceptable occupations for educated women. Tens of thousands made careers in the Red Cross,[18] military,[19] public health,[20] public schools,[21] clinics, and hospitals. When commercial air travel started in the 1930s, the airlines hired professional nurses to reassure passengers and attend to their medical needs.[22]

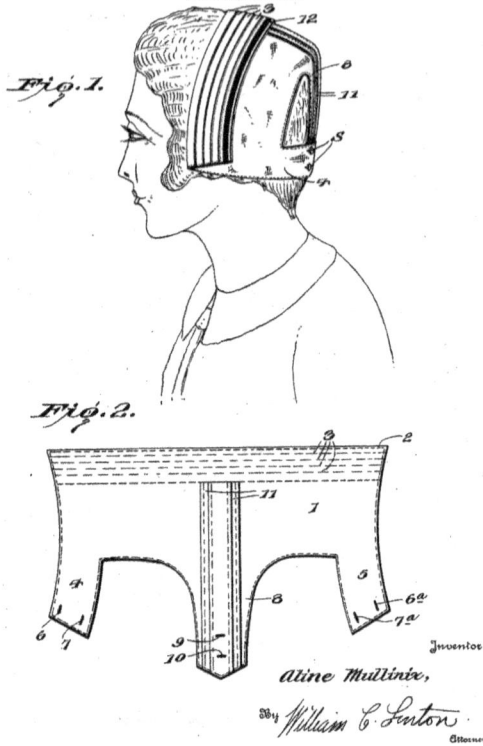

May 1, 1928.   1,668,331
A. MULLINIX
NURSE'S CAP
Filed June 23, 1927

Fig. 1.

Fig. 2.

Inventor
aline Mullinix,
By *William C. Linton.*
Attorney

Figure 4.6 Illustration for an innovative nurse's cap designed by Aline Mullinix, a nurse at Indianapolis City Hospital, US Patent 1,668,331, 1928.

It was even more socially admired to be a physician. A 1947 survey on occupational prestige found that it was one of the highest-rated professions among adults in the United States, just below US Supreme Court Justice and equivalent to being a state governor. Other jobs that were rated as slightly less prestigious included "cabinet member in the federal government," diplomat, mayor of a large city, professor, scientist, lawyer, banker, architect, and minister.[23] Notably, these occupations are associated with high levels of education, power, and personal autonomy—conditions that usually preclude the use of uniforms, unless they stem from long-standing traditions, such as judges' robes or the vestments worn by religious authorities.

In hospitals, sentiments against uniforms were overcome by needs for sterilization, efficiency, teamwork, and eventually by a new sense of prestige: earning the right to wear a nurse's cap or a doctor's jacket became a rite of passage for medical students. For staff who performed "unskilled" labor in hospitals—such as porters, maids, and waitresses—uniforms were already considered an essential part of the job. An article published in 1921 described uniforms for non-medical staff as being so common in hospitals that even unpaid volunteers should be supplied with uniforms.:

> A distinct uniform for the helpers is, of course, necessary, but it is a question whether they should be supplied by the hospital or provided by the helper. Most hospitals supply uniforms to maids and porters and could furnish them equally well to the helpers.[24]

In 1923, *The Modern Hospital*[25] published two back-to-back articles about uniforms. In the first article, the director of Mt. Sinai Hospital in Cleveland, Ohio, argued that uniforms for all ranks of staff working in hospitals were needed to establish standards of cleanliness, professional behavior, and distinguish employees from patients and visitors (Figure 4.7):

> Until recently only a few hospitals have required their employees to wear a distinctive garb. Now there is a marked tendency among progressive institutions to have the entire personnel appear in uniforms that have been selected to meet the individual requirements of the various groups.
>
> The effect of this tendency is clearly shown in three directions:
>
> (1) On the part of the institution, better discipline and higher morale are the natural results. A higher degree of cleanliness is readily secured when each employee is required to wear a uniform suitable to his duties.
>
> (2) On the part of the individual, well-designed and suitable uniforms are powerful factors in influencing conduct. A clean, freshly laundered uniform is an incentive to neatness in every duty. The donning of a distinctive uniform when going on duty and its removal at close of the day's service have a very distinct influence on the mental attitude of the employee. Proper uniforms give employees a certain pride in their work and a desire to live up to those standards that may be rightfully expected of them.
>
> (3) To the hospital patient or visitor, the general use of uniforms by the various classes of employees at once carries a suggestion of service efficiency. Confusion is overcome, employees are definitely separated from patients or visitors, and those in authority can be readily distinguished from subordinates.[26]

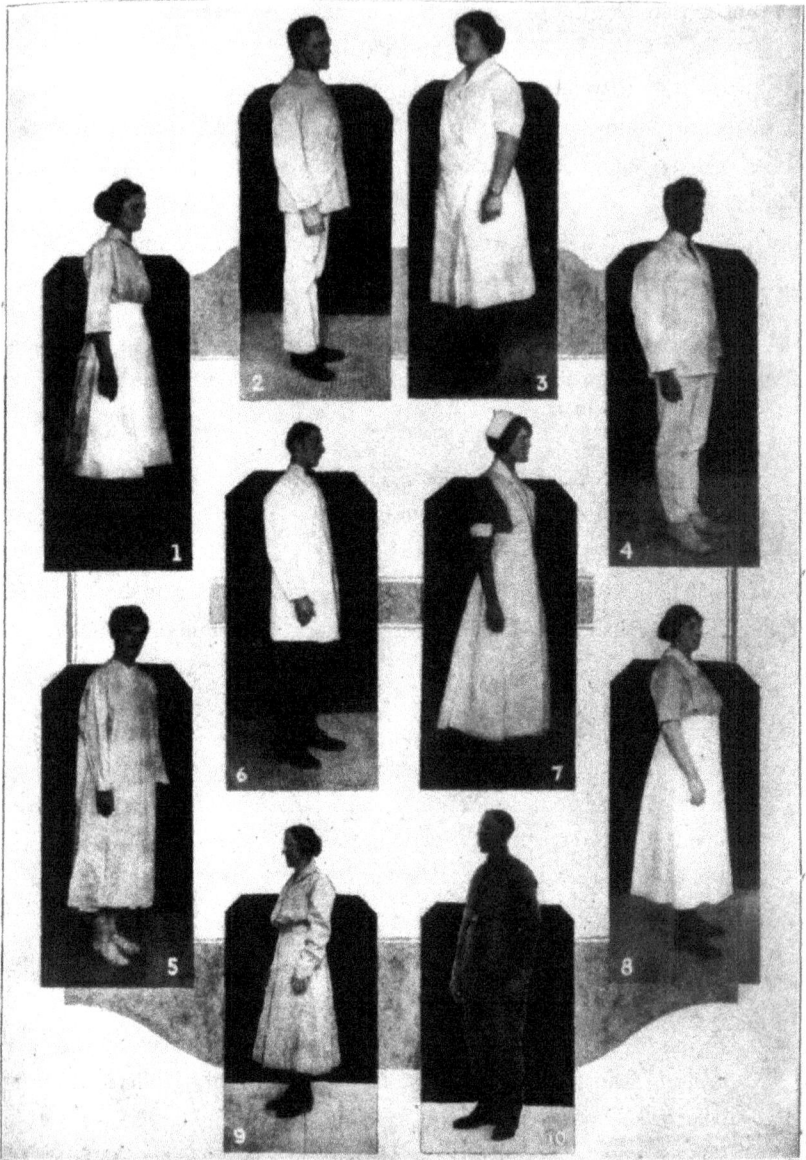

Figure 4.7 Uniforms for ten categories of staff at Mt. Sinai Hospital in Cleveland, Ohio, 1923. *The Modern Hospital*, 20 (4): 377.

The article was accompanied by an extensive chart outlining the numbers and types of staff employed by the hospital, including descriptions of their uniforms and notes about who was responsible for buying and laundering them. Notably, the jobs were split according to gender based on clothing: pants (doctors, interns, residents, storekeepers, porters, orderlies) vs. dresses (nurses, nursing students, dieticians, cooks, waitresses, and maids). Allowing a woman to work as a doctor or a man to work as a nurse—a change that took decades to achieve—would require shifts in both mindset and the design of the uniforms.[27] Only one category of workers at Mt. Sinai— laboratory and x-ray technicians—was not explicitly gendered since the regulations did not specify whether they should wear pants or dresses under their operating gowns.

Hierarchies of authority based on professional qualifications were reinforced through colors, upper-body garments, and head coverings. Only doctors and men who worked directly with patients (orderlies, elevator operators, and storekeepers) were allowed to wear jackets; porters and maintenance men were not. Only nurses were allowed to wear uniform caps; attendants, kitchen staff, and cleaning staff were not. Student nurses—who occupied a position in between nurses and non-medical staff—were allowed to wear caps, but were also required to wear aprons, collars, and cuffs to mark their subservient status.

Doctors and nurses were expected to wear white (except for student nurses, who wore gray dresses under their white aprons), but the author described other categories of workers as wearing solid-blue, blue-and-white (gingham or seersucker), cream, or olive drab. Even the weight of the fabric was specified: heavy cotton duck for the most prestigious ranks, sheeting and chambray (thinner, inexpensive fabrics) for the less prestigious.

The second article about uniforms in the same issue of *The Modern Hospital* was written by the superintendent for Bridgeport General Hospital in Bridgeport, Connecticut. Like the first, it describes the value of requiring uniforms for all types and ranks of hospital staff, however it is more specific about the cost and manner of acquiring, repairing, and laundering them. In 1921, the hospital created a "sewing room" to produce, repair, and replace uniforms as needed. For the position of food handler (gendered male) the author noted,

> The jackets and trousers cost two dollars each, the caps twenty-five cents, and the aprons, made by the hospital, cost for material forty-five cents a piece. Each man has four uniforms [...] and is allowed a maximum of three aprons per day. The life of a uniform is about six months.[28]

Waitresses (gendered female) were only allowed to have two uniforms made from five yards of "serviceable gray gingham" costing 22 cents per yard—less than the cost of one food handler's jacket.[29] Despite the cost of buying materials and staffing the sewing room, the author argued that the investment was producing financial value by impressing patients and visitors:

> The various luncheon clubs, the Rotary, Lions, Kiwanis, and Chamber of Commerce, are asked to visit the hospital each year and they are served with regular nurses' luncheon before their tour of inspection. The impression given by a uniformed personnel upon these business organizations, especially in regard to the kitchen help and food handlers, has been actually worth dollars and cents as judged from [their] financial and moral support . . .[30]

It is interesting that the author described these groups of visitors as business organizations and not philanthropies. The widespread use of uniforms in other business settings (hotels, theaters, restaurants, trains, etc.) likely gave visitors an impression that administrators were managing the hospital as if it were a modern business.

The widespread adoption of uniforms in hospitals created new opportunities for uniform manufacturers. When Morris Barker founded Barco in Los Angeles in 1929, his primary source of revenue was making uniforms for maids and beauty workers. When his stepson, Kenneth Donner, took over in 1936, he saw an opportunity to make more fashion-forward uniforms for nurses.[31] Throughout the 1940s, press releases in *Women's Wear Daily*—a trade journal for buyers and manufacturers in the fashion industry—emphasized how Barco was utilizing new materials and innovative details such as detachable shoulder pads,[32] French tucks, dolman sleeves, pastel colors,[33] nylon fabrics,[34] zippers,[35] set-in belts (to echo the popular post-war silhouette),[36] and Dacron polyester.[37] In 1951, an editorial in the journal observed,

> Styled-up uniforms in general are checking out twice as fast as staple styles, according to manufacturers, including Barco of California, Colonial Uniform Mfg. Co. and Angelica Uniform Co. Uniforms that have Peter Pan or stand-up collars, mandarin necklines, dolman sleeves, saddle shoulder styling, tucked yoke front, Dior pockets and set-in belts are proving most popular. The styled-up uniform is especially favored by nurses, beauticians, and doctor or dental assistants.[38]

In a move that was unusual for the uniform industry, Barco advertised in fashion magazines (*Mademoiselle* and *Cosmopolitan*) to flatter nurses and highlight the glamor of its uniforms.[39] However, in trade journals for nurses and hospital administrators, the company emphasized how its designs could make the hard work of nursing more comfortable and efficient:

> Hidden details of perfection in Barco uniforms are the Conmar zippers in the skirt plackets. These zippers are easy on the glide... up, down... down, up... with never a hitch to mar their smooth action. They're precision built with tiny teeth that simply mesh like magic... add so much to the trimness of these uniforms. Can't stick, can't jam, guaranteed flawless.[40]

For two decades, the company straddled the markets for uniforms and fashion with the slogan, "professional uniforms with a dressmaker's touch."

As it became more common for young women to finish high school, many hospitals introduced programs for teenagers to serve as volunteers during the summer. While supplying them with free labor for minor aspects of patient care such as filing, powdering surgical gloves, and taking patients' temperatures,[41] the larger goal was to introduce young women to nursing and attract them into the profession.[42] It is unclear when and where the volunteers first became known as "candy stripers,"[43] but the term reflects the common use of red-and-white seersucker fabric for their uniforms (resembling a candy cane). Blue-and-white seersucker was common for nurses' uniforms in the late 1800s, but by the time it was reintroduced for teenage volunteers the main purpose was to make them visually distinct from trained nurses wearing all-white uniforms (see Figure 4.8).

In the 1950s, sociologist Julius Roth conducted fieldwork in a tuberculosis hospital and found that there was still some resistance to uniforms, particularly among doctors and the highest-ranking nurses. To limit the spread of the disease,[44] the hospital had adopted surgical masks and operating gowns as part of the standard dress for all employees. However, the highest-ranking staff members were the least consistent about wearing protective clothing:

> [An] important factor is the likelihood that the employee can 'get away with' a violation. A doctor need not worry about a 'bawling out' for not protecting himself. A professional nurse might be criticized, but usually she is the highest authority on a ward. The chance of criticism increases down the scale. Students, who are new and unfamiliar with the situation [...] and who worry about possible 'demerits' wear protective clothing all the time in patients' rooms. Some ward employees, especially those of lower status, who are not 'properly dressed' hurriedly don a mask and gown if they see the supervisor of the nursing education program on the floor.[45]

Figure 4.8 "Candy Stripers in training in Tallahassee, Florida," 1957. Unknown photographer, originally published in the *Tallahassee Democrat*, Courtesy of the State Archives of Florida, floridamemory.com/items/show/261665.

The nurses complained "that the gown, and more especially the mask" were barriers to having good communication with their patients.[46]

In a survey of more than 1,000 nurses conducted in the mid-1950s, published in *The American Journal of Nursing*, 89 percent responded that their uniforms were mass manufactured. Some were getting the clothing from their employers, but more than half were expected to purchase their own uniforms, ranging in price from $5 to $16.[47] Of those questioned, 18 percent argued that the styles were becoming too fashionable and that it was damaging the professional image of nurses:

> They look like party dresses. I know one nurse who loaned her teenage sister a uniform to wear to a school dance and it looked perfectly all right—just like any other white dress. A nurse's uniform should be different, more dignified—you know, professional looking.[48]

Fit was also a concern, particularly for nurses who were unusually tall or short, overweight, or pregnant. Unlike waitresses, nurses could afford to solve problems with fit by paying extra to have their uniforms professionally altered.

The importance of professional qualifications in hiring and retention also gave them some leverage to bend hospital dress codes.

For doctors, white coats—also worn by scientists, pharmacists, and dentists—became widely viewed as the most appropriate uniform for interactions with patients, a style that remains in widespread use in the twenty-first century. In an article for the American Medical Association published in 2007, a doctor reflected on how the white coat had become a symbol of "medical authority and respect" as scientific advancements led to better healthcare:

> Probably the greatest development of medical science in the 20th century was the advent of antibiotics toward the end of World War II—the completion of Lord Lister's dream that bacteria could be successfully overcome. For the first time pneumonia, appendicitis, and infected blister or a toothache no longer condemned one to death.[49]

Even during the Second World War, a photograph of Japanese Americans held as political prisoners at an internment camp in California showed dentists and their assistants wearing white coats (Figure 4.9). While the photograph was

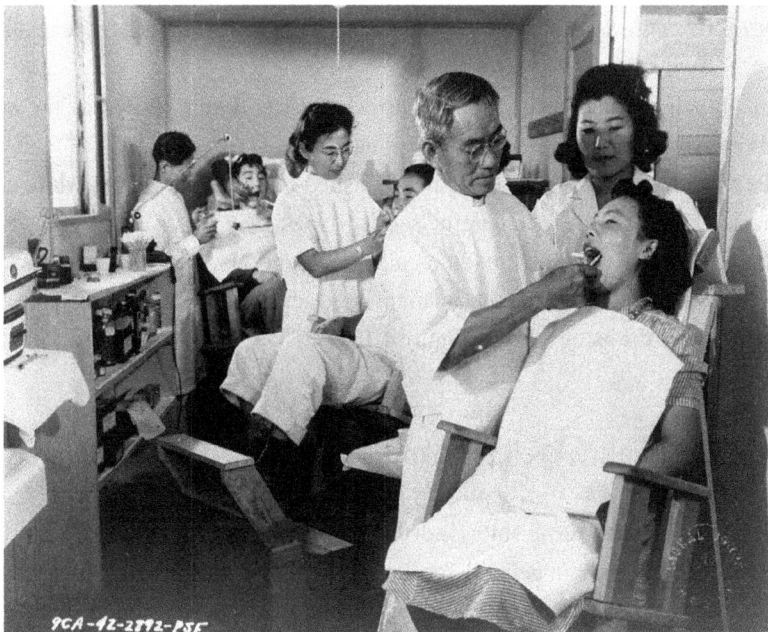

Figure 4.9 Japanese-American dentists serving patients at an internment camp in Pinedale, California, 1942. Photograph by the U.S. Army Signal Corps., Library of Congress Prints and Photograph Division, LC-USZ62-137388.

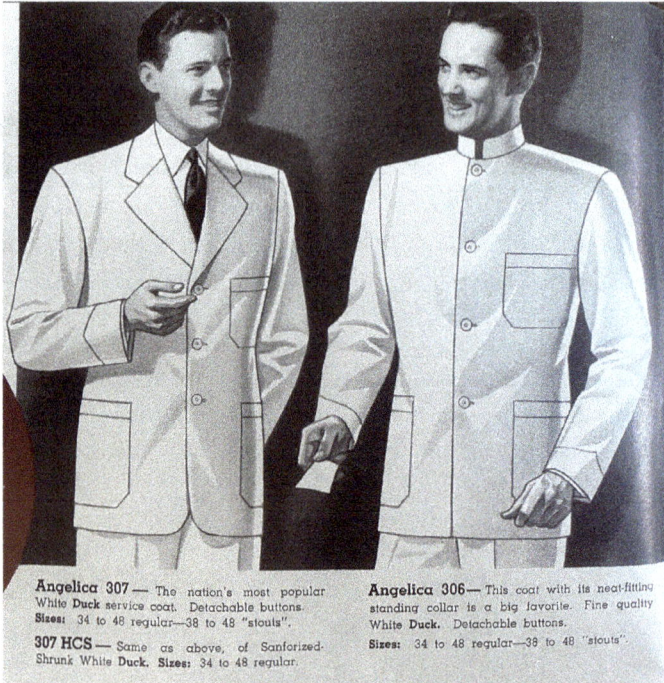

Angelica 307 — The nation's most popular   Angelica 306— This coat with its neat-fitting
White Duck service coat. Detachable buttons. standing collar is a big favorite. Fine quality
Sizes: 34 to 48 regular—38 to 48 "stouts".   White Duck. Detachable buttons.
307 HCS — Same as above, of Sanforized-   Sizes: 34 to 48 regular—38 to 48 "stouts".
Shrunk White Duck. Sizes: 34 to 48 regular.

Figure 4.10 Two styles of "service coats" for male medical professionals, 1962. *Angelica Washable Service Uniforms*, Angelica Jacket Co. of St. Louis, Missouri, 15.

probably staged to make life in the camp seem better than it really was, the white coats clearly signified "medical professionalism."

In its catalogues, Angelica Co. distinguished between hip-length white coats ("service coats") and knee-length "service frocks" by describing the latter as being "especially adapted" for blue-collar occupations such as "meat packers" and "garage men." However, the garments had identical pockets and collars and were made of the same fabrics (Figure 4.10).[50]

Equality, Wellness, and Protection 1970–2020

Like surgical masks, scrub suits (shortened to "scrubs") also migrated outside of the operating room.[51] In general, scrubs are two-piece outfits with a loose-fitting top and a pair of pants that has a drawstring or an elastic waistband. Their boxy construction is unisex and allows a small selection of sizes to fit a wide variety of bodies, which is convenient and cost-effective (Figure 4.11). A 1990 patent application for a "unisex scrub shirt" emphasized the high volume of scrubs

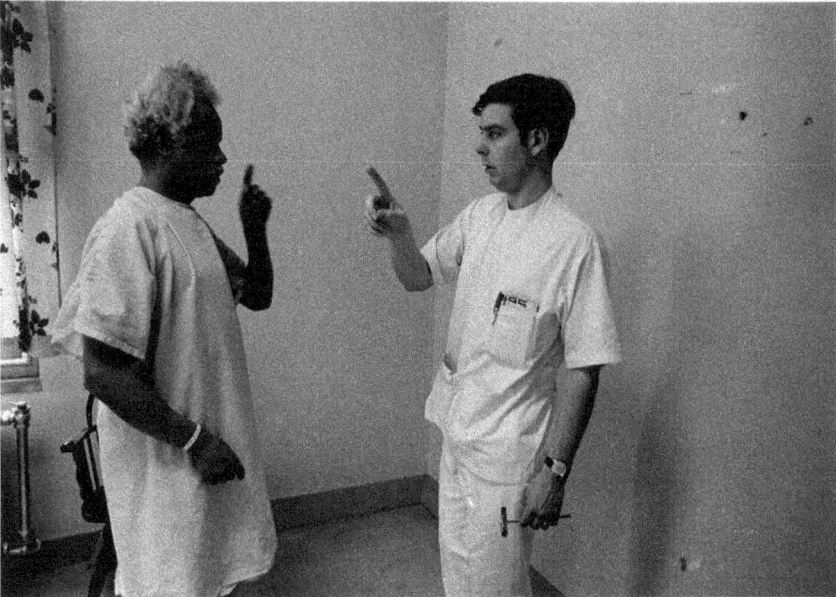

Figure 4.11 Doctor wearing scrubs outside of the operating room in Rochester, New York, *Untitled*, 1970–72. Photograph by Mitchell Payne (1944–1977), © Mitchell Payne Archive, Collection of the Center for Creative Photography, University of Arizona.

being used in healthcare facilities. "Reducing the cost of a single item by even a small amount can lead to tremendous cost savings if that item is used in sufficient quantity."[52]

The details of construction can vary. For example, Figure 4.12(a) shows the top of a scrub uniform worn by "Riley Physicians," pediatric medical staff who work for IU Health in the state of Indiana. It has snap closures, an embroidered logo, and two sets of pockets at hip level to hold tools and note pads. One pocket has the manufacturer's logo (Landau);[53] another pocket has a hidden piece of twill tape tacked inside to keep tools more securely in place (e.g., a pen light). The fabric is dark blue and made from a tightly woven blend of polyester and cotton.

Figure 4.12(b) shows a V-neck pullover scrub top worn by nursing students at Indiana University. The silhouette and fabric (polyester-cotton blend) are similar to the Riley uniform, but the student uniform is red and only has three pockets. The school's logo is embroidered on one sleeve and the manufacturer's logo (Cherokee)[54] is on the other. Some scrubs have more pockets at chest level (see Figure 4.11). Initially, the most common colors were white, surgical green, and "ceil blue" (a medium, sky-blue color).[55]

Figure 4.12 (a) Uniform scrub tops for IU Health Riley Physicians (blue); and (b) nursing students at Indiana University (red), both *c*. 2015. Author's research collection.

In 1982, a nurse administrator in California[56] published a chapter about sexism and uniforms. She observed that nurses were pushing back against traditional styles of uniforms because of the hierarchies they reflected and reinforced:

> The more a nurse specializes, the less traditional her appearance becomes. In the areas of intensive care, labor and delivery, the operating room, pediatrics, and psychiatry, in all of which nurses have increased autonomy, they seem to conform less to the traditional white uniform.[57]

Two major changes to medical uniforms in the 1970s and 80s were about gender equality: the acceptance of female staff wearing pants and nurses' rejection of wearing caps.[58]

On the television medical drama, *Quincy M.E.* (1976–83), a diverse cast of all-female nurses was shown wearing white dresses with white caps. There was tension among the staff; in a 1982 episode titled, "The Flight of the Nightingale,"[59] four nurses organized a strike when their nurse supervisor was wrongfully dismissed after being blamed for a doctor's mistake:

Nurse 1 (*Black*) What exactly are we gonna ask for [in the strike]? We have to be specific.

Nurse 2 (*Latina*) Diñero. More money.

Nurse 3 (*White*) More staff, so we can spend more time with the patients. I am tired of passing pills… on the phone trying to find doctors, or just dealing with hospital red tape.

Nurse 4 (*White organizer of the group*) What about the way doctors treat us?

Nurse 2 I'm with the patient much more than the doctor. There's a lot of input I could give, but would a doctor ever listen to me?

Nurse 1 Never.

Nurse 3 It's like the nineteenth century. We're like handmaidens. Yes, doctor. No, doctor. Whatever you say, doctor. It's like the only reason we exist is to do their bidding.

The uniforms did not change before the show ended in 1983, however, the doctors conceded to work jointly for better patient care. In the next major televised medical drama, *St. Elsewhere* (1982–8), the nurses did not wear caps. The cast also included several women as doctors, who dressed in scrubs or in street clothing with white coats.

In a short article about her first experience in an operating room as a medical student in 1987, surgeon Elizabeth Rider discovered color-coded scrubs:

Piled high on carts [in the women's locker room] are pink scrubs—not pastel, not fuchsia, but true pink—in all sizes. I look again through another small window into the operating room. Men in blue scrubs work with an air of authority. Buzzing around them are women in pink hats, pink scrubs, pink shoe covers. As far as I can ascertain, there are no pink female surgeons.

'Nope,' I think to myself, 'no way am I going out there in pink.' I walk out of the women's locker room and check the hall. No one is there. Not knowing what to expect, I open the door to the men's locker room. I fear I will come face to face with men in compromising stages of undress. Just inside, I find shelves of blue scrubs and grab a pair."[60]

Rider was not reprimanded for going into the men's locker room and the hospital eventually settled on green scrubs for all operating room staff, regardless of rank or gender.

Outside of hospitals, there was a growing trend to wear scrubs as an inexpensive form of casual wear and to emulate popular television shows. An article in the *Boston Globe* in 1980 quoted a twenty-three-year-old student (not a medical student) as saying, "I'll wear the pants around the house and on Cape Cod this summer."[61] In an interview for a blog on historic street fashions, a surgeon recalled how during his residency in the 1980s, it was "absolutely forbidden" to wear scrubs outside of the hospital. "Residents who would sneak out their scrubs and wear them off hours usually did it to attract women by letting them know they were doctors."[62] In the video for Prince's hit song "1999," released in 1982, one member of the band, Matt Fink, wore a set of green scrubs with a white surgical mask hanging by a strap over his chest.[63]

Since the 1960s, medical-themed series such as *General Hospital* (1963–present), *Marcus Welby, MD* (1969–76), *Trapper John, MD* (1979–86), *ER* (1994–2009), *Scrubs* (2001–10), *Nip/Tuck* (2003–10), *House* (2004–12), *Grey's Anatomy* (2005–present), and *Nurse Jackie* (2009–15) have been some of the most highly rated television shows in the United States, set mostly in Chicago, New York, or Los Angeles. In 1983, a uniform retailer in North Carolina observed that sales of scrubs had "skyrocketed as people prepared for the last episode of [the television show] M*A*S*H" (1972–83).[64] Doctors in particular have been portrayed as powerful, wealthy, and sexually desirable. In 1986, while playing the role of Dr. Caldwell on *St. Elsewhere*, Mark Harmon was featured as Sexiest Man Alive on the cover of *People Magazine*. George Clooney received the same title for the first time in 1997 while playing Dr. Ross on *ER*.[65]

As a result of these trends, in the 1980s hospitals around the country reported spending tens of thousands of dollars per year to replace stolen or missing scrubs. In Pennsylvania, a medical laundry service began stamping "HCSC" on scrubs to identify thieves after spending more than $100,000 in a single year to replace missing uniforms. In a newspaper feature, the company's director threatened, "Apparently it is a bit of a fad to have a scrub shirt because they are comfortable, popular and, up until now, free—but not anymore, because it could cost you a criminal record to wear them."[66] In 1987 the American Hospital Association reported that institutions were trying a variety of methods to reduce theft including inventory controls, "garish" colors, and selling scrubs in hospital gift shops, but without much success.[67]

Nurses in southern California were pushing the limits of uniforms in different ways by wearing athletic shoes and street clothing:

> Arlene Ucinski, a registered nurse in the cardiac rehabilitation department of Cedars-Sinai Medical Center, says she often wears white shorts and a T-shirt with a cow in running shoes pictured on the front, because, she says, "It makes the patients feel more comfortable and puts them in better spirits."
>
> She's quick to point out that what she wears is consistent with what she does: helping outpatients work on athletic equipment. In addition to monitoring their hearts, she may be called upon to demonstrate exercise equipment or help lift

patients from machine to machine. "When I worked at bedside, I wore white overalls and colorful T-shirts."[68]

In the emergency department at Midway Hospital in Los Angeles, nurses were asked to go back to wearing white after administrators received "complaints from patients who didn't know they had seen a nurse... obviously they had, but they weren't able to identify them."[69]

Pediatric nurses—who noticed that solid-color uniforms (especially white) were causing fear in their patients[70]—may have been the first to wear scrubs with characters from popular cartoons, films, and video games (see for example Figure 4.13). Koi by Kathy Peterson, a brand of "designer scrubs" based in California, has used a variety of proprietary and licensed patterns including

Figure 4.13 Scrub top featuring kittens from *The Aristocats* (1970) by Disney Corporation, *c.* 2000. Author's research collection.

florals, ombre, animal prints, characters from Kellogg's cereal, and Betsey Johnson graphics (Figure 4.14).[71] Although the company also sells to men, who now hold approximately 10 percent of all nursing jobs in the US,[72] most of the styles are feminine. To counteract the boxy/unisex fit of scrubs, the designs have features such as decorative ties, elastic, rib knit cuffs, and small amounts of spandex to make them fit more closely. In a throwback to the fashion-forward uniforms of the 1950s and 1960s, the company's website asks shoppers, "If you have to wear scrubs to work, shouldn't they make you look and feel amazing?"[73]

In 2007, Barco launched a new line of scrubs in collaboration with ABC, the television network that owns *Grey's Anatomy*.[74] A editorialist for *The New York Times*

Figure 4.14 Fashion scrub top from Koi by Kathy Peterson, featuring a leopard print, geometric accents, and a hidden elastic waistband, *c.* 2010. Author's research collection.

asked whether the new brand was going too far, blurring the lines between fiction (television) and reality (real-life medical staff).[75] As the show has become one of the longest-running medical dramas—second only to the soap opera, *General Hospital*—the line of scrubs has continued to be manufactured. The solid-color uniforms are visually unremarkable. Small labels on the pockets are the only way for patients to know that they have any connection to *Grey's Anatomy*.

Some brands that make scrubs (like Barco) have a long history specific to healthcare uniforms. Others have crossed over from other industries. For example, Dickies and Carhartt are better known among factory and construction workers.[76] Baby Phat, a streetwear brand founded by Kimora Lee Simmons[77] sells a line of scrubs, as does Vera Bradley, better known for its handbags and luggage in colorful printed patterns.[78] Since the basic construction of scrubs is so simple, individuals can even make their own using paper patterns and a vast array of colorful fabrics such as batik and African wax prints.

Another crossover is the "wellness industry," which blends fitness trends such as yoga and Pilates with complementary medicine (acupuncture, massage), the beauty industry, and workplace health programs.[79] In 2000, the *New York Times* published an article about a new clinic for cancer patients that was "part luxury hotel, part Zenlike retreat":[80]

> In the New York City area, health care institutions and a spate of wellness centers are wooing patients with amenities like on-the-site hair salons, Zen tearooms and lavish kimonos, which make chilly clinics and consulting rooms seem as dated as high-button shoes. [...]
>
> Even uniforms have been made over with cheery patterns and bright colors, reinforcing the impression that the hospital staff is as friendly and accessible as, say, one's favorite hairdresser.[81]

Healing Hands[82] sells only scrubs, but with a "yoga" line (Figure 4.15) that clearly nods to the wellness industry. Noel Asmar manufactures high-end "spa and wellness uniforms," but also describes "medical and dental uniforms" as one of its main categories of business.[83]

The AIDS crisis of the 1980s and early 1990s—as well as the arrival of Ebola in the US (2014)[84] and the COVID-19 pandemic (2020–3)[85]—have pushed hospitals to think more carefully about uniforms not just as a management tool or to limit the spread of infections in patients, but as protective gear for the workers themselves. In 1997, an article in the *American Journal of Infection Control* argued that OSHA regulations should not apply to scrubs, since the cloth is porous and does not protect the wearer from blood-borne

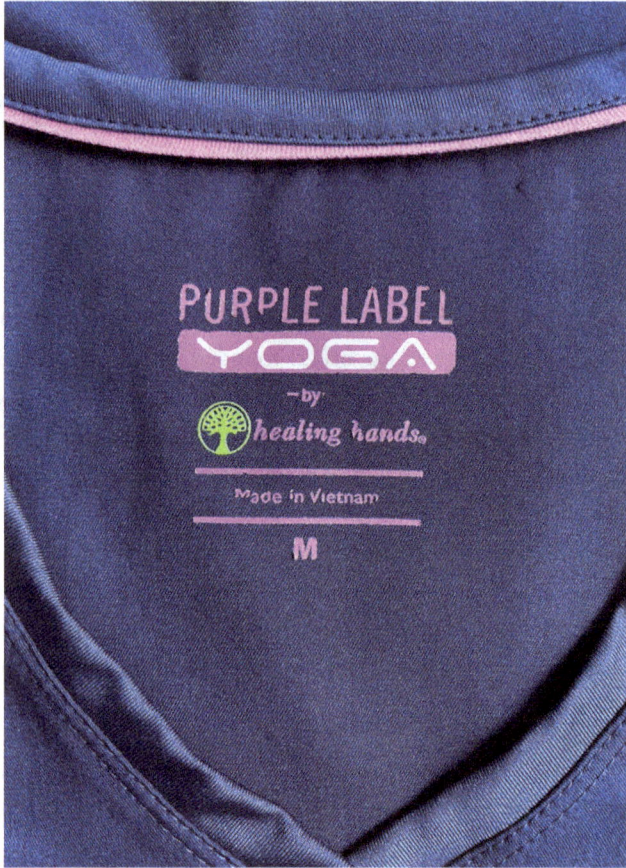

Figure 4.15 Label inside a scrub top by Healing Hands, a healthcare uniform manufacturer that crosses over into the wellness industry, *c.* 2015. Author's research collection.

pathogens.[86] Instead, the focus should be on extra layers of gear worn on top of clothing.

In the 1990s, manufacturers introduced disposable cover gowns, caps, shoe covers, and surgical masks made of polyester, polyethylene, and polypropylene—inexpensive, lightweight materials that do not absorb water (see Figure 4.16). Despite concerns about the environmental impact of the materials[87] and mixed research regarding its effectiveness,[88] disposable protective clothing has come into widespread use in hospitals in the US. In particularly high-risk situations, full-body suits made of PTFE (better known as Teflon) are worn.[89]

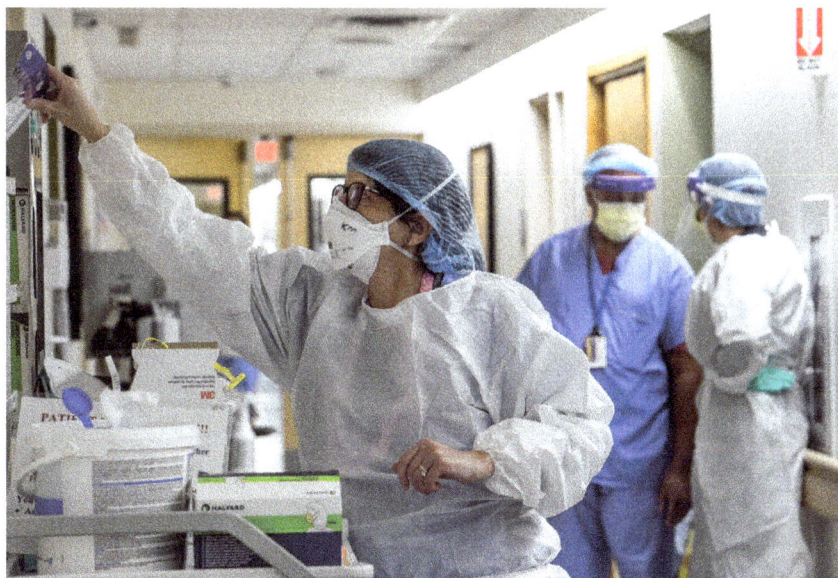

Figure 4.16 Medical worker at a hospital in Massachusetts donning a layer of PPE during the COVID-19 pandemic with another worker in the background wearing ceil blue scrubs, January 11, 2022. Photograph by Joseph Prezioso / AFP via Getty Images.

In 2014, Congress solicited testimony about how to handle Ebola after two nurses in Texas were infected while treating a patient who had contracted the disease in Liberia.[90] A statement from Deborah Burger, a registered nurse and co-president of National Nurses United, an organization representing 190,000 nurses in the United States, highlighted the importance of protective gear for ensuring the health and safety of workers:

> Initially the nurses who interacted with Mr. Duncan wore a non-impermeable gown front and back, three pairs of gloves, with no taping around the wrists, surgical masks, with the *option* of N-95s,[91] and face shields. Some supervisors even told the nurses the N-95 masks were not necessary. This is what happens when guidelines are insufficient and voluntary.[92] (Original emphasis)

Comparing nurses to soldiers, she argued. "We are your first line of defense. No leader would ever contemplate sending soldiers into the battlefield without armor and weapons."[93]

Similar language was used at the beginning of the COVID-19 pandemic in 2020 when hospitals around the country were struggling to obtain enough PPE for hospital staff. Analyzing the reasons for the crisis in *Preventative Medicine*, scholars Jennifer Cohen and Yana van der Meulen Rodgers noted that sizing and gender disparities contributed to the problem. Although 75 percent of healthcare workers in the US are women, most "PPE that is available is designed for men, meaning that women are often left grappling with poorly fitted PPE, especially oversized gloves, goggles, and masks.[94]

Conclusion

Compared to most other industrialized countries—where the training and placement of medical professionals is largely paid for and managed by the national government—healthcare in the US is profit-driven and highly decentralized. Regulations on uniforms and PPE are also handled on a case-by-case basis and are not standardized, even within states. In an industry where workers are in high demand and increasingly mobile,[95] scrubs and lab coats have become the universal uniform for medical professionals in the US, regardless of the wearer's gender and location, and whether the job is temporary or permanent, part-time or full-time. In cases where workplaces still provide uniforms, they are not that different from the uniforms workers buy on their own.

In 1992, sociologist Fred Davis published a book titled *Fashion, Culture, and Identity* which argued that "ambivalence" is one of the major causes of cyclical changes in fashion. Regarding gender, for example, he observed that while designers and consumers may play with masculine designs for women and feminine designs for men, the experiments never last. Fashion swings back and forth as women who wear masculine styles eventually return to less austere[96] options, while men who experiment with feminine styles of dress are pressured to stop looking like "gays and rock musicians."[97] Davis also argued that fashion had become so rigidly binary that it was almost impossible to imagine alternatives:

> Theoretically there is no need for women in business and the professions to opt for masculine dress insignia. They could conceivably move in a unisex direction that is avowedly neither masculine nor feminine (consider surgical gowns). However, the cultural linkage of "male = work, career, skill, mastery, authority" is so formidable, it is not at all surprising that this is the symbolic trajectory the identity negotiation assumes.[98]

While pointing to "surgical gowns" as an exception to fashion ambivalence, he did not explore the topic further, except to observe that since "lab coats, smocks, and surgical gowns" are layers that can easily be added or removed, they "seem to encourage a degree of liberality in the choice of whatever *other* [fashionable] clothes are worn to work"[99]

At the moment in the US, the healthcare industry is one of the few places where work uniforms typically do not say something about the wearer's gender. Healthcare uniforms will undoubtedly continue to change, but the reasons have little to do with fashion ambivalence.

Government Work

Postal Carriers, Meter Maids, and Park Rangers

In an article for the *Berg Companion to Fashion*, journalist Stefano Tonchi described numerous fashions in Europe and the US that have been inspired by military uniforms:

> Teenagers in cargo pants, men in flight jackets and hooded parkas, and women in safari jackets and sailor pants are common sights on the everyday scene. Fashion runways have featured seasonal flurries of camouflage: print chiffon evening gowns, multipocket vests in bright satin, white leather cinched trench coats, and armies of military cashmere greatcoats with gilded buttons where the initials of famous fashion designs and the logos of powerful brands have taken the place of the insignia of royal families, dictators, and military empires.[1]

Many of these styles have become classics that never really go "out of fashion," conveying a message of power, masculinity, and confidence. Military uniforms are also durable, functional, and have striking aesthetics. When divorced from their original use, military-inspired fashions can take on a range of other meanings. Camouflage, for example, "has paradoxical capabilities to both identify and disguise; whereas the military uses both traits to concurrently hide from the enemy while identifying national affiliation, fashion uses camouflage solely for its ability to make one stand out."[2] Military-inspired fashions can make anti-government statements (e.g., wearing combat boots to protest the Vietnam War),[3] but they can also make pro-government statements (e.g., President Biden wearing aviator glasses).[4] Context is everything.

Unsurprisingly, the influence of military uniforms is also visible in the uniforms of other government workers, particularly workers for the federal government such as postal carriers and National Park Service rangers. Figure 5.1 shows uniformed postal carriers marching in military formation on September 15, 1904, designated as "St. Louis Day" at the World's Fair. In the late 1800s and early 1900s, a popular pastime in middle-class households was to gaze at

Figure 5.1 "Mail Carriers of St. Louis in Parade" for the World's Fair in St. Louis, Missouri, 1904. Photograph by Richard R. Whiting (1872–1944), Library of Congress Prints and Photographs Division, LC-DIG-stereo-1s03784.

collections of stereograph cards, which were sold in sets to show viewers awe-inspiring flora and fauna, geographic features, buildings, and newsworthy events.[5] Using a device called a stereoscope, the viewer could look at two slightly different images as if they were a single, three-dimensional image, bringing the scene to life. Clearly, the photographer of Figure 5.1 thought it was awe-inspiring and/or newsworthy to show hundreds of postal carriers marching together in their identical uniforms. One of the spectacles at the 1904 World's Fair was an exhibit about the U.S. Post Office Department, which included a working post office, historic "relics" (such as an "old-fashioned stagecoach" riddled with bullet holes), and a display of "tabooed articles found in the mails, ranging from infernal machines to living serpents."[6]

While many government workers are proud to wear their uniforms and do their best to make a positive impact on society, their uniforms are some of the most conservative, require a great deal of conformity, and have the most direct connections to the military. One reason for this similarity is government procurement practices; when a manufacturer or vendor knows how to navigate one branch of the government, it becomes easier to work with others. However, the visual symbolism matters too. Being a government worker means being a visual representation of the government (city, state, or federal), which comes with unique rights, responsibilities, and sometimes dangers. UPS workers deliver packages, but they are not targets for anti-government violence. Their customer service has no impact on how citizens think about the government. On the other hand, a "meter maid" issuing a parking ticket can easily become a focus of rage over how government services are being handled. It is important to note that despite the legality and availability of firearms in American society, police officers and some park rangers are typically the only government workers who display them as part of their uniform.

Uniforms for Postal Carriers

Postal service began in North America long before the founding of the United States. Early colonial administrators (British, French, and Dutch) hired indigenous people to deliver mail, since they were willing to travel long distances on foot and had far better knowledge of the best overland routes. In particular, the Lenape (Delaware) were considered the fastest and most reliable,[7] which was important for military and political communications.

After the Revolution, the federal government organized a national postal system to make mail delivery affordable and widely available to the public.[8] However, it was not until after the Civil War that government letter carriers were required to wear uniforms. In 1868, Postmaster General Alexander W. Randall described in detail how the new uniforms should be constructed by tailors and manufacturers:

1. A single breasted Sack Coat[9] of "Cadet Gray" or technically "Blue mixed cadet cloth" extending two thirds the distance from the top of the hip bone to the knee, with a pocket at each side, and one on left breast – all outside – with flaps two and three fourths to three inches wide with length to suit – say 6½ to 7 inches. Coat to be bound entirely round with good plain black Alpaca binding one inch wide, to be put half over edges, with five brass buttons with the design of the seal of this Department (post-rider with mail bag across the saddle) down the front to button up to the neck, and once-half inch black braid round the sleeves 2½ inches from the bottom.
2. Pants of same material and color with fine black broadcloth stripe one half inch wide, down each leg.
3. A single-breasted vest of the same material and color with seven oval brass buttons (vest size) with the letters P.O. upon the face.
4. Cap of the same material and color, navy pattern, bound round with a fine black cloth band 1½ inches wide, with small size buttons at the sides of the

same material and design as those of the vest, and glazed cover for wet weather.

5.   A reversible cape (detached from the coat) reaching to the cuff of the coat sleeve when the arm is extended, of the same material and color on one side, and gutta percha cloth on the other side, with five buttons, the same as on the coat down the front, and bound entirely round with plain black Alpaca binding one inch wide put half over edges.[10]

From the beginning, the Post Office Department had no single, centralized system for manufacturing or distributing uniforms. Urban postmasters around the country were expected to choose their own contractors and make decisions about how local uniforms should be composed and adjusted seasonally. Issues of *The Postal Record*, published by the National Association of Letter Carriers (NALC)[11] in the late 1800s included reports about uniforms from postal officials and advertisements for uniform manufacturers located in the Northeast and Midwest. A few of the larger contractors, such as Browning, King & Co. in New York, mass-produced uniforms and sold them in retail stores.[12] Plymouth Rock Pants Company in Boston advertised a more tailor-like, customized approach:

> most anybody prefers to have their clothing CUT TO ORDER if it costs no more than to buy it READY MADE. That, then, is the secret of our business— instead of carrying immense stocks of ready-made clothing, cut into every imaginable size, we PREFER to keep our cloth in the roll, and cut and fit each man to order. We cut to order the famous $3 Pants, of which we need only say that if we sell a man ONCE we sell him AGAIN, and SUITS of same grade at $13.25. [...] Upon receipt of 6 cents, we mail samples to anyone in the United States, with careful rules for self-measurement.[13]

Like porters, postal carriers were initially forced to buy their own uniforms as a condition of employment. In 1890, carriers in Chicago sent a resolution to Congress complaining bitterly that after passing the civil service exam and purchasing their uniforms, they were forced to work as substitute carriers for a period of 9 to 12 months, making less than $15 dollars per month. Many could only cover the cost by going into debt.[14] At the time, the starting pay for an official, full-time postal carrier in Chicago was $600 per year (Figures 5.2 and 5.3.

Since they were expected to work regardless of the weather, carriers in Brooklyn complained about how the harsh conditions were destroying their expensive uniforms:

Figure 5.2 Postal carrier in New York City wearing a derby hat with an oval badge, 1896. Photograph by Alice Austen (1866–1952), New York Public Library Digital Collections, Miriam and Ira D. Wallach Division of Art, Prints and Photographs, at: https://digitalcollections.nypl.org/items/510d47d9-a8cf-a3d9-e040-e00a18064a99.

We took a vote among the Carriers this week to decide whether our headgear this winter shall be helmets, such as we are now wearing, or caps. The helmet is the best thing in the service, and greatly protects a fellow in stormy weather, while the cap is an abomination. The water soakes [sic] through the top and runs down the face and neck, and causes loud and sometimes strong language among the men.

Although the weather is still warm [in September] and the trees thick with foliage, stern hoary-headed old winter has sent ahead his card in the shape of an order from the [Postmaster], relating to winter uniforms. This uniform business twice a year is a fearful drain upon a man. Some times it's a positive hardship to pay for them. And how cheerful it makes one feel to put them on in all sorts of weather and distroy [sic] them in a few months; it's tough.[15]

In the late 1800s, advertised prices for three-piece uniforms (pants, jacket, and vest) ranged from $11.50 to $16.00, but carriers also had to pay for their own headwear, shoes, belts, neckwear, outerwear, and bags. In 1891 in Nashville, Tennessee, postal

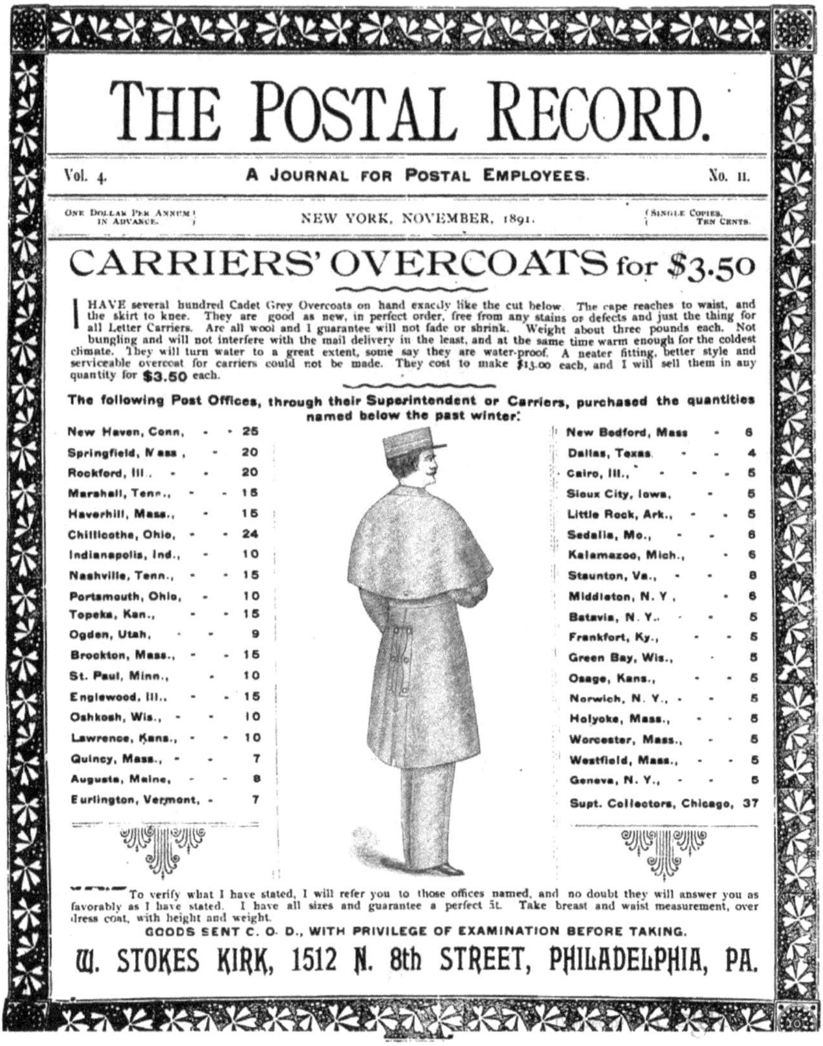

Figure 5.3 Advertisement for overcoats by W. Stokes Kirk, a manufacturer of postal uniforms based in Philadelphia, 1891. *The Postal Record*, 4 (1): 1.

carriers were able to negotiate a good price on overcoats because they were "made for some military company, but not being faced properly, were rejected by them."[16] Canvas bags for collecting and delivering mail were more affordable than leather bags, which some carriers complained were also "too heavy."[17]

Regional variations in headwear included Panama hats made of straw for hot weather,[18] cloth caps with "ear protectors" for harsh winters,[19] derby hats (Figure 5.2), railway caps (Figure 5.3), and police-style caps (Figure 5.8). In 1887,

Figure 5.4 Numbered badge worn by a postal carrier for the U.S. Post Office Department City Delivery Service, 1887. Collection of the Smithsonian National Postal Museum, 1992.2002.131.

numbered badges were added. German silver was selected for the metal due to its hardness and resistance to corrosion,[20] but likely also for its affordability. Early designs were ovals (Figure 5.2) and wreaths (Figure 5.4); during the 1920s, the badges were redesigned to feature an eagle, the national bird of the United States.[21]

In rural areas, the Post Office Department operated "star routes" where individuals were hired on four-year contracts to deliver the local mail. They had to be at least 16 years old, pay a bond to the government, and take an oath of office,[22] but some regulations were more flexible than for regular postal carriers. In 1859, the routes were declared open to both women and people of color. The first black woman known to have delivered official mail was "Stagecoach Mary" Fields (Figure 5.5), who had moved from Ohio to Montana to care for a friend, a Catholic nun running a mission school.[23] Mary's postal route ran between the mission and the closest town, which was 17 miles away. As the only carrier on her route (and perhaps the only female postal carrier in Montana at that time), it is unlikely that Mary's style of dress (Figure 5.5) was a true uniform. Since their regular travel schedules made rural postal carriers targets for thieves,[24] it would have been preferable to wear non-uniform clothing.

Figure 5.5 "Stagecoach Mary" Fields (1832–1914), the earliest-known black woman to work as a mail carrier in the United States, *c.* 1895. Wikimedia Commons.

A young woman identified as a "mail carrier" in Los Angeles in the early twentieth century was probably also working on a star route (Figure 5.6). Like soldiers in the US Army during the First World War, she wore pants designed for horseback riding: loose around the hips and thighs, with her calves covered by leather puttees to reduce wear from friction. Short-sleeve shirts were not allowed for official postal service uniforms until the 1940s.[25] When the first women were hired directly by the Post Office Department in 1917 (Figure 5.7), they wore the same uniforms as the men with long skirts instead of pants.

As late as the 1930s, some uniforms for carriers were still being made by tailors. A 1936-37 catalogue by Ed V. Price & Co.[26] based in Chicago featured

Figure 5.6 Young woman employed as a "mail carrier" in rural Los Angeles, *c.* 1915–20. Photograph by Bain News Service, Library of Congress Prints and Photographs Division, LC-DIG-ggbain-26023.

upper-class business suits, but a small section in the back advertised "uniforms for many purposes," including police, firemen, theater attendants, and bus drivers. The letter carriers' uniform featured a double-breasted jacket, straight pants, and a police-style cap with a wreath badge (Figure 5.8). The military uniform featured a Sam Browne belt, a British invention adopted in the 1920s and 1930s by US military officers, the National Park Service, and many police departments.[27]

Mid-century additions to official uniforms for postal carriers included sweaters, zippers, plastic buttons, Eisenhower jackets,[28] pith helmets, maroon accents, several new styles of hats (berets, fur and knit hats for winter, and

Figure 5.7 Photograph of Permilia S. Campbell (in uniform) and Nellie M. McGrath, the first two women to work directly for the U.S. Post Office Department as postal carriers, 1917. Photograph by Harris & Ewing, Library of Congress Prints and Photographs Division, LC-DIG-hec-09910.

pillbox hats), shorts, and slip-resistant shoes. Numbered metal badges were abandoned in favor of standardized embroidered patches, which featured a postal carrier on horseback to honor the Pony Express.[29] The style and placement of the patch echoed the use of shoulder sleeve insignia on US military uniforms.

In 1954, an alliance of unions representing 1.5 million postal workers (not just carriers)—including NALC, the United National Association of Post Office Clerks, National Rural Letter Carriers Association, and the National Postal Transport Association—petitioned Congress for pay increases and other benefits.[30] Although the Postmaster General opposed the salary increase, he

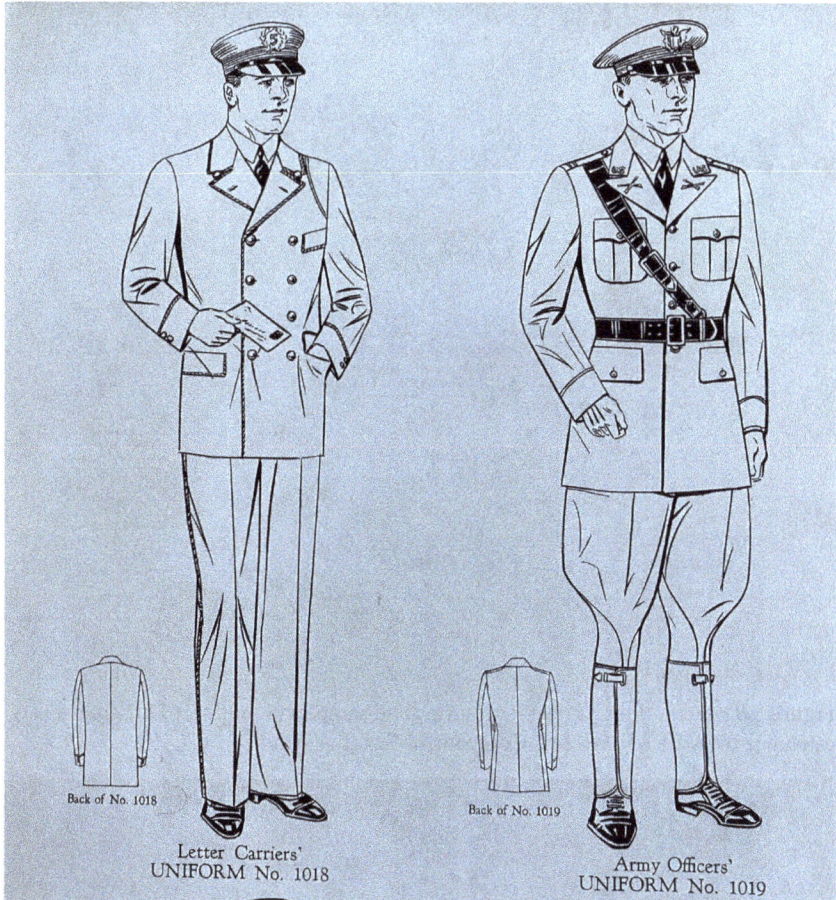

Letter Carriers'
UNIFORM No. 1018

Back of No. 1018

Army Officers'
UNIFORM No. 1019

Back of No. 1019

Figure 5.8 Tailored uniforms for letter carriers and (U.S.) Army officers, 1936–7. *Who's Your Tailor?* catalogue by E.V. Price & Co. of Chicago, 28.

conceded to give postal carriers an annual allowance to purchase uniforms. These allowances have continued with regular increases in the amount to keep pace with inflation.[31]

Although the Postal Service had begun using light blue for some parts of its uniforms in the 1970s (see, for example, Figure 5.9), in the early 1990s it completely abandoned "cadet gray" and maroon in favor of light blue, navy blue, and red accents (Figure 5.10). Maternity clothing was added, and some styles were updated to align with contemporary fashions. For example, the Eisenhower jacket was replaced by parkas, insulated vests, windbreakers, and bomber jackets.[32]

Figure 5.9 Illustrations of postal uniforms and samples of fabric, 1972. *Elbeco Shirts*, catalogue by Wide Awake Shirt Company of Reading, Pennsylvania, 2.

Figure 5.10 Postal carrier wearing a baseball cap and insulated vest with the "sonic eagle" logo in Chicago, October 2021. Photograph by Luke Sharrett / Bloomberg via Getty Images.

Instead of just revising the dress code, the Postal Service also began to standardize the process for becoming an official uniform supplier. This would allow individuals to select (from the list of approved vendors) whatever items of dress were best suited to meet their individual preferences and local weather conditions. Anticipating that changes would have a ripple effect on costs and labor conditions for uniform suppliers, in 1997 Congress asked the US Government Accountability Office[33] to investigate the update. Specific concerns included the preservation of manufacturing jobs in the US, whether there would be any cost savings from centralization, and whether small businesses would be able to compete effectively as vendors.[34] At the time, postal workers were buying clothing and accessories from more than 800 vendors; the Postal Service hoped that the number could be reduced to six or less.[35]

Centralization has led to a smaller number of vendors, but never as low as anticipated. In 2019, there were 115 official suppliers in 26 states.[36] Unlike small and private businesses, the Postal Service has an extensive manual for employees that is accessible to the public. Section 931.21 describes the purposes of postal uniforms:

a. To provide immediate visual identification with the Postal Service to the public
b. To project an appearance to the public that is neat, professional, and pleasing
c. To help develop in the employee a feeling of esprit de corps[37]
d. To meet standard professional practices (doctors, nurses, etc.)[38]

Although postal uniforms have much more in common with military uniforms in terms of how they look and function and how they are purchased,[39] it is interesting that this language nods to the prestige of the healthcare industry. Postal carriers must wear their uniforms while on duty but cannot wear them in other settings unless officially authorized "for activities in which the Postal Service participates, or which it sponsors, where identification with the Postal Service is beneficial to the Service" or while in transit to and from work.[40]

Behind the scenes, postal carriers give one another advice and support on dressing to the appropriate standards. An article published in a 2020 issue of *The Postal Record* cautioned new employees that:

Shopping for and buying the uniform items needed for all types of weather can take time and sometimes exceed the [$465] allowance, especially for carriers in extreme climate areas. 'As new carriers quickly learn, a letter carrier must have many uniform items. [...] You have to have something to wear to work while other items are in the laundry. You will need rain gear and perhaps heavy winter clothes and accessories. And good footwear is essential. The cost can add up.'[41]

In some cities, branches of NALC have clothing exchanges where new members can access "gently used and unwanted uniform items" donated by more senior and retired members.[42]

Because postal carriers routinely handle personal and confidential documents, US law forbids non-employees from wearing official uniforms, with an exception for "an actor or actress in a theatrical, television, or motion-picture production."[43] Not all items that postal carriers wear have emblems (for example, shoes) but to sell those that do, suppliers must demand proof of employment with the US Postal Service.[44] To comply with the law, eBay allows sellers to list "collectible" postal uniforms and accessories, but only if the item is at least ten years old and does not resemble the current uniform.[45]

Uniforms for Meter Maids

As the number of automobiles surged in the US in the early 1900s, cities adjusted by widening streets, building new roads, building off-street parking lots,[46] and hiring more police officers to patrol busy areas. Between 1913 and 1930, the number of automobiles in Oklahoma increased from 3,000 to 550,000.[47] As the state's capital and center of commerce, Oklahoma City tried to improve access to the downtown area by imposing time limits for parking, but the police found them difficult to enforce.[48] In 1935, a city official in charge of traffic, Carl Magee, filed a patent for a novel solution: a timed parking meter that would charge motorists upfront.[49]

After months of planning, 200 parking meters were installed in the retail district. City officials anticipated that it would make parking enforcement easier and generate a stream of revenue for the city,[50] but not everyone was convinced. An article in *The Oklahoma News* noted that, "There have been threats of a court battle against the meters on the grounds that the charge for parking is unconstitutional. Mr. Magee, however, insists that the charge is not a tax but a police supervision fee and therefore legal."[51]

By 1950, the invention had spread to more than 1,000 cities in the US.[52] In an article for *Public Administration Review*, an assistant to the Chicago superintendent of police described them as "a common source of irritation to both the public and the police."[53] Although parking meters generated revenue, enforcement was taking time away from other pressing concerns; Chicago was struggling with the question of how much parking enforcement was realistic:

[The city manager] suggested that the city could assign one police officer to enforce all of the meters throughout the city. If this was done, he anticipated that the frequency of checks would be low and the number of overtime violations and red flags would increase. On the other hand, he could assign one police officer to each parking meter in the city. With such extensive coverage, there would be reasonable assurance that a summons would be issued at the moment the meter expired. The city manager then suggested that the council determine through its appropriation, just how many police officers were to be provided and what level of enforcement was desired.[54]

Obviously, this issue was also connected to how many (trained and expensive) police officers the city was willing to pay for.

In 1954, Salt Lake City decided to solve the problem by hiring women (who were not as well trained and could be paid less), which were described for the first time as "meter maids." While officially part of the police department, their role was limited to parking enforcement. *The Salt Lake City Tribune* argued that "their employment has released a number of regular police officers for other more important duty."[55] In a report published in the *FBI Enforcement Bulletin*, the chief of police in Lincoln, Nebraska used similar language:

Our first four meter maids stepped on the streets of Lincoln on March 1, 1959, neat and trim in their uniforms. With ticket books and pencils in hand, they began this experiment in our parking enforcement program.

We soon found that they were performing their tasks with peak proficiency and public approval. Not only were the results favorable, as far as the quality of the work done, but the program also released four experienced uniformed police officers for other pressing duties of police service.[56]

Uniforms for meter maids varied depending on the city. Some (like postal uniforms) were simply modified versions of male police uniforms, but others were modeled after uniforms designed for women serving in the WAVES (US Navy) and WAAC (US Army) during the Second World War.[57] The WAVES uniform (Figure 5.11) was designed by Mainbocher, an American-born couturier who fled from Paris at the start of the war; his skill and reputation made the uniform seem especially appealing and prestigious.[58] It included a knee-length skirt and tailored jacket, a white blouse with a collar, white gloves, nude hosiery,[59] black shoes with heels, and a distinctive hat with a deeply curved brim.

A photograph of meter maids in Portland, Oregon shows a similar outfit (Figure 5.12). Subtle differences include a collarless shirt without a necktie, fabric-covered buttons, and an embroidered patch on the left jacket sleeve. These

Figure 5.11 Lieutenant Harriet Ida Pickens (left) and Ensign Francis Wills (right), the first two black women commissioned as officers in the WAVES, 1944. US Naval History and Heritage Command, Washington DC, NH 90006.

Figure 5.12 Detail of a photograph showing uniformed meter maids in the city of Portland, Oregon, 1962. Unknown photographer, City of Portland Archives, A2005-001.1381.

uniforms were probably mass-produced; however, it appears that some of the women altered their jackets for a better fit.

In Janesville, Wisconsin, meter maids walked an average of 15 miles per day and wore pants as a concession to the weather. An article in the local newspaper noted,

> [The newest hire, Dawn Trescher] said she did not consider the meter maid job as 'real police work.' 'I have never thought about getting any deeper into police work—as a detective or anything like that,' she said. The meter maid uniform consists of a light blue blouse and darker blue trousers with a women's military-type hat. Miss Trescher said that skirts would be more feminine, but on windy days could prove to be a problem.[60]

In Miami, Florida, the first meter maids also wore pants as part of the uniform (Figure 5.13), not because of the weather, but so they could ride motorcycles and

Figure 5.13 Meter maids in Miami, Florida, patrolling on motorcycles while wearing uniforms with pants and garrison caps, 1959. Photograph by Bob East for the *Miami Herald*. © 1959 McClatchy. All rights reserved. Used under license. At: https://flashbackmiami.com/2014/06/04/meter-maids/.

patrol larger areas. At the time, pants were not generally accepted as appropriate clothing for women.

Although police departments in the US had begun hiring small numbers of women in the early 1900s, they were typically confined to working as secretaries, dispatchers, social workers,[61] and as matrons for female prisoners—positions that were barely visible to the public. As much more public representatives of police authority, choices about uniforms for meter maids became proxies for larger conflicts over appropriate roles for women in US society.

In 1965, New York City doubled the number of meter maids, an investment of $500,000 that was expected to generate millions of dollars in revenue.[62] A few months later, a public battle erupted when the Traffic Commission tried to dismiss some of the meter maids based on their weight and how they fit into their uniforms:

> Traffic Commissioner Henry Barnes said that only two girls are being dismissed and they are 50 pounds overweight. One of them, he said, weighs more than 250 pounds. Barnes said both were hired on a six-month probation term with the promise they would try to reduce. 'They were warned several times,' Barnes said, 'that their uniforms didn't fit and that if they continued to put on weight, they would not be an asset to the department.'[63]

Journalists reported that one of the women "weighed 190 pounds when the department asked for her resignation."[64] Although she had lost weight by spending two weeks at a health spa, a staff member for the Traffic Commission said that it wasn't enough for his "trained eye."[65] The president of the local Teamsters Union (the meter maids' official representative) did not push back on whether it was appropriate to judge workers based on their physical appearance:

> The union leader said [one of the meter maids] "looks just like Kim Novak."[66] He said another meter maid alleged to be overweight has proportions of a Miss Universe: 38-28-38. "She is 5 feet tall and she's lovely." [...]
>
> "If they were overweight in the first instance," [the union leader] said, "they should not have been hired." He said the women had already spent almost $400 each on uniforms and other equipment.[67]

For weeks, reports about the battle appeared in newspapers around the country. In December 1965, the city's Civil Service Commission quietly announced that the Traffic Commission would no longer discriminate and that men were welcome to apply for jobs in parking enforcement.[68]

Due to events in the 1960s such as the passage of the Civil Rights Act (1964), founding of the Equal Employment Opportunity Commission (1965), a series of

Figure 5.14 Parking enforcement officer in Denver, Colorado, 2019. Photograph by RJ Sangosti / MediaNews Group / The Denver Post via Getty Images.

protests by the National Organization for Women (1966), and the advent of women working as patrol officers (1968),[69] many municipal governments dropped the term "meter maid " in favor of more gender-neutral alternatives such as "parking control assistant" or "parking enforcement officer" (Figure 5.14).[70] Some also moved parking enforcement to other agencies, such as public works or transportation.[71]

In the 1950s and 1960s, meter maids and their uniforms were viewed as somewhat glamorous, akin to stewardesses.[72] Today, the uniforms are designed more for safety and identification by the public. The city of San Francisco describes parking control officers as "civilian employees" who "wear a uniform and badge but do not carry weapons"[73]:

> The nature of the work involves considerable walking, standing, and sitting for extended periods of time, working in inclement weather, performing repetitive hand motion to chalk tires and direct traffic, repetitive bending, kneeling, squatting and exiting/entering vehicles, and requires normal color vision. Employees are required to lift and install/remove vehicle immobilization devices or traffic barricades weighing up to 50 pounds and wear equipment weighing up to 10 pounds while working. [. . .] [They must also] wear a departmental issued uniform, helmet and safety gear.[74]

Unlike the federal government, not all cities make their operations manuals available to the public. Those that do have extremely varied policies on uniforms. In Berkeley, California, for example, parking enforcement is part of the police department. The list of mandatory items that parking enforcement officers must wear is short:

- Light blue shirt; either long- or short-sleeved, by Flying Cross[75] w/badge tab
- Trousers, by Fechheimer (or any brand used to replace current brand, navy blue)
- Dress Coat, Eisenhower-style, navy blue w/ brass buttons
- Necktie, navy blue clip-on
- 1½" wide black basket weave belt w/brass buckle
- Socks, solid black
- Shoes, fully enclosed toe, solid black
- Patches on each upper garment[76]

The department also issues orange and yellow safety vests, rain gear, badges, and name tags and allows some variations such as maternity clothing, baseball caps, cargo shorts, skirts, and gloves ("solid black" without a logo).[77]

In Washington, DC, parking officers are supervised by the Department of Public Works, which also manages trash collection, street sweeping, and graffiti removal to make "streets and public spaces clean, safe, attractive and accessible."[78] A large portion of the uniform policy describes seasonal variations and exceptions for extreme weather, but the lists of "clothing and equipment" and "personal accessories" have some lengthy descriptions. For example,

> Footwear – When in uniform, plain solid black leather/vinyl tie up athletic shoes shall be worn. Shoe soles shall not exceed three-fourths of an inch in thickness. Heels shall not be more than one and one-half inches in height. The shoes shall be kept clean, in good repair, and shined to a luster. Shoes may be of a high top design provided that the top is close fitting; however, fashion footwear is not permitted (e.g. Jordan or LeBron sneakers). Loafers, shoes with buckles, Velcro, suede, [nubuck], mesh or any fabric other than leather or vinyl shall not be worn. Shoes with straps, wedge heels, or open heels are not permitted. During periods of cold or inclement weather, members may wear black insulated, water-repellent shoes or boots with a plain design that are oil treated that cannot be shined to a luster.[79]

Although the department issues (and apparently cleans) some clothing and equipment such as jackets, hats, helmets, reflective vests, and handheld devices,[80] variations are allowed for items that the workers must purchase themselves. They are not limited to a list of vendors or required to buy particular brands.

Uniforms for Park Rangers

Some park rangers are also city or county employees, but many work for the state or federal government. Their jobs are highly varied, combining law enforcement with customer service and academic-like responsibilities for educating visitors about local history and the physical environment. The Student Conservation Association describes two major types of rangers:

> **Interpretive rangers** provide information to visitors – either practical information such as directions, timetables and weather forecasts, or educational information in the form of guided tours, on-and-offsite talks, demonstrations, and reenactments. In addition to parks, interpretive rangers work at historic trails, national monuments, battlefields, and historic sites in both rural and urban settings.

> **Protection rangers** are tasked with keeping park and monument visitors safe through law enforcement, emergency medical services, firefighting, and search and rescue. Commission rangers are federal law enforcement officers who wear a Department of the Interior badge on their uniform, although not all protection rangers are commissioned. Many protection rangers are also certified as wilderness first responders, emergency medical technicians, or paramedics.[81]

Griffith Park in Los Angeles, founded in 1896 with more than 3,000 acres of land, is one of the largest municipal parks in the United States. Identified as a "park ranger," a photograph of the park's first motorcycle officer, Bob Brown, showed him wearing a three-piece suit, leather boots and gloves, and a police-style cap (Figure 5.15). While park rangers in Los Angeles now work for the Department of Recreation and Parks, they are also required to follow the city's code of ethics for law enforcement officers.[82]

The state of Wyoming—which has several famous national parks, including Yellowstone and Grand Teton—also has its own park system. Men and women are allowed to wear the same uniform components, however there are variations for "dress," work, and special events:

Figure 5.15 "Griffith Park motorcycle officer," Bob Brown, *c*. 1915. Unknown photographer, Los Angeles Public Library Legacy Collection, 00010223.

> The Field Staff "dress" uniform is worn during public or government meetings to present a highly visible and professional image. [It includes a] button-up shirt as listed on the uniform order form; dress pants or skirt in navy blue or khaki. [. . .]
>
> Class A Law Enforcement (LE) attire will be worn during parades, honor guard, special events and court. Class A attire includes a flak jacket, tie, striped slacks and cowboy hat. [. . .]
>
> The "work" uniform is worn [for] routine maintenance, construction activities, field trips, and/or the day-to-day activities associated with the functioning of our parks and historic sites. [It] includes the button-up shirt, t-shirts and polo shirts, shorts as listed on the uniform order form, as well as jean skirt (at knee length or below) or blue jeans. Footwear. . . will be brown or black western boot or brown or black dress shoe.[83]

Like the job of the park ranger, this uniform mixes the aesthetic language of law enforcement (flak jacket) with professional customer service (polo shirt) and cultural heritage (cowboy hat).

The order form is internal to the state government, which makes it difficult to determine the source(s) of items;[84] however, Wyoming park rangers are not restricted to a list of brands or vendors for the few items they need to purchase themselves, such as belts and neckties.

As federal employees, rangers for the National Park Service (NPS) wear much more standardized and conservative uniforms that have become iconic. The first "forest rangers" at Yellowstone (the oldest national park, established in 1872) were soldiers in the US Army who wore their official uniforms while on patrol.[85] When the first civilian "scouts" were hired to protect wildlife from poachers, individuals wore eclectic mixtures of civilian and military-inspired clothing with silver badges for identification.[86]

As more national parks were created and automobile traffic rapidly increased, park officials and rangers were eager to establish a uniform that would be consistent throughout the country. In 1911, the Superintendent for Glacier National Park in Montana wrote a letter to the Secretary of the Interior outlining a new uniform that he was planning to require for his rangers, consisting of "one Norfolk jacket, one wool shirt, one pair riding trousers, one pair leggings, and one felt camping hat after the Stetson style."[87] Sold by Parker, Bridget & Co.,[88] the "dark olive green" uniforms were modeled after the 1910 US Army uniform (Figure 5.16).[89] The Secretary informed all parks about the style and distributed order forms, but stopped short of making it obligatory.

During the first two decades, the jacket was redesigned several times to include pockets, lapels, and a more tailored shape with a defined waistline. When women began working for the NPS at the end of the First World War, opinions varied on how they should dress. Some were allowed to wear only the badge (with any practical clothing of their choice), while others wore the same uniforms as the men. In the 1930s, women who worked as tour guides at Carlsbad Caverns wore uniform jackets, shirts, and neckties with either pants or knee-length skirts, but were not allowed to wear the official Stetson hat (Figure 5.17).[90]

When the NPS established official regulations for women's uniforms in 1947, there were two significant changes: women would no longer be allowed to wear pants and required to wear a distinctive new "soft felt hat with small snap brim, turned up at back and sides and down over forehead in front, in matching color with narrow grosgrain ribbon on dark green color."[91] For reasons that are now unclear, female park rangers rejected the hat in favor of the "overseas cap" worn by women who served in the WAAC during the Second World War. Official photographs from the 1950s show only the latter style.[92]

By mid-century, most male park rangers had switched from wearing breeches to looser-fitting trousers. During hot weather, they were also allowed to wear a button-down shirt and tie without a jacket. Otherwise, their uniforms remained

Figure 5.16 Photograph from Glacier National Park comparing a U.S. Army uniform without insignia (left) to the newly designed NPS ranger uniform (right), 1915. U.S. National Park Service History Collection, HPC-001037.jpg.

largely unchanged. In the 1960s and 1970s, the uniforms for women were redesigned several times to reinforce distinctions between male and female park rangers—much like police officers and meter maids. The first major change was a suit modeled explicitly after the uniforms worn by stewardesses for Delta Airlines:[93] a tailored jacket with princess seams, calf-length skirt, a trim, fashionable cap, and pumps with heels up to two inches. The NPS Training Center even hired stewardesses to coach female park rangers on their grooming practices (Figure 5.18).[94]

In the early 1970s, the uniforms were radically redesigned by an NPS staff member with input from park rangers, to include sweaters, short sleeves,

Figure 5.17 NPS guides at Carlsbad Caverns, 1931. U.S. National Park Service, CAVE Women group picture_1930s_NPSHPC-CACA#7487_Cropped.jpg. U.S. National Park Service History Collection.

miniskirts, boots, bell-bottom pants, and decorative scarves with the NPS arrowhead emblem. Although the color was different from the men's uniforms—"sand" with orange and white accents vs. drab green and gray—women were finally allowed to wear a lightweight version of the official Stetson hat (Figure 5.19). The new uniforms gave women more options for their range of duties, for example, giving tours at urban historical sites vs. leading a hike through rugged terrain. However,

> It didn't take the women of the Park Service long to realize that the new uniforms were more fluff than substance. If anything they added to [their woes], not being as serviceable as those previously worn. The new uniforms were very stylish and

Figure 5.18 Airline stewardess (right) hired to coach female NPS rangers (left) on their uniforms and grooming practices, 1966. U.S. National Park Service History Collection, hfca_1607_airline stewardess_1966.

Figure 5.19 Female NPS ranger wearing a minidress uniform and Stetson hat, 1972. Photograph by Richard Frear, U.S. National Park Service History Collection, HFCA #1607_Fee Collection_014.jpg.

chic, for duty in the offices and visitor centers, but in the field they were useless. They didn't hold up very well, and it wasn't long before all of the enthusiasm of their introduction turned to ridicule. The public did not always realize that the women wearing these new uniforms were even in the Park Service. They still envisioned the ranger wearing forest green.[95]

In 1974, the main color was changed to dark green. Under pressure from the female park rangers (including the threat of a lawsuit),[96] by the end of the decade the NPS decided that women could wear the same uniforms as men. A photograph taken in 2021 at the Flight 93 National Memorial in Pennsylvania[97] shows all rangers wearing drab green trousers, light-gray button-down shirts without a tie, and identical Stetson hats (Figure 5.20). The man on the far left with a light blue shirt was part of the Student Conservation Association (a ranger-in-training, but not an official NPS ranger); the woman on the right wearing a bright blue shirt was an intern.

The NPS policy still contains some gender-specific regulations such as "men are not authorized to wear earrings" and "men may not wear nail polish." It argues that "This does not reflect any difference in the degree to which it is imperative that female or male employees are well groomed; rather it reflects norms and expectations by the public of grooming standards by the two sexes."[98] It also urges park rangers and other NPS employees to wear the uniform with pride and confidence and to uphold the traditions of the park system:

Figure 5.20 NPS rangers at the Flight 93 National Memorial wearing identical uniforms regardless of gender, 2021. U.S. National Park Service History Collection, 102A2707.png.

The appearance of uniformed NPS employees greatly influence public perceptions. The uniform and the men and women who wear it, are recognized and respected as symbols of excellence and dedication to resource stewardship and public service. The gray and green colors, distinctive hat, arrowhead patch, and sequoia cones[99] all help to identify NPS employees as stewards of America's special places. Wearing the uniform, therefore, is a privilege and imposes a great responsibility, steeped in tradition.[100]

In an interview for the Golden Gate National Parks Conservancy, a ranger described the uniform as conveying a more straightforward message: "I'm here, here to help."[101] While this is admirable as a sentiment of public service, not all members of the public (or even park rangers) have such a positive view of federal authority. In 2013, an indigenous Hawaiian woman working as an NPS park ranger published an article describing local "traditions that go back many hundreds, even thousands, of years" regarding land management:

> When national park units in Hawai'i were created beginning in 1916, the paternalistic intention of NPS (which, it must be remembered, was modeled on the military) was to preserve Hawaiian environments, culture, and history in encapsulated, delineated areas of the landscape—with dotted artificial boundary lines, operating within statues, laws, regulations, polices, and directives that were completely foreign to Native Hawaiians. The process set aside places and resources and created somewhat isolated pockets that serve, as we now know, as treasured spaces that are loved to death.[102]

While arguing that she is "proud to wear the green and gray," she encouraged specific changes in uniforms that would "allow employees to wear their family and traditional tattoos with pride while on duty, and to allow male employees to wear their hair as long as female employees."[103]

Like postal carriers, NPS park rangers receive annual allowances to purchase uniforms, however most items must be purchased though a website that is closed to the public. Operated by Workwear Outfitters,[104] it also supplies uniforms to the US Fish and Wildlife Service, US Park Police, and the US Army Corps of Engineers (USACE).[105] In 1970, USACE decided to hire park rangers to engage with the public in areas such as the Okeechobee Waterway:[106] giving tours, assisting with emergencies, and enforcing federal laws.[107] Interestingly, the agency decided to use the same basic uniform as the NPS, replacing the arrowhead emblem and sequoia cones with the Corps Castle emblem (Figure 5.21).[108] Due to this visual similarity, most people in the public

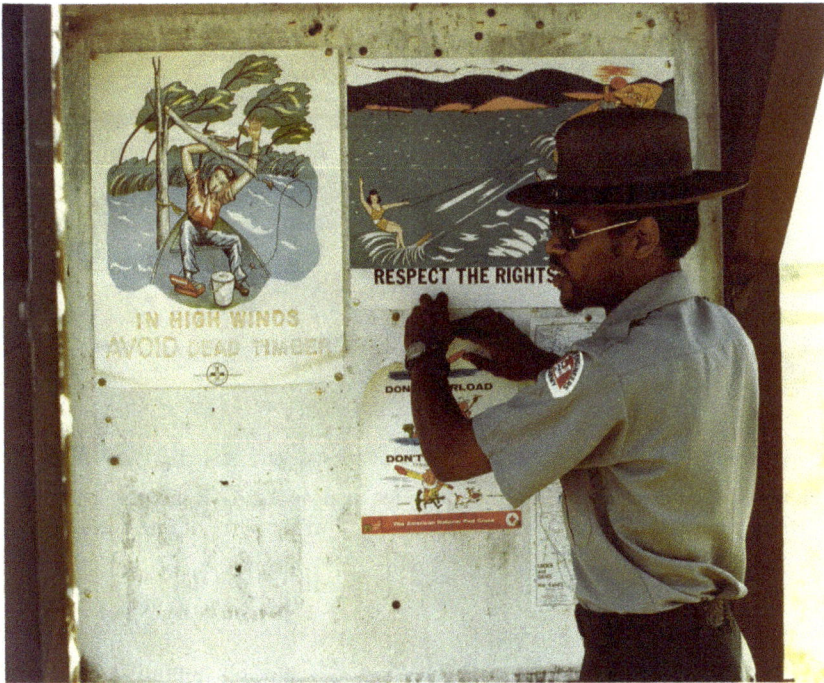

Figure 5.21 USACE park ranger wearing an NPS-style uniform with the Corps Castle emblem on his left sleeve, 1980s. Office of History, HQ, US Army Corps of Engineers, G1_Ranger posts water safety poster.jpg.

are unaware that there is any difference between NPS park rangers and USACE park rangers.

These military-style uniforms—along with park rangers' authority to carry firearms, execute warrants, and make arrests[109]—also invites comparisons to the police. Increasingly critical views on policing in US society as a whole[110] are understood (and perhaps shared) by park rangers. In 2010 and 2016, hundreds of USACE park rangers responded to a repeated internal survey about safety. One question asked, "Do you believe wearing the Corps park ranger uniform, compared to the way other Corps employees dress, makes you

Safer because being viewed as law enforcement personnel, or person of authority, and respected for such – 37.8% (2010), 30.3% (2016)
Less safe due to being viewed as law and/or other enforcement personnel but without legal authority – 35.1% (2010), 44.9% (2016)
Depends on situation – 21.1% (2010), 24.8% (2016)[111]

Figure 5.22 Screenshot from a YouTube video made by USACE showing a civilian staff member helping with disaster relief, 2018. US Army Corps of Engineers, OCLC #1248899457.

Soldiers in the US Army who work for USACE wear their camouflage uniforms while working with the public (for example, offering disaster relief); however, civilians wear hard hats and a mixture of shirts and jackets displaying the Corps Castle emblem. For instance, after Hurricane Michael hit the Gulf Coast of Florida in 2018, a civilian member of USACE who ordinarily worked as a biologist was filmed wearing a white hard hat with the Corps Castle emblem, a red polo shirt, gray hooded sweatshirt, a name badge, and a fluorescent vest with the Corps Castle emblem printed on the back (Figure 5.22). These "civilian" uniforms are made and sold by Human Technologies Corporation, based in New York,[112] another difference compared to the uniforms worn by USACE park rangers.

Conclusion

Embodying government authority through a uniform is a double-edged sword. It can instill a great sense of pride and responsibility, but it can also invite danger. Members of the public with grievances against the government sometimes take their frustrations out on the individuals who represent it. While police officers are probably the most frequent targets of violence,[113] postal carriers, meter maids, and park rangers have also experienced abuse and sometimes violence.

For example, in 2021 a man in southern Texas was convicted of shooting a postal worker as she was delivering mail and then setting her body and vehicle on fire.[114]

Overall, government uniforms are notable for being some of the slowest to change, but also for allowing input from workers, whether through dialogue, surveys, or union involvement. These features are in sharp contrast to the next chapter, focusing on corporate uniforms.

Corporate Branding

Receptionists, Bankers, and Baristas

While the United States has a rich history of entrepreneurship, today's economy is dominated by large corporations. In 2021, *Fortune* magazine observed that "the 500 [largest] corporations on this year's list generated $13.8 trillion in revenue, or some two-thirds of the US economy."[1] The largest single company, Walmart, offers an excellent example of how corporations use the bodies of their workers to reinforce their branding.

Figure 6.1 was taken by a photojournalist for the *Los Angeles Times* in 2005. It shows the CEO of Walmart Stores, Lee Scott (2000–2009), shaking hands with an unidentified worker at a store in Panorama City, California. Scott and three other executives (all white men) are wearing business suits. Although the suits look very similar with minor variations in color, they were freely chosen by the people wearing them. Business suits are also generic to white-collar workers in a variety of industries, not just retailing. On the other hand, the store worker (who appears to be Latino) is wearing a mandatory garment specific to Walmart: a "Walmart blue"[2] jacket with the company's logo on the upper chest. Visible on the left side of the photo, another employee (wearing a blue vest with a black shirt) can be seen with his back turned to the camera, revealing a printed statement, "How may I help you?" Unlike a business suit, this garment has a clear connection to Walmart customers and customer service.

Like many other corporations, Walmart frequently updates its branding (colors, fonts, packaging, interior furnishings, etc.) to appear fresh and more relevant. In 2014, the company decided to give workers the option of wearing black bottoms (pants or a skirt) instead of khaki. While mandating that all shirts (white or navy blue) should have collars, the company also decided that all workers in the stores would be required to wear the same, updated Walmart blue vest. The company would pay for the vest, but none of the other clothing. While workers described the whole outfit (pants, shirt, and vest) as a uniform, Walmart

Figure 6.1 Former CEO of Walmart Stores, Lee Scott (center right), shaking hands with an unidentified store employee in Panorama City, California, February 23, 2005. Photograph by Gary Friedman / Los Angeles Times via Getty Images.

executives described everything but the vest as a "dress code." A journalist for *Forbes* observed,

> by choosing a dress code, not a store uniform, Wal-Mart has completely and legally put the financial burden of the clothing intended to create a specific look on the employees and saved itself a lot of money, given that the company claims 1.3 million US workers alone.[3]

Anonymously—but in large numbers—Walmart workers complained to the media:

> Dozens of employees told Business Insider that they can't afford to buy clothes that fit the requirements. [...] More than half of the associates are on food stamps, can't afford to buy a vehicle to get to work so they have to bum rides from other employees," said one associate who works at a Texas Wal-Mart.
>
> A customer service manager at a Boise, Idaho, store said, "I have been an employee of Wal-Mart for the past three years and have gone through more required dress code changes than I can count. It is completely ridiculous."[4]

In terms of the impact on workers, these statements echo the experiences of waitresses in the twentieth century. However, the extreme imbalance in power between executives and store employees in corporate franchises is also a master–servant[5] dynamic as described in Chapter 2.

It took four years for Walmart to change its controversial uniform policy, a topic that I return to in the conclusion of this book. The executives who make decisions about branding do not spend much time interacting with store employees and do not care much about their working conditions as long as the corporation makes a profit.

Like many corporations in the US, Walmart actively works to keep labor costs as low as possible by lobbying politicians[6] and suppressing labor unions.[7] In a 2008 working paper about conditions for frontline workers in US retail stores,[8] policy analysts Françoise Carré and Chris Tilly observed that while corporations minimize costs through a variety of strategies, such as adopting new technologies for checking out and inventory management, wages are frequent targets for cost cutting because they are the "single largest operating cost." As an assistant manager at a chain of mid-priced grocery stores explained to them, "You have full control... you have little control of the beef you throw away. You have little control about your produce you throw away. You have control of your labor."[9]

This chapter explores three different industries—hospitality, banking, and food service—that were overtaken by corporatization in the late twentieth century. When viewed as a whole, there is an interesting paradox in corporate work uniforms. Corporations can afford to hire the best designers and have developed some of most aesthetically striking uniforms that are not inspired by the military. However, corporations are also big, risk-averse, and slow to change. Uniforms for their workers must be low cost and easy to reproduce in the thousands. They are not couture; they do not make political statements like anti-fashion. Corporate work uniforms have exemplified the clean lines and bold colors of modernism and more recently, minimalism. When those aesthetics are in fashion, corporate work uniforms are fashionable. However, if the trends shift to something that corporate work uniforms cannot accommodate (like maximalism) they are no longer fashionable. In many respects corporations dominate American society, but they cannot ignore trends in clothing without appearing irrelevant.

Uniforms for Receptionists

This section focuses on uniforms worn by receptionists (also known as front desk clerks) at corporate hotel chains. However, it is useful to start with a more general description since receptionists work in a variety of other settings including hospitals, nursing homes, fitness centers, schools, museums, and private offices:

What is a Receptionist?

Receptionists work for companies and organizations to help them run smoothly. They are often the first employee that a customer or the public comes in contact with, and are therefore responsible for making a good first impression.

What does a Receptionist do?

Receptionists perform various administrative tasks, such as greeting visitors, answering telephones, taking messages, scheduling appointments, filing and maintaining documents, providing information to various people, making travel arrangements, and running errands.[10]

Receptionists typically sit or stand behind a desk at the facility's entrance, making them highly visible. At hotels, they are not necessarily the first employees that guests encounter. In large, expensive hotels, that person might be a valet or a doorman. However, receptionists are also critical to the hotel's operation: they take payments from guests, answer their questions, give advice, and screen outside callers and visitors (Figure 6.2).

Figure 6.2 Receptionist at a hotel in San Augustine, Texas, 1939. Photograph by Russell Lee for the US Farm Security Administration, Library of Congress Prints and Photographs Division, LC-USF34-032895-D.

In the first half of the twentieth century, there were three major types of hotels in the US. The largest, known as "grand hotels" or "luxury hotels," catered primarily to business travelers, but also served as places where large numbers of middle- and upper-class visitors could gather for secular events such as banquets, balls, wedding receptions, and meetings.[11] Another type of urban hotel—typically smaller and less expensive—offered short-term and long-term lodging, like apartments but without kitchens.[12] While some guests had the financial means to own a house or apartment and simply preferred to live in a hotel, the cheapest became associated with extramarital affairs,[13] "shiftless laborers, social misfits, thieves, and prostitutes."[14]

The third type of hotel—also known as "motor hotels" or motels—blossomed along highways as many tourists and families began travelling by car. An article published in 1959 in a trade journal for accountants described how these roadside motels looked and functioned:

> The reader is undoubtedly familiar with the so-called tourist or motor courts which have been with us for some 25 years. The typical cluster of small cabins surrounding a driveway and an office can be seen on most of the secondary roads and older highways in this country. The term 'motel' began to have wide usage when those cabins were combined into one structure, the facilities were expanded and the style of operation and furnishings was upgraded.[15]

In 1951, Kemmons Wilson—a successful entrepreneur and builder who lived with his wife and five children in Memphis, Tennessee—took a family vacation to Washington, DC,[16] a driving distance of nearly 900 miles. As his business partner, Wallace Johnson, later recalled:

> He was both astonished and outraged by the poor accommodations they had found [staying at roadside motels] and the high prices they had to pay. It had cost him ten dollars a night for Mrs. Wilson and himself, plus two or three dollars extra for each of their five children. The motels were hot, dirty, noisy. Rooms were so small they had no place to sit. Some bathrooms were no larger than little closets, and often the plumbing fixtures were loud and defective.[17]

Wilson decided that he could do better by building a new kind of hotel—a nationwide chain where travelers could find predictable, comfortable, and affordable lodging. Many of Wilson's innovations set new standards in the hospitality industry: no extra charges for children, free ice, pools in every hotel, and a phone and television in every room. Guests could use their Gulf Oil credit cards[18] to pay for their rooms and get help booking another reservation for the next leg of the journey.[19] In the early 1960s, the company partnered with IBM to create a pre-internet electronic reservation system known as the Holidex.[20]

The chain expanded very rapidly. In his first year of business, Wilson built four hotels in the Memphis area. By 1968, there were more than 1,000 Holiday Inns. An article published in 1969 by a business professor noted a snowballing pattern of growth. "With each new Holiday Inn, an additional market of 100 to 200 travelers is fed into the system. Each new Holiday Inn also adds to the attractiveness of this system for the traveler [since] he has one more choice of a motel at which to stop."[21] Many of the new hotels were franchises, built and managed according to corporate specifications but funded by private owners.

In 1973, another article by a business professor about the pitfalls of franchising praised Holiday Inns of America for "epitomizing" good franchise management:

> In terms of the system afforded franchisees, Holiday Inns, for example, is acutely involved in all construction plans and site acquisitions, as it is in the maintaining of operating standards through the use of full-time investigators who make periodic, unannounced visits to most Inns throughout the year. During such visits, everything is examined—pool, restaurant, even the carpeting—according to a strict point system. Inns failing to secure above a predetermined figure have only a month to make things right. Moreover, all managers attend rigorous training sessions conducted in a university-like facility in Mississippi.[22]

Almost every aspect of the hotel was designed to fit the corporate brand, including the linens, furniture, wallpaper, appliances, toiletries, and even the candies offered to guests in the lobby. In 1967, Holiday Inn launched a subsidiary, Institutional Mart of America, to supply products to franchise owners and other hospitality businesses, operating from a showroom in Memphis with 300,000 square feet of floor space.[23] As described by Wallace Johnson,

> manufacturers, distributors and dealers display everything needed to furnish and operate a motel, hotel, dormitory, restaurant, cafeteria, institutions of various kinds. It is a complete shopping center for buyers. They find everything they need at our IMA—and a lot of things they want when they see them—furniture, fixtures, rugs and carpets, lamps, bedding, paintings and prints, drapes, china and tableware, stoves and utensils, air-conditioners and heaters, mirrors, plaques. And everything is so artistically displayed that the atmosphere is that of a world's fair instead of a merchandise mart.[24]

In 1972, the company opened three additional showrooms in Los Angeles, Miami, and Atlanta. A writer for the New York Times reported that it took "4,000 items to furnish a motel" and that everything could be purchased through the corporation.[25]

It is difficult to say when uniforms were established for the front desk, restaurant, and cleaning staff. A series of advertisements in 1969 included two illustrations of receptionists: one with a woman wearing a yellow blouse and green headband (Figure 6.3) and one that showed a man wearing a dark green blazer with a white button-down shirt and black necktie. These may have been uniforms since the corporation's color scheme was yellow and green. Judging from the availability of iron-on patches with the Holiday Inn logo (Figure 6.4) some branch hotels used them to embellish affordable, generic garments and create uniforms.

Figure 6.3 Holiday Inn advertisement with a receptionist wearing a yellow blouse and green headband, which may have been a uniform, 1969. Author's research collection.

Figure 6.4 Embroidered Holiday Inn patch with iron-on adhesive for attaching it to clothing, 6.5 cm x 9 cm, *c.* 1970s–80s. Author's research collection.

An advertisement from the 1970s—which ended with the tagline, "At every Holiday Inn, the best surprise is no surprise"—showed an executive in a business suit checking in at the front desk. Two receptionists behind him were wearing identical uniforms: dark blue blazers, white shirts with large collars, patterned scarves (worn like a loose necktie), and name tags. While the colors have changed over the last four decades, the business-like style has not (Figure 6.5).

Today, this chain is owned by IHG Hotels & Resorts based in the United Kingdom, but there are several other hospitality corporations that are just as large and iconic in American society including Choice Hotels (established in 1939 as a "marketing cooperative" for roadside motels),[26] Hilton (1946), Best Western (1946), Hyatt (1957), and Marriott (1957). Wyndham Hotels & Resorts (1981) has absorbed several older and smaller chains of hotels including Howard Johnson (established in 1925), Travelodge (1939), Ramada (1953), La Quinta (1968), Super 8 (1974), AmericInn (1984), Microtel (1989), and Days Inn (1992).[27]

One of the largest suppliers of hotel uniforms is Cintas, a Fortune 500 corporation based in Cincinnati, Ohio. In 2017, IHG Hotels & Resorts announced that it would debut a new line of uniforms for its upscale Crowne Plaza hotels at

Figure 6.5 Receptionist at a Holiday Inn in Kissimmee, Florida, 2015. Jeff Greenberg for Universal Images Group via Getty Images.

New York Fashion Week, developed through a collaboration between Cintas and fashion designer, Timo Weiland. As noted in a press release, "They named the collection *MOMENTUM* to represent the Crowne Plaza brand's commitment to being a design-led, culturally relevant and technology-driven brand. The uniforms are both fashion-forward and suitable for a day's work, providing hotel team members with a look that they can be proud of and comfortable in."[28] For its line of "direct purchase" uniforms, which it sells directly to employers—not retailers or individual staff—Cintas has invited executives to:

> Reinforce your brand image and positively impact your team's morale and productivity by creating a unique uniform program using our apparel that is on-trend and functional. We've created the most distinctive apparel and innovative designs to fit your industry and budget. With talented designers and the latest apparel technology, we're proud to be your source for hospitality uniforms that tell guests exactly who you are.[29]

For hotel staff members who are not as visible to guests, the company rents and launders more generic uniforms.[30] With more than one million customers, white delivery vans with the Cintas logo are a common sight in cities around the US.

Not every business that supplies uniforms to hotels is this large. Western Hotel Supply, owned by Corporate Image Group based in Aberdeen, South

Dakota,[31] sells uniforms to more than 40 hotel chains using password-protected web portals. One chain that it supplies is Best Western, which also contracts with RB Apparel, based in Indianapolis.[32] Executive Apparel, which started manufacturing elements of police uniforms in Philadelphia in 1934, has largely shifted to school uniforms and the hospitality industry.[33] In a blog post about hotels and restaurants reopening from COVID-19 lockdowns, the company advised buyers that "New, updated uniforms are the perfect way to give an immediate fresh impression to customers that this hospitality business takes pride in cleanliness, neatness, and forward-thinking."[34]

Hotel workers who interact the most directly with guests, such as receptionists, are the most likely to wear uniforms that resemble business suits. Top Hat Imagewear, based in New York, sells uniforms for "front desk staff" that are shaped like business suits, but more colorful, such as a sky-blue blazer with a light purple pocket square and plaid necktie.[35] The company advises that, "No matter the setting, corporate, residential, hotel or resort, our sophisticated line of modern apparel will be sure to impress your guests."[36] The company also carries touches of business suits through to the uniforms of less visible workers. For example, Figure 6.6 shows a black-and-white, calf-length coatdress for housekeeping staff that has a business-like pinstripe pattern, made of hard-wearing polyester instead of wool.

Uniforms for Bankers

In the US, pinstripe is a fabric that has a long association with bankers. A photograph taken in 1937 (Figure 6.7) shows three bankers from Buffalo, New York—all wearing pinstripe business suits—testifying before the Securities and Exchange Commission in Washington, DC.

In 1933, Congress enacted a federal law known as the Glass-Steagall Act, which would limit the sizes of banks for several decades by forcing them to choose between commercial banking and investment banking.[37] Consolidation started slowly in the 1950s as hotels, department stores, and restaurants began experimenting with credit cards. A law review article published in 1967 described how institutions were banding together to give consumers broad access to credit:

> Diners' Club [the first credit card in the hospitality industry] sells no goods. It provides the credit and collection services for merchant members of the plan and makes it possible for a card holder to purchase goods and services on credit

Figure 6.6 Uniform for hotel housekeeping staff with a business-like pinstripe fabric, made by Top Hat Imagewear, *c.* 2015. Author's research collection

at a large number of retailers without a prior arrangement with each merchant. Diners' Club and its direct competitors, American Express (which entered the credit-card field in 1958) and Carte Blanche (which was launched by the Hilton Hotel chain in 1959), are primarily used by travelers in hotels and restaurants.[38]

The first banks to issue credit cards were Bank of America and Chase Manhattan, but it would take time to develop networks of businesses where consumers could use them. Between 1965 and 1967, the number of merchants accepting the BankAmericard as payment ballooned from 50,000 to 90,000.[39] In 1966, groups of banks in Chicago and California formed alliances so they could reciprocally honor credit card transactions and clear them like paper checks.[40]

Figure 6.7 Bankers from Buffalo, New York wearing pinstripe suits, 1937. Photograph by Harris & Ewing, Library of Congress Prints and Photographs Division, LC-DIG-hec-22022.

As these alliances expanded nationwide, they consolidated into a handful of major networks. In 1969, the Interbank Card Association rebranded its card as Master Charge (now Mastercard); in 1976, BankAmericard rebranded as Visa.[41] While the new systems were not without problems, the success of credit cards led to the increasing deregulation of banks in the 1980s and 1990s.[42] In 1999, Congress repealed the Glass-Steagall Act, allowing banks to expand dramatically. Today, the banking industry in the US is dominated by just four corporations: JP Morgan Chase (which had assets of $3.31 trillion at the end of 2021), Bank of America, Wells Fargo, and Citibank. To get a better sense of this dominance, consider that Citibank (which is only half the size of JP Morgan Chase) has more assets than the next two largest banks combined (US Bank and PNC Bank). According to the FDIC, the total number of banks in the US fell from a peak of 14,469 in 1983 to just 4,236 in 2021.[43]

When an individual walks into a branch office to withdraw cash or talk to a loan officer, the first "banker" he or she is likely to encounter is a teller, also

Figure 6.8 Tellers at the grand opening of a US Century Bank in Miami, Florida, 2018. Photograph by Jeffrey Isaac Greenberg via Alamy.

known as a cashier (Figure 6.8). According to the US Bureau of Labor Statistics, the average teller is hired with a high school diploma and makes $32,620 per year working full-time.[44]

Like chains of hotels, corporate banks require uniforms for employees to make their branches predictable: cashiers at Chase banks in Phoenix wear the same colors and styles as cashiers in Cleveland. The "Chase Apparel Dress Code" tells newly hired workers that,

> As brand ambassadors, employees have a significant impact on customer perception of brand image and Chase's ability to provide high quality financial services and products. An employee's dress and etiquette are important components of projecting a professional image and engendering confidence and trust in the Chase brand by our customers.[45]

Chase employees—both branch and corporate—are given allowances to purchase uniforms supplied by Lands' End through a password-protected web portal. As a vertically integrated clothing manufacturer and retailer, Lands' End does a substantial amount of business selling uniforms for schools[46] and workplaces,[47] with regular updates that reflect the changing seasons and changing mainstream fashions in clothing. A portion of the website dedicated to "Custom

Bank & Financial Uniform Clothing" includes three dozen generic styles of garments that can be turned into proprietary uniforms by applying embroidered logos. Although the colors for pants, skirts, and blazers are very limited (black, navy, charcoal, and khaki), there are more available for polo shirts, button-down shirts, sweaters, and accessories to match the colors of corporate brands.[48] For Chase bank employees, uniforms are limited to white, light gray, and shades of blue, with small touches of red on scarves, neckties, and socks.[49]

In 2013, an article published by the American Banking Association noted that "dress codes can be difficult to enforce, so some banks choose easier-to-manage uniforms, or career apparel."[50] An executive for Lands' End Business reasoned that uniforms could function as advertisements. "Your employees are wearing this product not only to work, but before and after work.... It tends to be a walking billboard in the community."[51] While perhaps good for the corporations, in 2021 the Bank of America corporate office in New York City warned staff to be on alert while commuting since "wearing the company logo or dressing up" was putting them at risk of assault.[52] Ironically the highest-paid financial executives are far more likely to wear business suits (which do not have corporate logos) instead of uniforms.

Uniforms for Baristas, and Other Fast-Food Workers

The job of "barista" is relatively new in American society and is strongly (but not exclusively) associated with Starbucks, a corporation founded in Seattle in 1971. In 2020, anthropologist Sabine Parrish defined the term through comparison to other jobs in food service:

> "Barista" refers to anyone whose primary job is making and serving coffee—one can think of them as the coffee industry's version of bartenders—but this definition encompasses a broad range of sites of employment, from drive-thru kiosks on the sides of highways to cafes inside supermarkets, any Starbucks location, and upscale coffee houses.[53]

The Standard Occupational Classification system (used for taxes, labor laws, and reporting by the US Bureau of Labor Statistics) includes baristas in the category of "Fast Food and Counter Workers," which is distinguished from "Waiters and Waitresses":

35-3023 Fast Food and Counter Workers
Perform duties such as taking orders and serving food and beverages. Serve customers at counter or from a steam table. May take payment. May prepare

food and beverages. Counter attendants who also wait tables are included in "Waiters and Waitresses."

Illustrative examples: Barista, Cafeteria Server, Ice Cream Server, Mess Attendant, Snack Bar Attendant

35-3030 Waiters and Waitresses

Take orders and serve food and beverages to patrons at tables in dining establishment. Excludes "Fast Food and Counter Workers."

Illustrative examples: Cocktail Server, Dining Car Server, Wine Steward[54]

Both types of workers make an average of $11.60 per hour, but the positions are rarely full-time.[55] This limits their benefits (such as healthcare and retirement plans); it also means that many workers hold two or even three jobs at the same time.[56] However, workplaces can vary tremendously. While a counter worker at an airport coffee shop, for example, might do little more than collect payments and serve customers from a selection of pre-made beverages and food, baristas at upscale cafes can be highly skilled and knowledgeable about coffee, like wine sommeliers at expensive restaurants. They educate customers, make handcrafted beverages, receive sizeable tips, and enter competitions like the United States Coffee Championships.[57]

Fast-food restaurants—also known as Quick Service Restaurants (QSR)—are the opposite of upscale. Predictable, affordable, and accessible, they do not require or allow much creativity from workers. Although McDonalds (founded in 1955) is often credited as the first, there are several chains still operating in the US that are even older, including A&W (1919), White Castle (1921), Dairy Queen (1940), KFC (1952), and Sonic (1953). The term "fast food" did not emerge until the mid-twentieth century. In an interview with *Smithsonian Magazine*, Adam Chandler, author of *Drive-Thru Dreams*, described its place in American culture:

> Fast food [took off] in large part because of the highway system that we built in the 1950s and the 1960s. America started driving more than ever before and we rearranged our cities based on car travel, for better or worse. And it was a natural business response to the American on-the-go kind of lifestyle. [...] The food is terrible, and it's delicious, and it's completely ridiculous and we love it.[58]

Compared to uniforms worn by hotel receptionists and bankers, many uniforms worn by baristas and fast-food workers are more bold and colorful, sometimes even kitsch.[59] Fashion historian Valeria Nofri has described kitsch as "bad taste" that nevertheless has a "sense of both attraction and repulsion, similar to being punched in the stomach—a burst of elements that convey curiosity and disgust."[60] In the 1960s and 1970s, fast-food corporations turned to some of the largest uniform manufacturers for attention-grabbing designs.

After Dunkin' Donuts began selling franchises in 1955,[61] the company hired Angelica to design uniforms for its counter staff. It was a natural alliance since Angelica was already well-known for its waitress uniforms. An early design looked like a white, short-sleeved blouse covered by a pink vest or minidress. While it appears very feminine—and the top shown in Figure 6.9(a) was worn by a woman[62]—pink and orange are the signature colors of the brand (Figure 6.9(b)).

Barco—better known as a manufacturer of healthcare uniforms—entered the QSR market in 1970 by designing a "color block dress" for Denny's waitresses.[63] An early collaboration with Burger King (Figure 6.10) produced a uniform with a short-sleeved, plaid blouse covered by a faux-corduroy vest. While the colors (maroon and light yellow) were specific to the brand, it also featured the company's logo embroidered on the upper left chest. This uniform appeared in the film *Back to the Future*,[64] released in 1985. Worn by Marty McFly's brother, Dave, it came with matching maroon pants and a maroon visor with the Burger King logo (Figure 6.11).

Another iconic uniform from this time period was worn by employees at Pizza Hut. Designed by Crest Uniform Company, based in New York City,[65] the

Figure 6.9 (a) Dunkin' Donuts uniform top designed by Angelica Uniform Co.; (b) featuring a doughnut-shaped logo, early 1970s. Author's research collection.

Figure 6.10 Burger King uniform top designed by Barco, *c.* 1980. Author's research collection.

jacket is bright red and closes with a zipper. Panels of cloth on the jacket and hat (Figure 6.12) have the chain's iconic red-and-white checkerboard pattern, which was also used on tablecloths in Pizza Hut restaurants. The fabric is tricot (likely nylon, judging from the feel) and would have been easy to wash and wear without ironing, but it also would have been uncomfortable to wear around hot grills, ovens, and fryers. Furthermore, nylon (like other synthetics) is oleophilic, which makes the smells of body odor and oily food difficult to wash out.

In the 1980s and 1990s, many restaurant chains incorporated polo shirts into their uniforms. Burger King switched to light-yellow polos.[66] Barco manufactured color block polo shirts for Taco Bell employees (Figure 6.13(a)) with diagonal panels of maroon, navy blue, and dark green. Dunkin' Donuts used a variety of

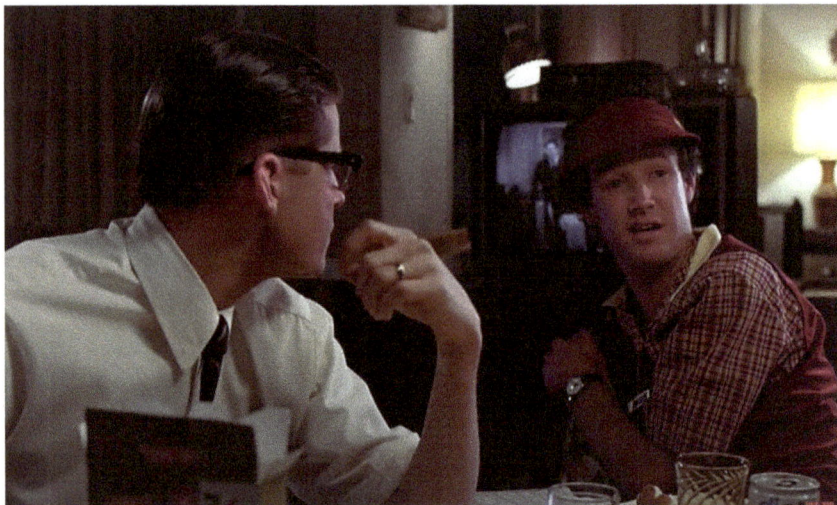

Figure 6.11 Still from *Back to the Future* (Amblin Entertainment, 1985), showing Marty McFly's father (left) and brother (right) wearing the Burger King uniform designed by Barco.

Figure 6.12 Pizza Hut (a) uniform jacket and (b) hat designed by Crest Uniform Company, *c.* 1980. Author's research collection.

Figures 6.13 (a) Taco Bell uniform polo shirt designed by Barco, and (b) a Dunkin' Donuts polo shirt designed by Uniforms to You, a Chicago-based division of Cintas, both *c*. 1995. Author's research collection.

polo shirts that were mostly bright purple, hot pink, maroon (Figure 6.13(b)), or gray accented with orange and pink stripes.

In 1999, a scholar of hospitality argued that "Most observers would say that chain restaurants are in the business of selling food. A strong counterargument is made that these restaurants sell experiences."[67] Bright colors are associated with excitement and happiness, encouraging fast-food consumers to eat more[68] and develop brand loyalty starting in childhood.[69] Some fast-food chains have retained these bright colors. After years of declining market share due to stiff competition from regional and national pizza chains, Pizza Hut has re-emerged as a nostalgic favorite. In 2021, the company launched a line of streetwear with the red-and-white checkerboard pattern from the 1980s.[70] McDonalds, on the other hand, has turned to more serious colors out of public concerns about childhood obesity.[71] In 2017, Barco completely re-designed the corporation's uniforms to include T-shirts, polo shirts, and button-down shirts in charcoal gray and slate blue.[72] A similar shirt for Wendy's (Figure 6.14(a)) is charcoal gray with subtle pinstripes. The only features that distinguish it from bank uniforms are the tiny logo on the left sleeve (Figure 6.14(b)) and the high-performance polyester-cotton blend.

Figures 6.14 Banker-style uniform for (a) Wendy's with pinstripes and (b) a subtle logo on one sleeve, designed by Barco, *c*. 2015. Author's research collection.

This shift also echoes a twenty-first century resurgence of interest in minimalism. In 2022, business scholars Anne Wilson and Silvia Bellezza synthesized contemporary marketing and consumer rhetoric about this trend, describing minimalism as "a preference for neutral or monochromatic colors, neatness and little clutter, and simplicity of appearance." Regarding clothing, they observed that some brands were offering capsule collections ("uniforms") with "limited colors, patterns, and designs"[73] as a response to consumers' interest in buying and owning less clothing. In 2019, the Museum at FIT in New York launched an exhibit putting minimalism (and its opposite, maximalism) into context within fashion history.[74]

In contrast to this trend towards minimalism, Subway workers wear lime green uniforms, symbolizing that the chain offers a healthy (green) option for a quick meal. A recent uniform T-shirt (Figure 6.15) has the corporation's logo on the front and "FRESH IS WHAT WE DO" on the back. Starbucks describes the color green as "fresh and inviting," but also visible from long distances,[75] which is useful for drawing in customers who are traveling. The red and blue color scheme used consistently by Domino's Pizza since the 1960s is not only eye-catching but reads as "patriotic" in the US.

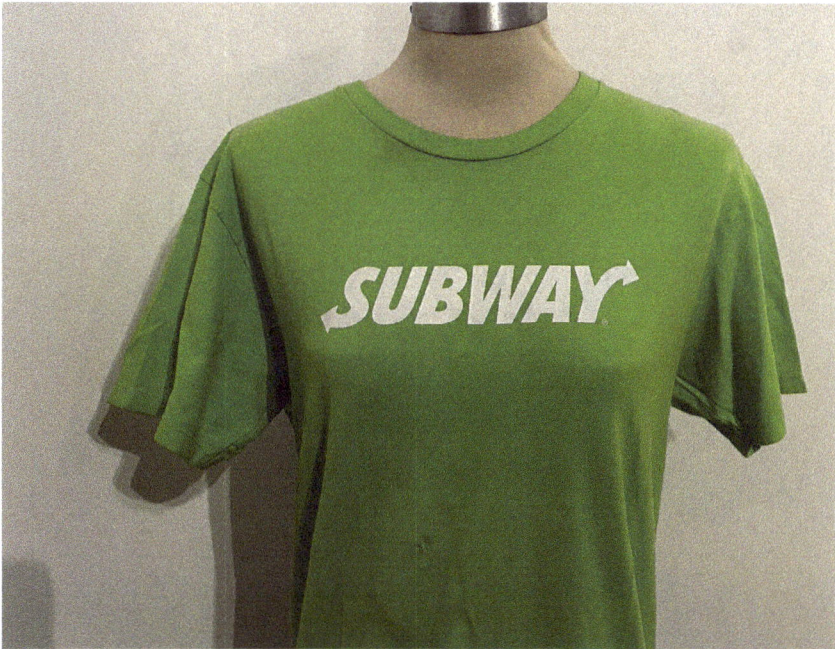

Figure 6.15 Subway uniform T-shirt, likely designed and distributed internally since there is no manufacturing tag, *c.* 2015. Author's research collection.

Like healthcare uniforms, food service uniforms must be washed frequently. Both industries were early adopters of nylon and polyester, materials that are durable, do not need ironing or dry cleaning, and do not lose color when laundered repeatedly. They also trap up to one-third of the wearer's sweat[76] causing itchy rashes and blisters.[77] To overcome this problem, fast-food uniforms in the twenty-first century are typically designed with one of three solutions: the addition of cotton (since cotton absorbs water and is more comfortable to wear), advanced synthetics that use capillary action to wick moisture away from the body,[78] and/or high-tech warp knits that increase the surface area of the fabric and allow more evaporation of sweat. A uniform that Barco designed for KFC (Figure 6.16) looks like an ordinary cotton T-shirt that a customer would wear, but on close inspection the polyester fabric is a warp knit resembling a honeycomb. The scale of corporate buying gives manufactures incentives to experiment with new technologies, since a markedly better design could be very lucrative.

On interactive websites like Reddit, Quora, Zippia, and Indeed, bloggers and workers share tips about uniforms at different corporations, including official

Figure 6.16 Uniform designed by Barco for KFC that looks like an ordinary cotton T-shirt but is actually a 100% polyester warp knit, *c.* 2015. Author's research collection.

policies, exceptions, and variations between stores. Zippia, for example, advises potential applicants that:

> McDonald's requires employees to wear black pants that aren't leggings, sweatpants, yoga pants, or jeans with wide legs or large stitching. Employees' shoes also need to be black, closed-toed, non-slip, sturdy, and polished, which means no nylon or canvas. This is to protect your feet from hot oil or other hazards while you work. You'll wear your McDonald's shirt, nametag, and hat during your shift as well. If it's cold, employees are often allowed to wear long sleeve shirts in approved colors under their short sleeve uniform shirts.[79]

These tips are important because of the thin line between uniforms and dress codes. Many counter workers and baristas are asked to supply their own pants and shoes and may need to cover up tattoos and remove jewelry. Even before applying, workers can judge whether they will be able to meet the requirements. Once the work begins, there may not be enough time (or money) for the worker to get into compliance if they are not already.

Black pants are a staple for many different jobs, but slip-resistant shoes are specific to work environments where the floors need to be cleaned frequently. In a research study about the causes of slip-related injuries at limited-service restaurants, a team of epidemiologists found that if "slip-resistant shoes were provided by the employer, 91 percent of participants wore them; whereas if they were neither provided nor encouraged, only 53.5 percent wore them."[80] Teenage workers were the least likely to own and wear the specialized shoes.[81]

Job advertisements for corporate fast-food chains often describe "free uniforms" as one of the perks of working there:

Pizza Hut

Nothing "uniform" about the way we do things, because our uniforms (which are actually just really cool t-shirts and hats that you get when you start) were made for team members by team members. We just ask that you keep them clean and come to work ready to rock the Pizza Hut look.[82]

Wendy's

As a Wendy's Crew Member, you'll enjoy the benefits of working in a fun, fast-paced environment where uniforms are provided, meal discounts are granted, and there is plenty of room for career advancement.[83]

Chipotle

Get your Chipotle uniform (aka shirts and hats) for free.[84]

Taco John's

When you're here, you're part of a crew that feels like family, and supported by a management team that truly wants to see you succeed. You'll also enjoy awesome perks like: free food during your shift, paid vacation, up to $3,200 toward college tuition, referral bonuses, quick & fun online training, free uniforms [...] and that's just the beginning.[85]

While Starbucks also serves food and beverages, the dress code is more personalized to match the handcrafted style of its products. A fifteen-page manual advises baristas on options that are allowed but keep the focus on the true uniform: an apron with the Starbucks logo. It advises that: "As ambassadors of the Starbucks brand, you should feel proud of your own look as you tie on the green apron. [...] We hope this Dress Code Lookbook gets you excited to open your closets and have fun."[86] Underlying clothing must be black, charcoal, gray, navy, brown, khaki, or white. Tiny accents of other colors are allowed on neckties, scarves, and socks. Workers can have visible tattoos and brightly colored hair as long as the hairstyle is "clean, brushed and kept back from the face."[87] Visors and caps with the Starbucks logo are available from a website that only employees can access,[88] but are not required at every location. Bucket hats and logos from other companies (for example, Nike) are forbidden.[89]

Figure 6.17 Stock photograph of a "barista" wearing a beige version of the standard apron. SDI Productions via Getty Images.

While the color of the Starbucks apron is part of the corporation's branding scheme, the basic style of the apron (based on the butcher apron) has been widely adopted by other coffee shops. Searching for stock photos of "baristas" inevitably shows workers behind a counter wearing an apron with thin straps that covers the front of the body from mid-chest to mid-thigh. Figure 6.17 shows a typical example.

Conclusion

By the 1990s, sociologists were lamenting the effects of corporatization on human interactions, most famously George Ritzer in *The McDonaldization of Society*:

> Easily consumed finger foods make the meal itself a quick one. Some fast-food restaurants use chairs that make customers uncomfortable after about twenty minutes. Much the same effect is produced by the colors used in the decor: 'Relaxation isn't the point. Getting the Hell out of there is the point. The interior colors have been chosen carefully with this end in mind. From the scarlet and yellow of the logo to the maroon of the uniform; everything clashes. It's designed to stop people from feeling so comfortable they might want to stay.'[90]

Sociologist Ray Oldenburg described corporate restaurants and coffee shops as "nonplaces" where workers and customers are depersonalized. "In nonplaces one cannot be an individual or become one, for one's individuality is not only irrelevant, it also gets in the way."[91] This is not always an intentional strategy. A decade later, two business professors argued that the best way to improve service for customers is to take better care of workers:

> Employees who provide the face-to-face service (e.g., the bank teller) are often the part-time, low paid, and high turnover positions in the company. An often neglected customer service principle is service to employees; employees are customers. Management must treat employees the way they want employees to treat their customers.[92]

Providing good customer service is the drumbeat of these jobs, characterized by phrases like "the customer is king" and "the customer is always right." As corporatization has advanced, a broad spectrum of employers and customers in the US have come to expect deference from front-line workers,[93] an attitude that scholars also refer to as "customer sovereignty." The worst abuses typically happen in industries where workers are poorly paid, have little job security, and are considered low-status (e.g., women and people of color), leading to high turnover and a lack of long-term relationships between workers and customers.[94]

In an article about why some service workers take revenge on customers, two scholars of business, Lloyd Harris and Emmanuel Ogbonna, argued that negative interactions arise most often in sectors with long-standing master–servant expectations, such as hospitality and food service.[95] An article by sociologist Elaine Hall described this dynamic in greater detail:

> To do personal service work means accepting one's subordination; waiters learn to 'accept one's place' and waitresses learn to 'humble' themselves each time they approach a table of customers. [...] As subordinated service providers, waiters and waitresses are expected to show deference, particularly by smiling to show they take pleasure in serving and by accepting being treated as 'non-persons.' Smiling applicants for waiting jobs are more likely to be hired, training programs emphasize a friendly smiling manner for table servers, and customers tip smiling servers better.[96]

Uniforms are not the primary reason that most workers select or reject jobs. However, they do play an important role in customer interactions. For corporate executives, uniforms are needed to make workers visible to customers, to standardize their appearance, and to make them part of the corporate brand. However, by limiting workers' ability to express their personalities and identities through their dress—a normal and healthy behavior that most adults engage in—they also (perhaps unintentionally) infantilize and dehumanize them. The workers themselves care more about "comfort, overall fit and the ease of maintenance and cleaning."[97] These goals are not necessarily opposites: satisfied workers provide better customer service.[98]

The services that corporations provide are more complicated than they first appear. A hotel is a safe and comfortable shelter. Through their appearance and behaviors, receptionists help to establish a welcoming atmosphere. However, the people who stay at hotels engage in a wide variety of behaviors: eating, sleeping, watching television, having sex, doing business, or even hiding illegal activities such as human trafficking.[99] The next chapter—focusing on sexualized uniforms—considers how the main service is not necessarily the only service.

7

Adult Entertainment

Sexualized and Embodied Uniforms

In her book, *The Managed Heart*, published in 1983, sociologist Arlie Hochschild coined the term "emotional labor" to describe how corporate airlines expected flight attendants (at the time, nearly all women) to provide much more than just physical caretaking of passengers. Observing a training session for newly hired workers, she noted:

> The young trainee sitting next to me wrote on her notepad, 'Important to smile. Don't forget to smile.' The admonition came from the speaker in the front of the room, a crew-cut pilot in his early fifties, speaking in a Southern drawl: 'Now girls, I want you to go out there and really *smile*. Your smile is your biggest *asset*. I want you to out there and really use it. Smile. *Really* smile. Really *lay it on*.'[1] (Original emphasis)

In academic terms, a genuine smile is called a "Duchenne smile," indicating that the person who is smiling is having a positive emotion.[2] In daily life in the US, a person who is smiling is most likely happy. It also influences the people around them to feel happy. Regardless of whether a smile is genuine (or the toll it takes on the worker's mental health) corporate airlines understand this psychology. As an extension of the corporate brand, a smiling flight attendant conveys the airline's "confidence that its planes will not crash, its reassurance that departures and arrivals will be on time, its welcome and its invitation to return."[3] The smile is part of the uniform.

Building on Hochschild's work, the concept of "aesthetic labor" goes even further to describe how the bodies and behaviors of workers are preselected and managed by employers. In a study focusing on how upscale retail stores attract workers, sociologists Christine Williams and Catherine Connell noted that,

> Aesthetic labor includes a worker's deportment, style, accent, voice, and attractiveness. Employees at these stores must embody particular styles of

standing, speaking, and walking. 'Looking good' and 'sounding right' are their jobs' primary requirements. In virtually every case, the right aesthetic is middle class, conventionally gendered, and typically white.[4]

In the twenty-first century, retail stores sell much more than products—they sell entertainment, sensory experiences, and feelings such as happiness, excitement, and belonging. A 2015 article in the *Journal of Fashion Marketing and Management* argued that, "What consumers want are products, communications, and marketing campaigns that dazzle their senses, touch their hearts, and stimulate their minds."[5] In physical stores, workers perform labor to keep the store running, but they also serve as educators and aesthetic role models.

Aesthetic Labor in Adult Entertainment

Aesthetic labor has always been an integral part of adult entertainment, which involves age-limited activities such as smoking, drinking, gambling, nudity, and sexual behavior. While not all workers in these industries are women—and this chapter includes examples of men who work in adult entertainment such as bouncers and exotic dancers—sexual attractiveness in both body and dress is the driving force behind adult entertainment uniforms. Curiously, there seems to be much more academic literature about uniforms as a type of sexual fetish[6] (concentrated in gender studies) than academic literature concerning sexual attractiveness as a dimension of work uniforms and dress codes (concentrated in business, hospitality, and legal studies).

The history of uniforms as a sexual fetish seems to be nearly as old as the existence of standardized uniforms. In 1895, an American inventor, Herman Casler, received a patent for a machine that he called a "mutoscope." In describing its purpose and function, he noted:

> My object is to produce a device for exhibiting pictures, photographs, or similar likenesses so arranged that by successively bringing them into the line of vision they will show the changing positions of the body or bodies and reproduce to the eye the acts of the performers.[7]

Commonly used in peep shows in the first half of the twentieth century, the viewer dropped a coin into the machine and then cranked it by hand. If done quickly, the effect was similar to a kinetoscope—an early "motion picture" device refined by Thomas Edison. If cranked slowly, the viewer could linger over individual cards.[8] Most featured women flirting and undressing.

A mutoscope card from the 1940s (Figure 7.1) shows a woman in a skimpy version of a nurse's uniform, holding a spoon and a mercury thermometer. Since she is not wearing a dress under the apron, her cleavage and the sides of her breasts are visible. The caption says, "easy to take," a double entendre for medical treatment and sexual domination. Throughout the twentieth century, nurses and their work uniforms were frequent subjects of pornographic illustrations and films,[9] invoking power dynamics (controlling nurse vs. helpless patient), pain as pleasure, and fetish materials (steel, latex, and PVC).[10] Fashion historian Valerie Steele briefly explored the sexual appeal of work uniforms in her book, *Fetish*:

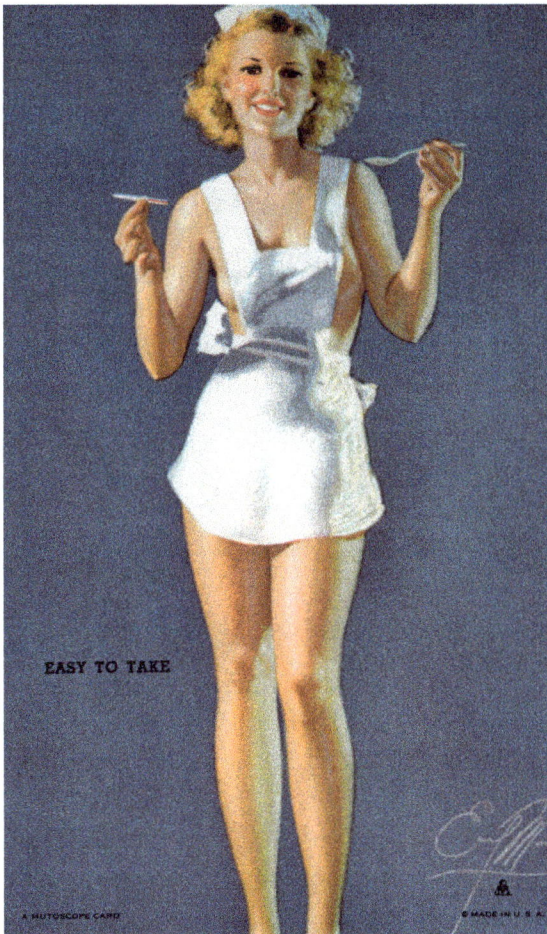

EASY TO TAKE

Figure 7.1 Mutoscope card featuring a sexy nurse wearing only a cap and short apron, 1940s. Universal History Archive via Getty Images.

Military uniforms are probably the most popular prototype for the fetishist uniform because they signify hierarchy (some command, others obey), as well as membership in what was traditionally an all-male group whose function involves the legitimate use of physical violence. Soldiers can shoot and stab without constraint. The erotic connotations of military uniforms derive, in part, from the sexual excitement that many people associate with violence and with the relationship between dominance and submission.[11]

This connection between uniforms and sexiness is not always conscious. In a 2012 article connecting the color of waitress uniforms and tipping practices in restaurants, hospitality scholars Nicolas Guéguen and Céline Jacob found evidence that when female waitresses wear red uniforms it seems to enhance their sexual attractiveness as demonstrated by increased tips, but only when the customers are men[12] (presumably cis-gender, heterosexual men).

In a 2013 article about male strippers in nightclubs patronized by women, sociologist Maren Scull observed that strippers use costumes to generate sexual excitement (e.g., by ripping off their pants during the performance), but also to encourage particular types of behavior among customers by dressing up as "soldiers, businessmen, doctors, sailors, football players, firemen, police officers, gladiators, and cowboys."[13] Uniforms make these roles easy to recognize and do not need to be very specific or accurate to be effective. Imitations for Halloween,[14] acting,[15] and sexual fantasies are widely available. In a study of police impersonators (mostly men), criminal justice scholars Callie Marie Rennison and Mary Dodge found that,

> The tools used by police impersonators are simple and easily obtained. [. . .] The clothing worn by the offender generally was described by victims as 'a dark blue t-shirt with white lettering in the breast area,' 'dark blue/black uniform with a gun belt and badge,' or 'dark blue pants, blue uniform shirt.' In the majority of cases, impersonators carried badges, wore patches, or carried police looking equipment (e.g., flashlight, Nextel cell phone, walkie-talkie).[16]

When strippers dress like police officers, they are not impersonating them to commit other crimes; everyone involved knows they are not actually police officers. The function of the uniform is to draw on stereotypes and to set a tone of sexual dominance and submission.

The purpose of this chapter is not to explore how uniforms are used in sexual fantasies or to shame sex workers and other consensual adults—although sexual attraction is an important subtext in this discussion. Instead, this chapter focuses on occupations and workplaces where uniforms are hypersexualized, but actual sex is uncommon and/or discouraged.

Barmaids and Cigarette Girls, 1880–1960

In the early twentieth century, very few women in the US worked as bartenders, however it was not uncommon for women to serve food and drinks in bars. Working as a "barmaid" was often stigmatized as dangerous and unsavory; a bar was "not the kind of place a 'self-respecting lady' would seek employment."[17] For Japanese women who came to the US as immigrants in the late 1800s and early 1900s, opportunities for paid employment were very limited, with many taking positions as maids or prostitutes. Some worked in brothels, but others

> worked in Japanese restaurants as barmaids (*shakufu*). Bar-restaurants began to appear in Pacific Coast Japanese communities in the 1890s, catering primarily to Japanese men. Barmaids served food and alcohol, talking to the customers over drinks, and dancing and playing *samisen* (Japanese guitar). [. . .] Overcome with homesickness, Japanese men were naturally attracted to Japanese sake, food, and songs in bar-restaurants after the day's work.[18]

The line between barmaid and prostitute was thin, not just in the US but in many parts of the world.[19] An image published in 1895 in *Police Gazette*—an early magazine for men that would inspire other adult publications like *Maxim* and *Playboy*[20]—published an illustration that gives us a glimpse into what barmaids wore (Figure 7.2). In what may have been an advertisement for Moët & Chandon champagne, a barmaid is entertaining a group of men by theatrically pouring a drink between two glasses. Several features of her outfit echo the uniforms worn by waitresses and maids—a frilly, white cap, a white bib apron, and a corseted dress with exaggerated sleeves. However, the material of the dress is a colorful red-and-white striped pattern,[21] her sleeves are pushed up past her elbows, and the neckline is cut very low to reveal cleavage, which is slightly covered by a piece of green foliage.

When Prohibition (1920–33) was established by an amendment to the US Constitution, alcohol consumption was driven underground, and conventional bars were forced to close. As a result, there was a surge in demand for other types of consumption and entertainment such as ice cream parlors,[22] soda fountains,[23] cafeterias,[24] jazz clubs,[25] and palatial movie theaters.[26] In venues where adults gathered at night, "cigarette girls" replaced barmaids—beautiful young women who circulated around the room selling candy, chewing gum, and cigarettes from trays. Films from the 1920s and 30s such as *Island Wives* (1922), *The Singing Fool* (1928), *Nothing but the Truth* (1929), *Sunset Murder Case* (1938), and *Cafe Society* (1939) drew attention to the occupation and glamorized the look of the cigarette girl.

BARMAID OF THE 20ᵀᴴ CENTURY.

Figure 7.2 Illustration of a barmaid from *Police Gazette*, a lifestyle magazine for adult men, 1895. Library of Congress Prints and Photographs Division, LC-DIG-ppmsca-44106.

Early depictions of cigarette girls (for example, Figure 7.3) were similar to maids and waitresses. By the 1940s, however, the costumes were more sexualized. When Virginia O'Brien was cast to a play a cigarette girl in *Du Barry Was a Lady* (1943), she was featured on the lobby cards wearing an exotic turban-style cap and cropped shirt that exposed her midriff. As the lead in *Cigarette Girl* (1947), Leslie Brooks wore black high heels and an extremely short black dress with a white apron. While it superficially resembled a maid's uniform, the sleeveless top was molded to fit her breasts. In *Lucky Losers* (1950), "cigarette girl" was a very minor role, however the actress, Wendy Waldron, was featured on lobby cards wearing a black top hat and bowtie, a tuxedo-style shirt, and a tight-fitting bodysuit made of red fabric covered in black lace (Figure 7.4). Like a one-piece swimsuit, the bottom half of the outfit did not cover her legs.

These outfits were not just Hollywood fantasies but reflections of real-life uniforms. In 1956, photographer Angelo Rizzuto captured an image of a cigarette girl working on a sidewalk in New York City (Figure 7.5). Her outfit—consisting of a sequined bodysuit, sequined high heels, dark stockings, and a mask—contrasts sharply with the more plain and modest clothing (less-sexualized)

Figure 7.3 Actress Evelyn Kahn, dressed for her role as a cigarette girl in *Nothing but the Truth* (Paramount Studios, 1929). Photograph by Bettmann via Getty Images.

Figure 7.4 Lobby card for *Lucky Losers* (Monogram Pictures, 1950), featuring actress Wendy Waldron as a cigarette girl. Photograph by LMPC via Getty Images.

Figure 7.5 Cigarette girl working on a sidewalk in New York City, 1956. Photograph by Angelo Rizzuto (1906–1967), Library of Congress Prints and Photographs Division, LC-DIG-ppmsca-70004.

worn by her female customer. Cigarette girls did not immediately disappear when Prohibition ended in 1933. Instead, they were slowly replaced by vending machines for candy and cigarettes,[27] which delivered higher profits to the owners of bars, casinos, and other adult entertainment venues. Today, cigarette girls exist only as novelties for special events.[28]

Carhops and Topless Dancers, 1920–85

In 1921, Jessie Kirby opened a new kind of roadside restaurant in Dallas, Texas, where motorists could enjoy meals without getting out of their cars:

> When a customer pulled into the Pig Stand parking lot, teenaged boys in white shirts and black bow ties jogged over to his car, hopped up on the running board—sometimes before the driver had even pulled into a parking space—and took his order. This daredevilry won the servers a nickname: carhops. Soon, the Pig Stand drive-ins replace the carhops with attractive young girls on roller skates, but the basic formula was the same: good-looking young people, tasty food, speedy service, and auto-based convenience.[29]

Figure 7.6 Carhop at a Clock-In restaurant in California wearing a short-sleeved blouse with a majorette-style skirt and plumed hat, *c.* 1955. Photograph by Graphic House / Archive Photos via Getty Images.

The business quickly expanded into a chain of restaurants, inspiring many competitors.[30] By the 1940s, drive-ins were common throughout the country.

In a move that newspapers described as a promotional stunt, Sivil's—a drive-in beer garden in Houston, Texas—changed the uniforms of its carhops to be much more revealing. As a reporter in Paris, Texas described, "Sivil's glorified drive-in stand undressed its pretty carhops as much as it could without bringing the reformers down en masse." The outfit consisted of "scanties" (short shorts), brassieres, and tall "shako" hats, similar to those worn by marching band majorettes.[31]

In 1942, one of the beer garden's carhops was murdered by a customer, who thought the young woman had rejected him as a love interest.[32] The day after the crime was discovered, the state liquor board held an emergency meeting to discuss the situation, focusing on whether it should set limits on uniforms for the carhops (which the chair described as "near-nakedness"). Under public pressure, the owner of Sivil's announced that he would add short skirts to the uniforms, however he "insisted he could see nothing indecent in the shorts."[33] Chains of drive-in restaurants like Big Boy, Checkers, In-N-Out Burger, Sonic, and Eat'n Park expanded rapidly in the 1940s and 50s, but many were overtaken by "rowdy teenagers" who were old enough to drive but not old enough for bars. Much of the restaurant business moved back indoors.[34]

Bars reopened when Prohibition ended in 1933, but the business was not as lucrative as it had been since so many other options for entertainment had been invented. In 1964, a bar in San Francisco called The Condor was facing bankruptcy when its featured dancer, Carol Doda, began wearing a new topless swimsuit invented by designer Rudi Gernreich.[35] The "gimmick" was an instant success and spread quickly in San Francisco and Los Angeles, with women working as "sketch-me-nude models, topless dancers, topless waitresses [and] topless barmaids."[36]

Despite hundreds of court challenges for violating laws on public nudity,[37] the trend lured many customers back into adult entertainment venues. In 1966, a journalist in Las Vegas noted that casinos were introducing "nearly-topless" uniforms, designed to push the limits of nudity laws without breaking them, with "female card dealers at the Silver Nugget casino" wearing "peek-a-boo transparent blouses and pasties."[38] With astonishment and humor, an opinion columnist for the *Oakland Tribune* noted:

> As a dedicated trend watcher, I am considering the topless trend. I think we're about to see an escalation, or a proliferation if you will, of bare bosoms. The latest

in San Francisco is a topless shoeshine girl and in Englewood, New Jersey, a service station owner wants to dress his female pump attendants in topless swimsuits. That's our topic for today. Children under 18 are not allowed to read this column unless accompanied by a Republican.[39]

The topless gas station attendants were called "bumper bunnies,"[40] undoubtedly based on the "bunnies" who served drinks at Playboy nightclubs,[41] most famously in New York where Gloria Steinem briefly worked as a waitress to write a feminist exposé about the club.[42] Articles about topless barbers began appearing in newspapers in the early 1970s:

> When Teri Moran starts to work at Bob's Torii Club Barber Shop, the door is locked and the shades are drawn. Owner Bob May jumps to the door to post a large 'Topless—Adults Only' sign. [...] since Mrs. Moran, a buxom blonde, started giving topless shampoos earlier this week his business is booming.[43]

The State Board of Barber Examiners questioned whether the "former topless dancer" and "divorced mother of two children" was qualified to work as a barber.[44] This may be why the neighboring state of Texas specifies that barbers may not integrate "lingerie or see-through fabric" into their uniforms.[45]

In 1983, the owner of a struggling doughnut shop near Denver, Colorado hired topless dancers to serve customers and periodically strip out of their "French maid" uniforms. The experiment failed when the dancers complained about low wages and slippery floors caused by the greasy doughnut machine.[46] In 1985, a similar shop opened in Fort Lauderdale, Florida:

> R Donuts—as in R-rated—will open next week in a former fast-food restaurant. Starting at 6am daily, a dozen topless waitresses will serve coffee, doughnuts and sandwiches. [The owner] got the idea from a shop near Yuma, Arizona, where customers wait in a line to pay a $2 cover charge before they can even order doughnuts.[47]

Protestors shattered one of the shop's windows, complaining that "these kinds of businesses bring in prostitutes, and they bring in crime."[48]

Carol Doda—who started dancing topless at The Condor in 1964—continued until the 1980s, earning the 2015 equivalent of $4,000 dollars per week.[49] In an interview near the end of her life she proudly claimed, "The minute I knew I existed in life was the night I started the Condor thing. The only thing that mattered to me was entertaining people."[50] She continued dancing professionally (more fully clothed) until 2009.

Chippendales, Bouncers, and Cocktail Waitresses, 1975–2020

In the late 1970s, Steve Bannerjee, an immigrant from India living in Los Angeles, was trying to turn his struggling bar into a successful business. After experiments with backgammon, dinner theater, and mud wrestling failed,[51] he decided to try an idea that he had seen at another bar: male dancers stripping for women. The concept quickly turned his fortunes around. He named the dancers "Chippendales" after an expensive style of furniture popular among the upper class and eventually renamed his business from Destiny II to Chippendales.[52] An article in a California newspaper in 1980 described one of the shows:

> The primarily female audience was jammed three and four deep around the dance floor railing, with several women standing on tables and chairs to get a better view. Amid high-pitched screams of 'Take it all off,' the dancers stomped to disco music clad—at first—in elaborate costumes ranging from an Indian chief's regalia to a space suit. At the end of the dance, women would stuff paper money into the only apparel left on—the male version of a G-string.[53]

By 1982, the dancers were wearing standardized, nearly topless uniforms (Figure 7.7)—black pants with a white collar, white cuffs, and a black bowtie.

Figure 7.7 Dancers at a Chippendales show in Los Angeles wearing the group's iconic uniform, 1982. Photograph by Steve Schapiro / Corbis via Getty Images.

While the uniforms superficially resemble livery (historically worn by servants in upper-class households), the pants are rigged with Velcro along the sides so they can be ripped off during performances, revealing the dancer's muscular legs and skimpy undergarment. Media Studies scholar, Clarissa Smith, has observed that the Chippendales uniform is not just about clothing, but the look of the dancers' bodies. "Although Chippendales' management claim to be offering men who appeal to the tastes of every audience member, there does seem to be a *look* which is favoured: clean cut, polished, manicured."[54] Like other male strippers, dancers are expected to manage their bodies through diet, exercise, and grooming techniques such as tanning, shaving off body hair, and applying body oil to achieve the look of a bodybuilder.[55]

In 1990, *Saturday Night Live* parodied the Chippendales in a sketch featuring the host, Patrick Swayze (whose body fit the look) competing for a job with cast member, Chris Farley (whose body did not). As one of the judges explained to Farley, "I guess in the end, we all thought that [Swayze's] body was just much, much better than yours. You see, it's just that at Chippendales, our dancers have traditionally had that lean, muscular, healthy physique, like [Swayze] whereas yours is. . . well. . . fat and flabby."[56] The sketch was memorable, but controversial. Chris Rock, a former member of the cast who worked with Farley, argued:

> I always hated [that sketch] . . . The joke of it is basically, 'We can't hire you because you're fat.' I mean, he's a fat guy, and you're going to ask him to dance with no shirt on. OK. That's enough. You're gonna get that laugh. But when he stops dancing you have to turn it in his favor. There's no turn there. There's no comic twist to it. It's just fucking mean.[57]

In the early 2000s, outside investors purchased and revived the Chippendales brand, which now includes a nightly performance at the Rio All-Suite Hotel and Casino in Las Vegas. Described on the website as a sexy entertainment activity for bachelorette parties and adult "birthday girls," audience members brought on stage during the act are allowed to have a bit of contact with the dancers, but no "groping or grinding":[58]

> Chippendales shows are very different from strip clubs. . . you don't have to make it rain[59] and there are no poles to climb. The men of Chippendales are dancers not strippers. Yes they take it all off, but it's done with style.[60]

In a study of gay strippers (male dancers who perform for male customers), writer Joseph R.G. DeMarco described a more aggressive style of interaction, where "the goal is to see as much of the stripper as one can, to have as much access to the stripper's body as possible, and to garner as much attention from the stripper as is feasible."[61] The customers compete with one another by paying large tips to the strippers, buying them drinks, making provocative comments, and by returning to the same clubs repeatedly so the strippers know them and pay them attention (in anticipation of receiving more tips). The stripper's clothing and body are essential parts of the performance, but the stripper himself is aware that his appearance is a kind of uniform, and the entire act is "just a job."[62]

In establishments where strippers work—such as bars, nightclubs, and casinos—the uniforms and bodies of other workers contribute to the sexualized atmosphere. Bouncers, for example, protect (and monitor) strippers, enforce the rules of the club, and use violence when necessary to maintain order.[63] As observed by sociologists Matthew DeMichele and Richard Tewksbury, "bouncers embody many stereotypical notions of masculinity that are attached to power and sexuality, which bolsters bouncers' abilities to enforce organizational rules."[64] Their uniforms make them easy to identify, but also establish their dominance over the environment (Figure 7.8):

> Often, [bouncers] are strategically stationed under pot lights, lit up through the haze of the nightclub to remind patrons, staff, and other bouncers of their presence. [...] Depending on the nightclub, they may be uniformed in bright yellow polo shirts with "SECURITY" emblazoned across the back or black T-shirts with white lettering. There is, of course, no single uniform of nightclub security; this varies depending on the sponsorship and whatever ambience or aesthetic the nightclub wishes to project.[65]

Typically chosen for their height, strength, and physical skills,[66] they sort "the docile and the useful revelers, from the troublesome and commercially worthless."[67] Dark clothing and dark glasses invite comparisons to the police, including sexual fantasies about them; tight clothing emphasizes the masculine shapes of their muscles. Sexiness and dominance are intertwined.

Uniforms worn by cocktail waitresses—invariably women—are also tight-fitting but emphasize the feminine curves of their hips and breasts (Figure 7.9). In her ethnographic study of cocktail waitresses who serve drinks in casinos, gender studies scholar Lorraine Bayard de Volo found a complex set of dynamics at play:

> cocktail waitresses' workplace identity and the value they attach to their job are in part based on a subjective sense of the attractiveness of their uniform. This in turn relies on its perceived sexual appeal and how much of the body it reveals.

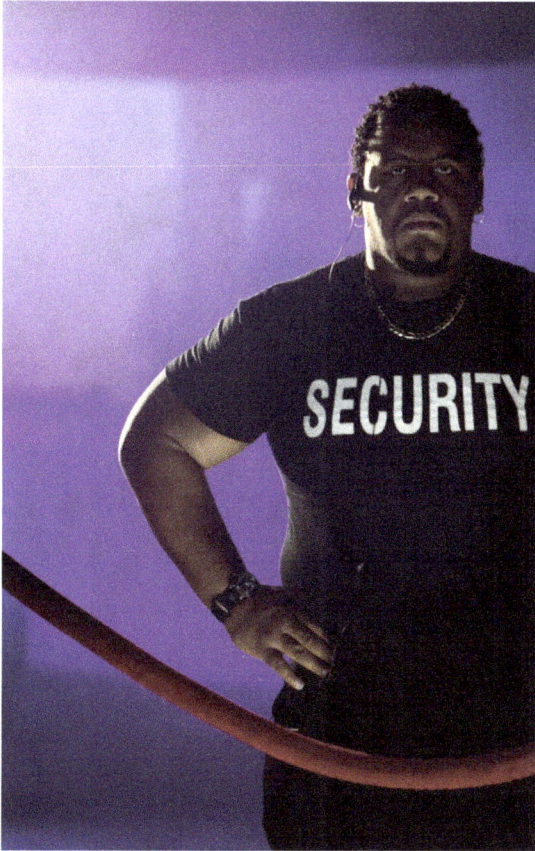

Figure 7.8 Stock photo of a bouncer wearing a dark uniform that emphasizes his muscles and security function. Photograph by PNC via Getty Images.

The difference between not enough and too much shifts in relation to cultural expectations linked with each cocktail waitress's perception of her own body (particularly in terms of weight, age, and breast size). Tip income is also thought to be linked to their attractiveness—sex sells in the sense that the prettiest girls get better tips.[68]

Over the last two decades, casinos (particularly in Las Vegas) have been sued repeatedly over their hiring practices, which often exclude applicants based on gender, age, race, and/or body size.[69] As explained by legal scholar Ann McGinley, the casinos have pointed to their uniforms and dress codes to prove that "being a woman is a bona fide occupational qualification" which legally allows them to discriminate against any male applicants:

Figure 7.9 Shenae Grimes, a cocktail waitress/model at MGM Casino in Las Vegas, 2014. Photograph by Gabe Ginsberg / Stringer via Getty Images.

Strict appearance and dress codes governing cocktail servers' uniforms are closely related to, but not determinate of, the question of whether Title VII[70] permits casinos to hire women exclusively to serve cocktails on the casino floors. Without the appearance codes and uniforms required of cocktail servers, the casino's argument that cocktail servers must be women would necessarily fail. It is not merely women, but women with a particular appearance, that casinos hire as cocktail servers. In most casinos, cocktail servers are young, shapely, smiling, and thin. The form-fitting uniforms enhance their sexuality and the illusion that the cocktail server exists merely to please the male casino customer.[71]

Casinos make most of their money from gambling, but they also use alcohol and visual access to sexualized workers to keep gamblers in their seats, particularly heterosexual men. This mixture of business strategies within a single establishment creates a gray area for the legal system.

In what may have been an effort to get ahead of potential lawsuits,[72] Rio Hotel and Casino fired all of its cocktail waitresses in 2003 and created the new job title of "bevertainer." This allowed management to hire different types of workers (both men and women) who could be trained to serve cocktails, but were primarily hired to give short musical performances. One employee— who had been a showgirl in *Jubilee!* for ten years—described how the women's uniforms were still much more sexualized: "The guys are gorgeous, but their uniform is not as risqué as ours. . . It's such a shame, they have such great bodies."[73] The uniform for women is essentially a black bikini with extra panels of lace to cover the buttocks and part of the midriff. The front panel hangs down provocatively over the dancer's crotch like an oversized necktie. Male "beverage ambassadors," however, wear conventional pants and a short-sleeve jacket without a shirt or necktie, revealing only the arms and a small bit of the upper chest.[74]

Breastaurant Workers, 1980–2020

In 1983—the same year that R Donuts opened in Fort Lauderdale, Florida—six men on the Gulf Coast side of the state opened "Hooters," a sexually charged bar and restaurant named after a slang word for women's breasts. A brief history on the company's website describes the chain as "delightfully tacky, yet unrefined," designed to be a place where the owners (and customers like them) "couldn't get kicked out" for their deviant interests and behavior:[75]

> Sometimes you hit on a big idea by accident—just by putting the stuff you love all in one place. Craveable food, cold beer, and all the sports you could possibly watch on wall-to-wall big screen TVs. And let's not forget the Hooters Girls. It all seems so simple, we can't believe nobody else ever thought of it.[76]

In reality, the concept of a "sports bar" had existed for decades.[77] The idea of hiring scantily clad waitresses to serve food and beverages was also not new. What was new, perhaps, was the combination of the two and the crassness of the name. The success of Hooters inspired several competing corporations including Show-Me's (founded in 1990 in St. Charles, Missouri), Bone Daddies (2000, Dallas), Tilted Kilt (2003, Las Vegas), Redneck Heaven (2008, Lewisville, Texas), and Ojos Locos (Spanish for "crazy eyes," 2010, Dallas). In 2011, Bikinis Bar and

Grill (founded in 2006 in Austin, Texas) legally trademarked the term "breastaurant" to describe this style of business.[78]

In 2022, Hooters had 302 locations in the US (Figure 7.10) concentrated in the Southeast, mid-Atlantic, and lower Midwest.[79] During the first three decades, the uniforms for waitresses and female bartenders barely changed: a white or black tank top with the company's logo and location, orange "runner shorts," "suntan" pantyhose, white athletic socks, and white sneakers. The tight fit of the outfit was designed to reveal the wearer's cleavage and thighs[80] and was manufactured in sizes "extra-extra small, extra-small, and small."[81] In an unusual move—perhaps because third-party uniform manufacturers did not (at the time) have the styles that Hooters was looking for—the company developed its own proprietary uniforms.[82]

In 2021, the company attempted to change the uniform to an equally tight short-sleeved shirt with a bowtie, high heels or platform shoes (no socks), and more revealing shorts,[83] a look that resembled Playboy bunnies instead of the "all-American cheerleader."[84] When several TikTok videos of Hooters Girls complaining about the "underwear" went viral, the company announced that workers could choose to wear either the old uniform or the new one.[85]

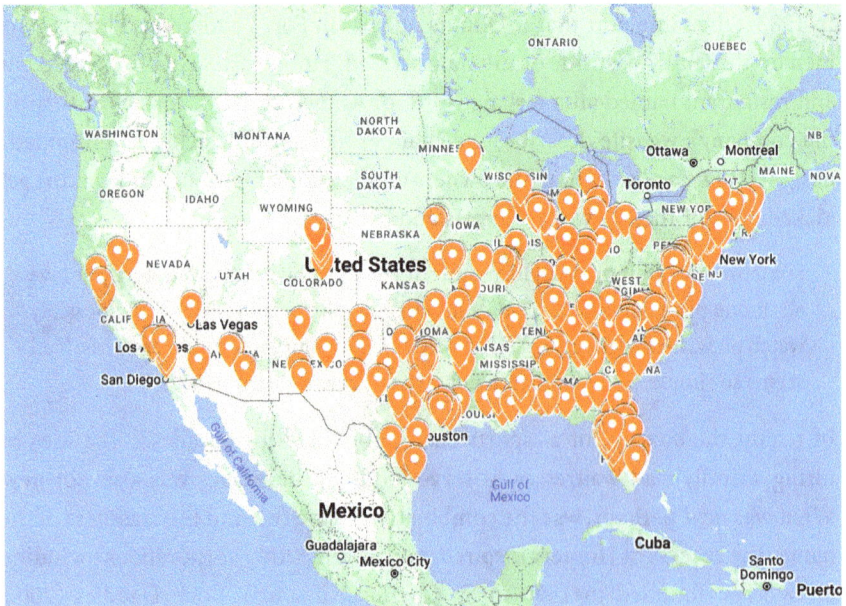

Figure 7.10 Hooters restaurants in the United States in May 2022. Map generated by author using location listings from hooters.com.

As the breastaurant trend accelerated, Terra Watson—who had worked as a cheerleader for the Dallas Cowboys before she started a business designing uniforms for professional dancers and cheerleaders[86]—was asked to develop the uniforms for Twin Peaks, a breastaurant that was opening in the Dallas suburb of Lewisville. As she described in a later interview,

> The CEO of what would become Twin Peaks told me, 'Hey, I'm thinking of this sexy uniform for this restaurant.' I almost didn't take the call because it sounded kind of peculiar. But the minute he told me about the idea of Twin Peaks, the very first idea I came up with was that lumberjack—well, lumbergirl—outfit. It went from there.[87]

Sensing opportunity, Watson launched a new division of her company, Terra's Dancewear and Dallaswear LLC and trademarked it as Waitressville.[88] In 2013, she appeared on CNBC's show *Crowd Rules* to pitch her new business,[89] focusing exclusively on women's uniforms for adult entertainment venues: sports bars, casinos, and breastaurants.

One of Waitressville's most innovative designs is the "Dream Corset." Like historical corsets, it fits tightly at the waist and lifts the breasts to emphasize the wearer's cleavage. However, it also closes with a zipper in the front, has a completely flexible construction, and is meant to be worn as a single layer, not as an undergarment. In 2015, Watson redesigned the uniforms for waitresses who work at the Tilted Kilt, a Scottish-themed breastaurant chain where the female waitresses wear plaid bikini tops and kilt-like skirts.[90]

Heart Attack Grill—which was founded in Arizona in 2005, but now has a single location in downtown Las Vegas—pushes the breastaurant concept to an extreme:

> Customers are referred to as "patients," orders as "prescriptions," and the waitresses as "nurses." All those who weigh over 350 pounds are invited to unlimited free food provided they weigh themselves on an electronic cattle scale affront a cheering restaurant crowd.
>
> "Patients" who are unable to finish their meals are subjected to brutal spankings publicly delivered by one of the Heart Attack Grill's attractive nursing staff. These spankings have been the subject of significant publicity. Thought of as being an erotic gimmick, Dr Jon refers to them as "Pain Management Therapy" and insists they are a very necessary part of the healing process only from which true growth can emerge.[91]

The waitresses wear tight-fitting mini dresses (mostly white, with red accents) and nurses' caps, modeled after the uniforms worn by actual nurses in the mid-twentieth century.[92] The Arizona Board of Nursing and the Center for Nursing Advocacy criticized the restaurant for the "naughty nurse uniforms, saying they degraded the profession."[93] While the Heart Attack Grill has taken aggressive legal action against competitors, such as the Flatline Grilll (Florida), Heart Stoppers Grill (Florida), and the Heart Attack Shack (Tennessee),[94] it clearly draws on decades of "sexy nurse" imagery from peep shows, adult magazines, and pornographic films.

Conclusion

Many of the uniforms in this chapter are unique to American culture and have not translated well to other parts of the world. Hooters, for example, is the only corporate breastaurant chain that has made any significant effort to expand outside of the US.[95] On its website, the company lists 75 locations in 23 countries, but only 56 are active and nearly half of those are in Mexico.[96] When the first Hooters opened in the UK (in the city of Nottingham) in 1998, the company was forced to scale back its plans for expansion due to widespread protests; two other locations in Cardiff and Bristol shut down after less than two years.[97] During the protests, a journalist for the *Daily Mail* wrote a long article about the chain for the newspaper's Sunday edition:

> I cannot believe that I am in Nottingham or that it is the year 2010. I remember, as a student in the Seventies, interviewing one of the last Playboy bunnies at a club on Park Lange. I asked the young woman in fishnet tights how it felt to be part of a dying breed. Peeling off her false eyelashes, she said the world had moved on—women were no longer viewed as objects. Fast forward 30 years and, again, I'm talking to a young woman in tights with false eyelashes.[98]

In early 2022, the company successfully sought approval to open a new location in Liverpool, despite objections from protestors.[99] In opposition, a local politician launched a petition on change.org titled, "Say No to Hooters Liverpool":

> Hooters is an archaic and chauvinistic brand and this [type] of venue is no longer reflective of today's society.
>
> Hooters employs women to promote its business activities in an exploitive manner. It demeans and degrades women and undermines female equality.
>
> We believe it will attract interest from a narrow unwanted demographic and will cause increased anti-social behavior.[100] [Figuure 7.11]

Figure 7.11 Hooters Girls posing at a fishing tournament in Miami Beach, 2012. Photograph by Jeff Greenberg for Universal Images Group via Getty Images.

On Twitter, the city's mayor encouraged residents to sign the petition, arguing: "This type of business undermines all the great work which our local organisations are doing to promote the eradication of violence against women and girls."[101]

In South America, locations in Paraguay, Argentina, and Venezuela have closed, with only four restaurants remaining in Columbia (Cali, Medellin) and Brazil (Sao Paolo). A chapter in *Global Beauty, Local Bodies*, notes that while Hooters in the US is affordable, casual, and "low brow," Hooters in Columbia is much more formal, a place where upper-class Columbians go to signal their elite status.[102] While the uniform is the same, the bodies are not: instead of being "blonde, busty, and lean," the typical Hooters Girl in Columbia has dark hair, dark eyes, and a more "voluptuous" bottom, enhanced by the use of foam padding.[103]

In 2015, Hooters proposed opening a restaurant in the Riverside neighborhood of Phnom Penh, Cambodia, an area full of bars that cater to Western tourists and expatriates.[104] In a blog post analyzing the failure of Hooters in southeast Asia, a British travel writer noted,

> The concept of Hooters is fairly simple, you get served decent food by fairly scantily clad women. Of course, you pay a premium to do so. Now whilst this tends to work well in places like Seattle or Vancouver, the concept of paying a

premium to be served by hot women made slightly less sense in Bangkok, one of the sex capitals of the world.

[The aim of the Cambodian location] appeared to be that it would appeal to middle-class Cambodians and families. This of course raises a lot of questions, such as what kind of family would pick Hooters for little Johnny's 7th birthday bash. Also, if the restaurant had nothing to do with sex, then why put it next to the sex capital of the capital?[105]

Prostitution is illegal in Cambodia, but common,[106] so a breastaurant—a place where food and drinks are literally consumed, but bodies are only visually consumed—offers little attraction.

Scholarship regarding "sexually objectifying portrayals of women" has tended to focus on films, television, music videos, magazines, and (more recently) social media.[107] A chapter in the *APA Handbook of the Psychology of Women* describes an extensive body of research showing that "experiences in objectifying environments or mere exposure to the sexually objectifying culture (media, marketing) provides a kind of instruction manual, cultivating self-objectification in girls and young women, who desire to embody idealized, appearance-focused femininity."[108] Taking a close look at occupational uniforms suggests that this phenomenon is in fact quite old, and that tens of thousands of women—and even some men—experience sexual objectification every year directly through employer-mandated uniforms and dress codes.

Envisioning the Future

In May 2018, a senior Vice President for Walmart, Karisa Sprague, announced online that the company was going to begin implementing a new set of "dress guidelines" in all 4,700 stores in the US. While still requiring a name badge and a standardized, dark blue vest with the corporate logo and text ("Proud Walmart Associate"), the company would give its workers more flexibility to make choices about their clothing and overall appearance:

> We've been listening to your feedback and are really excited to switch from the old, long text-based policy fully of "Don'ts" to a lookbook loaded with great color photos showing how you can make your personal style work *at work*. [Original emphasis]
>
> This is a big deal—and I'm speaking from experience. I started in the stores as an hourly intern and worked 16 years in the field. Growing up in stores, I always tried to make the dress code mine, like adding a necklace to the required blue shirt and khakis to try and dress them up a bit. But, no matter what you do, wearing the same clothes day after day gets boring.[1]

Sprague argued that the change would allow store managers to focus on performance instead of "playing fashion police" and improve conditions for all workers. "Safety and professionalism are still at the core, but relaxing the rules on style and letting people bring their whole selves to work just makes good sense for the business, for our people—and for fashion."[2] Uniforms have some entanglements with the aesthetics and production methods of fashion, but as this statement describes they are not quite the same as fashion. They require instruction (written, visual, and/or oral) to be worn effectively. They demand compliance and obedience. They are monotonous to wear. And above all, they limit individual choices about the body and clothing—one of the most intimate ways that human beings communicate with one another.

Policing Compliance

Choosing a uniform and writing a dress code is just one step in the process of creating a work uniform. As soon as the worker puts it on, the process shifts to analysis and enforcement. Is the worker wearing it correctly? Does it fit? Does it send the right message? How can it be improved or refined? New hires might make mistakes that can be corrected by coworkers and/or managers (a best-case scenario for policing), but what if correction is not possible? If the worker needs a size 3X, but the largest size available is 2X, what can be done? The worker might quit or be bullied into quitting, be forced to squeeze into the largest size available, be allowed to wear something else, or be forced to work in a position that is not visible to the public[3] (for example, stocking shelves at night). Some workers actively resist uniforms and dress codes for a variety of reasons—they resent being told what to wear, the style doesn't make them look or feel good, they can't afford to buy the required clothing, it goes against their religious beliefs, etc.

Employers can refuse to make exceptions to dress codes and uniforms if doing so would compromise health and safety.[4] However, federal law prohibits discrimination "based on race, color, religion, sex (including pregnancy, sexual orientation, or gender identity), national origin, age (40 or older), disability and genetic information (including family medical history)."[5] The list of these "protected categories" has been expanded several times and applies in all 50 states. City and state governments cannot disregard them but can choose to add more. For example, the state of Indiana (where I live) forbids employers from discriminating based on "off-duty tobacco use" and having a "sealed or expunged arrest or conviction record."[6] In 1945, the state of New York was the first in the US to pass a human rights law, originally known as the "Law Against Discrimination."[7] The most recent version, updated in 2019, includes several protected classes that go beyond federal law: "domestic violence victim status," "marital status," "military status," and "prior arrest or conviction record." It also prohibits discrimination and harassment based on "retaliation for opposing unlawful discriminatory practices."[8]

The effects of these laws can be better understood within the context of specific cases. In early 2023, for example, a journalist for *Business Insider* wrote about a controversial dress code policy at Sheetz, a chain of convenience stores and gas stations based in Pennsylvania:

> Like all retail workers, employees at Sheetz are expected to show up on time and provide pleasant customer service. But a more unusual policy in the company's employee handbook says that 'applicants with obvious missing, broken, or badly

discolored teeth (unrelated to a disability) are not qualified for employment with Sheetz.' Insider obtained a written version of the policy and confirmed it with three former employees who had or have access to it.[9]

Within days, other news outlets echoed the story and provided more information. A worker in Ohio claimed that she had been fired from Sheetz because she was unable to obtain temporary dentures from her insurance company; her front teeth had been knocked out by her abusive ex-husband.[10] Others complained that the policy was classist, discriminating against low-income workers who could not afford good dental care.[11] Less than two weeks after *Business Insider* published the article, Sheetz issued a press release:

> Our culture at Sheetz has always been centered on respect and putting our employees, customers and communities first. As a family-owned and operated company, nothing is more important than creating an environment that is inclusive and supportive of all of our employees. Recently through employee feedback, we have learned that the smile policy is not aligned with these values from their perspective. We agree. Effective immediately, this policy is discontinued. We are committed to ensuring our policies moving forward are equitable and celebrate the diverse experiences, individual identities and unique perspectives of our employees."[12]

The state of Pennsylvania prohibits discrimination based on disability but is silent about social class and victims of domestic violence.[13] Workers who file discrimination lawsuits when they are not part of a recognized protected class generally lose in court.[14]

That was exactly what happened in 1992 to a man who had been working as a firefighter for the city of Montgomery, Alabama. He filed a lawsuit after his supervisor punished him for noncompliance with the fire department's dress code:

> Following a roll-call inspection on April 6, 1990, Defendant Lieutenant M.E. Pitts informed Plaintiff that Plaintiff needed to either put on a t-shirt or shave the chest hair showing from under his uniform shirt. Plaintiff replied that the City of Montgomery did not issue t-shirts to fire fighters [as part of the uniform] and that chest hair was not facial hair.[15]

Although the dress code did not specifically mention chest hair (only that employees should be "cleanly shaved") the court dismissed the lawsuit by arguing that employers need not anticipate every possible variation in appearance but could set and enforce new policies ad hoc. The court did not make a distinction between uniforms and dress codes; it did not even decide who should pay for the

T-shirts in cases where employees have excessive chest hair. Men and "people with excessive body hair" are not protected classes of workers.

Still, being part of a protected class is no guarantee of success for a worker who files a lawsuit. In 2004, a federal court ruled against a worker who claimed that her employer (Costco, a corporate retailer of wholesale merchandise) had violated her religious beliefs as a member of the Church of Body Modification (CBM). When the company asked her to remove or cover her facial piercings to conform with a new dress code she refused, arguing that her faith required her to display her piercings at all times. She also refused to accept a less visible position where she would not interact directly with the public:

> In granting summary judgment on the Title VII claim,[16] the court stressed that 'the search for a reasonable accommodation goes both ways. Although the employer is required under Title VII to accommodate an employee's religious beliefs, the employee has a duty to cooperate with the employer's good faith efforts to accommodate.' The court also noted that Title VII does not require Costco to grant [the defendant's] preferred accommodation, but merely a reasonable one. While Costco's suggested accommodation balanced [the defendant's] beliefs with its interest in presenting a professional appearance, [the defendant] 'offered no accommodation whatsoever.'[17]

The court refused to judge the legitimacy of the Church or the worker's religious beliefs, simply arguing that both sides (employer and worker) needed to compromise.

Activism for Change

So, why are corporations like Walmart and Sheetz changing their dress codes even when they are not doing anything illegal or would likely prevail in court? Employers can lose workers and damage their brands when they refuse to make accommodations, while doing the right thing has the potential to attract workers, improve working conditions, improve the reputation of the brand, and increase company profits. In 2018, for example, Nike decided to publicly support Colin Kaepernick, who had been blackballed from the NFL for kneeling during the national anthem to protest racially motivated police brutality.[18] While some people protested Nike's move and burned Nike shoes, sales rose 31 percent compared to the year before.[19] Scholars of business have questioned the company's motivations:

Was Nike signaling the virtue of its brand by aligning itself with an important societal issue, or was it merely, and perhaps cynically, exploiting a newsworthy event? Should other brands emulate Nike's *virtue signaling* strategy [emphasis in the original], and are there strategic and financial benefits to be gained from these approaches? Or are there risks to brand health and the long-term survival of brands that are simply not worth taking?[20]

Cynically, all media coverage is free advertising, regardless of the tone. Edgy fashion brands and aspiring couture designers regularly engage in controversy to generate media coverage and increase public awareness.[21] Sheetz quickly turned negative media attention into an opportunity for virtue signaling. Without the initial controversy, the adoption of a more inclusive dress code policy would not have been front-page news.

Dove (a major manufacturer of grooming and hygiene products owned by Unilever) has pursued an even more unusual and proactive strategy for increasing brand awareness. In 2019, the company formed a coalition with three non-profit activist organizations (Color of Change, the Western Center on Law & Poverty, and National Urban League) with the goal of advancing "anti-hair discrimination legislation" in the US. As described on a page within the company's website dedicated to environmental and social responsibility projects:

> All women experience pressure to conform to certain beauty standards. But, for black women and girls in the US, many aspects of their daily lives are impacted by unfair judgment based on hair texture and discrimination against protective hairstyles include braids, locs[22] and twists.
>
> At the moment it is legal to discriminate against a person in the workplace or in schools because of their natural or protective hairstyles. This is the case in all states except for California, New York, New Jersey, Virginia, Colorado, Washington, and Maryland.[23]

Black activists had been pushing for reform for decades[24] to give black men and women more freedom for self- and cultural expression through their hairstyles.[25] Dove's support gave them funding and political traction. It also raised public awareness of the Dove brand while putting pressure on corporations to make their dress codes more inclusive, creating new opportunities to sell haircare products for diverse hair types. In July 2019, California—which has more than 39 million people (nearly 12% of the total US population)—became the first state in the US to sign the CROWN Act (Create a Respectful and Open Workplace for Natural Hair) into law.[26]

Similarly, workers are pushing back on employers' expectations for gender expression with help from activist organizations like Out & Equal, Pride at Work, and the Human Rights Campaign Foundation, which advocates that,

> If an employer has a dress code, it should modify it to avoid gender stereotypes and enforce it consistently. Requiring men to wear pant suits and women to wear skirts or dresses, is based on gender stereotypes. Alternatively, codes that require attire professionally appropriate to the office or unit in which an employee works and that apply to all employees in that office or unit are gender-neutral. Examples of gender-neutral dress codes include:
>
> – Employees may wear earrings no more than two inches in length or diameter.
> – Employees must wear a suit to meetings with clients.
> – Employees with hair below the chin must wear their hair tied back while working with or on the floor with machinery.[27]

One sector making big changes around gender expression is the airline industry.[28] In March 2022, Alaska Airlines became the first airline in the world to adopt gender-neutral uniforms (Figure 8.1).[29] Instead of dictating that men should wear pants and women should wear skirts (or that everyone should wear the same thing, like healthcare professionals), the airline began offering a menu of options for workers to choose from. It also began to allow any individual, regardless of gender, to wear "fingernail polish, makeup, two earrings per ear, and a single stud nose piercing."[30] An article in the *Wall Street Journal* argued that such changes are not only good for individuals, but necessary for the airlines: "Relaxing dress codes broadens the pool of candidates, and can make work more engaging for current employees in an industry struggling to hang on to workers."[31]

In September 2022, Virgin Atlantic (based in the UK) decided to follow the lead set by Alaska Airlines; regardless of gender, all members of flight crews would be allowed to mix the existing elements of the company's iconic red and burgundy uniforms, which had been designed by Vivienne Westwood. American actress Michelle Visage—better known as one of the judges on *RuPaul's Drag Race*—modeled the uniform for a press release and commented,

> As the mother of a non-binary child, and as an ally to the LGBTQ+ community, these efforts by Virgin Atlantic to further inclusivity for its people are extremely important and personal to me. People feel empowered when they are wearing what best represents them, and this gender identity policy allows people to embrace who they are and bring their full selves to work.[32]

Figure 8.1 Image from a press release by Alaska Airlines about the company's new uniforms and gender-inclusive dress code, March 2022. Photograph by Ingrid Barrentine, Courtesy of Alaska Airlines.

Despite facing a wave of anti-LGBTQ+ legislation in the US,[33] the major airlines cannot afford to limit their marketing and branding (including their uniforms) to the American market.

Expanding Health and Safety

When the COVID-19 pandemic began in 2020, front-line businesses that continued to operate such as grocery stores, childcare centers, and transportation services struggled to make decisions on how to protect workers, how to procure sufficient quantities of masks and gloves, how to handle resistance (and sometimes violence) from customers, and how to integrate PPE into their uniforms.[34] The federal government had stockpiled 30 million N95 masks;[35] however as the virus spread, it quickly became apparent that hundreds of millions more would be needed just to supply hospitals, let alone the general population.[36] The federal agency charged with handling disease outbreaks, the Centers for Disease Control and Prevention (CDC), provided guidance about how healthcare workers should ideally use N95 masks:

> N95 respirators are the PPE most often used to control exposures to infectious pathogens transmitted via the airborne route, though their effectiveness is highly dependent upon proper fit and use. N95 respirators are intended to be used once and then properly disposed of and replaced with a new N95 respirator.[37]

Recognizing that there would be severe shortages caused by global demand and manufacturing disruptions in China,[38] the CDC issued special "crisis capacity" guidelines for reusing the same mask up to five times and for storing used (but still functional) masks in paper bags.[39]

For many US employers outside of the healthcare industry, the pandemic was the first time they had been asked to consider—as part of their official dress code—whether to require, allow, or forbid the use of masks during work and if so, what type(s). The Occupational Health and Safety Administration (OSHA) took months to issue official guidance. In September 2020, an article in the *Journal of the American Medical Association* pointed to layers of policy failure:

> OSHA cannot make workplaces safe: that is the responsibility of employers. By law, every worker has the right to a safe workplace, and OSHA's mission is to protect this right by ensuring that employers eliminate hazards that could injure workers or increase their risk of illness. [...] Every workplace needs a clear COVID-19 prevention plan that includes the following: scheduling and workspace design to [avoid] crowding and allow physical distancing; PPE such as masks and respirators when needed; enhanced ventilation; hand sanitation and adequate facilities for washing; and disinfection of potentially contaminated surfaces. Screening should be conducted to identify workers with symptoms consistent with COVID-19 or who have had close contact with others who are infected. Screening programs will be more effective if workers who are kept out of workplaces because of COVID concerns have access to adequate paid sick leave or unemployment compensation.[40]

In the beginning, high-quality disposable masks such as surgical masks and N95s were simply unavailable to most employers outside of the healthcare industry.[41] Bombarded by a flurry of conflicting information about cloth masks and how they could or should be designed,[42] it took months for uniform manufacturers to offer them. While some employers decided to let workers make their own decisions about masks (and did not supply them), others were keen to customize them to match the rest of the uniform. For instance, Figure 8.2 shows

Figure 8.2 Grocery store manager in Pennsylvania wearing a uniform with a branded jacket, cap, and face mask, March 2021. Photograph by Ben Hasty / MediaNews Group / Reading Eagle via Getty Images.

a manager at a grocery store in Pennsylvania one year after the start of the pandemic, wearing a jacket, cap, and cloth mask in the same color scheme with variations of the company's logo.

Once items of dress are added to uniforms—such as the caps once worn by nurses and the hats worn by NPS park rangers—they tend to become long-term fixtures, regardless of whether they are functional and/or comfortable to wear. Now that Americans are familiar with wearing masks and COVID-19 has become impossible to contain, it is likely that masks will persist for some time in the uniforms of essential workers, not just in healthcare but in transportation, food service, retail, banking, and other industries where in-person contact is unavoidable. In a July 2022 press release that predicted a "bright future" for uniforms in the United States, the Network Association of Uniform Manufacturers & Distributors (NAUMD) included health and safety in the list of top reasons that employers require uniforms:

> Uniforms, whether for public safety, medical, industrial or corporate, strengthen the structures of organizations today. Workplace uniforms are associated with enhancing brand awareness, but they of course go beyond this. The uniforms

establish and support a business image, *prevent cross-contamination between workers and their environment*, build a team spirit, and improve client relationships.[43] (Emphasis added)

Based on information from the US Bureau of Labor Statistics, the press release also highlighted four industries that are expected to hire increasing numbers of workers within the next decade: law enforcement (7% growth), transportation (9%), food service (17%), and healthcare (16%).[44] Notably, uniforms are nearly universal within these industries.

OSHA now offers official guidelines on protecting workers from infectious diseases, including both general and industry-specific guidelines for COVID-19:

> Workers should wear a face covering that covers the nose and mouth to contain the wearer's respiratory droplets and to help protect others and potentially themselves. Face coverings should be made of at least two layers of a tightly woven breathable fabric, such as cotton, and should not have exhalation valves or vents. They should fit snugly over the nose, mouth, and chin with no large gaps on the outside of the face. Employers should provide face coverings to workers who request them at no cost (and make replacements available to workers when they request them). [...] When an employer determines that PPE is necessary to protect unvaccinated and otherwise at-risk workers from exposure to COVID-19, the employer must provide PPE in accordance with **relevant mandatory OSHA standards**.[45] (Original emphasis)

These policies apply to all workers in the US, not just to healthcare workers. They have not changed since August 2021, suggesting that this is now a long-term standard. While some workers and business owners will undoubtedly refuse to comply, many others will not only comply but go above and beyond, whether to retain workers, lower costs for insurance and healthcare, or to avoid the possibility of any lawsuits or punishments.[46]

Opportunities for Further Research

With rare exceptions, uniforms change slowly—certainly, more slowly than mainstream fashion. The benefits of a slow pace for both workers and employers can include predictability, safety protections that are built into the system (and do not need constant reconsideration), and a positive sense of tradition. For example, a fact sheet about the "white coat ceremony" featured on the website of the Association of American Medical Colleges (AAMC) features quotes from medical students about the symbolism of the doctor's uniform. One emphasizes how as a child the student looked up to doctors with a sense of awe:

> Growing up, doctors often felt superhuman to me. They must be, right? Not only do they dedicate themselves to lifelong learning and service, but they often serve as the voice of reason and as a comforting presence in difficult situations. But I've come to learn that the white coat is not a superhero cape. Instead, it is a symbol of something much greater; our commitment to take the best care of each other and of our patients.[47]

On the other hand, uniforms can also have very negative associations: they can stifle creativity, reduce individuality (sometimes to the point of dehumanization), and represent workers' lack of power to make their own decisions, often compounded by classism, racism, sexism, ageism, and other forms of discrimination. In *Hand to Mouth: Living in Bootstrap America*, worker-turned-journalist, Linda Tirado, described how working in a long series of minimum-wage jobs (mostly in food service) impacted her thinking about employers and work uniforms:

> I wouldn't even mind the degradations of my work life so much if the privileged and powerful were honest about it. [...] Instead, we're told to work harder and be grateful we have jobs, food, and a roof over our heads. And for fuck's sake, we are. But in exchange for all that work we're doing, and all our miserable work conditions, we're not allowed to demand anything in return. No sense of accomplishment, or respect from above, or job security. We are expected not to feel entitled to these things. [...]
>
> The result of all this? I just give up *caring* about work. I lose the energy, the bounce, the willingness. I'll perform as directed, but no more than that. *I've rarely had a boss who gave me any indication that he valued me more highly than my uniform*—we were that interchangeable—so I don't go out of my way for my bosses either. The problem I have isn't just being undervalued—it's that it feels as though people go out of their way to make sure you know how useless you are.[48] (Emphasis added)

What would occupational uniforms look like if workers had more input? Would they even exist at all? In most professions where workers have a great deal of autonomy, uniforms are not part of the job. Professors, wedding planners, social workers, and tattoo artists are all highly visible service workers, but they do not wear uniforms (at least not in the US). Prisoners—people with the least amount of autonomy—always wear uniforms. There is a lot of pride at stake.

This book has provided a foundation to understand how work uniforms are manufactured, sold, worn, and enforced in the US; the next major step I see is to concentrate on the experiences of workers—both those who wear uniforms and those who do not. For example, one comparison might be between barbers and tattoo artists. Both are licensed. Both are creative and attuned to aesthetics, yet barbers typically wear uniforms and tattoo artists do not. Are there workers who prefer to wear uniforms? If so, why? In a very novel article about self-identified women who appear to others as masculine, sociologist Raine Dozier found that women in these circumstances sometimes prefer to work in blue collar jobs that require masculine uniforms—when there is no pressure to look feminine it limits prying questions about their gender and sexuality, sometimes to the point that they "pass" as men (with better pay and increased opportunities).[49]

Figure 8.3 Uniform-inspired fashion design by Craig Green for Spring/Summer 2023, shown on the runway at Paris Men's Fashion Week in June 2022. Photograph by Victor VIRGILE / Gamma-Rapho via Getty Images.

Another area for further research is the typically anonymous individuals who design work uniforms. I have touched on a few examples such as Theresa Dell Angelica, Timo Weiland, and Stan Herman, but for the most part uniform designers are not household names. It would be interesting to investigate why individual fashion designers choose to engage with or avoid the uniform industry and to uncover more uniform designers who have previously been unknown to the public. I have barely delved into the influences of uniforms on fashion, but examples include military-inspired clothing,[50] denim jeans,[51] bib overalls,[52] workwear brands,[53] and the designs of UK-based designer Craig Green who is frequently inspired by work uniforms (see Figure 8.3).

There are certainly more professions with uniforms that I did not get a chance to explore in this book, such as toll booth operators, bus drivers, restaurant chefs, ski instructors, Catholic priests, and soda jerks. Police uniforms are so complicated that they could (and I believe should) be the focus of an entire book. It would be interesting to consider whether people who work for professional sports teams (coaching staff, clerical staff, etc.) feel like "part of the team" when elements of the players' uniforms are incorporated into their work uniforms. Although I did not include any examples of religious employers in this book, I suspect that entanglements between religious dress and work uniforms create unique tensions and satisfactions.

This book is really just the tip of the iceberg on exploring work uniforms in the United States. How do laws, traditions, and attitudes towards uniforms compare to the experiences of workers in other countries? Are Americans too individualistic to fully embrace uniforms?[54] Or conversely, have Americans been so crushed by corporations and mass manufacturing that work uniforms now seem inescapable and mundane? There are many questions to answer. I hope that this book inspires a great deal of new research.

Notes

Chapter 1

1   Kim Parker, Juliana Menasce Horowitz, and Rachel Minkin, "How the Coronavirus Outbreak Has—and Hasn't—Changed the Way Americans Work," Pew Research Center, December 9, 2020, at: https://www.pewresearch.org/social-trends/2020/12/09/how-the-coronavirus-outbreak-has-and-hasnt-changed-the-way-americans-work/.

2   Derek Thompson, "Workism is Making Americans Miserable," *The Atlantic*, February 24, 2019, at: https://www.theatlantic.com/ideas/archive/2019/02/religion-workism-making-americans-miserable/583441/.

3   Aaron Barlow, *The Cult of Individualism: A History of an Enduring American Myth* (Santa Barbara, California: ABC-CLIO, 2013). Alex Zakaras, *The Roots of American Individualism: Political Myth in the Age of Jackson* (Princeton, New Jersey: Princeton University Press, 2022).

4   Adrie S. Kusserow, *American Individualisms: Child Rearing and Social Class in Three Neighborhoods* (New York: Palgrave Macmillan, 2004).

5   Grant McCracken, *Culture & Consumption: New Approaches to the Symbolic Character of Consumer Goods and Activities* (Bloomington, Indiana: Indiana University Press, 1988).

6   Jennifer Kite-Powell, "Here's the Real Story of Issey Miyake and Steve Jobs' Iconic Turtleneck," Forbes, August 10, 2022, at: https://www.forbes.com/sites/jenniferhicks/2022/08/10/heres-the-real-story-of-issey-miyake-and-steve-jobs-iconic-turtleneck/?sh=ae72480303f5.

7   Harriette Richards and Fabio Mattioli, "Fashioning Founders: Dress and Gender in the Entrepreneurial Ecosystem," *Gender, Work & Organization* 28, no. 4 (2021): 1367.

8   Kite-Powell, "Here's the Real Story".

9   Lennart Lennerlöf, "Learned Helplessness at Work," in *The Psychosocial Work Environment: Work Organization, Democratization and Health*, edited by Jeffrey V. Johnson, Bertil Gardell, and Gunn Johannson (New York: Routledge, 2020), 73–88.

10 Linda Tirado, *Hand to Mouth: Living in Bootstrap America* (New York: Berkley Books, 2015).

11 Barbara Ehrenreich, *Nickel and Dimed: On (Not) Getting by in America* (New York: Picador USA, 2011).

12 Nathan Joseph, *Uniforms and Nonuniforms: Communication through Clothing* (Westport, Connecticut: Greenwood Press, 1986), 114–16.

13 Paul Fussell, *Uniforms* (New York: Houghton Mifflin, 2002), 3–4.

14 Jennifer Craik, *Uniforms Exposed: From Conformity to Transgression* (Oxford: Berg Publishers, 2005).

15 Ibid., 115.

16 Chantal Fernandez, "How Stan Herman, Father of Fashion Week, Changed the US Fashion Industry," *Fashionista*, June 29, 2015, at: https://fashionista.com/2015/06/stan-herman-father-of-fashion-week.

17 Tom Post, "Mr. Uniform," *Forbes*, November 16, 1998, 84.

18 San Francisco Airport Commission, "Fashion in Flight: A History of Airline Uniform Design," SFO Museum, 2016, at: https://www.sfomuseum.org/exhibitions/fashion-flight-history-airline-uniform-design.

19 Fashion is not confined to clothing or the fashion industry. For example, fashion changes also occur in packaging, architecture, and paradigms of scientific knowledge. See Thomas S. Kuhn, *The Structure of Scientific Revolutions* (Chicago, Illinois: University of Chicago Press, 1962).

20 Prudence Black, "A Cast of Thousands: Martin Grant and the New Qantas Uniform," in *Uniform: Clothing and Discipline in the Modern World*, edited by Jane Tynan and Jane Godson (London: Bloomsbury Visual Arts, 2019), 179–98.

21 James Laver, *British Military Uniforms* (London: Penguin Books, 1948); Joep van Hoof, *Military Uniforms in the Netherlands, 1752–1800* (Vienna: Militaria, 2011); and William K. Emerson, *Encyclopedia of United States Army Insignia and Uniforms* (Norman, Oklahoma: University of Oklahoma Press, 1996).

22 Christina Bates, *A Cultural History of the Nurse's Uniform* (Gatineau: Canadian Museum of Civilization, 2012).

23 Brian J. McVeigh, *Wearing Ideology: State, Schooling and Self-Presentation in Japan* (Oxford: Berg Publishers, 2000); David L. Brunsma, *The School Uniform Movement and What It Tells Us About American Education* (Lanham, Maryland: Rowman & Littlefield, 2004); and Todd A. DeMitchell, *The Challenges of Mandating School Uniforms in the Public Schools: Free Speech, Research, and Policy* (Lanham, Maryland: Rowman & Littlefield, 2015.)

24 Eric Michael Pickhartz, *Look Good, Play Good: The World of American Sports Uniforms* (Austin Texas: University of Texas Press, 2011); Linda K. Fuller (ed.), *Sportswomen's Apparel Around the World: Uniformly Discussed* (New York: Palgrave Macmillan, 2020).

25 Linda B. Arthur, *Religion, Dress and the Body* (Oxford: Berg Publishers, 1999); Sally Dwyer-McNulty, *Common Threads: A Cultural History of Clothing in American Catholicism* (Chapel Hill, North Carolina: University of North Carolina Press, 2014).

26 Toni Pfanner, "Military Uniforms and the Law of War," *International Review of the Red Cross* 86, no. 853 (2004): 94.

27 Fabien Beaumont et al., "Aerodynamic Study of Time-Trial Helmets in Cycling Racing Using CFD Analysis," *Journal of Biomechanics* 67, no. 23 (2018): 1–8.

28 Brad Partridge, "Fairness and Performance-Enhancing Swimsuits at the 2009 Swimming World Championships: The 'Asterisk' Championships," *Sports, Ethics and Philosophy* 5, no. 1 (2011): 63–74.

29 John Paul and Michael L. Birzer, "Images of Power: An Analysis of the Militarization of Police Uniforms and Messages of Service," *Free Inquiry in Creative Sociology* 32, no. 2 (2004): 121–8.

30 Target Corporation, "Let's Hear It For the Stores! Target Store Team Members Can Now Rock Denim All Week Long," target.com, February 14, 2019, at: https://corporate.target.com/article/2019/02/employee-dress-code-policy.

31 Fussell, *Uniforms*, 4–5.

32 Joseph, *Uniforms and Nonuniforms*, 114–16.

33 Andrew Ross, "No-Collar Labour in America's 'New Economy'," *Socialist Register* 37 (2001): 77–87.

34 Erynn Masi de Casanova, *Buttoned Up: Clothing, Conformity, and White-Collar Masculinity* (Ithaca, New York: ILR Press, 2015).

35 Valerie Steele, "Dressing for Work," in *Men and Women: Dressing the Part*, edited by Claudia Kidwell and Valerie Steele (Washington, DC: Smithsonian Institution Press, 1989), 78.

36 Cesar Hernandez-Villanueva, "Dress Code and Religious Accommodations through the Lens of EEOC v. Kroger," *Rutgers Journal of Law & Religion* 22, no. 1 (2021): 161–99.

37 Clyde W. Summers, "Employment at Will in the United States: The Divine Right of Employers," *University of Pennsylvania Journal of Labor and Employment Law* 3, no. 1 (2000): 65–86.

38 Restricting a partner's clothing choices is a common tactic of "coercive control" in intimate relationships. Evan Stark, *Coercive Control: The Entrapment of Women in Personal Life* (Oxford: Oxford University Press, 2009).

39 Thorstein Veblen, *The Theory of the Leisure Class: An Economic Study of Institutions* (New York: The Macmillan Company, 1899).

40 Georg Simmel, "Fashion," *International Quarterly* 10 (1904): 130–55.

41 Charles W. King, "Fashion Adoption: A Rebuttal to 'Trickle-Down' Theory," in *Toward Scientific Marketing*, edited by Stephen A. Greyser (Chicago, Illinois: American Marketing Association, 1963), 108–25; and Dwight Robinson, "The Rules of Fashion Cycles," *Harvard Business Review* 1, no. 4 (1958): 62.

42 A rare exception to this is shown in the television series, *Undercover Boss*, where managers and owners of large companies disguise themselves as low-level employees in order to avoid being recognized, so they can observe their workers impartially and either reward or punish them. The deception is usually successful; the manager's disguise is only temporary.

43 Everett M. Rogers, *Diffusion of Innovations* (New York: The Free Press, 1962). This highly influential book was revised several times; the last (fifth) edition was published in 2003.

44 In this body of scholarship, less attention is given to non-clothing aspects of dress such as jewelry, shoes, cosmetics, and hairstyles.

45 Marilyn Revell DeLong, "Fashion, Theories of," in *The Berg Companion to Fashion*, edited by Valerie Steele (London: Bloomsbury Academic, 2010), 323.

46 Dorothy U. Behling, "Three and a Half Decades of Fashion Adoption Research: What Have We Learned?" *Clothing and Textiles Research Journal* 10, no. 2 (1992): 40.

47 Ted Polhemus, *Street Style: From Sidewalk to Catwalk* (London: Thames & Hudson, 1994); Caroline Evans, "Street Style, Subculture and Subversion," *Costume* 31, no. 1 (1997): 105–10; David Muggleton, *Inside Subculture: The Postmodern Meaning of Style* (Oxford: Berg Publications, 2000).

48 Jane E. Workman and Seung-Hee Lee, "What Do We Know about Fashion Adoption Groups? A Proposal and Test of a Model of Fashion Adoption," *International Journal of Consumer Studies* 41, no. 1 (2017): 61.

49 Many groups of people resist consumerism for environmental, ideological, and/or religious reasons. Fashion and dress are not synonyms.

50 Elizabeth Wilson, *Adorned in Dreams: Fashion and Modernity* (Berkeley, California: University of California Press, 1985), 3.

51 Ibid., 8.

52 Clayton M. Christensen et al., "Disruptive Innovation for Social Change," *Harvard Business Review* 84, no. 12 (2006): 94–103.

53 Joanne Entwistle, *The Fashioned Body: Fashion, Dress and Social Theory*, second edition (Cambridge: Polity Press, 2015), xiv.

54 Malcolm Barnard, *Fashion Theory: A Reader*, second edition (Abingdon: Routledge, 2020), 2.

55 Joanne Eicher, "Dress," in *Routledge International Encyclopedia of Women: Global Women's Issues and Knowledge*, edited by Cheris Kramarae and Dale Spender (New York: Routledge, 2000), 422–3.

56 Herbert Blumer, "Fashion: From Class Differentiation to Collective Selection," *Sociological Quarterly* 10, no. 3 (1969): 275–91.

57 Ibid., 279.

58 Ibid., 275.

59 Ted Polhemus and Lynn Procter, *Fashion & Anti-Fashion: Anthropology of Clothing and Adornment* (London: Thames & Hudson, 1978).

60 Emma Tarlo and Annelies Moors (eds.), *Islamic Fashion and Anti-Fashion: New Perspectives from Europe and North America* (London: Bloomsbury Academic, 2013); and Nickolas Pappas, *The Philosopher's New Clothes: The Theaetetus, the Academy, and Philosophy's Turn Against Fashion* (London: Taylor & Francis, 2015).

61 Nickolas Pappas, "Anti-Fashion: If not Fashion, Then What?" in *Philosophical Perspectives on Fashion*, edited by Giovanni Matteucci and Stefano Marino (London: Bloomsbury Academic, 2017), 82.

62 Nicolas Cambridge, "Cherry-Picking Sartorial Identities in Cherry-Blossom Land: Uniforms and Uniformity in Japan," *Journal of Design History* 24, no. 2 (2011): 179.

63 Kat Eschner, "How Hoop Skirts Led to Tape Measures," *Smithsonian Magazine*, July 14, 2017, at: https://www.smithsonianmag.com/smart-news/how-hoop-skirts-led-tape-measures-180963995/.

64 Andrew Godley, "The Global Diffusion of the Sewing Machine, 1850-1914," *Research in Economic History* 20 (2001): 1–45.

65 Joy Spanabel Emery, *A History of the Paper Pattern Industry: The Home Dressmaking Fashion Revolution* (London: Bloomsbury Academic 2014).

66 Jean L. Druesedow, "Ready-to-Wear," in *The Berg Companion to Fashion*, edited by Valerie Steele (Oxford: Bloomsbury Academic, 2010), 591–6.

67 Kaleb Dissinger, Rodney Foytik, David Accetta, David Cole, and Fort McHenry Guard, "Common Threads: Army," US Department of Defense, 2021, https://www.defense.gov/Experience/Common-Threads/Common-Threads-Army/.

68 Mark R. Wilson, *The Business of Civil War: Military Mobilization and the State, 1861–1865* (Baltimore, Maryland: Johns Hopkins University Press, 2006).

69 "The Latest News," *The Sun* (New York), May 18, 1861, 2.

70 Jessica Iredale, "Zac Posen on Creative Directing for a Conservative Customer," *Women's Wear Daily*, April 25, 2018, 26, at: https://wwd.com/fashion-news/fashion-features/zac-posen-on-creative-directing-a-conservative-customer-1202657064/.

71 Brooks Brothers, "Outfitting a Nation," *Brooks Brothers Magazine*, 2021, at: https://magazine.brooksbrothers.com/outfitting-a-nation/.

72 "Boston A City of Uniforms," *Boston Daily Globe*, July 31, 1898, 25.

73 The Fair Labor Standards Act (FLSA), passed by Congress in 1938, ended most paid labor for children under the age of 14 and restricted labor for children between the ages of 14 and 17.

74 In his will, recorded in the probate court of St. Louis on June 28, 1898, Cherubino left equal shares of the company to his wife, Theresa, and to the children from his first marriage.

75 Angelica, "History," angelica.com, 2021, at: http://www.angelica.com/about-us/history/.

76 Stephen Fried, *Appetite for America: Fred Harvey and the Business of Civilizing the Wild West—One Meal at a Time* (New York: Bantam Books, 2010).

77 Lesley Poling-Kempes, *The Harvey Girls: Women Who Opened the West* (New York: Marlowe & Company, 1991), 55.

78 Joshua Simon and Michael Mamp, "'Nostalgic Elegance': The Enduring Style of the Gibson Girl," *Dress* 47, no. 1 (2021): 61–77.

79 Craik, *Uniforms Exposed*, 128.

80 Many thanks to Jane Tynan for drawing my attention to how non-state combatants (rebels, guerillas, insurgents) develop and use uniforms. There is a fascinating body of literature on this topic, for example: Artur Beifuss and Francesco Trivini Bellini, *Branding Terror: The Logotypes and Iconography of Insurgent Groups and Terrorist Organizations* (London: Merrell Publishers, 2013).

81 Jane Tynan and Suzannah Biernoff, "Making and Remaking the Civilian Soldier: The World War I Photographs of Horace Nicholls," *Journal of War & Culture Studies* 5, no. 3 (2013): 277–93.

82 Carolyn Purnell, *Blue Jeans* (London: Bloomsbury Academic, 2023).

83 The term "unskilled" is often used for jobs that have no special requirements for training and/or licensure, but it devalues the skills that workers develop on the job. Emma Dowling, "The Waitress: On Affect, Method, and (Re)presentation," *Cultural Studies s Critical Methodologies* 12, no. 2 (2012): 109–17.

84 Amy S. Wharton, "The Sociology of Emotional Labor," *Annual Review of Sociology* 35 (2009): 146–65.

85 "Service Industry," *Encyclopaedia Britannica*, 2018, at: https://www.britannica.com/topic/service-industry.

86 US Bureau of Labor Statistics, "Employment, Hours, and Earnings from the Current Employment Statistics," bls.gov, January 9, 2023, at: https://data.bls.gov/timeseries/CES0700000001?amp%253bdata_tool=XGtable&output_view=data&include_graphs=true.

87 The Uniform Retailers Association specifies that "membership is for independent retailers who specialize in hospital scrubs." Uniform Retailers Association, "Homepage," uniformretailers.org, 2021, at: https://uniformretailers.org/aws/URA/pt/sp/home_page.

88 Joseph Locker, "The Secret to Success of the Only Hooters in the UK and What It's Like to Work There," NottinghamshireLive, August 27, 2019, at: https://www.nottinghampost.com/news/nottingham-news/secret-success-only-hooters-uk-3249244.

Chapter 2

1 Sarah Field Splint, *The Art of Cooking and Serving* (Cincinnati, Ohio: Proctor & Gamble, 1929).

2 Mary Romero, *Maid in the U.S.A.* (New York: Routledge, 1992).

3 A copyright statement at the end of the column credits Henry W. Fischer, who may have been a ghostwriter, a translator, or the real author.

4 Elsa von Rauch, "The Servant Girl for the Well-to-Do Family," *Washington Post*, June 9, 1901, 30.

5   Thorstein Veblen, *The Theory of the Leisure Class: An Economic Study of Institutions* (London: George Allen & Unwin, Ltd., 1899).

6   Minnesota Historical Society, "About the House," James J. Hill House, 2021, at: https://www.mnhs.org/hillhouse/learn/house.

7   US Census Bureau, "Twelfth Census of the United States," City of St. Paul in Ramsey County, Minnesota, 1900, Enumeration District No. 116, Sheet No. 17.

8   Aileen Ribeiro, *Dress in Eighteenth Century Europe* (New Haven, Connecticut: Yale University Press, 2002), 82.

9   After migrating to the United States in 1892 with his wife and three children, his surname was shortened from Dickstein to Dix.

10 Mark H. Dix, *An American Business Adventure: The Story of Henry A. Dix* (New York: Harper & Brothers Publishers, 1928).

11 "Trading in Houses," *New-York Daily Tribune*, October 2, 1907, 16.

12 *The Work of the National Consumers' League.* (Philadelphia, Pennsylvania: American Academy of Political and Social Science, 1910).

13 Dix, *American Business Adventure*, 30.

14 Ibid., 39.

15 Kaufman-Straus, Co., "The Christmas Store," *The Courier-Journal* (Louisville, Kentucky), November 26, 1922, 5.

16 Dix, *American Business Adventure*, 34.

17 Margaret Wallace, "Queries Raised Over Uniforms for the Maids," *Washington Post*, December 6, 1936, S11.

18 "Proper Dress for Servants Aids Home Harmony," *Los Angeles Times*, October 23, 1935, 35.

19 "Want a Stage Beauty for a Cook?" *Philadelphia Inquirer*, March 19, 1922, 73.

20 Emily Post, "Household—Dressing the Butler and the Maid," *The Sun* (Baltimore, Maryland), February 2, 1936, SC6.

21 Phyllis Palmer, *Domesticity and Dirt: Housewives and Domestic Servants in the United States, 1920–1945* (Philadelphia, Pennsylvania: Temple University Press, 1989), 68.

22 Bonnie Thornton Dill, *Across the Boundaries of Race and Class: An Exploration of Work and Family among Black Female Domestic Servants* (New York: Routledge, 1994).

23 Kellie Carter Jackson, "'She Was a Member of the Family': Ethel Phillips, Domestic Labor, and Employer Perceptions," *Women's Studies Quarterly* 45, no. 3/4 (2017): 160–73.

24 Loren Miller, "On Second Thought," *California Eagle* (Los Angeles, California), May 26, 1933, 12.

25 Palmer, *Domesticity and Dirt*, 141.

26 Advertisement for maids' uniforms at a department store in Wilkes-Barre, Pennsylvania, Isaac Long, "Maids' Uniforms," *The Wilkes-Barre Record* (Wilkes-Barre, Pennsylvania), June 9, 1941, 10.

27 Stacie McCormick, "'I'm Every Woman': The Cultural Influence and Afterlife of Florence Johnston of *The Jeffersons*," in *The 25 Sitcoms that Changed Television: Turning Points in American Culture*, edited by Laura Westengard and Aaron Barlow (Santa Barbara, California: ABC-CLIO, 2018), 94–107.

28 Angela Brown, "Our Story," Savvy Cleaner, 2021, at: https://savvycleaner.com.

29 Angela Brown, "Why Uniforms Work: The Psychology of Uniforms," Ask a House Cleaner, February 21, 2021, at: https://askahousecleaner.com/why-uniforms-work/.

30 Angela Brown, "Why Uniforms Work—The Psychology of Cleaning Uniforms," YouTube, February 22, 2021, at: https://www.youtube.com/watch?v=tLafHPs70p4.

31 Jack Santino, *Miles of Smiles, Years of Struggle: Stories of Black Pullman Porters* (Champaign, Illinois: University of Illinois Press, 1991).

32 Larry Tye, *Rising from the Rails: Pullman Porters and the Making of the Black Middle Class* (New York: Henry Holt, 2004), 2–3.

33 Malca Chall and Joyce A. Henderson, "A Maid with the Pullman Company, 1926–1931," interview by Frances Mary Albrier, University of California, 1979, at: https://oac.cdlib.org/view?docId=hb696nb3ht;NAAN=13030&doc.view=frames&chunk.id=div00046&toc.depth=1&toc.id=div00046&brand=oac4.

34 Santino, *Miles of Smiles*, 21–2.

35 "R.R. Porters Must Buy Their Suits at Fields Even if They Cost More," *The Day Book* (Chicago, Illinois) second edition, March 1, 1917, 11–12.

36 Tye, *Rising from the Rails*, 90.

37 Santino, *Miles of Smiles*, 8.

38 Ibid., 33.

39 The Smithsonian National Museum of African American History and Culture has a complete set of buttons from a Pullman uniform, 2021.46.75.18a-d.

40 Pullman Company, *Car Service Rules of the Operating Department of Pullman's Palace Car Company* (Chicago, Illinois: W.H. Pottinger, 1893).

41 "R.R. Porters," 12.

42 Amy Vanderbilt, "Amy's Etiquette: Differences Between Train, Pullman Conductors Told," *The Wichita Beacon* (Wichita, Kansas), November 14, 1956, 36.

43 One example is a photograph of porter J. W. Mays, taken between 1894 and 1901, Library of Congress Prints & Photographs Division, LC-B5-44842.

44 Charles L. Upton, "Los Angeles Pullman Porters Should Have Locker Space for Uniforms," *California Eagle* (Los Angeles), September 5, 1930, 11.

45 Ibid.

46 Beth Tompkins Bates, *Pullman Porters and the Rise of Protest Politics in Black America, 1925–1945* (Chapel Hill, North Carolina: University of North Carolina Press, 2001). Melinda Chateauvert, *Marching Together: Women of the Brotherhood of Sleeping Car Porters* (Urbana, Illinois: University of Illinois Press, 1998).

47 Eric Arnesen, *Brotherhoods of Color: Black Railroad Workers and the Struggle for Equality* (Cambridge, Massachusetts: Harvard University Press, 2001).

48 Brotherhood of Sleeping Car Porters, "Report of the Proceedings of the Brotherhood of Sleeping Car Porters, Convention Held in St. Louis, Missouri, on September 13–18, 1942," Chicago Historical Society, 1942, 103.

49 Brotherhood of Sleeping Car Porters, "BSCP Agreements, 1941–1953," Library of Congress, Manuscript Division, A. Philip Randolph Papers, 1951.

50 Peter Lyth, "'Think of Her as Your Mother': Airline Advertising and the Stewardess in America, 1930–1980," *Journal of Transport History* 30, no. 1 (2009): 1–21.

51 Arnesen, *Brotherhoods of Color*, 240–1.

52 Eric Porter, "'A Black Future in the Air Industry?': Liberation and Complicity at San Francisco International Airport," *California History* 97, no. 2 (2020): 88–111.

53 "Employment Opportunities," *The Brooklyn Daily Eagle* (New York), May 19, 1943, 22.

54 Jens Wietschorke, "Caretakers, Doormen, Concierges: Negotiating Intermediate Spaces," in *The Routledge History of the Domestic Sphere in Europe*, edited by Joachim Eibach and Margareth Lanzinger (New York: Routledge, 2020), 397–414.

55 *Oxford English Dictionary*, "Livery, n.," *OED Online*, June 2021.

56 Maria Hayward, *Rich Apparel: Clothing and the Law in Henry VIII's England* (Farnham: Ashgate Publishing, 2009), 147.

57 Urvashi Chakravarty, "Livery, Liberty, and Legal Fictions," *English Literary Renaissance* 42, no. 3 (2012): 373.

58 John Styles, "Involuntary Consumers? Servants and Their Clothes in Eighteenth-Century England," *Textile History* 33, no. 1 (2002): 9–21.

59 Alexandra Kim, "Class, Work, and Dress," in *Berg Encyclopedia of World Dress and Fashion: West Europe*, edited by Lise Skov (Oxford: Bloomsbury Academic, 2010), 444–51.

60 Leslie Dorsey and Janice Devine, *Fare Thee Well: A Backward Look at Two Centuries of Historic American Hostelries, Fashionable Spas & Seaside Resorts* (New York: Crown Publishers, 1964), 80.

61 Frances Benjamin Johnson, "Two men, one a doorman, standing at the F. Street entrance to the Willard Hotel," *c.* 1901–1910, Library of Congress Prints and Photographs Division, LC-DIG-ppmsca-10456. Also, National Photo Company, "Doorman Willard," 1921, Library of Congress Prints and Photographs Division, LC-DIG-npcc-05433.

62 National Photo Company, "Mayflower Hotel (doorman)," *c.* 1916–1917, Library of Congress Prints and Photographs Division, LC-DIG-npcc-32511.

63 National Photo Company, "Doorman Wardman," 1921, Library of Congress Prints and Photographs Division, LC-DIG-npcc-05429.

64 National Photo Company, "Doorman Lafayette," 1921, Library of Congress Prints and Photographs Division, LC-DIG-npcc-05430.

65 National Photo Company, "Doorman Prohatan," 1921, Library of Congress Prints and Photographs Division, LC-DIG-npcc-05431.

66 Peter Bearman, *Doormen* (Chicago, Illinois: University of Chicago Press, 2005), 20.

67 James Collins, "Why Doormen?" *New York Times*, April 26, 2010, A23.

68 Edward Grimm, *The Doorman*, illustrated by Ted Lewin (New York: Orchard Books, 2000).

69 "Well-Dressed Doorman Trades Epaulets for Ivy League Look," *New York Times*, July 21, 1963, 187.

70 Dee Wedemeyer, "In Fashion for Doormen: Few Frills, Some Fray," *New York Times*, June 25, 1978, R1.

71 Robin Finn, "The Latest (or Not) in Doorman Fashion," *New York Times*, January 17, 2010, NJ8.

72 Sarah Kramer, "Keeping Peace in a Vertical Village," *New York Times*, May 12, 2013, L12.

73 Atlanta Urban Design Commission, "The Ten Park Place Building (Thornton Building)," City of Atlanta, 2021, at: https://www.atlantaga.gov/government/departments/city-planning/office-of-design/urban-design-commission/the-ten-park-place-building-thornton-building.

74 Laura Itzkowitz, "The Little-Known Story Behind Cincinnati's Terrace Plaza Hotel," *Architectural Digest*, February 3, 2021, at: https://www.architecturaldigest.com/story/the-little-known-story-behind-cincinnatis-terrace-plaza-hotel.

75 Kathy S. Koops, "Terrace Hilton Hotel," The Cincy Blog: Cincinnati Real Estate, September 9, 2015, at: https://thecincyblog.com/tag/terrace-hilton-hotel/.

76 Itzkowitz, "The Little-Known Story."

77 Postcard in author's research collection.

78 Scott Sandell, "L.A.'s Answer to the Doorman," *Los Angeles Times*, October 16, 2003, at: https://www.latimes.com/local/la-hm-concierge16oct16203418-story.html.

Chapter 3

1 Minjee Kim and Tingyu Zhou, "Does Restricting the Entry of Formula Businesses Help Mom-and-Pop Stores? The Case of Small American Towns with Unique Community Character," *Economic Development Quarterly* 35, no. 2 (2021): 157–73.

2 Office of Size Standards, "SBA's Size Standards Methodology," Small Business Administration, April 2019, 7, at: https://www.sba.gov/sites/default/files/2021-02/SBA%20Size%20Standards%20Methodology%20April%2011%2C%202019-508.pdf.

3 Under the North American Industry Classification System (NAICS), this sector includes businesses that "prepare meals, snacks, and beverages to customer order for immediate on-premises and off-premises consumption." This includes bars, coffee

shops, food trucks, and restaurants, but does not include service within hotels, recreational facilities, or schools (where food and beverage service is not the primary business). "722 – Food Services and Drinking Places," NAICS, 2018, at: https://www.naics.com/naics-code-description/?code=722.

4 US Census Bureau, "The Number of Firms and Establishments, Employment, and Annual Payroll by State, Industry, and Enterprise Employment Size," census.gov, 2018, at: https://www.census.gov/data/tables/2018/econ/susb/2018-susb-annual. html.

5 Brian Headd, "The Characteristics of Small-Business Employees," *Monthly Labor Review*, April 2000, 13–18, at: https://www.bls.gov/opub/mlr/2000/04/art3full.pdf.

6 "Franchising," *Entrepreneur*, 2021, at: https://www.entrepreneur.com/encyclopedia/ franchising.

7 Stephen C. Root, "The Meaning of Franchise Under the California Franchise Investment Law: A Definition in Search of a Concept," *McGeorge Law Review* 30, no. 4 (1999): 1163–220.

8 James O. Robinson, "The Barber-Surgeons of London," *Archives of Surgery* 119, no. 10 (1984): 1171–5.

9 Samuel X. Radbill, "The Barber Surgeons Among the Early Dutch and Swedes Along the Delaware," *Bulletin of the Institute of the History of Medicine* 4, no. 9 (1936): 718–44.

10 Quincy T. Mills, *Cutting Along the Color Line: Black Barbers and Barber Shops in America* (Philadelphia, Pennsylvania: University of Pennsylvania Press, 2013), 4.

11 David E. Bernstein, "Licensing Laws: A Historical Example of the Use of Government Regulatory Power Against African-Americans," *San Diego Law Review* 31, no. 1 (1994): 89–104.

12 Mills, *Cutting Along the Color Line*, 6–7.

13 American Barber Association, "A History of Entrepreneurship, Freedom, and Professionalism," americanbarber.org, 2021, at: https://americanbarber.org/history/.

14 Arthur B. Moler, *Standardized Barbers' Manual*, revised edition (Chicago, Illinois: National Educational Council of the Associated Master Barbers of America, 1928), 25.

15 Isadore Goldman and Jacob Cohen, 1932, "Barber's Coat," US Patent 1,8878,275, filed December 12, 1931, and issued September 20, 1932.

16 This quote (the earliest mention I've found of the "Mr. Barco" label) is from a store advertisement for Dunn Professional Uniforms that appeared in the *El Paso Herald-Post* (El Paso, Texas) on May 3, 1957, 18.

17 Randy Alfred, "May 8, 1951: DuPont Debuts Dacron," Wired, May 8, 2009, at: https://www.wired.com/2009/05/dayintech-0508/.

18 Department of Labor, "Title 46: Professional and Occupational Standards: Barbers (Part VII)," State of Louisiana, Board of Barber Examiners, July 1964, at: https:// www.doa.la.gov/media/uwabz4p3/46v07.pdf.

19 Tom Beer, "Journeyman Barbers in Minnesota," Minnesota Historical Society, 2015, at: https://www.mnopedia.org/journeymen-barbers-minnesota.

20 "Barbers Will Feast in Celebration of Their Recent Victory and Birthday," *The Saint Paul Globe* (St. Paul, Minnesota), May 18, 1897, 12.

21 The last was Alabama, which regulated barbers at the county level (instead of the state level) until 2013. See US Bureau of Labor Statistics, "The De-Licensing of Occupations in the United States," *Monthly Labor Review*, 2015, at: https://www.bls.gov/opub/mlr/2015/article/the-de-licensing-of-occupations-in-the-united-states.htm.

22 Edward J. Timmons and Robert J. Thornton, "The Licensing of Barbers in the USA," *British Journal of Industrial Relations* 48, no. 4 (2010): 740–57.

23 "18 AAC 23.230 – Practitioner Hygiene," State of Alaska, 2002, at: http://www.legis.state.ak.us/basis/folioproxy.asp?url=http://www.legis.state.ak.us/cgi-bin/folioisa.dll/aac/query=*/doc/%7B@81957%7D?prev.

24 State Board of Barber Examiners, "Amendment to Rule 023.00.92-001," State of Arkansas, 2018, at: http://170.94.37.152/REGS/023.00.18-002P-18172.pdf.

25 Mississippi Barber Board, "Title 30, Part 1801, Chapter 6: Barber Shops/Schools Regulations," State of Mississippi, 2018, at: http://www.msbarberboard.com/sites/default/files/00000504c.pdf.

26 New Hampshire Board of Barbering, Cosmetology and Esthetics, "302.07 Licensee," State of New Hampshire, 2016, at: http://gencourt.state.nh.us/rules/state_agencies/bar100-700.html.

27 Division of Licensing Services, "Appearance Enhancement," New York Department of State, 2020, at: https://dos.ny.gov/system/files/documents/2021/05/appearance_enhancement_feb_2021.pdf.

28 State of Texas, "Title 16, Part 4, Chapter 82, Rule §82.70," Texas Administrative Code, 2020, at: https://texreg.sos.state.tx.us/public/readtac$ext.TacPage?sl=R&app=9&p_dir=&p_rloc=&p_tloc=&p_ploc=&pg=1&p_tac=&ti=16&pt=4&ch=82&rl=70.

29 Board of Cosmetology and Barber Examiners, "Proposed Rule: 20 CSR 2085-11.010 Barber Sanitation Rules," *Missouri Register* 32, no. 18 (2007): 1733, at: https://www.sos.mo.gov/CMSImages/adrules/moreg/2007/v32n18/v32n18(part2)a.pdf.

30 Division of Professional Regulation, "24 Delaware Code, Section 5100 Board of Cosmetology and Barbering," Delaware Department of State, 2017, at: https://regulations.delaware.gov/register/may2017/final/20%20DE%20Reg%20916%2005-01-17.htm.

31 LIC Salon Apparel, "About LIC," licsalonapparel.com, 2021, at: https://licsalonapparel.com/about-lic/.

32 W. D. King, "When Theater Becomes History: Final Curtains on the Victorian Stage," *Victorian Studies* 36, no. 1 (1992): 53–61.

33 "The Iroquois," *Chicago Tribune*, November 9, 1903, 4.

34 The fire of 1871, one of the defining moments in the city's history, burned more than three square miles and left 100,000 people homeless. Frank Alfred Randall and John D. Randall, *History of the Development of Building Construction in Chicago*, second edition (Champaign, Illinois: University of Illinois Press, 1999).

35 "Damage Suits Great 'Graft;' Theaters Hit," *Chicago Tribune*, October 17, 1903, 1–2.

36 "Fire in the Iroquois Theater Kills 571 and Injures 350 Persons," *Chicago Tribune*, December 31, 1903, 1–8.

37 Marshall Everett, *The Great Chicago Theater Disaster: The Complete Story Told by the Survivors* (Chicago, Illinois: Publishers Union of America, 1904), 77–8.

38 C. H. Blackall, "Theater Fires," *The Sanitarian* 43 (April 1, 1904): 340.

39 Douglas Gomery, *Shared Pleasures: A History of Movie Presentation in the United States* (Madison, Wisconsin: University of Wisconsin Press, 1992), 49.

40 Although the scarf/necktie and color of the vest are not mentioned in the policy, the uniforms are visible in an article written by the theater's manager of volunteer and internship services. See Nicole Smith, "Truly Integrating Volunteers and Interns into Your Organization," Tessitura Network, July 31, 2019, at: https://www.tessituranetwork.com/Items/Articles/Innovator-Series/2019/Nicole-Smith.

41 "Front of House Usher Training Handbook," Adrienne Arsht Center for the Performing Arts, 2021, 5, at: https://www.arshtcenter.org/Documents/Volunteer/Seasoned%20Usher%20Training%20Handbook%20.pdf.

42 "Paramount Theater," Digital Library of Georgia, 2021, at: https://dlg.usg.edu/record/geh_athpc_2444.

43 Kate Stephenson, "Uniform Adoption in English Public Schools, 1830–1930," in *Uniform: Clothing and Discipline in the Modern World*, edited by Jane Tynan and Lisa Godson (London: Bloomsbury Visual Arts, 2019), 67–86.

44 Description from *Angelica Galaxy of Uniforms* (St. Louis, Missouri: Angelica Uniform Co., 1988), 51.

45 *Angelica Washable Service Uniforms* (St. Louis, Missouri: Angelica Jacket Co., 1962), 48. This page lists the patent number, US115117. Viola S. Levy, 1939, "Uniform Dress," US Patent 115,117S, filed February 23, 1939, and issued June 6, 1939.

46 Charles B. Weinberg et al., "Technological Change and Managerial Challenges in the Movie Theater Industry," *Journal of Cultural Economics* 45 (2021): 239–62.

47 Rasha Salti, "Do Not Go Gentle into That Good Night: Film Festivals, Pandemic, Aftermath," *Film Quarterly* 74, no. 1 (2020): 88–96.

48 Nolan Ellmore Barrick, "The Architectural Development of the Automobile Filling Station in America" (MA thesis, Rice Institute, Houston, Texas, 1937), 2.

49 "America on the Move: Fill 'Er Up!" Smithsonian National Museum of American History, 2003, at: https://americanhistory.si.edu/america-on-the-move/fill-up.

50 Barrick, "Architectural Development," 6–7.

51 "Painting, 'The First Gas Station in the World, Seattle, 1907,' by Robert Addison," Museum of History & Industry (Seattle, Washington), 2021, at: https://digitalcollections.lib.washington.edu/digital/collection/imlsmohai/id/13486/.

52 Tim Steil, *Fantastic Filling Stations* (Saint Paul, Minnesota: MBI Publishing Company, 2002), 13.

53 This was particularly important for black motorists, who were prevented from accessing many other businesses. For more, see Erin Elizabeth Scott, "Mississippi Motoring: Mom and Pops and Entrepreneurs" (MA thesis, University of Mississippi, 2014). Also, Mia Bay, "Traveling Black/Buying Black: Retail and Roadside Accommodations during the Segregation Era," in *Race and Retail: Consumption across the Color Line*, edited by Mia Bay and Ann Fabian (New Brunswick, New Jersey: Rutgers University Press, 2015), 15–33.

54 The collecting term "petroliana" refers to historic artifacts from gas stations (typically 1910–1970) such as pumps, signage, packaging, advertising materials, and uniforms.

55 Scott, "Mississippi Motoring," 11.

56 Ronald N. Johnson and Charles J. Romeo, "The Impact of Self-Service Bans in the Retail Gasoline Market," *Review of Economics and Statistics* 82, no. 4 (2000): 625.

57 Ibid., 625–6.

58 As of 2021, New Jersey and Oregon still have statewide bans on self-service gas stations. Some municipalities in other states also ban the practice. For more about the rationale behind these laws (which are not just about fire safety), see: Robert Scott III, "Fill 'er Up: A Study of Statewide Self-Service Gasoline Station Bans," *Challenge* 50, no. 5 (2007): 103–14.

59 "Unitog Co.," *International Directory of Company Histories*, Volume 19 (Detroit, Michigan: St. James Press, 1998), 457.

60 Ibid.

61 *Approved Esso Uniforms* (Kansas City, Missouri, Unitog Co., 1954), catalogue and mail-in order form.

62 Ibid.

63 "Trucker caps" and "baseball caps," are very similar. They fit closely to the head and have a visor in the front that is several inches long. Trucker caps typically have mesh panels on the sides to provide ventilation. Baseball caps typically have eyelets for ventilation. This brochure describes the cap as a "baseball cap" and shows how a "gripper-snap adjustment" in the back can be adjusted, making it "ideal for part-time help."

64 *The Great Race*, directed by Blake Edwards (Warner Brothers, 1965).

65 Elisabetta Bini, "Selling Gasoline with a Smile: Gas Station Attendants between the United States, Italy, and the Third World, 1945–1970," *International Labor and Working-Class History* 81 (2012): 78.

66 Ibid.

67 Dorothy Sue Cobble, *Dishing It Out: Waitresses and Their Unions in the Twentieth Century* (Champaign, Illinois: University of Illinois Press, 1991), 3.

68 Ibid., 2.

69 Heather Paul Kurent, "Frances R. Donovan and the Chicago School of Sociology: A Case Study in Marginality" (PhD diss., University of Maryland, 1982).

70 Frances R. Donovan. *The Woman Who Waits* (Boston, Massachusetts: Gorham Press, 1920).

71 Cobble, *Dishing It Out*, 36.

72 Shane Company manufactured uniforms in Evansville, Indiana, from 1936 to 1974. The owner of the company, Norman A. Shane, was originally from Chicago. As a prominent member of the Jewish community in Indiana, he was mentioned repeatedly in *The Jewish Post*, a newspaper still published in Indianapolis. See also Pat Sides, "Shane Uniform Company," *The City-County Observer* (Evansville, Indiana), December 10, 2018, at: https://city-countyobserver.com/shane-uniform-company/.

73 Mikyoung Whang and Sherry Haar, "Nelly Don's 1916 Pink Gingham Apron Frock: An Illustration of the Middle-Class American Housewife's Shifting Role from Producer to Consumer," *Fashion and Textiles* 1, no. 18 (2014), Doi: 10.1186/s40691-014-0018-1.

74 *Pennsylvania Farmer*, founded in 1912, is one of the longest-operating farm journals in the United States. For more, see: "Pennsylvania: Historical Essay on Agriculture and Rural Life," part of a proposal submitted by Pennsylvania State University to the National Endowment for the Humanities, 1962, at: https://ecommons.cornell.edu/bitstream/handle/1813/54904/PENNSYLVANIA_ESSAY.pdf?sequence=1&isAllowed=y.

75 Pennsylvania Farmer, *Book of Patterns* (New York: Pennsylvania Farmer Pattern Department, New York, c. early 1940s), 19–22 and the back cover.

76 Andrew P. Haley, "Dining in High Chairs: Children and the American Restaurant Industry, 1900–1950," *Food & History* 7, no. 2 (2009): 69–94.

77 *Angelica Washable Service Uniforms*, 24.

78 Ibid., 30. Arm shields are strategically placed fabric inserts that keep sweat from showing on the outside of the garment. They are better known today as "dress shields" or "sweat shields."

79 Industrial Uniform Co., founded in 1938 in Wichita, Kansas, now operates under the name "Logo Depot." It no longer manufactures uniforms, but focuses on designing printed and embroidered logos for other manufacturers of work uniforms. Logo Depot, "A Wichita Legacy of Excellence," logodepotweb.com, 2020, at: https://logodepotweb.com/our-story/.

80 Cobble, *Dishing It Out*, 38.

81 Although the term "gender non-conforming" is quite new, it is clear that waiter/ess uniforms (and many other work uniforms) reflected and shaped a sharp gender binary in US society. I return to this topic in Chapter 8.

82 *Angelica Washable Service Uniforms*, 39.

83 Greta Foff Paules, *Dishing It Out: Power and Resistance Among Waitresses in a New Jersey Restaurant* (Philadelphia: Temple University Press, 1991), 3.

84 Ibid., 9.

85 Dowling, "The Waitress," 113.

86 Wage and Hour Division, "Fact Sheet #15: Tipped Employees Under the Fair Labor Standards Act (FLSA)," US Department of Labor, 2018, https://www.dol.gov/agencies/whd/fact-sheets/15-flsa-tipped-employees.

87 Elise Gould and David Cooper, "Seven Facts about Tipped Workers and the Tipped Minimum Wage," Economic Policy Institute, May 31, 2018, https://www.epi.org/blog/seven-facts-about-tipped-workers-and-the-tipped-minimum-wage/?gclid=CjwKCAiAp8iMBhAqEiwAJb94z4hac9ry1GRDwm8VlpFLV_B7d3fl4ZyPb6AHB9GUOtxkT01go6hM6BoC2FMQAvD_BwE.

Chapter 4

1 Alex Attewell, "Florence Nightingale (1820–1910)," *Prospects* 28 (1998): 151–66.

2 Irene Schuessler Poplin, "Nursing Uniforms: Romantic Idea, Functional Attire, or Instrument of Social Change?" *Nursing History Review* 2 (1994): 153–67.

3 Susan Reverby, *Ordered to Care: The Dilemma of American Nursing, 1850–1945* (Cambridge: Cambridge University Press, 1987).

4 Christina Bates, "The Nurse's Cap and its Rituals," *Dress* 36, no. 1 (2010): 21–40. See also Bates, *A Cultural History*.

5 Patricia M. Donahue, *Nursing, the Finest Art: An Illustrated History* (St. Louis, Missouri: C.V. Mosby, 1985).

6 Janie Brown Nowak, *The Forty-Seven Hundred: The Story of the Mount Sinai Hospital School of Nursing* (Canaan, New Hampshire: Phoenix Publishing, 1981), 114.

7 Ibid.

8 Susan Hardy and Anthony Corones, "Dressed to Heal: The Changing Semiotics of Surgical Dress," *Fashion Theory* 20, no. 1 (2016): 27–49.

9 The term refers to the practice of careful washing or "scrubbing in" before surgery.

10 Nathan L. Belkin, "Use of Scrubs and Related Apparel in Health Care Facilities," *American Journal of Infection Control*, 25 (1997): 401–4.

11 Harry M. Sherman, "The Green Operating Room at St. Luke's Hospital," *California State Journal of Medicine* 12, no. 5 (1914): 181–3.

12 In the 1980s, *Showing Your Colors*, a popular guide to mixing colors in fashion observed that "hospital green has always been either [an] esoteric fashion color or a very common color closely associated with institutional uniforms." Jeanne Allen, *Showing Your Colors: A Designer's Guide to Coordinating Your Wardrobe* (San Francisco, California: Chronicle Books, 1986).

13 Kendra Van Cleave, "'A Style All Her Own': Fashion, Clothing Practices, and Female Community at Smith College, 1920–1929," *Dress* 32, no. 1 (2005): 56–65.

14 For example, the Smithsonian National Museum of American History has a nurse's cap worn by a 1945 graduate of Johns Hopkins Hospital School of Nursing (2005.0171.01), which is made of stiff, white organdy. It has a heavily pleated band with a pleated crown that is several inches high.

15 The "wings" led to comparisons between nurses and angels. Sandy Summers, *Saving Lives: Why the Media's Portrayal of Nurses Puts All of Us At Risk* (New York: Kaplan Publications, 2010).

16 The 1940 US census lists her occupation as "nurse" and her place of residence as Indianapolis. Aline Mullinix, 1927, "Nurse's Cap," US Patent 1,668,331A filed June 23, 1927, and issued May 1, 1928.

17 Stella Freidinger, "Maintaining Standards in Small Hospitals and Training Schools," *American Journal of Nursing* 20, no. 7 (1920): 535–8.

18 Julia F. Irwin, "Connected by Calamity: The United States, the League of Red Cross Societies, and Transnational Disaster Assistance after the First World War," *Moving the Social*, 57 (2017): 57–76.

19 Susan H. Godson, *Serving Proudly: A History of Women in the U.S. Navy* (Annapolis, Maryland: Naval Institute Press, 2001).

20 Elizabeth A. Toon, "Managing the Conduct of Individual Life: Public Health Education and American Public Health, 1910 to 1940," (PhD diss., University of Pennsylvania, 1998).

21 Rima D. Apple, "School Health is Community Health: School Nursing in the Early Twentieth Century in the USA," *History of Education Review* 46, no. 2 (2016): 136–49.

22 Suzanne Lee Kolm, "Women's Labor Aloft: A Cultural History of Airline Flight Attendants in the United States, 1930–1978" (PhD diss., Brown University, Providence, Rhode Island, 1995).

23 Robert W. Hodge, Paul M. Siegel, and Peter H. Rossi, "Occupational Prestige in the United States, 1925–63," *American Journal of Sociology* 70, no. 3 (1964): 286–302.

24 Claribel A. Wheeler, "Hospital Helpers," *The Modern Hospital* 16, no. 2 (1921): 153.

25 *The Modern Hospital* (1913–74) was a trade journal published by the American Hospital Association.

26 Frank E. Chapman, "Clothes Make the Man," *The Modern Hospital* 20, no. 4 (1923): 376.

27 Elizabeth Blackwell, the first woman in the US to earn an MD (in 1849) was shunned by most employers. In an essay she recalled, "When I entered college in 1847, the ladies of the town pronounced the undertaking crazy, or worse, and declared they would die rather than employ a woman as a physician." Elizabeth Blackwell and Emily Blackwell, *Address on the Medical Education of Women* (New York: Baptist & Taylor, 1864), 5.

28 John F. Bresnahan and Harriet L. Borman, "A Uniformed Hospital Personnel," *The Modern Hospital* 20, no. 4 (1923): 379.

29 Ibid.

30 Ibid., 381.

31 Barco Uniforms, "Barco Uniforms Celebrates 90th Anniversary," PRN News Wire, August 2, 2019, at: https://www.prnewswire.com/news-releases/barco-uniforms-celebrates-90th-anniversary-300895530.html.

32 "Detachable Shoulder Pads in Uniforms," *Women's Wear Daily*, December 6, 1945, 22.

33 "Pastel Nylon in Coast Line of Nurse's Uniforms," *Women's Wear Daily*, July 1, 1948, 28.

34 "L.A. Hospital Prescribes Pastel Nylon Uniforms," *Women's Wear Daily*, June 27, 1949, 29.

35 "Nylon Seersucker," *Women's Wear Daily*, May 22, 1950, 28.

36 "Unmounted Sleeves in New Uniform," *Women's Wear Daily*, September 25, 1950, 34.

37 "In Los Angeles Uniforms Lines: Less 'Uniformity' Spurs Orders," *Women's Wear Daily*, April 21, 1952, 30.

38 "Defense Plans Boom Uniform Preparations on West Coast," April 30, 1951, 16.

39 Barco Uniforms, "Barco Uniforms Celebrates."

40 Advertisement for Barco of California in *RN* 13, no. 1 (October 1949): 4–5.

41 "Candy Stripers Provide Cheery Note in Washington University Clinics," *Hospital Record* 12, no. 9 (September 1958): 13–16.

42 Betsey R. Carroll, "From Candy Stripers to Nursing Career—Well-Planned Program Does It," *Hospital Topics* 42, no. 7 (1964): 44–6.

43 The earliest use of this term I have found was in 1921. "Bellevue Teens Donate Candy Striper Hours," *The Wayne Herald* (Wayne, Nebraska), September 16, 1921, 13.

44 Centers for Disease Control and Prevention, "How TB Spreads," US Department of Health & Human Services, 2016, at: https://www.cdc.gov/tb/topic/basics/howtbspreads.htm.

45 Julius A. Roth, "Ritual and Magic in the Control of Contagion," *American Sociological Review* 22, no. 3 (1957): 312.

46 Ibid., 314.

47 With inflation, the equivalent prices today would be roughly US$50–US$160.

48 Cordelia W. Kelly, "What Nurses Want in a Uniform," *American Journal of Nursing* 57, no. 10 (1957): 1282–4.

49 Mark S. Hochberg, "The Doctor's White Coat: An Historical Perspective," *AMA Journal of Ethics*, 2007, at: https://journalofethics.ama-assn.org/article/doctors-white-coat-historical-perspective/2007-04.

50 *Angelica Washable Service Uniforms*, 16. "Duck" is now better known as canvas.

51 Belkin, "Use of Scrubs."

52 John L. Dillon, Jr., 1990, "Unisex Scrub Shirt and Methods for Making Same," US Patent 5,083,315A, filed December 13, 1990, and issued January 28, 1992.

53 Rudolph Landau founded his business (which is still family owned) in Memphis, Tennessee, in 1938. Although his first market was uniforms for mechanics and gas station attendants, Landau is now known primarily for its medical uniforms. Landau Uniforms, "Landau: Our Story," landau.com, 2022, at: https://www.landau.com/about.

54 Cherokee, founded in Venice Beach, California, in 1973, described itself as "an iconic American family lifestyle brand, offering classic, casual comfort at great value." See Cherokee USA, "Our Story," cherokeeusa.com, 2022, at: http://www.cherokeeusa.com/our-story.

55 Likely a corruption of the French word for sky (*ciel*), "ceil blue" is a medium blue tint.

56 Janet Muff, *Socialization, Sexism, and Stereotyping: Women's Issues in Nursing* (St. Louis, Missouri: Mosby, 1982), ix.

57 Shermalayne Southard Szasz, "The Tyranny of Uniforms," in *Socialization, Sexism, and Stereotyping: Women's Issues in Nursing*, edited by Janet Muff (St. Louis, Missouri: Mosby, 1982), 400–1.

58 "Capless Nurse Reinstated in Dispute Over Uniforms," *American Journal of Nursing* 71, no. 1 (1971): 12.

59 "The Flight of the Nightingale" aired in 1982, season 7, episode 17.

60 Elizabeth Rider, "Pink Scrubs," *British Medical Journal*, 336, no. 7638 (2008): 277.

61 Julie Hatfield, "Hospital Scrubs Suits Hit the Streets," *Boston Globe*, May 29, 1980, 61.

62 Interview with Dr. Charles Rosen, clinical professor of orthopedic surgery at UC-Irvine, for "Scrubs as Streetwear." *AllWays in Fashion*, November 5, 2015, at: http://allwaysinfashion.blogspot.com/2015/11/scrubs-as-streetwear.html.

63 Prince, "Prince – 1999 (Official Music Video)," YouTube, 1982, at: https://www.youtube.com/watch?v=rblt2EtFfC4.

64 Kim Best, "Hospitals Crack Down on Scrub Suit Pilfering," *The Herald-Sun* (Durham, North Carolina), April 30, 1983, 68.

65 "All of the Sexiest Man Alive Covers," *People Magazine*, November 10, 2021, at: https://people.com/celebrity/all-the-sexiest-man-alive-covers/?slide=b7c2cf75-809b-438c-aa24-8ccfb5e87cdf#b7c2cf75-809b-438c-aa24-8ccfb5e87cdf.

66 David M. Erdma, "Medical Scrub Garment Thieves May Face Change in Uniform," *The Morning Call* (Allentown, Pennsylvania), January 6, 1986, 6.

67 Scripps Howard News Service, "Scrub Suit Dispensers Stop Thefts," *The Salina Journal* (Salina, Kansas), December 24, 1987, 10.

68 Paddy Calistro, "For Some Modern Nurses, Clara Barton Look is Out," *Los Angeles Times*, July 22, 1988, G1.

69 Ibid.

70 Piera Sanna et al., "The Nurses' Uniform in Pediatrics, The Opinion of Children and Nurses," *Acta Biomedica* 91, supplement 2 (2020): 67–76. In adults, this fear is known as "white coat syndrome."

71 The collaboration with Kellogg's was for a limited time in 2016. The collaboration with Betsey Johnson, a fashion brand based in New York City, started in 2019 and is ongoing, even though Betsey Johnson also produces its own line. Koi Design, "About Us," Koi by Kathy Peterson, 2021, at: https://www.koihappiness.com/our-story/.

72 Suzanne Kronsberg, Josephine Rachel Bouret, and Anne Liners Brett, "Lived Experiences of Male Nurses: Dire Consequences for the Nursing Profession," *Journal of Nursing Education and Practice* 8, no. 1 (2018): 46–53.

73 Ibid.

74 Barco Uniforms, "Our Story," Grey's Anatomy Scrubs, 2022, at: https://www.greysanatomyscrubs.com/our-story/.

75 Rob Walker, "Branding Operation: Reference a Fictional TV Hospital Drama in Real-Life Hospital Scrubs," *New York Times*, October 3, 2010, SM19.

76 Dickies, "Dickies Heritage: On the Job Since 1922," dickies.com, 2022, at: https://www.dickies.com/history.html. Carhartt, "Outworking Them All Since 1889," carhartt.com, 2022, https://www.carhartt.com/carhartt-history?icid=abouthistory_042721_carhartt-history_allvisitors.

77 Vanessa Hsieh, "A Brief History of Baby Phat, the Cult 00s Label Bringing Sexy Back," *Dazed*, March 12, 2019, at: https://www.dazeddigital.com/fashion/article/43682/1/baby-phat-cult-00s-y2k-fashion-label-hip-hop-kimora-lee-simmons-lil-kim-aaliyah.

78 Vera Bradley, "About Us," verabradley.com, 2022, at: https://verabradley.com/pages/about-us.

79 Janina Lynn Misiewicz, "Conditional Recognition and the Popularization of the Contemporary Wellness Industry," (MA thesis, Dartmouth College, Hanover, New Hampshire, 2021).

80 Ruth La Ferla, "Hospitals are Discovering Their Inner Spa," *New York Times*, August 13, 2000, ST1.

81 Ibid.

82 Healing Hands Scrubs, "Our Story," healinghandsscrubs.com, 2022, at: https://healinghandsscrubs.com/pages/our-story.

83 Noel Asmar Uniforms, "Medical and Dental Uniforms," noelasmaruniforms.com, 2022, at: https://www.noelasmaruniforms.com/collections/industries-medical-dental-all.

84 Sydney Lupkin, "Ebola in America: Timeline of the Deadly Virus," ABC News, November 17, 2014, at: https://abcnews.go.com/Health/ebola-america-timeline/story?id=26159719.

85 Eugene Furman et al., "Prediction of Personal Protective Equipment Use in Hospitals During COVID-19," *Health Care Management Science* 24 (2021): 439–53.

86 Belkin, "Use of Scrubs," 403. The Occupational Safety and Health Act (OSHA) was established in 1970 to "ensure safe and healthful working conditions for workers by setting and enforcing standards." Occupational Safety and Health Administration, "About OSHA," US Department of Labor, 2022, at: https://www.osha.gov/aboutosha#:~:text=OSHA's%20Mission,%2C%20outreach%2C%20education%20and%20assistance.

87 Elissa J. Zhang, et al., "Protecting the Environment from Plastic PPE," *British Medical Journal* 372, no. 109 (2021), Doi: 10.1136/bmj.n109.

88 F. Selcen Kilinc Balci, "Isolation Gowns in Health Care Settings: Laboratory Studies, Regulations and Standards, and Potential Barriers of Gown Selection and Use," *American Journal of Infection Control* 44, no. 1 (2016): 104–11.

89 W. Nocker, "Evaluation of Occupational Clothing for Surgeons: Achieving Comfort and Avoiding Physiological Stress Through Suitable Gowns," in *Handbook of Medical Textiles*, edited by V. T. Bartels (Cambridge: Woodhead Publishing, 2011), 443–60.

90 Jon Herskovitz, "Texas Hospital Reaches Settlement with Nurse Infected with Ebola," Reuters, October 24, 2016, at: https://www.reuters.com/article/us-health-ebola-texas-nurse/texas-hospital-reaches-settlement-with-nurse-infected-with-ebola-idUSKCN12O2AF.

91 N95 masks fit more closely than surgical masks and provide better protection against airborne and bloodborne diseases. US Food and Drug Administration, "N95 Respirators, Surgical Masks, Face Masks, and Barrier Face Coverings," Medical Devices, September 15, 2021, at: https://www.fda.gov/medical-devices/personal-protective-equipment-infection-control/n95-respirators-surgical-masks-face-masks-and-barrier-face-coverings.

92 Committee on Oversight and Government Reform, "The Ebola Crisis: Coordination of a Multi-Agency Response," Serial No. 113-163, Washington, DC: US House of Representatives, October 24, 2014, 75, at: https://www.govinfo.gov/content/pkg/CHRG-113hhrg94053/pdf/CHRG-113hhrg94053.pdf.

93 Ibid., 78.

94 Jennifer Cohen and Yana van der Meulen Rodgers, "Contributing Factors to Personal Protective Equipment Shortages During the COVID-19 Pandemic," *Preventative Medicine* 141 (2020): 6, Doi: 10.1016/j.ypmed.2020.106263.

95　Timothy N. Snavely, "A Brief Economic Analysis of the Looming Nursing Shortage in the United States," *Nursing Economics* 34, no. 2 (2016): 98–100; and Lauren Hilgers, "The Future of Work Issue: 'Nurses Have Finally Learned What They're Worth,'" *New York Times*, February 15, 2022, at: https://www.nytimes.com/2022/02/15/magazine/traveling-nurses.html.

96　Fred Davis, *Fashion, Culture, and Identity* (Chicago, Illinois: University of Chicago Press), 70.

97　Ibid., 66.

98　Ibid., 85.

99　Ibid., 98.

Chapter 5

1　Stefano Tonchi, "Military Style," in *The Berg Companion to Fashion*, ed. Valerie Steele (Oxford: Bloomsbury Academic, 2010), 507–8.

2　Sarah Scaturro, "From Combat to Couture: Camouflage in Fashion" (MA thesis, Fashion Institute of Technology, New York), i.

3　Betty Luther Hillman, *Dressing for the Culture Wars: Style and the Politics of Self-Presentation in the 1960s & 1970s* (Lincoln, Nebraska: University of Nebraska Press, 2015).

4　Arthur Asa Berger, *Searching for a Self: Identity in Popular Culture, Media and Society* (Wilmington, Delaware: Vernon Press, 2022).

5　Leon Gurevitch, "The Stereoscopic Attraction: Three-Dimensional Images and the Spectacular Paradigm, 1850–2013," *Convergence: The International Journal of Research into New Media Technologies* 19, no. 4 (2013): 396–405.

6　J. W. Hanson, *The Official History of the Fair, St. Louis, 1904: The Sights and Scenes of the Louisiana Purchase Exposition* (St. Louis: St. Louis Fair Officials, 1904), 461–2.

7　Marshall Joseph Becker, "Lenape ('Delaware') Mail Carriers and the Origins of the US Postal Service," *American Indian Culture and Research Journal* 39, no. 3 (2015): 99–121.

8　Winifred Gallagher, *How the Post Office Created America: A History* (New York: Penguin Books, 2016).

9　Until the late 1800s, "frock coats" were more common for men's suits, a long jacket with a seam at the waist and pleats at the hips (allowing the wearer to ride a hose without taking his jacket off). "Sack coats," which are shorter, less expensive, and easier to construct, are now the dominant style.

10　US Postal Service, "Letter Carriers' Uniform: Overview," usps.com, 2002, at: https://about.usps.com/who-we-are/postal-history/letter-carrier-uniform-overview.pdf.

11　NALC, a national labor union established in 1889 in Milwaukee, was a charter member of the ALF-CIO and is still in operation today. National Association of

Letter Carriers, "About NALC: Labor Ties," nalc.org, 2022, at: https://www.nalc.org/about/labor-ties.

12 In 1880, Browning, King & Co. had retail shops in St. Louis, Philadelphia, Chicago, and Milwaukee selling millions of dollars in wool suits. Dan C. Young, "A Card to Buyers of Stylish and Artistic Clothing," *St. Louis Post-Dispatch* (St. Louis, Missouri), March 24, 1880, 4.

13 Plymouth Rock Pants Company, advertisement in *The Boston Globe*, April 24, 1888, 2.

14 "Substitute Carriers' Association Formed," *The Postal Record* 3, no. 3 (1890): 51.

15 "Brooklyn Notes," *The Postal Record* 3, no. 9 (1890): 190.

16 "Nashville, Tenn.," *The Postal Record* 4, no. 2 (1891): 36.

17 "Brooklyn Notes," 190.

18 US Postal Service, "Letter Carrier's Uniform," 1.

19 "Malden, Mass.," *The Postal Record* 3, no. 10 (1890): 217.

20 "German silver" is a mixture of copper, zinc, and nickel. Note associated with object 1992.2002.131, Smithsonian National Postal Museum.

21 US Postal Service, "Letter Carrier's Uniform," 3.

22 US Postal Service, "Star Routes," usps.com, 2007, at: https://about.usps.com/who-we-are/postal-history/star-routes.pdf.

23 Miantae Metcalf McConnell, "Mary Field's Road to Freedom," in *Black Cowboys in the American West: On the Range, On the Stage, Behind the Badge*, edited by Bruce A. Glasrud and Michael N. Searles (Norman, Oklahoma: University of Oklahoma Press, 2016), 149–68.

24 US Postal Service, "Star Routes," 1.

25 US Postal Service, "Letter Carriers' Uniform," 3.

26 *Who's Your Tailor?* (Chicago, Illinois: Ed. V. Price & Company, 1936–7).

27 See note associated with a First World War officer's uniform 2009.300.2986a-t at the Metropolitan Museum of Art. Also, B. Granville Baker, "The Mirror of Fashion," *Journal of the Society for Army Historical Research* 17, no. 68 (1938): 205–7.

28 Named after a popular style of jacket commissioned by General Eisenhower during the Second World War, the Eisenhower jacket is shorter than a sack coat and fits closely at the waist.

29 US Postal Service, "Letter Carriers' Uniforms," 4–5.

30 "Postal Rates, Postal Pay Hikes," *Congressional Quarterly Almanac*, Volume 10 (Washington, DC: Congressional Quarterly News Features, 1954), 385–8.

31 The first allowance was $100 per year, regardless of the individual's length of service. National Association of Letter Carriers, "Looking the Part: The Letter Carrier Uniform," *The Postal Record* 133, no. 9 (2020): 20–1.

32 US Postal Service, "Letter Carriers' Uniforms," 5–6.

33 The US GAO is an independent agency that provides financial advice to Congress and investigates government spending. US Government Accountability Office, "The

Role of the GAO in Assisting Congressional Oversight," gao.gov, 2002, at: https://www.gao.gov/products/gao-02-816t.

34 US Government Accountability Office, "US Postal Service: Information on Centralized Procurement of Uniforms, Report #B-279075," gao.gov, January 28, 1998, at: https://www.gao.gov/assets/ggd-98-58r.pdf.

35 Ibid., 5.

36 US Postal Service, "Updated Uniform Allowance Vendor Listing," usps.gov, 2019, at: https://liteblue.usps.gov/humanresources/ourworkforce/uniforms/pdf/updated-uniform-allowance-vendor-listing-may2019.pdf.

37 "Esprit de corps" is French for "spirit of the body," which the US Marine Corps describes as good "individual and group morale." Dan Stallard, "Esprit de Corps: Moral and Force Preservation," *Marine Corps Gazette* (2018): 78, at: https://www.hqmc.marines.mil/Portals/61/Users/254/50/4350/Esprit%20de%20Corps_Morale_Force%20Preservation_Stallard_Gazzette_April%2018.pdf.

38 US Postal Service, "930: Work Clothes and Uniforms," *Employee and Labor Relations Manual*, 2022, at: https://about.usps.com/manuals/elm/html/elmc9_009.htm#ep96853.

39 In 2014, Congress passed a law known as the Berry Amendment, requiring the Department of Defense to procure military uniforms (and many other items) from domestic sources out of concerns about short-term and long-term security. See Valerie Bailey Grasso, "The Berry Amendment: Requiring Defense Procurement to Come from Domestic Sources," Washington, DC: Congressional Research Service, February 24, 2014.

40 Ibid., "931.263: When to Wear Uniforms."

41 In 2020, the allowance was US$464 per year. National Association of Letter Carriers, "Looking the Part," 20.

42 Ibid.

43 18 US Code §1730, "Uniforms of Carriers," 1948, at: https://www.law.cornell.edu/uscode/text/18/1730.

44 For example, Postal Uniforms Direct, an online supplier, requires buyers to have an activated Postal Allowance Credit Card to buy anything with an emblem. Postal Uniforms Direct, "Frequently Asked Questions," postaluniformsdirect.com, 2022, at: https://www.postaluniformsdirect.com/Pages/FAQS.

45 eBay, "Government Items Policy," ebay.com, 2022, at: https://www.ebay.com/help/policies/prohibited-restricted-items/government-items-policy?id=4318&st=12&pos=1&query=Government%20items%20policy&intent=government&context=9010_BUYER&docId=HELP1254.

46 Walter Curt Behrendt, "Off-Street Parking: A City Planning Problem," *Journal of Land & Public Utility Economics* 16, no. 4 (1940): 464–7.

47 Robert Emmett Smith, "The Development and Impact of the Parking Meter Before World War II" (MA thesis, Oklahoma State University, 1960).

48 Ibid., 5.

49 Carl Magee, 1935, "Coin Controlled Parking Meter," US Patent 2,118,318, filed May 13, 1935, and issued May 24, 1938.

50 "City Ready to Try Parking Meters," *The Oklahoma News* (Oklahoma City, Oklahoma), February 25, 1935, 2.

51 "Have Your Nickel Handy Tuesday and Don't Expect to Get Gum Out of Parking Meters," *The Oklahoma News* (Oklahoma City, Oklahoma), July 14, 1935, 3.

52 William V. Bachelder, "Limitations on the Municipal Use of Parking Meters," *Journal of Criminal Law and Criminology* 40, no. 5 (1950): 601–6.

53 Herman Goldstein, "Police Discretion: The Ideal Versus the Real," *Public Administration Review* 23, no. 3 (1963): 140.

54 Ibid.

55 "Meter Maids Lauded," *The Salt Lake Tribune* (Salt Lake City, Utah), December 21, 1954, 14.

56 Joseph T. Carroll, "Recruiting and Training of Police Personnel," *FBI Enforcement Bulletin* 33, no. 12 (1964): 7.

57 Although women had been serving in the military as nurses for several decades, the WAVES (Women Accepted for Volunteer Emergency Service) and WAACs (Women's Army Auxiliary Corps) were established in 1942 to allow other types of service such as weather forecasting, code breaking, rigging parachutes, and flying cargo planes. Doris Weatherford, *American Women During World War II: An Encyclopedia* (New York: Routledge, 2010).

58 Kathleen M. Ryan, "Uniform Matters: Fashion Design in World War II Women's Recruitment," *Journal of American Culture* 37, no. 4 (2014): 419–29.

59 Ibid, 420.

60 "New Meter Maid Getting Used to 15-Mile Walks," *Janesville Daily Gazette* (Janesville, Wisconsin), July 1, 1964, 9.

61 Kerry Segrave, *Policewomen: A History* (Jefferson, North Carolina: McFarland & Company, Inc., 2014).

62 "Meter Maids," *Abilene Reporter-News* (Abilene, Texas), January 4, 1965, 6.

63 "Meter Maids Too Fat: Battle of Scales Erupts in New York," *Wilkes-Barre Times Leader* (Wilkes-Barre, Pennsylvania), July 31, 1965, 11.

64 "Meter Maids Lose Battle of Bulge," *The Daily Notes* (Canonsburg, Pennsylvania), September 9, 1965, 7.

65 Ibid.

66 Kim Novak was best known for her role in Alfred Hitchcock's film, *Vertigo* (Alfred J. Hitchcock Productions, 1958).

67 "Meter Maids Too Fat."

68 "Male Meter Maids," *The Times Record* (Troy, New York), December 8, 1965, 8.

69 Robert L. Snow, *Policewomen Who Made History: Breaking Through the Ranks* (Lanham, Maryland: Rowman & Littlefield, 2010).

70 Pittsburg, Kansas changed the job title to "parking assistant." "Pittsburg Takes on New Aim for Its Meter Maids," *Great Bend Tribune* (Great Bend, Kansas), December 17, 1965, 7.

71 In the 1960s in Abilene, Texas, "the meter maids [were] transferred from the police department to the traffic department." Tanya Eiserer, "First 'Police Women' Limited in Duties," *Abilene Reporter-News* (Abilene, Texas), August 3, 1997, 10.

72 Victoria Vantoch, *The Jet Sex: Airline Stewardesses and the Making of an American Icon* (Philadelphia, Pennsylvania: University of Pennsylvania Press, 2013). SFO Museum, *Fashion in Flight: A History of Airline Uniform Design* (San Francisco, California: San Francisco Airports Commission, 2020).

73 "Parking Control Officer (#8214)," City and County of San Francisco, September 12, 2012, at: https://www.jobapscloud.com/SF/specs/classspecdisplay.asp?ClassNumber=8214.

74 Ibid.

75 Flying Cross is a division of Fechheimer Brothers Co. Established in 1842, Fechheimer began manufacturing uniforms during the Civil War, 1861–5. Fechheimer Brothers Co., "About Us," fechheimer.com, 2013, at: https://www.fechheimer.com/.

76 Berkeley Police Department, "Parking Enforcement Operations Manual," City of Berkeley, California, February 4, 2015, 28, at: https://www.cityofberkeley.info/uploadedFiles/Police/Level_3_-_General/PEOManual111814rev3.pdf.

77 Ibid.

78 Department of Public Works, "About DPW," District of Columbia, 2022, at: https://dpw.dc.gov/page/about-dpw.

79 District of Columbia, "Standard Operating Procedures for Parking Officers and Supervisory Parking Officers," dpw.gov, 2011, 13, at: https://dpw.dc.gov/sites/default/files/dc/sites/dpw/publication/attachments/Parking%20Enforcement%20SOP%20final%20edition%202011.rev%2011%202%2011.pdf.

80 Ibid., 15.

81 Student Conservation Association, "Everything You Wanted to Know about Park Rangers... But Were Afraid to Ask," thesca.org, 2021, at: https://www.thesca.org/connect/blog/everything-you-wanted-know-about-park-rangers...-were-afraid-ask.

82 Park Ranger Division, "Policies and Procedures Manual," City of Los Angeles Department of Recreation and Parks, October 5, 2019, 1, at: https://www.laparks.org/sites/default/files/ranger/pdf/2020%20Manual%20for%20Web.pdf.

83 Department of State Parks and Cultural Resources, "Uniform Policy," State of Wyoming, March 8, 2010, 2, at: http://spcrintranet.wyo.gov/UNIFORM%20POLICY%20-%20updated%203-8-10.pdf.

84 In many states, public agencies are allowed (or even required) to purchase items such as furniture and uniforms from state prison industries. For an overview of how these programs work, see US Government Accountability Office, "Federal Prison Industries: Actions Needed to Evaluate Program Effectiveness," gao.gov, July 2020, at: https://www.gao.gov/assets/gao-20-505.pdf.

85 Sara Jernigan, Steve Austin, and Amanda Palmer, "USACE Natural Resource Management Uniform Program," US Army Corps of Engineers, April 18, 2017, at: https://corpslakes.erdc.dren.mil/employees/conferences/17National/Park%20 Ranger%20Uniforms.pdf.

86 R. Bryce Workman, *National Park Service Uniforms: In Search of an Identity (1872–1920)* (Harpers Ferry, West Virginia: National Park Service, 1994), 3.

87 Ibid., 16.

88 Parker, Bridget & Co. was a large department store in Washington, DC. Like the uniforms of Pullman porters sold by Marshall Fields department store, it is unclear who actually manufactured the uniforms.

89 Workman, *In Search of an Identity*, 17.

90 R. Bryce Workman, *National Park Service Uniforms: Breeches, Blouses and Skirts (1918–1991)* (Harpers Ferry, West Virginia: National Park Service, 1998), 4–10.

91 Ibid., 14.

92 Ibid., 15–16.

93 Ibid., 17–21.

94 Note associated with Figure 5.18, at: https://npgallery.nps.gov/AssetDetail/ e2e170c8-3f6f-4aeb-b1de-3745ea9b40d2.

95 Workman, *Breeches, Blouses and Skirts*, 42.

96 Ibid., 52.

97 The Flight 93 Memorial was established in 2002 to commemorate one of the flights hijacked on 9/11, which crashed into a field in Pennsylvania. It opened to the public in 2015. William J. White and Lisa A. Emili, "Purification and Translation in Public Memory: 'Healing the Landscape' at the Flight 93 National Memorial," *Emotion, Space and Society* 29 (2018): 32–47.

98 *Reference Manual 43: Uniforms* (Washington, DC: US National Park Service, October 2000), 29.

99 "Arrowhead patch" refers to the official insignia of the NPS. Pairs of metal "sequoia cones" (pinecones) are used as used as ornaments on NPS hats and belts.

100 Robert Stanton, "Director's Order #43: Uniform Program," US National Park Service, October 2000, at: https://www.nps.gov/policy/DOrders/DOrder43.htm.

101 Ryan Curran White, "What's the Story of the Iconic National Park Service Ranger 'Flat Hat'?" Golden Gate National Parks Conservancy, June 21, 2019, at: https:// www.parksconservancy.org/gateways-article/what-is-story-iconic-nps-ranger-flat-hat.

102 M. Melia Lane-Kamahele, "Considerations of Culture, Community, Change, and the Centennial," *George Wright Forum* 30, no. 2 (2013): 109.

103 Ibid, 113.

104 Workwear Outfitters, "Who We Are," wwof.com, 2022, at: https://test.wwof.com/who-we-are.

105 VF Imagewear, "LMA Online Uniform System," vfimagewear.com, 2022, at: https://uniforms.vfimagewear.com/vfweb/rwdprogram/coms/index_lma.htm.

106 The Okeechobee Waterway was designing to control flooding in the Everglades but allows recreational boat travel across southern Florida from the Gulf of Mexico to the Atlantic Ocean.

107 US Office of Personnel Management, "Classification & Qualifications: Park Ranger Series, 0025," opm.gov, 2022, at: https://www.opm.gov/policy-data-oversight/classification-qualifications/general-schedule-qualification-standards/0000/park-ranger-series-0025/.

108 Alexander S. Gorzalski and Anne L. Spiesman, "Washington Aqueduct: Serving Our Nation's Capital for Over 150 Years," *Journal (American Water Works Association)* 108, no. 2 (2016): 40–7.

109 Fran P. Mainella, "Director's Order #9: Law Enforcement Program," US National Park Service, March 23, 2006, at: https://www.nps.gov/policy/DOrders/DOrder9.html.

110 Sandra E. Weissinger and Dwayne A. Mack (eds.), *Law Enforcement in the Age of Black Lives Matter: Policing Black and Brown Bodies* (Lanham, Maryland: Lexington Books, 2021).

111 Jernigan, "USACE," slide 35.

112 Human Technologies Corporation, "USACE Press Release," htcorp.net, 2021, at: https://htcorp.net/usace/.

113 Candice Batton and Steve Wilson, "Police Murders: An Examination of Historical Trends in the Killing of Law Enforcement Officers in the United States, 1947 to 1998," *Homicide Studies* 10, no. 2 (2006): 79–97. Edward R. Maguire, Justin Nix, and Bradley A. Campbell, "A War on Cops? The Effects of Ferguson on the Number of US Police Officers Murdered in the Line of Duty," *Justice Quarterly* 34, no. 5 (2017): 739–58.

114 Department of Justice, "Coldspring Man Gets Life in Postal Carrier Death Case," US Attorney's Office, Southern District of Texas, December 6, 2021, at: https://www.justice.gov/usao-sdtx/pr/coldspring-man-gets-life-postal-carrier-death-case.

Chapter 6

1 "Fortune 500," *Fortune*, 2021, at: https://fortune.com/fortune500/.

2 Internal documents define "Walmart blue" as Pantone 285C. "Associate Brand Visual Identity," Walmart Stores, Inc., 2020, at: https://one.walmart.com/content/dam/px/associate_brand_center/all-company-brand-guidelines/AssociateBrand_VISID_200203.pdf.

3 Erik Sherman, "How Wal-Mart's 'Dress Code' Costs Employees," *Forbes*, September 8, 2014, at: https://www.forbes.com/sites/eriksherman/2014/09/08/how-walmarts-dress-code-costs-employees/?sh=1db6aea07e00.

4 Hayley Peterson, "Wal-Mart Employees Explain Why the New Dress Code is So Infuriating," *Business Insider*, September 5, 2014, at: https://www.businessinsider.com/wal-mart-employees-protest-dress-code-2014-9.

5 Thanks to legal historian Laura Edwards for drawing my attention to "master–servant" as a legal category for understanding certain types of workers (not just household servants).

6 Al Norman, "Wal-Mart's 'Invisible Army' of Lobbyists," *Huffington Post*, September 21, 2013, at: https://www.huffpost.com/entry/walmart-lobbyists_b_3632526.

7 Lloyd Klein and Steve Lang. "Truth, Justice and the Walmart Way: Consequences of a Retailing Behemoth," in *The Routledge International Handbook of the Crimes of the Powerful*, edited by Gregg Barak (Abingdon: Routledge, 2015), 121–31. John Logan, "The Mounting Guerilla War Against the Reign of Walmart," *New Labor Forum* 23, no. 1 (2014): 22–9.

8 Françoise Carré and Chris Tilly, "America's Biggest Low-Wage Industry: Continuity and Change in Retail Jobs," Center for Social Policy at the University of Massachusetts Boston, 2008, 1, at: https://scholarworks.umb.edu/cgi/viewcontent.cgi?article=1021&context=csp_pubs.

9 Ibid, 10.

10 "Overview: Receptionist," Sokanu Interactive, 2022, at: https://www.careerexplorer.com/careers/receptionist/.

11 Habbo Knoch, "Life on Stage: Grand Hotels as Urban Interzones Around 1900," in *Creative Urban Milieus: Historical Perspectives on Cultures, Economy, and the City*, eds. Martina Heßler and Clemens Zimmermann (Frankfurt: Campus Verlag, 2008), 137–57.

12 Paul E. Groth, *Living Downtown: The History of Residential Hotels in the United States* (Berkeley, California: University of California Press, 1994), 7.

13 J. Robert Lilly and Richard A. Ball, "No-Tell Motel: The Management of Social Invisibility," *Urban Life* 10, no. 2 (1981): 179–98.

14 Groth, *Living Downtown*, 202.

15 John D. Lesure, "Motor Hotels and Market Studies: The Accountant's Role," *New York Certified Public Accountant* 29, no. 7 (1959): 499–504.

16 Kemmons Wilson, "How to Make Your Guests Happy," *Business Perspectives* 12, no. 4 (2000): 32.

17 Wallace E. Johnson, *Together We Build: The Life and Faith of Wallace E. Johnson* (New York: Hawthorn Books, 1978), 2.

18 Eric E. Bergsten, "Credit Cards: A Prelude to the Cashless Society," *Boston College Industrial and Commercial Law Review* 8, no. 3 (1967): 485–518.

19 Donald E. Lundberg, "Kemmons Wilson: The Key to Marketing Success Might Well Be Defined as Holiday Inns of America," *Cornell Hotel and Restaurant Administration Quarterly* 9, no. 4 (1969): 100–3.

20 Note associated with object THF287361 at the Henry Ford Museum of American Innovation, press kit from Holiday Inns of America, Inc. *c.* 1979, at: https://www.thehenryford.org/collections-and-research/digital-collections/artifact/455755/~ide=gs-431723.

21 Lundberg, "Kemmons Wilson," 101.

22 Leonard L. Berry, "Franchising: Some Words of Caution for the Small Businessman," *Journal of Small Business Management* 11, no. 4 (1973): 3.

23 For comparison, this is the average size of an IKEA store.

24 Johnson, *Together We Build*, 106.

25 Marylin Bender, "The Hospitality Crusade: Holiday Inns Spreading from Kyoto to Paducah," *New York Times*, August 26, 1973, 1 and 11.

26 Choice Hotels International, "A History of Innovation," choicehotels.com, 2022, at: https://www.choicehotels.com/about/corporate-history.

27 Wyndham Hotels & Resorts, "Our Brands," wyndhamhotels.com, 2022, at: https://www.wyndhamhotels.com/wyndham-rewards/our-brands.

28 IHG Hotels & Resorts, "Haute Hospitality: Uniform Collection MOMENTUM by Timo Weiland for Crowne Plaza Debuts at New York Fashion Week," ihgplc.com, August 10, 2017, at: https://www.ihgplc.com/news-and-media/news-releases/2017/haute-hospitality-uniform-collection-momentum-by-timo-weiland-for-crowne-plaza.

29 Cintas Corporation, "Direct Purchase Uniforms," cintas.com, 2022, at: https://www.cintas.com/industries/hospitality/uniforms/.

30 Cintas Corporation, "Hotel Uniform Rental," cintas.com, 2022, at: https://www.cintas.com/industries/hospitality/rental-uniforms/.

31 Corporate Image Group, "Custom Apparel," corporateimagegroup.com, 2022, at: https://corporateimagegroup.com/services/custom-apparel/.

32 RB Apparel, "Home Page," rbapparel.com, 2022, at: https://www.rbapparel.com/bwlogoshop/default.asp.

33 Executive Apparel, "About Us," executiveapparel.com, 2021, at: https://executiveapparel.com/about-us/.

34 Executive Apparel, "Hospitality: Rising from the Ashes," executiveapparel.com, March 10, 2021, at: https://executiveapparel.com/hospitality-rising-from-the-ashes/.

35 Top Hat Imagewear, "Front Desk Collection: Style ID FD358," tophatimagewear.com, 2022, at: https://tophatimagewear.com/collections/front-desk.

36 Ibid.

37 Eugene Nelson White, "Before the Glass-Steagall Act: An Analysis of the Investment Banking Activities of National Banks," *Explorations in Economic History* 23, no. 1 (1986): 33–55.

38 Bergsten, "Credit Cards," 485.

39 Ibid., 486.

40 Victor Savikas and Fred Shandling, "Credit Cards: A Survey of the Bank Card Revolution and Applicability of the Uniform Commercial Code," *DePaul Law Review* 16, no. 2 (1967): 389–408.

41 David L. Stearns, *Electronic Value Exchange: Origins of the Visa Electronic Payment System* (London: Springer, 2011).

42 Charles W. Calomiris, *US Bank Deregulation in Historical Perspective* (Cambridge: Cambridge University Press, 2000).

43 Federal Deposit Insurance Corporation, "Historical Bank Data," fdic.gov, December 31, 2021, at: https://banks.data.fdic.gov/explore/historical.

44 US Bureau of Labor Statistics, "Occupational Outlook Handbook: Tellers," bls.gov, 2021, at: https://www.bls.gov/ooh/office-and-administrative-support/tellers.htm.

45 JP Morgan Chase, "Chase Apparel Dress Code," Between My Peers, 2010, at: http://betweenmypeers.com/wp-content/uploads/2010/06/chase_dressguidelines.doc.

46 Lands' End, "School Uniforms," landsend.com, 2022, at: https://www.landsend.com/shop/school-uniform/S-ytp.

47 Categories of business uniforms sold by Lands' End include trade shows, convenience stores, grocery stores, and property management. Lands' End, "Lands' End Business," landsend.com, 2022, at: https://business.landsend.com/?cm_mmc=lecom-_-corenavs.

48 Lands' End, "Custom Bank & Financial Uniform Clothing," landsend.com, 2022, at: https://business.landsend.com/Finance/c/78?&pageSize=72.

49 Lands' End, "Chase Store," landsend.com, 2022, at: https://business.landsend.com/store/chasestorena/.

50 Ashley Bray, "Dressing the Part," *ABA Banking Journal* 105, no. 3 (2013): 11.

51 Ibid.

52 Alyssa Guzman, "Bank of America Tells its Workers to DRESS DOWN," *Daily Mail*, December 3, 2021, at: https://www.dailymail.co.uk/news/article-10272073/Bank-America-tells-workers-DRESS-head-NYCs-Bryant-Park-office.html.

53 Sabine Parrish, "Competitive Coffee Making and the Crafting of the Ideal Barista," *Gastronomica: The Journal for Food Studies* 20, no. 2 (2020): 80.

54 Executive Office of the President of the United States, "Standard Occupational Classification Manual," US Bureau of Labor Statistics, 2018, 124–5, at: https://www.bls.gov/soc/2018/soc_2018_manual.pdf.

55 US Bureau of Labor Statistics, "Food and Beverage Serving and Related Workers," bls.gov, September 8, 2021, at: https://www.bls.gov/ooh/food-preparation-and-serving/food-and-beverage-serving-and-related-workers.htm#tab-1.

56 Businesses with fifty or more employees are obligated to provide health insurance to those who work full-time, defined as an "average at least 30 hours of service per week, or 130 hours of service per month." Many workers are limited to no more than 29 hours per week to avoid crossing this threshold. US Internal Revenue Service, "Identifying Full-time Employees," irs.gov, 2021, at: https://www.irs.gov/affordable-care-act/employers/identifying-full-time-employees#:~:text=Definition%20of%20Full%2DTime%20Employee,hours%20of%20service%20per%20month.

57 Parrish, "Competitive Coffee Making," 79.

58 Anna Diamond, "A Crispy, Salty, American History of Fast Food," *Smithsonian Magazine*, June 24, 2019, at: https://www.smithsonianmag.com/history/crispy-salty-american-history-fast-food-180972459/.

59 Marcia A. Morgado, "From Kitsch to Chic: The Transformation of Hawaiian Shirt Aesthetics," *Clothing and Textiles Research Journal* 21, no. 2 (2003): 75–88.

60 Valeria Nofri, "The Aesthetics of Kitsch: From Versace to Prada," in *Fashion Through History: Costumes, Symbols, Communication*, volume 2, edited by Giovanna Motta and Antonello Biagini (Newcastle upon Tyne: Cambridge Scholars Publishing, 2017), 280.

61 Dunkin' Donuts, "Dunkin' Donuts History," dunkindonuts.com, 2016, at: https://news.dunkindonuts.com/internal_redirect/cms.ipressroom.com.s3.amazonaws.com/285/files/201610/Dunkin%27%20Donuts%20History_11%203%2016.pdf.

62 The original owner of the uniform was Kathy Hoffman, who worked at the Mt. Penn Dunkin' Donuts in Reading, Pennsylvania in the early 1970s. Communication with seller via eBay, April 2022.

63 Barco Uniforms, "Our Story," barcouniforms.com, 2021, at: https://www.barcouniforms.com/about-us/.

64 Robert Zemeckis, *Back to the Future* (Universal Pictures, 1985).

65 The first advertisements for Crest Uniforms (also known as Crest Career Images) appeared in US newspapers in the 1960s. Based in New York City, the company closed in 2000 and workers received retraining as compensation for the North American Free Trade Agreement. National Archives, "Crest Uniform Company, New York, NY: Notice of Termination of Investigation," Federal Register, October, 22, 2002, at: https://www.federalregister.gov/documents/2002/10/22/02-26747/crest-uniform-company-new-york-ny-notice-of-termination-of-investigation.

66 I have an example of the Burger King polo shirt, worn in Eau Claire, Wisconsin, in my research collection.

67 Stephani K.A. Robson, "Turning the Tables: The Psychology of Design for High-volume Restaurants," *Cornell Hotel and Restaurant Administration Quarterly* 40, no. 3 (1999): 56.

68 Jenna R. Cummings et al., "Extending Expectancy Theory to Food Intake: Effect of a Simulated Fast-Food Restaurant on Highly and Minimally Processed Food Expectancies," *Clinical Psychological Science* 9, no. 6 (2021): 1115–27.

69 Thomas N. Robinson et al., "Effects of Fast Food Branding on Young Children's Taste Preferences," *Archives of Pediatric Adolescent Medicine* 161, no. 8 (2007): 792–7.

70 "Pizza Hut Launches Bold Streetwear Collection," *QSR Magazine*, July 28, 2021, at: https://www.qsrmagazine.com/news/pizza-hut-launches-bold-streetwear-collection.

71 Michelle M. Mello, Eric B. Rimm, and David M. Studdert, "The McLawsuit: The Fast-Food Industry and Legal Accountability for Obesity," *Health Affairs* 22, no. 6 (2003): 207–16.

72 Tracy Saelinger, "Out with the Red, in with the Gray: See McDonald's New Uniforms," *Today*, April 24, 2017, at: https://www.today.com/food/mcdonald-s-unveils-new-uniforms-t110736.

73 Anne V. Wilson and Silvia Bellezza, "Consumer Minimalism," *Journal of Consumer Research* 48, no. 5: 796–816.

74 Melissa Marra-Alvarez, "Minimalism/Maximalism," The Museum at FIT, May 28, 2019, to November 16, 2019, at: https://www.fitnyc.edu/museum/exhibitions/minimalism-maximalism.php.

75 Starbucks Corporation, "Starbucks Creative Expression: Color," starbucks.com, 2020, at: https://creative.starbucks.com/color/.

76 Lindsay B. Baker et al., "Trapped Sweat in Basketball Uniforms and the Effect on Sweat Loss Estimates," *Physiological Reports* 5, no. 18 (2017): e13463, Doi: 10.14814/phy2.13463.

77 Jon Johnson, "Prickly Heat: What You Need to Know," *Medical News Today*, October 4, 2017, at: https://www.medicalnewstoday.com/articles/319612.

78 Y. Zhang, H. P. Wang, and Y. H. Chen, "Capillary Effect of Hydrophobic Polyester Fiber Bundles with Noncircular Cross Section," *Journal of Applied Polymer Science* 102 (2006): 1405–12.

79 Zippia, "McDonald's Dress Code," zippia.com, 2022, at: https://www.zippia.com/mcdonald-s-careers-7238/dress-code/.

80 Santosh K. Verma et al., "Workers' Experience of Slipping in US Limited-Service Restaurants," *Journal of Occupational and Environmental Hygiene* 7, no. 9 (2010): 491.

81 Ibid., 497.

82 Pizza Hut, Inc., "Drive for Dough," pizzahut.com, 2022, at: https://jobs.pizzahut.com/restaurants/drivers.php?gclid=Cj0KCQjwxtSSBhDYARIsAEn0thT2aa0ZkpkHjd3H0rvY6lNB2jNxvP93WjOoH8bKv9b2H1Gka48F6FcaAuUsEALw_wcB#hero.

83 Wendy's, "Crew Member," wendys.com, 2021, at: https://wendys-careers.com/job-search/posting/Crew-Member/31598/, job opening in Ammon, Idaho.

84 Chipotle Mexican Grill, "Chipotle Careers," chipotle.com, 2022, at: https://jobs.chipotle.com/benefits.

85 Taco John's International, "Join our Team!" tacojohns.com, 2022, at: https://careers. tacojohns.com.

86 Starbucks Corporation, "Starbucks Dress Code Lookbook," starbucks.com, 2019, 2, at: https://stories.starbucks.com/wp-content/uploads/2019/01/Dress_Code_Look_ Book_-_US_English.pdf.

87 Ibid., 7.

88 Starbuckscoffeegear.com.

89 "Starbucks Corporation, "Starbucks Dress Code Lookbook," 12.

90 The first edition of *The McDonaldization of Society* was published in 1993. George Ritzer, *The McDonaldization of Society*, New Century edition (Thousand Oaks, California: Pine Forge Press, 2000), 114.

91 Ray Oldenburg, *The Great Good Place: Cafés, Coffee Shops, Community Centers, Beauty Parlors, General Stores, Bars, Hangouts, and How They Get You Through the Day* (New York: Paragon House, 1989).

92 Anthony T. Allred and H. Lon Addams, "Service Quality at Banks and Credit Unions: What do Their Customers Say?" *Managing Service Quality* 10, no. 1 (2000): 56.

93 Elaine J. Hall, "Smiling, Deferring, and Flirting: Doing Gender by Giving 'Good Service,'" *Work and Occupations* 20, no. 4 (1993): 452–71.

94 Marek Korczynski and Claire Evans, "Customer Abuse to Service Workers: An Analysis of its Social Creation Within the Service Economy," *Work, Employment and Society* 27, no. 5 (2013): 768–84.

95 Lloyd C. Harris and Emmanuel Ogbonna, "Motives for Service Sabotage: An Empirical Study of Front-line Workers," *The Service Industries Journal* 32, no. 13 (2012): 2027–46.

96 Hall, "Smiling, Deferring, and Flirting," 456.

97 Guenther E. Karch and Mike Peters, "The Impact of Employee Uniforms on Job Satisfaction in the Hospitality Industry," *Journal of Hotel & Business Management* 6, no. 1 (2017): 5, Doi: 10.4172/2169-0286.1000157.

98 Ibid.

99 Alexandros Paraskevas and Maureen Brookes, "Human Trafficking in Hotels: An 'Invisible' Threat for a Vulnerable Industry," *International Journal of Contemporary Hospitality Management* 30, no. 3 (2018): 1996–2014; Katarzyna Minor and Andy Heyes, "50 Shades of the Luxury Hospitality Industry," in *The Emerald Handbook of Luxury Management for Hospitality and Tourism*, edited by Anupama S. Kotur and Saurabh Kumar Dixit (Bingley: Emerald Publishing Limited, 2022), 425–42.ck

Chapter 7

1 Arlie Russell Hochschild, *The Managed Heart: Commercialization of Human Feeling* (Berkeley, California: University of California Press, 1983), 4.

2   Kareem J. Johnson, Christian E. Waugh, and Barbara L. Fredrickson, "Smile to See the Forest: Facially Expressed Positive Emotions Broaden Cognition," *Cognitive Emotion* 24, no. 2 (2010): 299–321.

3   Hochschild, *The Managed Heart*, 4.

4   Christine L. Williams and Catherine Connell, "'Looking Good and Sounding Right': Aesthetic Labor and Social Inequality in the Retail Industry," *Work and Occupations* 37, no. 3 (2010): 350.

5   Ishita Sachdeva and Suhsma Goel, "Retail Store Environment and Customer Experience: A Paradigm," *Journal of Fashion Marketing and Management* 19, no. 3 (2015): 291.

6   Dinesh Bhugra and Padmal De Silva, "Uniforms—Fact, Fashion, Fantasy and Fetish," *Sexual and Marital Therapy* 11, no. 4 (1996): 393–406; Anne McClintock, "Maid to Order: Commercial Fetishism and Gender Power," *Social Text* 37 (1993): 87–116; and Jesse Paul Crane-Seeber, "Sexy Warriors: The Politics and Pleasures of Submission to the State," in *Embodying Militarism*, edited by Synne L. Dyvik and Lauren Greenwood (New York: Routledge, 2018), 41–55.

7   Herman Casler, 1895, "Mutoscope," US Patent 683,910A, filed on February 4, 1896, and issued on October 8, 1901, 4.

8   Erkki Huhtamo, "Slots of Fun, Slots of Trouble: An Archaeology of Arcade Gaming," in *Handbook of Computer Games Studies*, eds. Joost Raessens and Jeffrey Goldstein (Cambridge, Massachusetts: MIT Press, 2005), 11–12.

9   Beatrice J. Kalisch, Philip A. Kalisch, and Mary L. McHugh, "The Nurse as a Sex Object in Motion Pictures, 1930 to 1980," *Research in Nursing & Health* 5, no. 3 (1982): 147–54; and Brenda S. Gardenour Walter, "Pricked, Probed and Possessed: Medical Pornography and the Birth of the Fetish Clinic," in *Pornographies: Critical Positions*, edited by Katherine Harrison and Cassandra A. Ogden (Chester: University of Chester Press, 2018), 264–86.

10 Valerie Steele, *Fetish: Fashion, Sex, and Power* (New York: Oxford University Press, 1996), 182–3.

11 Ibid., 180.

12 Nicolas Guéguen and Céline Jacob, "Clothing Color and Tipping: Gentlemen Patrons Give More Tips to Waitresses with Red Clothes," *Journal of Hospitality and Tourism Research* 38, no. 2 (2014): 275–80.

13 Maren T. Scull, "Reinforcing Gender Roles at the Male Strip Show: A Qualitative Analysis of Men Who Dance for Women," *Deviant Behavior* 34, no. 7 (2013): 565.

14 Susan M. Alexander, "The Corporate Masquerade: Branding Masculinity through Halloween Costumes," *Journal of Men's Studies* 22, no. 3 (2014): 180–93; Sharron J. Lennon, Zhiying Zheng, and Aziz Fatnassi, "Women's Revealing Halloween Costumes: Other-Objectification and Sexualization," *Fashion and Textiles* 3, no. 21 (2016): 1–19.

15 Nicole Rogers, "Law and the Fool," *Law Text Culture* 14, no. 1 (2010): 286–309.

16 Callie Marie Rennison and Mary Dodge, "Police Impersonation: Pretenses and Predators," *American Journal of Criminal Justice* 37 (2012): 505–22.

17 Linda A. Detman, "Women Behind Bars: The Feminization of Bartending," in *Job Queues, Gender Queues: Explaining Women's Inroads into Male Occupations*, edited by Barbara F. Reskin and Patricia A. Roos (Philadelphia, Pennsylvania: Temple University Press, 1990), 241.

18 Kazuhiro Oharazeki, "Listening to the Voices of 'Other' Women in Japanese North America: Japanese Prostitutes and Barmaids in the American West, 1887–1920," *Journal of American Ethnic History* 32, no. 4 (2013): 12.

19 Diane Kirkby, "Writing the History of Women Working: Photographic Evidence and the 'Disreputable Occupation of Barmaid,'" *Labour History*, 61 (1991): 3–16.

20 "Welcome to the National Police Gazette: Covering Crime, Sports, Celebrities, and All Things Sensational Since 1845," *Police Gazette*, 2021, at: http://policegazette.us.

21 French historian Michel Pastoureau has argued that in Western cultures, striped fabrics have an association with deviant social figures such as court jesters, prostitutes, and criminals. Michel Pastoureau, *The Devil's Cloth: A History of Stripes*, translated by Jody Gladding (New York: Columbia University Press, 2001).

22 Anne Cooper Funderburg, *Chocolate, Strawberry, and Vanilla: A History of American Ice Cream* (Bowling Green, Ohio: Bowling Green State University Press, 1995).

23 Gia Giasullo and Peter Freeman, *The Soda Fountain: Floats, Sundaes, Eggs Cream & More—Flavors and Traditions of an American Original* (Berkeley, California: Ten Speed Press, 2014).

24 Herman Feldman. *Prohibition: Its Economic and Industrial Aspects* (New York: D. Appleton and Company, 1930), 96-–100.

25 Kathy J. Ogren, *The Jazz Revolution: Twenties America & the Meaning of Jazz* (Oxford: Oxford University Press, 1989).

26 David Naylor, *Great American Movie Theaters* (Washington, DC: Preservation Press, 1989).

27 Kerry Segrave, *Vending Machines: An American Social History* (Jefferson, North Carolina: McFarland & Company, 2003).

28 For example, Casino Party Experts in Detroit offers a range of "party extras" for corporate events and private celebrations, including cigarette girls who serve vintage bubblegum and candy cigarettes: https://detroitcasinoparty.com/cigarette-cigar-girls/. Screaming Queens Entertainment in New York City offers a similar service: https://www.screamingqueens.com/cigar-girls-theme.

29 History Channel, "Last Day for Texas' Celebrated Drive-in Pig Stands," A&E Television Networks, November 14, 2000, at: http://www.history.com/this-day-in-history/last-day-for-texas-celebrated-drive-in-pig-stands.

30 Michael Karl Witzel, *The American Drive-In* (Osceola, Wisconsin: Motorbooks International, 1994).

31 The shako was originally worn by European military units in the early nineteenth century and often includes a plume to exaggerate the wearer's height. See Alex R. Cattley, "The British Infantry Shako," *Journal of the Society for Army Historical Research* 15, no. 60 (1936): 188–208.

32 "Carhop and Houston Man Found Slain," *The Marshall News* (Marshall, Texas), February 17, 1942, 1.

33 "Carhops' Shorts and Brassieres Give Liquor Board a Headache," *Pampa Daily News* (Pampa, Texas), February 18, 1942, 8.

34 Brian Bulko, "Carhoppin' at Eat'n Park," *Western Pennsylvania History: 1918–2018* 82, no. 2 (1999): 84–93.

35 Alan Levy, "The West Passes the Topless Test: A Morality Play in Three Acts," *LIFE Magazine*, March 11, 1966, 79–87. Gernreich's swimsuit was conventional from the waist down, however it had two suspender-like straps that crossed between (but did not cover) the wearer's breasts. For images and more details, see William Poundstone, "Rudi Gernreich and the Monokini," Los Angeles County Museum on Fire, July 15, 2019, at:: http://lacmaonfire.blogspot.com/2019/07/rudi-gernreich-and-monokini.html.

36 Ibid., 82.

37 Judith Lynne Hanna, *Strip Clubs, Democracy, and a Christian Right* (Austin, Texas: University of Texas Press, 2013).

38 "Casino Risks Topless Deal," *Daily Independent Journal* (San Rafael, California), April 16, 1966, 2.

39 Al Martinez, "A Trend Watcher Watches a Trend," *Oakland Tribune* (Oakland, California), July 28, 1966, 23.

40 "To Top It Off There's. . . No Top at All," *The Salt Lake Tribune*, July 22, 1966, 1.

41 Áine Cain, "A Day in the Life of a Playboy Bunny, and How the Controversial Job Has Changed Over 60 Years," *Business Insider*, September 28, 2017, at: https://www.businessinsider.com/playboy-bunnies-history-2017-9.

42 Rachel Chang, "Inside Gloria Steinem's Month as an Undercover Playboy Bunny," *Biography*, March 23, 2020, at: https://www.biography.com/news/gloria-steinem-undercover-playboy-bunny.

43 "'Qualifications' of Topless Barber's Helper Questioned," *The Salina Journal* (Salina, Kansas), June 28, 1975, 1.

44 Ibid.

45 Rule §83.70, "Cosmetologists: Responsibilities of Individuals," Texas Administrative Code, 2005, at: https://casetext.com/regulation/texas-administrative-code/title-16-economic-regulation/part-4-texas-department-of-licensing-and-regulation/chapter-83-cosmetologists/section-8370-responsibilities-of-individuals.

46 "Doughnut Shop Quits Topless Dance Routine," *The Paris News* (Paris, Texas), October 12, 1983, 3.

47 "71-Year-Old Man to Start Topless Doughnut Shop in Lauderdale," *St. Lucie News Tribune* (St. Lucie, Florida), November 21, 1985, 6.

48 "Topless Doughnut Shop Opens," *St. Lucie News Tribune*, November 28, 1985, 6.

49 Sam Roberts, "Carol Doda, Pioneer of Topless Entertainment, Dies at 78," *The New York Times*, November 11, 1985, at: https://www.nytimes.com/2015/11/12/arts/dance/carol-doda-pioneer-of-topless-entertainment-dies-at-78.html.

50 Ibid.

51 Michael Kaplan, "The Shockingly Dark History of Chippendales," *New York Post*, February 7, 2021, at: https://nypost.com/article/dark-history-of-chippendales/.

52 Chippendales, "About Chippendales," chippendales.com, 2022, at: https://www.chippendales.com/about-chippendales.

53 "Feminists Use Male Strippers to Raise Funds," *Santa Cruz Sentinel* (Santa Cruz, California), May 9, 1980, 8.

54 Clarissa Smith, "Shiny Chests and Heaving G-Strings: A Night Out with the Chippendales," *Sexualities* 5, no. 1 (2022): 71.

55 Katherine Liepe-Levinson, *Strip Show: Performances of Gender and Desire* (New York: Routledge, 2001).

56 Saturday Night Live, "Chippendales Audition," YouTube, 2019, at: https://www.youtube.com/watch?v=stqG2ihMvP0. Originally broadcast in 1990 (Season 16).

57 Nate Rogers, "'So Elegant, So Sensual': Chris Farley Should Be Remembered for His Grace, Not His Falls," *The Ringer*, March 31, 2020, at: https://www.theringer.com/tv/2020/3/31/21200801/chris-farley-chippendales-patrick-swayze-skating-snl-sketch.

58 Chippendales, "Frequently Asked Questions," chippendales.com, 2022, at: https://www.chippendales.com/Hard-FAQs.

59 "Making it rain" refers to showering dancers/strippers with paper money.

60 Chippendales, "Frequently Asked Questions."

61 Joseph R. G. DeMarco, "Power and Control in Gay Strip Clubs," in *Male Sex Work: A Business Doing Pleasure*, edited by Todd G. Morrison and Bruce W. Whitehead (Philadelphia, Pennsylvania: Haworth Press, 2007), 117.

62 Ibid., 125.

63 Kim Price, "'Keeping the Dancers in Check': The Gendered Organization of Stripping Work in the Lion's Den," *Gender & Society* 22, no. 3 (2008): 367–89.

64 Matthew T. DeMichele and Richard Tewksbury, "Sociological Explorations in Site-Specific Social Control: The Role of the Strip Club Bouncer," *Deviant Behavior* 25 (2004): 555.

65 George Rigakos, *Nightclub: Bouncers, Risk, and the Spectacle of Consumption* (Montreal: McGill-Queen's University Press, 2008).

66 Price, "Keeping the Dancers in Check."

67 Kristy Doyle, John O'Brien, and Niamh Maguire, "Precarity in the Night-time Economy," *Irish Journal of Anthropology* 20, no. 2 (2017): 39.

68 Lorraine Bayard de Volo, "Service and Surveillance: Infrapolitics at Work among Casino Cocktail Waitresses," *Social Politics: International Studies in Gender, State & Society* 10, no. 3 (2003): 357.

69 Ariella Rotramel, Megan Tracy, and Emma Coles, "Weighing the Value of Femininity: Casino Cocktail Personal Appearance Standards," *Fat Studies* (2021), Doi: 10.1080/21604851.2021.2009682.

70 Title VII of the 1964 Civil Rights Act forbids US employers from discriminating on the basis of characteristics such as gender, race, ethnicity, and religion with exceptions for issues such as safety and the inherent nature of the job. For example, film directors can exclude women from playing male characters and vice versa.

71 Ann C. McGinley, "Babes and Beefcake: Exclusive Hiring Arrangements and Sexy Dress Codes," *Duke Journal of Gender Law & Policy* 14, no. 4 (2007): 259.

72 McGinley hints that it was also a strategy to get rid of older workers and to disrupt the waitresses' labor union.

73 Aleza Freeman, "Chronology of the Cocktail Waitress," Vegas.com, August 31, 2008, at: https://www.vegas.com/alwaysopen/pdfs/icon-cocktail-waitress.pdf.

74 Traci Dauphin, "How One Vegas Casino Uses iPads to Loosen Up Gamblers," *Cult of Mac*, January 12, 2013, at: https://www.cultofmac.com/209180/how-one-vegas-casino-uses-ipads-to-loosen-up-gamblers/.

75 Hooters Incorporated, "The Official Saga: Hooters History," originalhooters.com, 2022, at: https://www.originalhooters.com/saga.

76 Hooters of America, "The Recipe for a Good Time," hooters.com, 2022, at: https://www.hooters.com/about/history/.

77 Tammy S. Gordon, "History, Heritage and the Museum Function of a Sports Bar," in *The Dynamics of Interconnections in Popular Culture(s)*, edited by Ray B. Browne and Ben Urish (Newcastle upon Tyne: Cambridge Scholars Publishers, 2014), 36–54; Lawrence A. Wenner, "In Search of the Sports Bar: Masculinity, Alcohol, Sports, and the Mediation of Public Space," in *Sport and Postmodern Times*, edited by Geneviève Rail (Albany, New York: State University of New York Press, 1998), 301–32.

78 Bikinis Bar and Grill LLC, 2011, "Breastaurant," US Trademark 85,416,160, filed on September 6, 2011, and issued on October 23, 2012.

79 This figure represents a decline from 2015, when Hooters was one of the top-50 largest chain restaurants in the US with nearly 600 locations. See Michelle Newton-Francis and Gay Young, "Now Winging It at Hooters: Conventions for Producing a Cultural Object of Sexual Fantasy," *Poetics* 52 (2015): 1–17.

80 In the 1980s, the uniform tank top was also tied in a knot to expose the wearer's midriff. It is unclear exactly when and why the practice ended.

81 Linda L. Barkacs and Craig B. Barkacs, "She's Not Heavy, She's My Sister: Does Anyone Really Give a Hoot About Obesity and Weight Discrimination? The Case of the 'Heavy' Hooters Girls," *Journal of Legal, Ethnical, and Regulatory Issues* 14, no. 2 (2011): 110.

82 Although Hooters' corporate headquarters is now in Atlanta, Georgia, the manufacturer listed on garment tags, "Provident Manufacturing," has the same address as the original Hooters restaurant in Clearwater, Florida. The design and sale of private-label merchandise can be more tightly controlled than third-party merchandise.

83 "Hooters Dress Code: A Complete Guide," *How I Got the Job*, September 5, 2021, at: https://howigotjob.com/dress-code/hooters-dress-code-a-complete-guide/.

84 Michelle Newton-Francis and Salvador Vidal-Ortiz, "¡Más Que un Bocado! (More Than a Mouthful): Comparing Hooters in the United States and Columbia," in *Global Beauty, Local Bodies*, eds. Afshan Jafar and Erynn Masi de Casanova (New York: Palgrave Macmillan, 2013), 59–82.

85 Chelsea Ritschel, "Hooters Amends Uniform Policy After Employees Condemn 'Disturbing' New Shorts," *Yahoo! News,* October 17, 2021, at: https://www.yahoo.com/news/hooters-amends-uniform-policy-employees-154321145.html.

86 Watson's clients prior to the contract with Twin Peaks included the Los Angeles Lakers, Dallas Cowboys, and the San Francisco 49ers. Ian Froeb, "Breastaurant Uniforms Owner Terra Watson: The Gut Check Interview," *Riverfront Times*, July 2, 2012, at: https://www.riverfronttimes.com/food-drink/breastaurant-uniforms-owner-terra-watson-the-gut-check-interview-2620123.

87 Ibid.

88 Terra's Dancewear and Dallaswear LLC, 2011, "Breastaurant Uniforms," US Trademark 85,273,851, filed March 22, 2011, and issued November 8, 2011. Terra's Dancewear and Dallaswear LLC, 2013, "Waitressville," US Trademark 85,899,895, filed April 10, 2013, and issued November 19, 2013. Terra's Dancewear and Dallaswear LLC, 2013, "Serving Up Style," US Trademark 85,899,897, filed April 10, 2013, and issued November 19, 2013. Terra's Dancewear and Dallaswear LLC, 2015, "Dream Corset," US Trademark 86, 601, 461, filed April 17, 2015, abandoned February 23, 2016.

89 Cynthia Smoot, "Terra Saunders brings Waitressville to CNBC's Crowd Rules," *Oh So Cynthia*, May 28, 2013, at: https://www.ohsocynthia.com/2013/05/terra-saunders-brings-waitressville-to.html.

90 "Tilted Kilt Pub & Eatery Set to Debut New Costume," *Businesswire*, April 15, 2015, at: https://www.businesswire.com/news/home/20150415005191/en/Tilted-Kilt-Pub-Eatery-Set-to-Debut-New-Costume. Watson is now known by her married name, Terra Saunders.

91 Heart Attack Grill, "Press," heartattackgrill.com, 2022, at: https://www.heartattackgrill.com/press.html.

92 Debra Kelly, "The Untold Truth of Heart Attack Grill," *Mashed*, July 15, 2020, at: https://www.mashed.com/210610/the-untold-truth-of-heart-attack-grill/.

93 Kristin Edelhauser, "Cashing in on Controversy," *Entrepreneur*, February 26, 2007, at: https://www.entrepreneur.com/article/175144.

94 Heart Attack Grill, "Licensing," heartattackgrill.com, 2022, at: https://www.heartattackgrill.com/license.html.

95 Twin Peaks has two locations in Mexico. The other breastaurant chains listed in this chapter have no locations outside of the US.

96 As of May 2022, 19 locations are listed as "temporarily closed," including all restaurants in the Bahamas, Czech Republic, Dominican Republic, Panama, Singapore, Switzerland, and the United Kingdom. Details can be seen by clicking through the links on the company's list of locations. Hooters of America, "All Locations," hooters.com, 2022, at: https://www.hooters.com/location-list/. In 2016, Hooters announced that it was opening a new location in the Philippines and hoping for additional sites in Vietnam, Hong Kong, Malaysia, Cambodia, and Burma. None of these plans have come to fruition. Hooters of America, "Hooters Continues Expansion in Asia with New Location in Manila," hooters.com, June 15, 2016, at: https://www.hooters.com/about/news/hooters-continues-expansion-in-asia-with-new-location-in-manila.

97 Locker, "The Secret to the Success."

98 Liz Jones, "Sorry, I Found This Burger Bar More Offensive Than a Lapdancing Club," *Daily Mail* (London), October 7, 2010, at: https://www.dailymail.co.uk/femail/article-1318258/Hooters--offensive-bar-Britain-Asks-Liz-Jones.html.

99 "Hooters Restaurant Approved for Liverpool Despite Objections," BBC News, February 15, 2022, at: https://www.bbc.com/news/uk-england-merseyside-60391024.

100 Maria Toolan, "Say No to Hooters Liverpool," Change.org, 2022, at: https://www.change.org/p/liverpool-city-council-say-no-to-hooters-liverpool?utm_source=share_petition&utm_medium=custom_url&recruited_by_id=1c6078d0-d5ed-11e8-b7c0-352bdcade225.

101 Christian Smith, "Second Hooters Restaurant Approved for UK Despite Backlash," *The Drinks Business*, February 16, 2022, at: https://www.thedrinksbusiness.com/2022/02/second-hooters-restaurant-approved-for-uk-despite-backlash/.

102 Newton-Francis and Vidal-Ortiz, "¡Más Que un Bocado!" 70.

103 Ibid, 71–72.

104 Desmond Yap, "Phnom Penh's Riverside District," *Retalk Asia*, April 7, 2017, at: https://www.retalkasia.com/blog/desmond-yap/phnom-penhs-riverside-district/phnom-penh/riverside.

105 Gareth Johnson, "The Strange Tale of Hooters Cambodia," *Khmer Knights*, June 15, 2021, at: https://www.khmernights.com/the-strange-tale-of-hooters-cambodia/.

106 Larissa Sandy (ed.), *Women and Sex Work in Cambodia: Blood, Sweat and Tears* (London: Routledge, 2014).

107 L. Monique Ward, "Media and Sexualization: State of Empirical Research, 1995–2015," *Journal of Sex Research* 53, no. 4/5 (2016): 560–77; Sharla D. Biefield, Ellen A. Stone, and Christia Spears Brown, "Sexy, Thin, and White: The Intersection of Sexualization, Body Type, and Race on Stereotypes About Women," *Sex Roles* 85 (2021): 287–300.

108 Tomi-Ann Roberts, Rachel M. Calogero, and Sarah J. Gervais, "Objectification Theory: Continuing Contributions to Feminist Psychology," in *APA Handbook of the Psychology of Women: History, Theory, and Battlegrounds*, edited by Cheryl B. Travis et al. (Washington, DC: American Psychological Association, 2018), 252.

Chapter 8

1 Karisa Sprague, "Express Yourself: Walmart Introduces Relaxed Dress Guidelines in Stores," Walmart, May 30, 2018, at: https://corporate.walmart.com/newsroom/business/20180530/express-yourself-walmart-introduces-relaxed-dress-guidelines-in-stores.

2 Ibid.

3 Kristina Benson, "The Freedom to Believe and the Freedom to Practice: Title VII, Muslim Women, and Hijab," *UCLA Journal of Islamic and Near Eastern Law* 13, no. 1 (2014): 1–19.

4 Debbie Kaminer, "Uniforms, Dress Codes and an Employee's Religious Observance," *New York State Bar Association Journal* 84, no. 8 (2012): 26–31.

5 "Who is Protected from Employment Discrimination?" US Equal Employment Opportunity Commission, 2022, at:: https://www.eeoc.gov/employers/small-business/3-who-protected-employment-discrimination.

6 Indiana Civil Rights Commission, "What is a Protected Class?" IN.gov, 2022, at: https://faqs.in.gov/hc/en-us/articles/115005057627-What-is-a-protected-class-.

7 "New York State Human Rights Law," City of New York, 2022, at; https://www1.nyc.gov/site/mopd/laws/state-laws.page.

8 Division of Human Rights, "Important Updates to the New York State Human Rights Law," State of New York, 2019, at: https://dhr.ny.gov/sites/default/files/pdf/nysdhr-legal-updates-10112019.pdf.

9 Alex Bitter, "Sheetz is Reviewing its Controversial 'Smile Policy' that Prohibits Employees from Having 'Missing, Broken, or Badly Discolored Teeth," *Business Insider*, January 24, 2023, at: https://www.businessinsider.com/sheetz-reviewing-smile-policy-bars-hiring-employees-bad-teeth-2023-1.

10 Lee Brown, "Abuse Victim Who Lost Teeth Says She Was Booted from Job Over Sheetz 'Smile Policy,' *New York Post*, January 31, 2023, at: https://nypost.com/2023/01/31/ohio-woman-claims-she-lost-sheetz-job-because-her-teeth-violated-its-smile-policy/.

11 "Sheetz to Review 'Smile Policy,' Which States Employees Can't Have Teeth Issues," CBS Pittsburgh, January 25, 2023, at: https://www.cbsnews.com/pittsburgh/news/sheetz-review-smile-policy-employees-bad-teeth/.

12 Bill Shannon, "Sheetz Pulls Controversial 'Smile Policy' From Handbook," *The Hill*, February 2, 2023, at: https://thehill.com/homenews/3840323-sheetz-pulls-controversial-smile-policy-from-handbook/.

13 Tom Wolf, "Executive Order: Equal Employment Opportunity," Commonwealth of Pennsylvania Governor's Office, April 7, 2016, at: https://www.oa.pa.gov/Policies/eo/Documents/2016_04.pdf.

14 Nancy Levit, "Changing Workforce Demographics and the Future of the Protected Class Approach," *Lewis & Clark Law Review* 16, no. 2 (2012): 497–8.

15 Stalter v. City of Montgomery, 796 F. Supp. 489 (M.D. Ala. 1992).

16 "Summary judgement" means that the judge deemed a trial unnecessary due to lack of dispute about the facts or overwhelming evidence. "Title VII" refers to the Civil Rights Act of 1964.

17 Kimberly M. Cloutier, Plaintiff, Appellant, v. Costco Wholesale Corp., Defendant, Appellee, 390 F.3d 126, U.S. Court of Appeals for the First Circuit (2004).

18 In a statement to the media, Kaepernick explained, "I am not going to stand up to show pride in a flag for a country that oppresses black people and people of color." See Steve Wyche, "Colin Kaepernick Explains Why He Sat During National Anthem," *NFL Media*, August 27, 2016, at: https://web.archive.org/web/20160827165405/http://www.nfl.com/news/story/0ap3000000691077/article/colin-kaepernick-explains-protest-of-national-anthem.

19 Greg Sterling, "Report: Nike's Sales Jump 31% in Wake of Kaepernick Ad Campaign," MarTech, September 11, 2018, at: https://martech.org/report-nikes-sales-jump-31-in-wake-of-kaepernick-ad-campaign/.

20 Pierre R. Berthon et al., "The Virtuous Brand: The Perils and Promises of Brand Virtue Signaling," *Business Horizons* 66, no. 1 (2023): 28.

21 Caroline Evans, *Fashion at the Edge: Spectacle, Modernity & Deathliness* (New Haven, Connecticut: Yale University Press, 2003).

22 "Locs" is short for dreadlocks, rope-like strands of hair that are formed by twisting or braiding the hair and letting it naturally adhere together. In the US, dreadlocks are most common among people of African descent.

23 "Create a Respectful and Open World for Natural Hair (US)," Unilever Corporation, 2023, at; https://www.unilever.com/planet-and-society/take-action/initiative/create-a-respectful-and-open-world-for-natural-hair-us/.

24 Chime Edwards, "The Impact of the 'Fro in the Civil Rights Movement," *Essence*, October 27, 2020, at: https://www.essence.com/holidays/black-history-month/impact-fro-civil-rights-movement/.

25 Jantina Anderson, "Hair Discrimination is Racist: Why Black Communities Advocate for Hair Peace," *ENGAGE! Co-created Knowledge Serving the Public Good* 1, no. 3 (2020), Doi: 10.18060/24813.

26 Senate Bill No. 188, signed into law on July 3, 2023, at: https://leginfo.legislature.ca.gov/faces/billNavClient.xhtml?bill_id=201920200SB188.

27 "Workplace Dress Codes and Transgender and Non-Binary Employees," Human Rights Campaign Foundation, 2022, at: https://www.thehrcfoundation.org/professional-resources/workplace-dress-codes-and-transgender-employees.

28 Katie Deighton, "Some Flight Attendants Can Bring Their Full Selves to Work—Tattoos, Sneakers, Nose Studs, and All," *Wall Street Journal*, June 9, 2022, at: https://www.wsj.com/articles/some-flight-attendants-can-bring-their-full-selves-to-worktattoos-sneakers-nose-studs-and-all-11654768800.

29 Ali Garbino, "From Our Employees: What More Inclusive Gender-Neutral Uniforms and Policies Mean for Bringing Our Best Selves to Work," Alaska Airlines, March 28, 2022, at: https://news.alaskaair.com/diversity-equity-and-inclusion/alaska-airlines-gender-neutral-uniforms-pronouns/.

30 Ibid.

31 Deighton, "Some Flight Attendants."

32 "Virgin Atlantic Updates Gender Identity Policy," Virgin Atlantic Airways Ltd, September 28, 2022, at: https://corporate.virginatlantic.com/gb/en/media/press-releases/virgin-atlantic-updates-gender-identity-policy.html.

33 "Mapping Attacks on LGBTQ Rights in the U.S. State Legislatures," American Civil Liberties Union, March 24, 2023, at: https://www.aclu.org/legislative-attacks-on-lgbtq-rights.

34 Heather Marie Akou, "Food Service Uniforms and the Symbolism(s) of Wearing a Mask," *Clothing Cultures* 7, no. 2 (2020): 147–63.

35 N95 masks (also known as N95 respirators) are designed to filter 95% of airborne particles.

36 John Bacon, "Surgeon General Jerome Adams in March Said to Reserve Masks for Healthcare Providers," *USA Today*, March 1, 2020, at: https://www.usatoday.com/story/news/nation/2020/03/01/coronavirus-surgeon-general-stop-buying-face-masks/4922614002/.

37 "Optimizing N95 Respirator Supplies," Centers for Disease Control and Prevention, September 16, 2021, at: https://www.cdc.gov/coronavirus/2019-ncov/hcp/respirators-strategy/index.html.

38 Gary Gereffi, "What Does the COVID-19 Pandemic Teach Us About Global Value Chains? The Case of Medical Supplies," *Journal of International Business Policy* 3 (2020): 287–301.

39 "Optimizing N95 Respirator Supplies."

40 David Michaels and Gregory R. Wagner, "Occupational Safety and Health Administration (OSHA) and Worker Safety During the COVID-19 Pandemic," *Journal of the American Medical Association* 324, no. 14 (2020): 1389–90.

41 Clare Hammonds, Jasmine Kerrissey, and Donald Tomaskovic-Devey, "Stressed, Unsafe, and Insecure: Essential Workers Need a New, New Deal," University of Massachusetts Amherst Labor Center, June 5, 2020, at: https://www.umass.edu/lrrc/sites/default/files/Stressed%2C%20Unsafe%2C%20and%20Insecure-%20Essential%20Workers%20Need%20A%20New%2C%20New%20Deal%20.pdf.

42 See, for example, Jason Abaluck et al., "The Case for Universal Cloth Mask Adoption and Policies to Increase Supply of Medical Masks for Health Workers," Social Science Research Network, April 1, 2020, at: https://papers.ssrn.com/sol3/papers.cfm?abstract_id=3567438; Tom Li et al., "Mask or No Mask for COVID-19: A Public Health and Market Study," *PLoS One* 15, no. 8: e0237691; and Shovon Bhattacharjee et al., "Last-Resort Strategies During Mask Shortages: Optimal Design Features of Cloth Masks and Decontamination of Disposable Masks During the COVID-19 Pandemic," *BMJ Open Respiratory Research* 7 (2020): e000698.

43 "Bright Future for Post Pandemic U.S. Uniform Industry, Says BLS," Network Association of Uniform Manufacturers and Distributors, July 5, 2022, at: https://naumd.com/bright-future-for-post-pandemic-u-s-uniform-industry/.

44 Ibid.

45 "Protecting Workers: Guidance on Mitigating and Preventing the Spread of COVID-19 in the Workplace," US Department of Labor, Occupational Safety and Health Administration, August 13, 2021, at: https://www.osha.gov/coronavirus/safework.

46 Sidney A. Shapiro and Randy Rabinowitz, "Voluntary Regulatory Compliance in Theory and Practice: The Case of OSHA," *Administrative Law Review* 52, no. 1 (2000): 97–156.

47 "Medical Student Perspective: The White Coat Ceremony," American Association of Medical Colleges, 2022, at: https://students-residents.aamc.org/aspiring-docs-fact-sheets-what-medical-school/medical-student-perspective-white-coat-ceremony.

48 Linda Tirado, *Hand to Mouth: Living in Bootstrap America* (New York: Berkley Books, 2015), 48–9.

49 Raine Dozier, "Female Masculinity at Work: Managing Stigma on the Job," *Psychology of Women Quarterly* 41, no. 2 (2017): 197–209.

50 Denise N. Rall (ed.), *Fashion and War in Popular Culture* (Bristol: Intellect, 2014); Jane Tynan, *Trench Coat* (London: Bloomsbury Academic, 2022); and Jude Stewart, *Patternalia: An Unconventional History of Polka Dots, Stripes, Plaid, Camouflage, & Other Graphic Patterns* (London: Bloomsbury Academic, 2015).

51 Emma McClendon, *Denim: Fashion's Frontier* (New Haven, Connecticut: Yale University Press, 2016).

52 Susan Strawn, Jane Farrell-Beck and Ann R. Hemken, "Bib Overalls: Function and Fashion," *Dress* 32, no. 1 (2005): 43–55.

53 Lauren Miralles-Snow, "An Exploration of Origins and Appropriations: How Workwear Has Traveled and Transformed," unpublished thesis (Temple University, 2019), at: https://sites.temple.edu/emerge/files/2021/09/Vol4-Y-Miralles-Snow.pdf; and Oliviero Toscani and Olivier Saillard, *Workwear: Work Fashion Seduction* (Milan: Rizzoli International, 2009).

54 Claude S. Fischer, "Paradoxes of American Individualism," *Sociological Forum* 23, no. 2 (2008): 363–72.

Bibliography

"18 AAC 23.230 – Practitioner Hygiene." State of Alaska, 2002, at: http://www.legis.state.
ak.us/basis/folioproxy.asp?url=http://www.legis.state.ak.us/cgi-bin/folioisa.dll/aac/
query=*/doc/%7B@81957%7D?prev.

"71-Year-Old Man to Start Topless Doughnut Shop in Lauderdale." *St. Lucie News
Tribune* (St. Lucie, Florida), November 21, 1985.

"722 – Food Services and Drinking Places." NAICS, 2018, at: https://www.naics.com/
naics-code-description/?code=722.

"All of the Sexiest Man Alive Covers." *People Magazine*, November 10, 2021, at: https://
people.com/celebrity/all-the-sexiest-man-alive-covers/?slide=b7c2cf75-809b-438c-
aa24-8ccfb5e87cdf#b7c2cf75-809b-438c-aa24-8ccfb5e87cdf.

"America on the Move: Fill 'Er Up!" Smithsonian National Museum of American
History, 2003, at: https://americanhistory.si.edu/america-on-the-move/fill-up.

Angelica Galaxy of Uniforms. St. Louis, Missouri: Angelica Uniform Co., 1988.

Angelica Washable Service Uniforms. St. Louis, Missouri: Angelica Jacket Co., 1962.

Approved Esso Uniforms. Kansas City, Missouri, Unitog Co., 1954.

"Associate Brand Visual Identity." Walmart Stores, Inc., 2020, at: https://one.walmart.
com/content/dam/px/associate_brand_center/all-company-brand-guidelines/
AssociateBrand_VISID_200203.pdf. See also: https://web.archive.org/
web/20230807181223/https://one.walmart.com/content/dam/px/associate_brand_
center/all-company-brand-guidelines/AssociateBrand_VISID_200203.pdf.

"Barbers Will Feast in Celebration of Their Recent Victory and Birthday." *The Saint Paul
Globe* (St. Paul, Minnesota), May 18, 1897.

"Bellevue Teens Donate Candy Striper Hours." *The Wayne Herald* (Wayne, Nebraska),
September 16, 1921.

"Boston: A City of Uniforms." *Boston Daily Globe*, July 31, 1898.

"Bright Future for Post Pandemic U.S. Uniform Industry, Says BLS." Network
Association of Uniform Manufacturers and Distributors, July 5, 2022, at: https://
naumd.com/bright-future-for-post-pandemic-u-s-uniform-industry/. See also:
https://web.archive.org/web/20230807190058/https://naumd.com/bright-future-for-
post-pandemic-u-s-uniform-industry/.

"Brooklyn Notes." *The Postal Record* 3, no. 9 (1890): 190.

"Candy Stripers Provide Cheery Note in Washington University Clinics." *Hospital
Record* 12, no. 9 (September 1958): 13–16.

"Capless Nurse Reinstated in Dispute Over Uniforms." *American Journal of Nursing* 71,
no. 1 (1971): 12.

"Carhop and Houston Man Found Slain," *The Marshall News* (Marshall, Texas), February 17, 1942.

"Carhops' Shorts and Brassieres Give Liquor Board a Headache." *Pampa Daily News* (Pampa, Texas), February 18, 1942.

"Casino Risks Topless Deal." *Daily Independent Journal* (San Rafael, California), April 16, 1966.

"City Ready to Try Parking Meters." *The Oklahoma News* (Oklahoma City, Oklahoma), February 25, 1935.

"Create a Respectful and Open World for Natural Hair (US)." Unilever Corporation, 2023, at: https://www.unilever.com/planet-and-society/take-action/initiative/create-a-respectful-and-open-world-for-natural-hair-us/. See also: https://web.archive.org/web/20230807185604/https://www.unilever.com/planet-and-society/take-action/initiative/create-a-respectful-and-open-world-for-natural-hair-us/.

"Damage Suits Great 'Graft;' Theaters Hit." *Chicago Tribune*, October 17, 1903.

"Defense Plans Boom Uniform Preparations on West Coast." April 30, 1951.

"Detachable Shoulder Pads in Uniforms." *Women's Wear Daily*, December 6, 1945.

"Doughnut Shop Quits Topless Dance Routine." *The Paris News* (Paris, Texas), October 12, 1983.

"Employment Opportunities." *The Brooklyn Daily Eagle* (New York), May 19, 1943.

"Feminists Use Male Strippers to Raise Funds." *Santa Cruz Sentinel* (Santa Cruz, California), May 9, 1980.

"Fire in the Iroquois Theater Kills 571 and Injures 350 Persons." *Chicago Tribune*, December 31, 1903.

"Fortune 500." *Fortune*, 2021, at: https://fortune.com/fortune500/.

"Franchising." *Entrepreneur*, 2021, at: https://www.entrepreneur.com/encyclopedia/franchising.

"Front of House Usher Training Handbook." Adrienne Arsht Center for the Performing Arts, 2021, at: https://www.arshtcenter.org/Documents/Volunteer/Seasoned%20Usher%20Training%20Handbook%20.pdf.

"Have Your Nickel Handy Tuesday and Don't Expect to Get Gum Out of Parking Meters." *The Oklahoma News* (Oklahoma City, Oklahoma), July 14, 1935.

"Hooters Dress Code: A Complete Guide." *How I Got the Job*, September 5, 2021, at: https://howigotjob.com/dress-code/hooters-dress-code-a-complete-guide/. See also: https://web.archive.org/web/20230807184516/https://howigotjob.com/dress-code/hooters-dress-code-a-complete-guide/.

"Hooters Restaurant Approved for Liverpool Despite Objections." BBC News, February 15, 2022, at: https://www.bbc.com/news/uk-england-merseyside-60391024.

"In Los Angeles Uniforms Lines: Less 'Uniformity' Spurs Orders." *Women's Wear Daily*, April 21, 1952.

"L.A. Hospital Prescribes Pastel Nylon Uniforms." *Women's Wear Daily*, June 27, 1949.

"Malden, Mass." *The Postal Record* 3, no. 10 (1890): 217.

"Male Meter Maids." *The Times Record* (Troy, New York), December 8, 1965.

"Mapping Attacks on LGBTQ Rights in the U.S. State Legislatures." American Civil Liberties Union, March 24, 2023, at: https://www.aclu.org/legislative-attacks-on-lgbtq-rights. See also: https://web.archive.org/web/20230807185935/https://www.aclu.org/legislative-attacks-on-lgbtq-rights.

"Medical Student Perspective: The White Coat Ceremony." American Association of Medical Colleges, 2022, at: https://students-residents.aamc.org/aspiring-docs-fact-sheets-what-medical-school/medical-student-perspective-white-coat-ceremony. See also: https://web.archive.org/web/20230807190121/https://students-residents.aamc.org/aspiring-docs-fact-sheets-what-medical-school/medical-student-perspective-white-coat-ceremony.

"Meter Maids." *Abilene Reporter-News* (Abilene, Texas), January 4, 1965.

"Meter Maids Lauded," *The Salt Lake Tribune* (Salt Lake City, Utah), December 21, 1954.

"Meter Maids Lose Battle of Bulge." *The Daily Notes* (Canonsburg, Pennsylvania), September 9, 1965.

"Meter Maids Too Fat: Battle of Scales Erupts in New York." *Wilkes-Barre Times Leader* (Wilkes-Barre, Pennsylvania), July 31, 1965.

"Nashville, Tenn." *The Postal Record* 4, no. 2 (1891): 36.

"New Meter Maid Getting Used to 15-Mile Walks." *Janesville Daily Gazette* (Janesville, Wisconsin), July 1, 1964.

"New York State Human Rights Law." City of New York, 2022, at: https://www1.nyc.gov/site/mopd/laws/state-laws.page.

"Nylon Seersucker." *Women's Wear Daily*, May 22, 1950.

"Optimizing N95 Respirator Supplies." Centers for Disease Control and Prevention, September 16, 2021, at: https://www.cdc.gov/coronavirus/2019-ncov/hcp/respirators-strategy/index.html.

"Overview: Receptionist." Sokanu Interactive, 2022, at: https://www.careerexplorer.com/careers/receptionist/. See also: https://web.archive.org/web/20230807181259/https://www.careerexplorer.com/careers/receptionist/.

"Painting, 'The First Gas Station in the World, Seattle, 1907,' by Robert Addison." Museum of History & Industry (Seattle, Washington), 2021, at: https://digitalcollections.lib.washington.edu/digital/collection/imlsmohai/id/13486/.

"Paramount Theater." Digital Library of Georgia, 2021, at: https://dlg.usg.edu/record/geh_athpc_2444.

"Parking Control Officer (#8214)." City and County of San Francisco, September 12, 2012, at: https://www.jobapscloud.com/SF/specs/classspecdisplay.asp?ClassNumber=8214.

"Pastel Nylon in Coast Line of Nurse's Uniforms." *Women's Wear Daily*, July 1, 1948.

"Pittsburg Takes on New Aim for Its Meter Maids." *Great Bend Tribune* (Great Bend, Kansas), December 17, 1965.

"Pizza Hut Launches Bold Streetwear Collection." *QSR Magazine*, July 28, 2021, at: https://www.qsrmagazine.com/news/pizza-hut-launches-bold-streetwear-collection.

"Postal Rates, Postal Pay Hikes." *Congressional Quarterly Almanac*, Volume 10 (Washington, DC: Congressional Quarterly News Features, 1954), 385–8.

"Proper Dress for Servants Aids Home Harmony." *Los Angeles Times*, October 23, 1935.

"Protecting Workers: Guidance on Mitigating and Preventing the Spread of COVID-19 in the Workplace." US Department of Labor, Occupational Safety and Health Administration, August 13, 2021, at: https://www.osha.gov/coronavirus/safework.

"'Qualifications' of Topless Barber's Helper Questioned." *The Salina Journal* (Salina, Kansas), June 28, 1975.

"R.R. Porters Must Buy Their Suits at Fields Even if They Cost More." *The Day Book* (Chicago) second edition, March 1, 1917.

Reference Manual 43: Uniforms. Washington, DC: US National Park Service, October 2000.

"Scrubs as Streetwear?" *AllWays in Fashion*, November 5, 2015, at: http://allwaysinfashion. blogspot.com/2015/11/scrubs-as-streetwear.html. See also: https://web.archive.org/ web/20230807155902/http://allwaysinfashion.blogspot.com/2015/11/scrubs-as-streetwear.html

"Service Industry." *Encyclopaedia Britannica*, 2018, at: https://www.britannica.com/ topic/service-industry.

"Sheetz to Review 'Smile Policy,' Which States Employees Can't Have Teeth Issues." CBS Pittsburgh, January 25, 2023, at: https://www.cbsnews.com/pittsburgh/news/ sheetz-review-smile-policy-employees-bad-teeth/.

"Substitute Carriers' Association Formed." *The Postal Record* 3, no. 3 (1890): 51.

"The Iroquois." *Chicago Tribune*, November 9, 1903.

"The Latest News." *The Sun* (New York), May 18, 1861.

The Work of the National Consumers' League. Philadelphia, Pennsylvania: American Academy of Political and Social Science, 1910.

"Tilted Kilt Pub & Eatery Set to Debut New Costume." *Businesswire*, April 15, 2015, at: https://www.businesswire.com/news/home/20150415005191/en/Tilted-Kilt-Pub-Eatery-Set-to-Debut-New-Costume.

"To Top It Off There's. . . No Top at All." *The Salt Lake Tribune*, July 22, 1966.

"Topless Doughnut Shop Opens." *St. Lucie News Tribune*, November 28, 1985.

"Trading in Houses." *New-York Daily Tribune*, October 2, 1907, 16.

"Unitog Co." *International Directory of Company Histories*, Volume 19, 457–60. Detroit: St. James Press, 1998.

"Unmounted Sleeves in New Uniform." *Women's Wear Daily*, September 25, 1950.

"Virgin Atlantic Updates Gender Identity Policy." Virgin Atlantic Airways Ltd, September 28, 2022, at: https://corporate.virginatlantic.com/gb/en/media/press-releases/virgin-atlantic-updates-gender-identity-policy.html. See also: https://web. archive.org/web/20230807185847/https://corporate.virginatlantic.com/gb/en/media/ press-releases/virgin-atlantic-updates-gender-identity-policy.html.

"Want a Stage Beauty for a Cook?" *The Philadelphia Inquirer*, March 19, 1922.

"Welcome to the National Police Gazette: Covering Crime, Sports, Celebrities, and All Things Sensational Since 1845." *Police Gazette*, 2021, at: http://policegazette.us.

"Well-Dressed Doorman Trades Epaulets for Ivy League Look." *New York Times*, July 21, 1963.

"Who is Protected from Employment Discrimination?" US Equal Employment Opportunity Commission, 2022, at: https://www.eeoc.gov/employers/small-business/3-who-protected-employment-discrimination.

Who's Your Tailor? Chicago, Illinois: Ed. V. Price & Company, 1936–7.

"Workplace Dress Codes and Transgender and Non-Binary Employees." Human Rights Campaign Foundation, 2022, at: https://www.thehrcfoundation.org/professional-resources/workplace-dress-codes-and-transgender-employees. See also: https://web.archive.org/web/20230807185716/https://www.thehrcfoundation.org/professional-resources/workplace-dress-codes-and-transgender-employees.

Abaluck, Jason, Judith A. Chevalier, Nicholas A. Christakis, Howard Paul Forman, Edward H. Kaplan, Albert Ko, and Sten H. Vermund. "The Case for Universal Cloth Mask Adoption and Policies to Increase Supply of Medical Masks for Health Workers." Social Science Research Network, April 1, 2020, at: https://papers.ssrn.com/sol3/papers.cfm?abstract_id=3567438.

Akou, Heather Marie. "Food Service Uniforms and the Symbolism(s) of Wearing a Mask." *Clothing Cultures* 7, no. 2 (2020): 147–63.

Alexander, Susan M. "The Corporate Masquerade: Branding Masculinity through Halloween Costumes." *Journal of Men's Studies* 22, no. 3 (2014): 180–93.

Alfred, Randy. "May 8, 1951: DuPont Debuts Dacron." Wired, May 8, 2009, at: https://www.wired.com/2009/05/dayintech-0508/.

Allen, Jeanne. *Showing Your Colors: A Designer's Guide to Coordinating Your Wardrobe.* San Francisco, California: Chronicle Books, 1986.

Allred, Anthony T. and H. Lon Addams. "Service Quality at Banks and Credit Unions: What do Their Customers Say?" *Managing Service Quality* 10, no. 1 (2000): 52–60.

American Barber Association. "A History of Entrepreneurship, Freedom, and Professionalism." americanbarber.org, 2021, at: https://americanbarber.org/history/. See also: https://web.archive.org/web/20230807153844/https://americanbarber.org/about/.

Amtrack. "More Than Meets the Eye: A Conductor's Uniform." blog.amtrack.com, 2021, at: http://blog.amtrak.com/2013/02/more-than-meets-the-eye-a-conductors-uniform/.

Anderson, Jantina. "Hair Discrimination is Racist: Why Black Communities Advocate for Hair Peace," *ENGAGE! Co-created Knowledge Serving the Public Good* 1, no. 3 (2020). Doi: 10.18060/24813.

Angelica. "History." angelica.com, 2021, at: http://www.angelica.com/about-us/history/.

Apple, Rima D. "School Health is Community Health: School Nursing in the Early Twentieth Century in the USA." *History of Education Review* 46, no. 2 (2016): 136–49.

Arnesen, Eric. *Brotherhoods of Color: Black Railroad Workers and the Struggle for Equality.* Cambridge, Massachusetts: Harvard University Press, 2001.

Arthur, Linda B., ed. *Religion, Dress and the Body.* Oxford: Berg Publishers, 1999.

Atlanta Urban Design Commission. "The Ten Park Place Building (Thornton Building)." City of Atlanta, 2021, at: https://www.atlantaga.gov/government/departments/

city-planning/office-of-design/urban-design-commission/the-ten-park-place-building-thornton-building. See also: https://web.archive.org/web/20230807153056/ https://www.atlantaga.gov/government/departments/city-planning/office-of-design/ urban-design-commission/the-ten-park-place-building-thornton-building.

Attewell, Alex. "Florence Nightingale (1820–1910)." *Prospects* 28 (1998): 151–66.

Bachelder, William V. "Limitations on the Municipal Use of Parking Meters." *Journal of Criminal Law and Criminology* 40, no. 5 (1950): 601–6.

Bacon, John. "Surgeon General Jerome Adams in March Said to Reserve Masks for Healthcare Providers." *USA Today*, March 1, 2020, at: https://www.usatoday.com/ story/news/nation/2020/03/01/coronavirus-surgeon-general-stop-buying-face-masks/4922614002/.

Baker, B. Granville. "The Mirror of Fashion." *Journal of the Society for Army Historical Research* 17, no. 68 (1938): 205–7.

Baker, Lindsay B., Adam J. Reimel, Bridget C. Sopeña, Kelly A. Barnes, Ryan P. Nuccio, Peter John D. De Chavez, John R. Stofan, and James M. Carter. "Trapped Sweat in Basketball Uniforms and the Effect on Sweat Loss Estimates." *Physiological Reports* 5, no. 18 (2017): e13463. Doi: 10.14814/phy2.13463.

Balci, F. Selcen Kilinc. "Isolation Gowns in Health Care Settings: Laboratory Studies, Regulations and Standards, and Potential Barriers of Gown Selection and Use." *American Journal of Infection Control* 44, no. 1 (2016): 104–11.

Barco Uniforms. "Barco Uniforms Celebrates 90th Anniversary." PRN News Wire, August 2, 2019, at: https://www.prnewswire.com/news-releases/barco-uniforms-celebrates-90th-anniversary-300895530.html. See also: https://web.archive.org/ web/20230807155432/https://www.prnewswire.com/news-releases/barco-uniforms-celebrates-90th-anniversary-300895530.html.

Barco Uniforms. "Our Story." barcouniforms.com, 2021, at: https://www.barcouniforms. com/about-us/. See also: https://web.archive.org/web/20230807182637/https:// barcomade.com/pages/our-story.

Barco Uniforms. "Our Story." Grey's Anatomy Scrubs, 2022, at: https://www. greysanatomyscrubs.com/our-story/.

Barkacs, Linda L. and Craig B. Barkacs. "She's Not Heavy, She's My Sister: Does Anyone Really Give a Hoot About Obesity and Weight Discrimination? The Case of the 'Heavy' Hooters Girls." *Journal of Legal, Ethnical, and Regulatory Issues* 14, no. 2 (2011): 105–16.

Barlow, Aaron. *The Cult of Individualism: A History of an Enduring American Myth.* Santa Barbara, California: ABC-CLIO, 2013.

Barnard, Malcolm, ed. *Fashion Theory: A Reader*, second edition. Abingdon: Routledge, 2020.

Barrick, Nolan Ellmore. "The Architectural Development of the Automobile Filling Station in America." MA thesis, Rice Institute, Houston, Texas, 1937.

Bates, Beth Tompkins. *Pullman Porters and the Rise of Protest Politics in Black America, 1925–1945.* Chapel Hill, North Carolina: University of North Carolina Press, 2001.

Bates, Christina. *A Cultural History of the Nurse's Uniform*. Gatineau: Canadian Museum of Civilization, 2012.

Bates, Christina. "The Nurse's Cap and Its Rituals." *Dress* 36, no. 1 (2010): 21–40.

Batton, Candice and Steve Wilson. "Police Murders: An Examination of Historical Trends in the Killing of Law Enforcement Officers in the United States, 1947 to 1998." *Homicide Studies* 10, no. 2 (2006): 79–97.

Bay, Mia. "Traveling Black/Buying Black: Retail and Roadside Accommodations during the Segregation Era." In *Race and Retail: Consumption across the Color Line*, edited by Mia Bay and Ann Fabian, 15–33. New Brunswick, New Jersey: Rutgers University Press, 2015.

Bearman, Peter. *Doormen*. Chicago, Illinois: University of Chicago Press, 2005.

Beaumont, Fabien, R. Taiar, G. Polidori, H. Trenchard, and F. Grappe. "Aerodynamic Study of Time-Trial Helmets in Cycling Racing Using CFD Analysis." *Journal of Biomechanics* 67, no. 23 (2018): 1–8.

Becker, Marshall Joseph. "Lenape ('Delaware') Mail Carriers and the Origins of the US Postal Service." *American Indian Culture and Research Journal* 39, no. 3 (2015): 99–121.

Beer, Tom. "Journeyman Barbers in Minnesota." Minnesota Historical Society, 2015, at: https://www.mnopedia.org/journeymen-barbers-minnesota. See also: https://web.archive.org/web/20230807154030/https://www.mnopedia.org/journeymen-barbers-minnesota.

Behling, Dorothy U. "Three and a Half Decades of Fashion Adoption Research: What Have We Learned?" *Clothing and Textiles Research Journal* 10, no. 2 (1992): 34–41.

Behrendt, Walter Curt. "Off-Street Parking: A City Planning Problem." *Journal of Land & Public Utility Economics* 16, no. 4 (1940): 464–7.

Beifuss, Artur and Francesco Trivini Bellini. *Branding Terror: The Logotypes and Iconography of Insurgent Groups and Terrorist Organizations*. London: Merrell Publishers, 2013.

Belkin, Nathan L. "Use of Scrubs and Related Apparel in Health Care Facilities." *American Journal of Infection Control*, 25 (1997): 401–4.

Bender, Marylin. "The Hospitality Crusade: Holiday Inns Spreading from Kyoto to Paducah." *New York Times*, August 26, 1973.

Benson, Kristina. "The Freedom to Believe and the Freedom to Practice: Title VII, Muslim Women, and Hijab." *UCLA Journal of Islamic and Near Eastern Law* 13, no. 1 (2014): 1–19.

Berger, Arthur Asa. *Searching for a Self: Identity in Popular Culture, Media and Society*. Wilmington, Delaware: Vernon Press, 2022.

Bergsten, Eric E. "Credit Cards: A Prelude to the Cashless Society." *Boston College Industrial and Commercial Law Review* 8, no. 3 (1967): 485–518.

Berkeley Police Department. "Parking Enforcement Operations Manual." City of Berkeley, California, February 4, 2015, at: https://www.cityofberkeley.info/uploadedFiles/Police/Level_3_-_General/PEOManual111814rev3.pdf.

Bernstein, David E. "Licensing Laws: A Historical Example of the Use of Government Regulatory Power Against African-Americans." *San Diego Law Review* 31, no. 1 (1994): 89–104.

Berry, Leonard L. "Franchising: Some Words of Caution for the Small Businessman." *Journal of Small Business Management* 11, no. 4 (1973): 1–7.

Berthon, Pierre R, Sarah T. Lord Ferguson, Leyland F. Pitt, and Emma Wang. "The Virtuous Brand: The Perils and Promises of Brand Virtue Signaling." *Business Horizons* 66, no. 1 (2023): 27–36.

Best, Kim. "Hospitals Crack Down on Scrub Suit Pilfering." *The Herald-Sun* (Durham, North Carolina), April 30, 1983.

Bhattacharjee, Shovon, Prateek Bahl, Abrar Ahmad Chughtai, and C. Raina MacIntyre. "Last-Resort Strategies During Mask Shortages: Optimal Design Features of Cloth Masks and Decontamination of Disposable Masks During the COVID-19 Pandemic." *BMJ Open Respiratory Research* 7 (2020): e000698.

Bhugra, Dinesh and Padmal De Silva. "Uniforms—Fact, Fashion, Fantasy and Fetish." *Sexual and Marital Therapy* 11, no. 4 (1996): 393–406.

Biefield, Sharla D., Ellen A. Stone, and Christia Spears Brown. "Sexy, Thin, and White: The Intersection of Sexualization, Body Type, and Race on Stereotypes About Women." *Sex Roles* 85 (2021): 287–300.

Bikinis Bar and Grill LLC. 2011. "Breastaurant." US Trademark 85,416,160, filed on September 6, 2011, and issued on October 23, 2012.

Bini, Elisabetta. "Selling Gasoline with a Smile: Gas Station Attendants between the United States, Italy, and the Third World, 1945–1970." *International Labor and Working-Class History* 81 (2012): 69–93.

Bitter, Alex. "Sheetz is Reviewing its Controversial 'Smile Policy' that Prohibits Employees from Having 'Missing, Broken, or Badly Discolored Teeth." *Business Insider*, January 24, 2023, at: https://www.businessinsider.com/sheetz-reviewing-smile-policy-bars-hiring-employees-bad-teeth-2023-1.

Black, Prudence. "A Cast of Thousands: Martin Grant and the New Qantas Uniform." In *Uniform: Clothing and Discipline in the Modern World*, edited by Jane Tynan and Jane Godson, 179–98. London: Bloomsbury Visual Arts, 2019.

Blackall, C.H. "Theater Fires." *The Sanitarian* 43 (April 1, 1904): 340.

Blackwell, Elizabeth and Emily Blackwell. *Address on the Medical Education of Women.* New York: Baptist & Taylor, 1864.

Blumer, Herbert. "Fashion: From Class Differentiation to Collective Selection." *Sociological Quarterly* 10, no. 3 (1969): 275–91.

Board of Cosmetology and Barber Examiners. "Proposed Rule: 20 CSR 2085-11.010 Barber Sanitation Rules," *Missouri Register* 32, no. 18 (2007): 1733, at: https://www.sos.mo.gov/CMSImages/adrules/moreg/2007/v32n18/v32n18(part2)a.pdf.

Bray, Ashley. "Dressing the Part." *ABA Banking Journal* 105, no. 3 (2013): 11.

Bresnahan, John F. and Harriet L. Borman. "A Uniformed Hospital Personnel." *The Modern Hospital* 20, no. 4 (1923): 379–381.

Brooks Brothers. "Outfitting a Nation." *Brooks Brothers Magazine*, 2021, at: https://magazine.brooksbrothers.com/outfitting-a-nation/.

Brotherhood of Sleeping Car Porters, "BSCP Agreements, 1941–1953," Library of Congress, Manuscript Division, A. Philip Randolph Papers, 1951.

Brotherhood of Sleeping Car Porters. "Report of the Proceedings of the Brotherhood of Sleeping Car Porters, Convention Held in St. Louis, Missouri, on September 13–18, 1942." Chicago Historical Society, 1942.

Brown, Angela. "Our Story." Savvy Cleaner, 2021, at: https://savvycleaner.com. See also: https://web.archive.org/web/20230807152528/https://savvycleaner.com/.

Brown, Angela. "Why Uniforms Work: The Psychology of Uniforms." Ask a House Cleaner, February 21, 2021, at: https://askahousecleaner.com/why-uniforms-work/. ee also: https://web.archive.org/web/20230804124833/https://askahousecleaner.com/why-uniforms-work/.

Brown, Angela. "Why Uniforms Work—The Psychology of Cleaning Uniforms." YouTube, February 22, 2021, at: https://www.youtube.com/watch?v=tLafHPs70p4.

Brown, Lee. "Abuse Victim Who Lost Teeth Says She Was Booted from Job Over Sheetz 'Smile Policy.'" *New York Post*, January 31, 2023, at: https://nypost.com/2023/01/31/ohio-woman-claims-she-lost-sheetz-job-because-her-teeth-violated-its-smile-policy/.

Brunsma, David L. *The School Uniform Movement and What it Tells Us About American Education*. Lanham, Maryland: Rowman & Littlefield, 2004.

Bulko, Brian. "Carhoppin' at Eat'n Park." *Western Pennsylvania History: 1918–2018* 82, no. 2 (1999): 84–93.

Cain, Áine. "A Day in the Life of a Playboy Bunny, and How the Controversial Job Has Changed Over 60 Years." *Business Insider*, September 28, 2017, at: https://www.businessinsider.com/playboy-bunnies-history-2017-9.

Calistro, Paddy. "For Some Modern Nurses, Clara Barton Look is Out." *Los Angeles Times*, July 22, 1988.

Calomiris, Charles W. *US Bank Deregulation in Historical Perspective*. Cambridge: Cambridge University Press, 2000.

Cambridge, Nicolas. "Cherry-Picking Sartorial Identities in Cherry-Blossom Land: Uniforms and Uniformity in Japan." *Journal of Design History* 24, no. 2 (2011): 171–86.

Carhartt. "Outworking Them All Since 1889." carhartt.com, 2022, at: https://www.carhartt.com/carhartt-history?icid=abouthistory_042721_carhartt-history_allvisitors.

Carré, Françoise and Chris Tilly, "America's Biggest Low-Wage Industry: Continuity and Change in Retail Jobs." The Center for Social Policy at the University of Massachusetts Boston, 2008, 1, at: https://scholarworks.umb.edu/cgi/viewcontent.cgi?article=1021&context=csp_pubs.

Carroll, Betsey R. "From Candy Stripers to Nursing Career—Well-Planned Program Does It." *Hospital Topics* 42, no. 7 (1964): 44–6.

Carroll, Joseph T. "Recruiting and Training of Police Personnel." *FBI Enforcement Bulletin* 33, no. 12 (1964): 3–8.

Casler, Herman. 1895. "Mutoscope." US Patent 683,910A, filed on February 4, 1896, and issued on October 8, 1901.

Cattley, Alex R. "The British Infantry Shako." *Journal of the Society for Army Historical Research* 15, no. 60 (1936): 188–208.

Centers for Disease Control and Prevention. "How TB Spreads," US Department of Health & Human Services, 2016, at: https://www.cdc.gov/tb/topic/basics/howtbspreads.htm.

Chakravarty, Urvashi. "Livery, Liberty, and Legal Fictions." *English Literary Renaissance* 42, no. 3 (2012): 365–90.

Chall, Malca and Joyce A. Henderson. "A Maid with the Pullman Company, 1926–1931." Interview by Frances Mary Albrier, University of California, 1979, at: https://oac.cdlib.org/view?docId=hb696nb3ht;NAAN=13030&doc.view=frames&chunk.id=div00046&toc.depth=1&toc.id=div00046&brand=oac4.

Chang, Rachel. "Inside Gloria Steinem's Month as an Undercover Playboy Bunny." *Biography*, March 23, 2020, at: https://www.biography.com/news/gloria-steinem-undercover-playboy-bunny.

Chapman, Frank E. "Clothes Make the Man." *The Modern Hospital* 20, no. 4 (1923): 376–9.

Chateauvert, Melinda. *Marching Together: Women of the Brotherhood of Sleeping Car Porters*. Urbana, Illinois: University of Illinois Press, 1998.

Cherokee USA. "Our Story." cherokeeusa.com, 2022, at: http://www.cherokeeusa.com/our-story. See also: https://web.archive.org/web/20230807155753/http://www.cherokeeusa.com/our-story.

Chipotle Mexican Grill. "Chipotle Careers." chipotle.com, 2022, at: https://jobs.chipotle.com/benefits. See also: https://web.archive.org/web/20230807183432/https://jobs.chipotle.com/benefits.

Chippendales. "About Chippendales." chippendales.com, 2022, at: https://www.chippendales.com/about-chippendales. See also: https://web.archive.org/web/20230807184003/https://chippendales.com/.

Chippendales. "Frequently Asked Questions." chippendales.com, 2022, at: https://www.chippendales.com/Hard-FAQs.

Choice Hotels International. "A History of Innovation." choicehotels.com, 2022, at: https://www.choicehotels.com/about/corporate-history. See also: https://web.archive.org/web/20230807181405/https://www.choicehotels.com/about/corporate-history.

Christensen, Clayton M., Heiner Baumann, Rudy Ruggles, and Thomas M. Sadtler. "Disruptive Innovation for Social Change." *Harvard Business Review* 84, no. 12 (2006): 94–103.

Cintas Corporation. "Direct Purchase Uniforms." cintas.com, 2022, at: https://www.cintas.com/industries/hospitality/uniforms/.
See also: https://web.archive.org/web/20230807181513/https://www.cintas.com/industries/hospitality/hospitality-uniforms-apparel/.Cintas Corporation. "Hotel Uniform Rental." cintas.com, 2022, at: https://www.cintas.com/industries/hospitality/rental-uniforms/.

Cobble, Dorothy Sue. *Dishing It Out: Waitresses and Their Unions in the Twentieth Century.* Champaign, Illinois: University of Illinois Press, 1991.

Cohen, Jennifer and Yana van der Meulen Rodgers. "Contributing Factors to Personal Protective Equipment Shortages During the COVID-19 Pandemic." *Preventative Medicine* 141 (2020): 1–7. Doi: 10.1016/j.ypmed.2020.106263.

Collins, James. "Why Doormen?" *New York Times*, April 26, 2010.

Committee on Oversight and Government Reform. "The Ebola Crisis: Coordination of a Multi-Agency Response." Serial No. 113-163, Washington, DC: US House of Representatives, October 24, 2014, at: https://www.govinfo.gov/content/pkg/CHRG-113hhrg94053/pdf/CHRG-113hhrg94053.pdf.

Corporate Image Group. "Custom Apparel." corporateimagegroup.com, 2022, at: https://corporateimagegroup.com/services/custom-apparel/. See also: https://web.archive.org/web/20230807181625/https://www.corporateimagegroup.com/apparel.

Craik, Jennifer. *Uniforms Exposed: From Conformity to Transgression.* Oxford: Berg Publishers, 2005.

Crane-Seeber, Jesse Paul. "Sexy Warriors: The Politics and Pleasures of Submission to the State." In *Embodying Militarism*, edited by Synne L. Dyvik and Lauren Greenwood, 41–55. New York: Routledge, 2018.

Cummings, Jenna R., Lindzey V. Hoover, Meredith I. Turner, Kalei Glozier, Jessica Zhao, and Ashley N. Gearhardt. "Extending Expectancy Theory to Food Intake: Effect of a Simulated Fast-Food Restaurant on Highly and Minimally Processed Food Expectancies." *Clinical Psychological Science* 9, no. 6 (2021): 1115–27.

Dauphin, Traci. "How One Vegas Casino Uses iPads to Loosen Up Gamblers." *Cult of Mac*, January 12, 2013, at: https://www.cultofmac.com/209180/how-one-vegas-casino-uses-ipads-to-loosen-up-gamblers/. See also: https://web.archive.org/web/20230807184156/https://www.cultofmac.com/209180/how-one-vegas-casino-uses-ipads-to-loosen-up-gamblers/.

Davis, Fred. *Fashion, Culture, and Identity.* Chicago, Illinois: University of Chicago Press.

De Casanova, Erynn Masi. *Buttoned Up: Clothing, Conformity, and White-Collar Masculinity.* Ithaca, New York: ILR Press, 2015.

de Volo, Lorraine Bayard. "Service and Surveillance: Infrapolitics at Work among Casino Cocktail Waitresses." *Social Politics: International Studies in Gender, State & Society* 10, no. 3 (2003): 346–76.

DeLong, Marilyn Revell. "Fashion, Theories of." In *The Berg Companion to Fashion*, edited by Valerie Steele, 321–8. London: Bloomsbury Academic, 2010.

DeMarco, Joseph R.G. "Power and Control in Gay Strip Clubs." In *Male Sex Work: A Business Doing Pleasure*, edited by Todd G. Morrison and Bruce W. Whitehead, 111–28. Philadelphia, Pennsylvania: Haworth Press, 2007.

DeMichele, Matthew T. and Richard Tewksbury, "Sociological Explorations in Site-Specific Social Control: The Role of the Strip Club Bouncer." *Deviant Behavior* 25 (2004): 537–58.

DeMitchell, Todd A. *The Challenges of Mandating School Uniforms in the Public Schools: Free Speech, Research, and Policy*. Lanham, Maryland: Rowman & Littlefield, 2015.

Deighton, Katie. "Some Flight Attendants Can Bring Their Full Selves to Work—Tattoos, Sneakers, Nose Studs, and All." *Wall Street Journal*, June 9, 2022, at: https://www.wsj.com/articles/some-flight-attendants-can-bring-their-full-selves-to-worktattoos-sneakers-nose-studs-and-all-11654768800.

Department of Justice. "Coldspring Man Gets Life in Postal Carrier Death Case." US Attorney's Office, Southern District of Texas, December 6, 2021, at: https://www.justice.gov/usao-sdtx/pr/coldspring-man-gets-life-postal-carrier-death-case.

Department of Labor. "Title 46: Professional and Occupational Standards: Barbers (Part VII)." State of Louisiana, Board of Barber Examiners, July 1964, at: https://www.doa.la.gov/media/uwabz4p3/46v07.pdf.

Department of Public Works. "About DPW." District of Columbia, 2022, at: https://dpw.dc.gov/page/about-dpw.

Department of State Parks and Cultural Resources. "Uniform Policy." State of Wyoming, March 8, 2010, 2, at: http://spcrintranet.wyo.gov/UNIFORM%20POLICY%20-%20updated%203-8-10.pdf.

Detman, Linda A. "Women Behind Bars: The Feminization of Bartending." In *Job Queues, Gender Queues: Explaining Women's Inroads into Male Occupations*, edited by Barbara F. Reskin and Patricia A. Roos, 241–56. Philadelphia, Pennsylvania: Temple University Press, 1990.

Diamond, Anna. "A Crispy, Salty, American History of Fast Food." *Smithsonian Magazine*, June 24, 2019, at: https://www.smithsonianmag.com/history/crispy-salty-american-history-fast-food-180972459/.

Dickies. "Dickies Heritage: On the Job Since 1922." dickies.com, 2022, at: https://www.dickies.com/history.html. See also: https://web.archive.org/web/20230807160837/https://www.dickies.com/history.html.

Dill, Bonnie Thornton. *Across the Boundaries of Race and Class: An Exploration of Work and Family among Black Female Domestic Servants*. New York: Routledge, 1994.

Dillon, Jr., John L. 1990. "Unisex Scrub Shirt and Methods for Making Same." US Patent 5,083,315A, filed December 13, 1990, and issued January 28, 1992.

Dissinger, Kaleb, Rodney Foytik, David Accetta, and David Cole. "Common Threads: Army." US Department of Defense, 2021, at: https://www.defense.gov/Experience/Common-Threads/Common-Threads-Army/.

District of Columbia, "Standard Operating Procedures for Parking Officers and Supervisory Parking Officers," dpw.gov, 2011, at: https://dpw.dc.gov/sites/default/files/dc/sites/dpw/publication/attachments/Parking%20Enforcement%20SOP%20final%20edition%202011.rev%2011%202%2011.pdf.

Division of Human Rights. "Important Updates to the New York State Human Rights Law." State of New York, 2019, at: https://dhr.ny.gov/sites/default/files/pdf/nysdhr-legal-updates-10112019.pdf.

Division of Licensing Services, "Appearance Enhancement," New York Department of State, 2020, at: https://dos.ny.gov/system/files/documents/2021/05/appearance_enhancement_feb_2021.pdf.

Division of Professional Regulation. "24 Delaware Code, Section 5100 Board of Cosmetology and Barbering." Delaware Department of State, 2017, at: https://regulations.delaware.gov/register/may2017/final/20%20DE%20Reg%20916%2005-01-17.htm.

Dix, Mark H. *An American Business Adventure: The Story of Henry A. Dix.* New York: Harper & Brothers Publishers, 1928.

Donahue, Patricia M. *Nursing, the Finest Art: An Illustrated History.* St. Louis, Missouri: C.V. Mosby, 1985.

Donovan, Frances R. *The Woman Who Waits.* Boston, Massachusetts: Gorham Press, 1920.

Dorsey, Leslie and Janice Devine. *Fare Thee Well: A Backward Look at Two Centuries of Historic American Hostelries, Fashionable Spas & Seaside Resorts.* New York: Crown Publishers, 1964.

Dowling, Emma. "The Waitress: On Affect, Method, and (Re)presentation." *Cultural Studies Critical Methodologies* 12, no. 2 (2012): 109–17.

Doyle, Kristy, John O'Brien, and Niamh Maguire. "Precarity in the Night-time Economy." *Irish Journal of Anthropology* 20, no. 2 (2017): 39–51.

Dozier, Raine. "Female Masculinity at Work: Managing Stigma on the Job." *Psychology of Women Quarterly* 41, no. 2 (2017): 197–209.

Druesedow, Jean L. "Ready-to-Wear." In *The Berg Companion to Fashion*, edited by Valerie Steele, 591–96. Oxford: Bloomsbury Academic, 2010.

Dunkin' Donuts. "Dunkin' Donuts History." dunkindonuts.com, 2016, at: https://news.dunkindonuts.com/internal_redirect/cms.ipressroom.com.s3.amazonaws.com/285/files/201610/Dunkin%27%20Donuts%20History_11%203%2016.pdf. See also: https://web.archive.org/web/20230807182608/https://news.dunkindonuts.com/internal_redirect/cms.ipressroom.com.s3.amazonaws.com/285/files/201610/Dunkin%27%20Donuts%20History_11%203%2016.pdf.

Dwyer-McNulty, Sally. *Common Threads: A Cultural History of Clothing in American Catholicism.* Chapel Hill, North Carolina: University of North Carolina Press, 2014.

eBay. "Government Items Policy." ebay.com, 2022, at: https://www.ebay.com/help/policies/prohibited-restricted-items/government-items-policy?id=4318&st=12&pos=1&query=Government%20items%20policy&intent=government&context=9010_BUYER&docId=HELP1254. See also: https://web.archive.org/web/20230807174807/https://www.ebay.com/help/policies/prohibited-restricted-items/government-items-policy?id=4318&st=12&pos=1&query=Government%20items%20policy&intent=government&context=9010_BUYER&docId=HELP1254.

Edelhauser, Kristin. "Cashing in on Controversy." *Entrepreneur*, February 26, 2007, at: https://www.entrepreneur.com/article/175144.

Edwards, Blake, director. *The Great Race.* Warner Brothers, 1965.

Edwards, Chime. "The Impact of the 'Fro in the Civil Rights Movement." *Essence*, October 27, 2020, at: https://www.essence.com/holidays/black-history-month/impact-fro-civil-rights-movement/.

Ehrenreich, Barbara. *Nickel and Dimed: On (Not) Getting by in America*. New York: Picador USA, 2011.

Eicher, Joanne. "Dress." In *Routledge International Encyclopedia of Women: Global Women's Issues and Knowledge*, edited by Cheris Kramarae and Dale Spender, 422–3. New York: Routledge, 2000.

Eiserer, Tanya. "First 'Police Women' Limited in Duties." *Abilene Reporter-News* (Abilene, Texas), August 3, 1997.

Emerson, William K. *Encyclopedia of United States Army Insignia and Uniforms*. Norman, Oklahoma: University of Oklahoma Press, 1996.

Emery, Joy Spanabel. *A History of the Paper Pattern Industry: The Home Dressmaking Fashion Revolution*. London: Bloomsbury Academic, 2014.

Entwistle, Joanne. *The Fashioned Body: Fashion, Dress and Social Theory*, second edition. Cambridge: Polity Press, 2015.

Erdma, David M. "Medical Scrub Garment Thieves May Face Change in Uniform." *The Morning Call* (Allentown, Pennsylvania), January 6, 1986.

Eschner, Kat. "How Hoop Skirts Led to Tape Measures." *Smithsonian Magazine*, July 14, 2017, at: https://www.smithsonianmag.com/smart-news/how-hoop-skirts-led-tape-measures-180963995/.

Evans, Caroline. *Fashion at the Edge: Spectacle, Modernity & Deathliness*. New Haven, Connecticut: Yale University Press, 2003.

Evans, Caroline. "Street Style, Subculture and Subversion." *Costume* 31, no. 1 (1997): 105–10.

Everett, Marshall. *The Great Chicago Theater Disaster: The Complete Story Told by the Survivors*. Chicago, Illinois: Publishers Union of America, 1904.

Executive Apparel. "About Us." executiveapparel.com, 2021, at: https://executiveapparel.com/about-us/. See also: https://web.archive.org/web/20230807181838/https://executiveapparel.com/about-us/.

Executive Apparel. "Hospitality: Rising from the Ashes." executiveapparel.com, March 10, 2021, at: https://executiveapparel.com/hospitality-rising-from-the-ashes/.

Executive Office of the President of the United States. "Standard Occupational Classification Manual." US Bureau of Labor Statistics, 2018, at: https://www.bls.gov/soc/2018/soc_2018_manual.pdf.

Fechheimer Brothers Co. "About Us," fechheimer.com, 2013, at: https://www.fechheimer.com/. See also: https://web.archive.org/web/20230807180042/https://www.fechheimer.com/.

Federal Deposit Insurance Corporation. "Historical Bank Data." fdic.gov, December 31, 2021, at: https://banks.data.fdic.gov/explore/historical.

Feldman, Herman. *Prohibition: Its Economic and Industrial Aspects*. New York: D. Appleton and Company, 1930.

Fernandez, Chantal. "How Stan Herman, Father of Fashion Week, Changed the US Fashion Industry." *Fashionista*, June 29, 2015, at: https://fashionista.com/2015/06/stan-herman-father-of-fashion-week.

Finn, Robin. "The Latest (or Not) in Doorman Fashion," *New York Times*, January 17, 2010.

Fischer, Claude S. "Paradoxes of American Individualism." *Sociological Forum* 23, no. 2 (2008): 363–72.

Freeman, Aleza. "Chronology of the Cocktail Waitress." Vegas.com, August 31, 2008, at: https://www.vegas.com/alwaysopen/pdfs/icon-cocktail-waitress.pdf. See also: https://web.archive.org/web/20230807184127/https://www.vegas.com/alwaysopen/pdfs/icon-cocktail-waitress.pdf.

Freidinger, Stella. "Maintaining Standards in Small Hospitals and Training Schools." *American Journal of Nursing* 20, no. 7 (1920): 535–8.

Fried, Stephen. *Appetite for America: Fred Harvey and the Business of Civilizing the Wild West—One Meal at a Time*. New York: Bantam Books, 2010.

Froeb, Ian. "Breastaurant Uniforms Owner Terra Watson: The Gut Check Interview." *Riverfront Times,* July 2, 2012, at: https://www.riverfronttimes.com/food-drink/breastaurant-uniforms-owner-terra-watson-the-gut-check-interview-2620123. See also: https://web.archive.org/web/20230807184617/https://www.riverfronttimes.com/food-drink/breastaurant-uniforms-owner-terra-watson-the-gut-check-interview-2620123.

Fuller, Linda K., ed. *Sportswomen's Apparel Around the World: Uniformly Discussed*, New York: Palgrave Macmillan, 2020.

Funderburg, Anne Cooper. *Chocolate, Strawberry, and Vanilla: A History of American Ice Cream*. Bowling Green, Ohio: Bowling Green State University Press, 1995.

Furman, Eugene, Alex Cressman, Saeha Shin, Alexey Kuznetsov, Fahad Razak, Amol Verma, and Adam Diamant. "Prediction of Personal Protective Equipment Use in Hospitals During COVID-19." *Health Care Management Science* 24 (2021): 439–53.

Fussell, Paul. *Uniforms*. New York: Houghton Mifflin, 2002.

Gallagher, Winifred. *How the Post Office Created America: A History*. New York: Penguin Books, 2016.

Garbino, Ali. "From Our Employees: What More Inclusive Gender-Neutral Uniforms and Policies Mean for Bringing Our Best Selves to Work." Alaska Airlines, March 28, 2022, at: https://news.alaskaair.com/diversity-equity-and-inclusion/alaska-airlines-gender-neutral-uniforms-pronouns/. See also: https://web.archive.org/web/20230807185817/https://news.alaskaair.com/diversity-equity-and-inclusion/alaska-airlines-gender-neutral-uniforms-pronouns/.

Gereffi, Gary. "What Does the COVID-19 Pandemic Teach Us About Global Value Chains? The Case of Medical Supplies." *Journal of International Business Policy* 3 (2020): 287–301.

Giasullo, Gia and Peter Freeman. *The Soda Fountain: Floats, Sundaes, Eggs Cream & More—Flavors and Traditions of an American Original*. Berkeley, California: Ten Speed Press, 2014.

Godley, Andrew. "The Global Diffusion of the Sewing Machine, 1850–1914." *Research in Economic History* 20 (2001): 1–45.

Godson, Susan H. *Serving Proudly: A History of Women in the U.S. Navy*. Annapolis, Maryland: Naval Institute Press, 2001.

Goldman, Isadore and Jacob Cohen. 1932. "Barber's Coat." US Patent 1,8878,275, filed December 12, 1931, and issued September 20, 1932.

Goldstein, Herman. "Police Discretion: The Ideal Versus the Real." *Public Administration Review* 23, no. 3 (1963): 140–8.

Gomery, Douglas. *Shared Pleasures: A History of Movie Presentation in the United States*. Madison, Wisconsin: University of Wisconsin Press, 1992.

Gordon, Tammy S. "History, Heritage and the Museum Function of a Sports Bar." In *The Dynamics of Interconnections in Popular Culture(s)*, edited by Ray B. Browne and Ben Urish, 36–54. Newcastle upon Tyne: Cambridge Scholars Publishers, 2014.

Gorzalski, Alexander S. and Anne L. Spiesman, "Washington Aqueduct: Serving Our Nation's Capital for Over 150 Years," *Journal (American Water Works Association)* 108, no. 2 (2016): 40–7.

Gould, Elise and David Cooper. "Seven Facts about Tipped Workers and the Tipped Minimum Wage." Economic Policy Institute, May 31, 2018, at: https://www.epi.org/blog/seven-facts-about-tipped-workers-and-the-tipped-minimum-wage/?gclid=CjwKCAiAp8iMBhAqEiwAJb94z4hac9ry1GRDwm8VlpFLV_B7d3fI4ZyPb6AHB9GUOtxkT01go6hM6BoC2FMQAvD_BwE.

Grasso, Valerie Bailey. "The Berry Amendment: Requiring Defense Procurement to Come from Domestic Sources." Washington, DC: Congressional Research Service, February 24, 2014.

Grimm, Edward. *The Doorman*. New York: Orchard Books, 2000.

Groth, Paul E. *Living Downtown: The History of Residential Hotels in the United States*. Berkeley, California: University of California Press, 1994.

Guéguen, Nicolas and Céline Jacob. "Clothing Color and Tipping: Gentlemen Patrons Give More Tips to Waitresses with Red Clothes." *Journal of Hospitality and Tourism Research* 38, no. 2 (2014): 275–80.

Gurevitch, Leon. "The Stereoscopic Attraction: Three-Dimensional Images and the Spectacular Paradigm, 1850–2013." *Convergence: The International Journal of Research into New Media Technologies* 19, no. 4 (2013): 396–405.

Guzman, Alyssa. "Bank of America Tells its Workers to DRESS DOWN." *Daily Mail*, December 3, 2021, at: https://www.dailymail.co.uk/news/article-10272073/Bank-America-tells-workers-DRESS-head-NYCs-Bryant-Park-office.html.

Haley, Andrew P. "Dining in High Chairs: Children and the American Restaurant Industry, 1900–1950." *Food & History* 7, no. 2 (2009): 69–94.

Hall, Elaine J. "Smiling, Deferring, and Flirting: Doing Gender by Giving 'Good Service.'" *Work and Occupations* 20, no. 4 (1993): 452–71.

Hammonds, Clare, Jasmine Kerrissey, and Donald Tomaskovic-Devey, "Stressed, Unsafe, and Insecure: Essential Workers Need a New, New Deal," University of Massachusetts

Amherst Labor Center, June 5, 2020, at: https://www.umass.edu/lrrc/sites/default/files/Stressed%2C%20Unsafe%2C%20and%20Insecure-%20Essential%20Workers%20Need%20A%20New%2C%20New%20Deal%20.pdf.

Hanna, Judith Lynne. *Strip Clubs, Democracy, and a Christian Right*. Austin, Texas: University of Texas Press, 2013.

Hanson, J. W. *The Official History of the Fair, St. Louis, 1904: The Sights and Scenes of the Louisiana Purchase Exposition*. St. Louis, Missouri: St. Louis Fair Officials, 1904.

Hardy, Susan and Anthony Corones. "Dressed to Heal: The Changing Semiotics of Surgical Dress." *Fashion Theory* 20, no. 1 (2016): 27–49.

Harris, Lloyd C. and Emmanuel Ogbonna. "Motives for Service Sabotage: An Empirical Study of Front-line Workers." *Service Industries Journal* 32, no. 13 (2012): 2027–46.

Hatfield, Julie. "Hospital Scrubs Suits Hit the Streets." *Boston Globe*, May 29, 1980.

Hayward, Maria. *Rich Apparel: Clothing and the Law in Henry VIII's England*. Farnham: Ashgate Publishing, 2009.

Headd, Brian. "The Characteristics of Small-Business Employees." *Monthly Labor Review*, April 2000, at: https://www.bls.gov/opub/mlr/2000/04/art3full.pdf.

Healing Hands Scrubs. "Our Story." healinghandsscrubs.com, 2022, at: https://healinghandsscrubs.com/pages/our-story. See also: https://web.archive.org/web/20230807173220/https://www.healinghandsscrubs.com/our-story.html

Heart Attack Grill. "Licensing." heartattackgrill.com, 2022, at: https://www.heartattackgrill.com/license.html. See also: https://web.archive.org/web/20230807185034/https://www.heartattackgrill.com/license.html.

Heart Attack Grill. "Press." heartattackgrill.com, 2022, at: https://www.heartattackgrill.com/press.html. See also: https://web.archive.org/web/20230807184839/https://www.heartattackgrill.com/press.html.

Henry Ford Museum of American Innovation. Press kit from Holiday Inns of America, Inc. c. 1979, at: https://www.thehenryford.org/collections-and-research/digital-collections/artifact/455755/#slide=gs-431723.

Hernandez-Villanueva, Cesar. "Dress Code and Religious Accommodations through the Lense of EEOC v. Kroger." *Rutgers Journal of Law & Religion* 22, no. 1 (2021): 161–99.

Herskovitz, Jon. "Texas Hospital Reaches Settlement with Nurse Infected with Ebola." Reuters, October 24, 2016, at: https://www.reuters.com/article/us-health-ebola-texas-nurse/texas-hospital-reaches-settlement-with-nurse-infected-with-ebola-idUSKCN12O2AF.

Hilgers, Lauren. "The Future of Work Issue: 'Nurses Have Finally Learned What They're Worth.'" *New York Times*, February 15, 2022, at: https://www.nytimes.com/2022/02/15/magazine/traveling-nurses.html.

History Channel. "Last Day for Texas' Celebrated Drive-in Pig Stands." A&E Television Networks, November 14, 2000, at: http://www.history.com/this-day-in-history/last-day-for-texas-celebrated-drive-in-pig-stands. See also: https://web.archive.org/web/20230807183829/https://www.history.com/this-day-in-history/last-day-for-texas-celebrated-drive-in-pig-stands.

Hitchcock, Alfred, director. *Vertigo*. Alfred J. Hitchcock Productions, 1958.

Hochberg, Mark S. "The Doctor's White Coat: An Historical Perspective." *AMA Journal of Ethics*, 2007, at: https://journalofethics.ama-assn.org/article/doctors-white-coat-historical-perspective/2007-04.

Hochschild, Arlie Russell. *The Managed Heart: Commercialization of Human Feeling*. Berkeley, California: University of California Press, 1983.

Hodge, Robert W., Paul M. Siegel, and Peter H. Rossi. "Occupational Prestige in the United States, 1925–63." *American Journal of Sociology* 70, no. 3 (1964): 286–302.

Hooters of America. "All Locations." hooters.com, 2022, at: https://www.hooters.com/location-list/. See also: https://web.archive.org/web/20230807185046/https://www.hooters.com/location-list/.

Hooters of America. "Hooters Continues Expansion in Asia with New Location in Manila." hooters.com, June 15, 2016, at: https://www.hooters.com/about/news/hooters-continues-expansion-in-asia-with-new-location-in-manila. See also: https://web.archive.org/web/20230807185058/https://www.hooters.com/about/news/hooters-continues-expansion-in-asia-with-new-location-in-manila.

Hooters of America. "The Recipe for a Good Time." hooters.com, 2022, at: https://www.hooters.com/about/history/. See also: https://web.archive.org/web/20230807184407/https://www.hooters.com/about/history/.

Hooters Incorporated. "The Official Saga: Hooters History." originalhooters.com, 2022, at: https://www.originalhooters.com/saga. See also: https://web.archive.org/web/20230807184320/https://www.originalhooters.com/saga.

Hsieh, Vanessa. "A Brief History of Baby Phat, the Cult 00s Label Bringing Sexy Back." *Dazed*, March 12, 2019, at: https://www.dazeddigital.com/fashion/article/43682/1/baby-phat-cult-00s-y2k-fashion-label-hip-hop-kimora-lee-simmons-lil-kim-aaliyah.

Huhtamo, Erkki. "Slots of Fun, Slots of Trouble: An Archaeology of Arcade Gaming." In *Handbook of Computer Games Studies*, edited by Joost Raessens and Jeffrey Goldstein, 3–21. Cambridge, Massachusetts: MIT Press, 2005.

Human Technologies Corporation. "USACE Press Release." htcorp.net, 2021, at: https://htcorp.net/usace/.

IHG Hotels & Resorts. "Haute Hospitality: Uniform Collection MOMENTUM by Timo Weiland for Crowne Plaza Debuts at New York Fashion Week." ihgplc.com, August 10, 2017, at: https://www.ihgplc.com/news-and-media/news-releases/2017/haute-hospitality-uniform-collection-momentum-by-timo-weiland-for-crowne-plaza. See also: https://web.archive.org/web/20230807181438/https://www.ihgplc.com/en/news-and-media/news-releases/2017/haute-hospitality-uniform-collection-momentum-by-timo-weiland-for-crowne-plaza.

Indiana Civil Rights Commission. "What is a Protected Class?" IN.gov, 2022, at: https://faqs.in.gov/hc/en-us/articles/115005057627-What-is-a-protected-class-.

Iredale, Jessica. "Zac Posen on Creative Directing for a Conservative Customer." *Women's Wear Daily*, April 25, 2018, at: https://wwd.com/fashion-news/fashion-features/zac-posen-on-creative-directing-a-conservative-customer-1202657064/.

Irwin, Julia F. "Connected by Calamity: The United States, the League of Red Cross Societies, and Transnational Disaster Assistance after the First World War." *Moving the Social*, 57 (2017): 57–76.

Isaac Long, "Maids' Uniforms," *The Wilkes-Barre Record* (Wilkes-Barre, Pennsylvania), June 9, 1941.

Itzkowitz, Laura. "The Little-Known Story Behind Cincinnati's Terrace Plaza Hotel." *Architectural Digest*, February 3, 2021, at: https://www.architecturaldigest.com/story/the-little-known-story-behind-cincinnatis-terrace-plaza-hotel.

Jackson, Kellie Carter. "'She Was a Member of the Family': Ethel Phillips, Domestic Labor, and Employer Perceptions." *Women's Studies Quarterly* 45, no. 3/4 (2017): 160–73.

Jernigan, Sara, Steve Austin, and Amanda Palmer, "USACE Natural Resource Management Uniform Program." US Army Corps of Engineers, April 18, 2017, at: https://corpslakes.erdc.dren.mil/employees/conferences/17National/Park%20Ranger%20Uniforms.pdf.

Johnson, Gareth. "The Strange Tale of Hooters Cambodia." *Khmer Knights*, June 15, 2021, at: https://www.khmernights.com/the-strange-tale-of-hooters-cambodia/. See also: https://web.archive.org/web/20230807185347/https://www.khmernights.com/the-strange-tale-of-hooters-cambodia/.

Johnson, Jon. "Prickly Heat: What You Need to Know." *Medical News Today*, October 4, 2017, at: https://www.medicalnewstoday.com/articles/319612.

Johnson, Kareem J., Christian E. Waugh, and Barbara L. Fredrickson. "Smile to See the Forest: Facially Expressed Positive Emotions Broaden Cognition." *Cognitive Emotion* 24, no. 2 (2010): 299–321.

Johnson, Ronald N. and Charles J. Romeo. "The Impact of Self-Service Bans in the Retail Gasoline Market." *Review of Economics and Statistics* 82, no. 4 (2000): 625–33.

Johnson, Wallace E. *Together We Build: The Life and Faith of Wallace E. Johnson*. New York: Hawthorn Books, 1978.

Jones, Liz. "Sorry, I Found This Burger Bar More Offensive Than a Lapdancing Club." *Daily Mail* (London, UK), October 7, 2010, at: https://www.dailymail.co.uk/femail/article-1318258/Hooters--offensive-bar-Britain-Asks-Liz-Jones.html.

Joseph, Nathan. *Uniforms and Nonuniforms: Communication through Clothing*. Westport, Connecticut: Greenwood Press, 1986.

JP Morgan Chase. "Chase Apparel Dress Code." Between My Peers, 2010, at: http://betweenmypeers.com/wp-content/uploads/2010/06/chase_dressguidelines.doc.

Kalisch, Beatrice J., Philip A. Kalisch, and Mary L. McHugh. "The Nurse as a Sex Object in Motion Pictures, 1930 to 1980." *Research in Nursing & Health* 5, no. 3 (1982): 147–54.

Kaminer, Debbie. "Uniforms, Dress Codes and an Employee's Religious Observance." *New York State Bar Association Journal* 84, no. 8 (2012): 26–31.

Kaplan, Michael. "The Shockingly Dark History of Chippendales." *New York Post*, February 7, 2021, at: https://nypost.com/article/dark-history-of-chippendales/.

Karch, Guenther E. and Mike Peters. "The Impact of Employee Uniforms on Job Satisfaction in the Hospitality Industry." *Journal of Hotel & Business Management* 6, no. 1 (2017): 1–6. Doi: 10.4172/2169-0286.1000157.

Kaufman-Straus, Co. "The Christmas Store." *The Courier-Journal* (Louisville, Kentucky), November 26, 1922.

Kelly, Cordelia W. "What Nurses Want in a Uniform." *The American Journal of Nursing* 57, no. 10 (1957): 1282–4.

Kelly, Debra. "The Untold Truth of Heart Attack Grill." *Mashed*, July 15, 2020, at: https://www.mashed.com/210610/the-untold-truth-of-heart-attack-grill/.

Kim, Alexandra. "Class, Work, and Dress." In *Berg Encyclopedia of World Dress and Fashion: West Europe*, edited by Lise Skov, 444–51. Oxford: Bloomsbury Academic, 2010.

Kim, Minjee and Tingyu Zhou. "Does Restricting the Entry of Formula Businesses Help Mom-and-Pop Stores? The Case of Small American Towns with Unique Community Character." *Economic Development Quarterly* 35, no. 2 (2021): 157–73.

King, Charles W. "Fashion Adoption: A Rebuttal to 'Trickle-Down' Theory." In *Toward Scientific Marketing*, edited by Stephen A. Greyser, 108–25. Chicago, Illinois: American Marketing Association, 1963.

King, W. D. "When Theater Becomes History: Final Curtains on the Victorian Stage." *Victorian Studies* 36, no. 1 (1992): 53–61.

Kirkby, Diane. "Writing the History of Women Working: Photographic Evidence and the 'Disreputable Occupation of Barmaid.'" *Labour History*, 61 (1991): 3–16.

Kite-Powell, Jennifer. "Here's the Real Story of Issey Miyake and Steve Jobs' Iconic Turtleneck." Forbes, August 10, 2022, at: https://www.forbes.com/sites/jenniferhicks/2022/08/10/heres-the-real-story-of-issey-miyake-and-steve-jobs-iconic-turtleneck/?sh=ae72480303f5.

Klein, Lloyd and Steve Lang. "Truth, Justice and the Walmart Way: Consequences of a Retailing Behemoth." In *The Routledge International Handbook of the Crimes of the Powerful*, edited by Gregg Barak, 121–31. Abingdon: Routledge, 2015.

Knoch, Habbo. "Life on Stage: Grand Hotels as Urban Interzones Around 1900." In *Creative Urban Milieus: Historical Perspectives on Cultures, Economy, and the City*, edited by Martina Heßler and Clemens Zimmermann, 137–57. Frankfurt: Campus Verlag, 2008.

Koi Design. "About Us." Koi by Kathy Peterson, 2021, at: https://www.koihappiness.com/our-story/. See also: https://web.archive.org/web/20230807160113/https://www.koihappiness.com/pages/about-koi.

Kolm, Suzanne Lee. "Women's Labor Aloft: A Cultural History of Airline Flight Attendants in the United States, 1930–1978." PhD diss., Brown University, Providence, Rhode Island, 1995.

Koops, Kathy S. "Terrace Hilton Hotel." The Cincy Blog: Cincinnati Real Estate, September 9, 2015, at: https://thecincyblog.com/tag/terrace-hilton-hotel/ See also: https://web.archive.org/web/20230807153234/https://thecincyblog.com/tag/terrace-hilton-hotel/..

Korczynski, Marek and Claire Evans. "Customer Abuse to Service Workers: An Analysis of its Social Creation Within the Service Economy." *Work, Employment and Society* 27, no. 5 (2013): 768–84.

Kramer, Sarah. "Keeping Peace in a Vertical Village." *New York Times*, May 12, 2013.

Kronsberg, Suzanne, Josephine Rachel Bouret, and Anne Liners Brett. "Lived Experiences of Male Nurses: Dire Consequences for the Nursing Profession." *Journal of Nursing Education and Practice* 8, no. 1 (2018): 46–53.

Kuhn, Thomas S. *The Structure of Scientific Revolutions*. Chicago, Illinois: University of Chicago Press, 1962.

Kurent, Heather Paul. "Frances R. Donovan and the Chicago School of Sociology: A Case Study in Marginality." PhD diss., University of Maryland, 1982.

Kusserow, Adrie S. *American Individualisms: Child Rearing and Social Class in Three Neighborhoods*. New York: Palgrave Macmillan, 2004.

La Ferla, Ruth. "Hospitals are Discovering Their Inner Spa." *New York Times*, August 13, 2000.

Landau Uniforms. "Landau: Our Story." landau.com, 2022, at: https://www.landau.com/about. See also: https://web.archive.org/web/20230807155643/https://www.landau.com/about .

Lands' End. "Chase Store." landsend.com, 2022, at: https://business.landsend.com/store/chasestorena/. See also: https://web.archive.org/web/20230807182504/https://business.landsend.com/store/chasestorena/.

Lands' End. "Custom Bank & Financial Uniform Clothing." landsend.com, 2022, at: https://business.landsend.com/Finance/c/78?&pageSize=72. See also: https://web.archive.org/web/20230807182335/https://business.landsend.com/Finance/c/78?&pageSize=72.

Lands' End. "Lands' End Business." landsend.com, 2022, at: https://business.landsend.com/?cm_mmc=lecom-_-corenavs. See also: https://web.archive.org/web/20230807182424/https://business.landsend.com/?cm_mmc=lecom-_-corenavs.

Lands' End. "School Uniforms." landsend.com, 2022, at: https://www.landsend.com/shop/school-uniform/S-ytp. See also: https://web.archive.org/web/20230807182223/https://www.landsend.com/shop/school-uniform/S-ytp.

Lane-Kamahele, M. Melia. "Considerations of Culture, Community, Change, and the Centennial." *George Wright Forum* 30, no. 2 (2013): 107–16.

Laver, James. *British Military Uniforms*. London: Penguin Books, 1948.

Leidenberger, Georg. *Chicago's Progressive Alliance: Labor and the Bid for Public Streetcars*. DeKalb, Illinois: Northern Illinois University Press, 2006.

Lennerlöf, Lennart. "Learned Helplessness at Work." In *The Psychosocial Work Environment: Work Organization, Democratization and Health*, edited by Jeffrey V. Johnson, Bertil Gardell, and Gunn Johannson, 73–88. New York: Routledge, 2020.

Lennon, Sharron J., Zhiying Zheng, and Aziz Fatnassi. "Women's Revealing Halloween Costumes: Other-Objectification and Sexualization." *Fashion and Textiles* 3, no. 21 (2016): 1–19.

Lesure, John D. "Motor Hotels and Market Studies: The Accountant's Role." *New York Certified Public Accountant* 29, no. 7 (1959): 499–504.

Levit, Nancy. "Changing Workforce Demographics and the Future of the Protected Class Approach." *Lewis & Clark Law Review* 16, no. 2 (2012): 463–98.

Levy, Alan. "The West Passes the Topless Test: A Morality Play in Three Acts." *LIFE Magazine*, March 11, 1966.

Levy, Viola S. 1939. "Uniform Dress." US Patent 115,117S, filed February 23, 1939, and issued June 6, 1939.

Li, Tom, Yan Liu, Xiaoning Qian, and Susie Y. Dai. "Mask or No Mask for COVID-19: A Public Health and Market Study." *PLoS One* 15, no. 8: e0237691.

LIC Salon Apparel. "About LIC," licsalonapparel.com, 2021, at: https://licsalonapparel.com/about-lic/. See also: https://web.archive.org/web/20230807154219/https://licsalonapparel.com/about-lic/.

Liepe-Levinson, Katherine. *Strip Show: Performances of Gender and Desire*. New York: Routledge, 2001.

Lilly, J. Robert and Richard A. Ball. "No-Tell Motel: The Management of Social Invisibility." *Urban Life* 10, no. 2 (1981): 179–98.

Locker, Joseph. "The Secret to Success of the Only Hooters in the UK and What It's Like to Work There." NottinghamshireLive, August 27, 2019, at: https://www.nottinghampost.com/news/nottingham-news/secret-success-only-hooters-uk-3249244.

Logan, John. "The Mounting Guerilla War Against the Reign of Walmart." *New Labor Forum* 23, no. 1 (2014): 22–9.

Logo Depot. "A Wichita Legacy of Excellence." logodepotweb.com, 2020, at: https://logodepotweb.com/our-story/. See also: https://web.archive.org/web/20230807155216/https://logodepotweb.com/our-story/.

Lundberg, Donald E. "Kemmons Wilson: The Key to Marketing Success Might Well Be Defined as Holiday Inns of America." *Cornell Hotel and Restaurant Administration Quarterly* 9, no. 4 (1969): 100–3.

Lupkin, Sydney. "Ebola in America: Timeline of the Deadly Virus." ABC News, November 17, 2014, at: https://abcnews.go.com/Health/ebola-america-timeline/story?id=26159719.

Lyth, Peter. "'Think of Her as Your Mother': Airline Advertising and the Stewardess in America, 1930–1980." *Journal of Transport History* 30, no. 1 (2009): 1–21.

Magee, Carl. 1935. "Coin Controlled Parking Meter." US Patent 2,118,318 filed May 13, 1935, and issued May 24, 1938.

Maguire, Edward R., Justin Nix, and Bradley A. Campbell. "A War on Cops? The Effects of Ferguson on the Number of US Police Officers Murdered in the Line of Duty." *Justice Quarterly* 34, no. 5 (2017): 739–58.

Mainella, Fran P. "Director's Order #9: Law Enforcement Program." US National Park Service, March 23, 2006, at: https://www.nps.gov/policy/DOrders/DOrder9.html.

Martinez, Al. "A Trend Watcher Watches a Trend." *Oakland Tribune* (Oakland, California), July 28, 1966.

McClendon, Emma. *Denim: Fashion's Frontier*. New Haven, Connecticut: Yale University Press, 2016.

McClintock, Anne. "Maid to Order: Commercial Fetishism and Gender Power." *Social Text* 37 (1993): 87–116.

McConnell, Miantae Metcalf. "Mary Field's Road to Freedom." In *Black Cowboys in the American West: On the Range, On the Stage, Behind the Badge*, edited by Bruce A. Glasrud and Michael N. Searles, 149–68. Norman, Oklahoma: University of Oklahoma Press, 2016.

McCormick, Stacie. "'I'm Every Woman': The Cultural Influence and Afterlife of Florence Johnston of *The Jeffersons*" In *The 25 Sitcoms that Changed Television: Turning Points in American Culture*, edited by Laura Westengard and Aaron Barlow, 94–107. Santa Barbara, California: ABC-CLIO, 2018.

McCracken, Grant. *Culture & Consumption: New Approaches to the Symbolic Character of Consumer Goods and Activities*. Bloomington, Indiana: Indiana University Press, 1988.

McGinley, Ann C. "Babes and Beefcake: Exclusive Hiring Arrangements and Sexy Dress Codes." *Duke Journal of Gender Law & Policy* 14, no. 4 (2007): 257–83.

McVeigh, Brian J. *Wearing Ideology: State, Schooling and Self-Presentation in Japan*. Oxford: Berg Publishers, 2000.

Mello, Michelle M., Eric B. Rimm, and David M. Studdert. "The McLawsuit: The Fast-Food Industry and Legal Accountability for Obesity." *Health Affairs* 22, no. 6 (2003): 207–16.

Michaels, David and Gregory R. Wagner. "Occupational Safety and Health Administration (OSHA) and Worker Safety During the COVID-19 Pandemic." *Journal of the American Medical Association* 324, no. 14 (2020): 1389–90.

Miller, Loren. "On Second Thought." *California Eagle* (Los Angeles, California), May 26, 1933.

Mills, Quincy T. *Cutting Along the Color Line: Black Barbers and Barber Shops in America*. Philadelphia, Pennsylvania: University of Pennsylvania Press, 2013.

Minnesota Historical Society. "About the House." James J. Hill House, 2021, at: https://www.mnhs.org/hillhouse/learn/house.

Minor, Katarzyna and Andy Heyes. "50 Shades of the Luxury Hospitality Industry." In *The Emerald Handbook of Luxury Management for Hospitality and Tourism*, edited by Anupama S. Kotur and Saurabh Kumar Dixit, 425–42. Bingley: Emerald Publishing Limited, 2022.

Miralles-Snow, Lauren. "An Exploration of Origins and Appropriations: How Workwear Has Traveled and Transformed." MA thesis, Temple University, Philadelphia, Pennsylvania, 2019, at: https://sites.temple.edu/emerge/files/2021/09/Vol4-Y-Miralles-Snow.pdf.

Misiewicz, Janina Lynn. "Conditional Recognition and the Popularization of the Contemporary Wellness Industry." MA thesis, Dartmouth College, Hanover, New Hampshire, 2021.

Mississippi Barber Board. "Title 30, Part 1801, Chapter 6: Barber Shops/Schools Regulations." State of Mississippi, 2018, at: http://www.msbarberboard.com/sites/default/files/00000504c.pdf.

Moler, Arthur B. *Standardized Barbers' Manual*, revised edition. Chicago, Illinois: National Educational Council of the Associated Master Barbers of America, 1928.

Morgado, Marcia A. "From Kitsch to Chic: The Transformation of Hawaiian Shirt Aesthetics." *Clothing and Textiles Research Journal* 21, no. 2 (2003): 75–88.

Muff, Janet. *Socialization, Sexism, and Stereotyping: Women's Issues in Nursing*. St. Louis, Missouri: Mosby, 1982.

Muggleton, David. *Inside Subculture: The Postmodern Meaning of Style*. Oxford: Berg Publications, 2000.

Mullinix, Aline. 1927. "Nurse's Cap." US Patent 1,668,331A filed June 23, 1927, and issued May 1, 1928.

National Archives. "Crest Uniform Company, New York, NY: Notice of Termination of Investigation." Federal Register, October, 22, 2002, at: https://www.federalregister.gov/documents/2002/10/22/02-26747/crest-uniform-company-new-york-ny-notice-of-termination-of-investigation.

National Association of Letter Carriers. "About NALC: Labor Ties." nalc.org, 2022, at: https://www.nalc.org/about/labor-ties. See also: https://web.archive.org/web/20230807173815/https://www.nalc.org/about/labor-ties.

National Association of Letter Carriers. "Looking the Part: The Letter Carrier Uniform." *The Postal Record* 133, no. 9 (2020): 20–1.

Naylor, David. *Great American Movie Theaters*. Washington, DC: Preservation Press, 1989.

New Hampshire Board of Barbering, Cosmetology and Esthetics. "302.07 Licensee." State of New Hampshire, 2016, at: http://gencourt.state.nh.us/rules/state_agencies/bar100-700.html.

Newton-Francis, Michelle and Salvador Vidal-Ortiz. "¡Más Que un Bocado! (More Than a Mouthful): Comparing Hooters in the United States and Columbia." In *Global Beauty, Local Bodies*, edited by Afshan Jafar and Erynn Masi de Casanova, 59–82. New York: Palgrave Macmillan, 2013.

Newton-Francis, Michelle and Gay Young. "Now Winging It at Hooters: Conventions for Producing a Cultural Object of Sexual Fantasy." *Poetics* 52 (2015): 1–17.

Nocker, W. "Evaluation of Occupational Clothing for Surgeons: Achieving Comfort and Avoiding Physiological Stress Through Suitable Gowns." In *Handbook of Medical Textiles*, edited by V. T. Bartels, 443–60. Cambridge: Woodhead Publishing, 2011.

Noel Asmar Uniforms. "Medical and Dental Uniforms." noelasmaruniforms.com, 2022, at: https://www.noelasmaruniforms.com/collections/industries-medical-dental-all. See also: https://web.archive.org/web/20230807173401/https://www.noelasmaruniforms.com/collections/medical-scrubs.

Nofri, Valeria. "The Aesthetics of Kitsch: From Versace to Prada." In *Fashion Through History: Costumes, Symbols, Communication*, volume 2, edited by Giovanna Motta and Antonello Biagini, 279–316. Newcastle upon Tyne: Cambridge Scholars Publishing, 2017.

Norman, Al. "Wal-Mart's 'Invisible Army' of Lobbyists." *Huffington Post*, September 21, 2013, at: https://www.huffpost.com/entry/walmart-lobbyists_b_3632526.

Nowak, Janie Brown. *The Forty-Seven Hundred: The Story of the Mount Sinai Hospital School of Nursing.* Canaan, New Hampshire: Phoenix Publishing, 1981.

Occupational Safety and Health Administration. "About OSHA." US Department of Labor, 2022, at: https://www.osha.gov/aboutosha#:~:text=OSHA's%20 Mission,%2C%20outreach%2C%20education%20and%20assistance.

Office of Size Standards, "SBA's Size Standards Methodology," Small Business Administration, April 2019, at: https://www.sba.gov/sites/default/files/2021-02/ SBA%20Size%20Standards%20Methodology%20April%2011%2C%202019-508.pdf.

Ogren, Kathy J. *The Jazz Revolution: Twenties America & the Meaning of Jazz.* Oxford: Oxford University Press, 1989.

Oharazeki, Kazuhiro. "Listening to the Voices of 'Other' Women in Japanese North America: Japanese Prostitutes and Barmaids in the American West, 1887–1920." *Journal of American Ethnic History* 32, no. 4 (2013): 5–40.

Oldenburg, Ray. *The Great Good Place: Cafés, Coffee Shops, Community Centers, Beauty Parlors, General Stores, Bars, Hangouts, and How They Get You Through the Day.* New York: Paragon House, 1989.

Oxford English Dictionary, "Livery, n.," *OED Online*, June 2021.

Palmer, Phyllis. *Domesticity and Dirt: Housewives and Domestic Servants in the United States, 1920–1945.* Philadelphia, Pennsylvania: Temple University Press, 1989.

Pappas, Nickolas. "Anti-Fashion: If not Fashion, Then What?" In *Philosophical Perspectives on Fashion*, edited by Giovanni Matteucci and Stefano Marino, 73–90. London: Bloomsbury Academic, 2017.

Pappas, Nickolas. *The Philosopher's New Clothes: The Theaetetus, the Academy, and Philosophy's Turn Against Fashion.* London: Taylor & Francis, 2015.

Paraskevas, Alexandros and Maureen Brookes. "Human Trafficking in Hotels: An 'Invisible' Threat for a Vulnerable Industry." *International Journal of Contemporary Hospitality Management* 30, no. 3 (2018): 1996–2014.

Park Ranger Division. "Policies and Procedures Manual." City of Los Angeles Department of Recreation and Parks, October 5, 2019, at: https://www.laparks.org/ sites/default/files/ranger/pdf/2020%20Manual%20for%20Web.pdf.

Parker, Kim, Juliana Menasce Horowitz, and Rachel Minkin, "How the Coronavirus Outbreak Has—and Hasn't—Changed the Way Americans Work." Pew Research Center, December 9, 2020, at: https://www.pewresearch.org/social-trends/2020/12/09/how-the-coronavirus-outbreak-has-and-hasn't-changed-the-way-americans-work/.

Parrish, Sabine. "Competitive Coffee Making and the Crafting of the Ideal Barista." *Gastronomica: The Journal for Food Studies* 20, no. 2 (2020): 79–90.

Partridge, Brad. "Fairness and Performance-Enhancing Swimsuits at the 2009 Swimming World Championships: The 'Asterisk' Championships." *Sports, Ethics and Philosophy* 5, no. 1 (2011): 63–74.

Pastoureau, Michel. *The Devil's Cloth: A History of Stripes*, translated by Jody Gladding. New York: Columbia University Press, 2001.

Paul, John and Michael L. Birzer. "Images of Power: An Analysis of the Militarization of Police Uniforms and Messages of Service." *Free Inquiry in Creative Sociology* 32, no. 2 (2004): 121–8.

Paules, Greta Foff. *Dishing It Out: Power and Resistance Among Waitresses in a New Jersey Restaurant*. Philadelphia: Temple University Press, 1991.

Pennsylvania Farmer. *Book of Patterns*. New York: Pennsylvania Farmer Pattern Department, New York, c. early 1940s.

Peterson, Hayley. "Wal-Mart Employees Explain Why the New Dress Code is So Infuriating." *Business Insider*, September 5, 2014, at: https://www.businessinsider.com/wal-mart-employees-protest-dress-code-2014-9.

Pfanner, Toni. "Military Uniforms and the Law of War." *International Review of the Red Cross* 86, no. 853 (2004): 93–124.

Pickhartz, Eric Michael. *Look Good, Play Good: The World of American Sports Uniforms*. Austin, Texas: University of Texas Press, 2011.

Pizza Hut, Inc. "Drive for Dough." pizzahut.com, 2022, at: https://jobs.pizzahut.com/restaurants/drivers.php?gclid=Cj0KCQjwxtSSBhDYARIsAEn0thT2aa0Zkpk Hjd3H0rvY6lNB2jNxvP93WjOoH8bKv9b2H1Gka48F6FcaAuUsEALw_wcB#hero.

Polhemus, Ted. *Street Style: From Sidewalk to Catwalk*. London: Thames & Hudson, 1994.

Polhemus, Ted and Lynn Procter. *Fashion & Anti-Fashion: Anthropology of Clothing and Adornment*. London: Thames & Hudson, 1978.

Poling-Kempes, Lesley. *The Harvey Girls: Women Who Opened the West*. New York: Marlowe & Company, 1991.

Poplin, Irene Schuessler. "Nursing Uniforms: Romantic Idea, Functional Attire, or Instrument of Social Change?" *Nursing History Review* 2 (1994): 153–67.

Porter, Eric. "'A Black Future in the Air Industry?': Liberation and Complicity at San Francisco International Airport." *California History* 97, no. 2 (2020): 88–111.

Post, Emily. "Household—Dressing the Butler and the Maid." *The Sun* (Baltimore, Maryland), February 2, 1936, SC6.

Post, Tom. "Mr. Uniform." *Forbes*, November 16, 1998, 84.

Postal Uniforms Direct. "Frequently Asked Questions." postaluniformsdirect.com, 2022, at: https://www.postaluniformsdirect.com/Pages/FAQS.

Poundstone, William. "Rudi Gernreich and the Monokini." Los Angeles County Museum on Fire, July 15, 2019, at: http://lacmaonfire.blogspot.com/2019/07/rudi-gernreich-and-monokini.html.

Price, Kim. "'Keeping the Dancers in Check': The Gendered Organization of Stripping Work in the Lion's Den." *Gender & Society* 22, no. 3 (2008): 367–89.

Prince. "Prince – 1999 (Official Music Video)." YoutTube, 1982, at: https://www.youtube.com/watch?v=rblt2EtFfC4.

Pullman Company. *Car Service Rules of the Operating Department of Pullman's Palace Car Company*. Chicago, Ilinois: W.H. Pottinger, 1893.

Purnell, Carolyn. *Blue Jeans*. London: Bloomsbury Academic, 2023.

Radbill, Samuel X. "The Barber Surgeons Among the Early Dutch and Swedes Along the Delaware." *Bulletin of the Institute of the History of Medicine* 4, no. 9 (1936): 718–44.

Rall, Denise N., ed. *Fashion and War in Popular Culture*. Bristol: Intellect, 2014.

Randall, Frank Alfred and John D. Randall. *History of the Development of Building Construction in Chicago*, second edition. Champaign, Illinois: University of Illinois Press, 1999.

RB Apparel. "Home Page." rbapparel.com, 2022, at: https://www.rbapparel.com/bwlogoshop/default.asp.

Rennison, Callie Marie and Mary Dodge. "Police Impersonation: Pretenses and Predators." *American Journal of Criminal Justice* 37 (2012): 505–22.

Reverby, Susan. *Ordered to Care: The Dilemma of American Nursing, 1850–1945*. Cambridge: Cambridge University Press, 1987.

Ribeiro, Aileen. *Dress in Eighteenth Century Europe*. New Haven, Connecticut: Yale University Press, 2002.

Richards, Harriette and Fabio Mattioli. "Fashioning Founders: Dress and Gender in the Entrepreneurial Ecosystem." *Gender, Work & Organization* 28, no. 4 (2021): 1363–78.

Rider, Elizabeth. "Pink Scrubs." *British Medical Journal*, 336, no. 7638 (2008): 277.

Rigakos, George. *Nightclub: Bouncers, Risk, and the Spectacle of Consumption*. Montreal: McGill-Queen's University Press, 2008.

Ritschel, Chelsea. "Hooters Amends Uniform Policy After Employees Condemn 'Disturbing' New Shorts." *Yahoo! News*, October 17, 2021, at: https://www.yahoo.com/news/hooters-amends-uniform-policy-employees-154321145.html. See also: https://web.archive.org/web/20230807184514/https://www.yahoo.com/news/hooters-amends-uniform-policy-employees-154321145.html.

Ritzer, George. *The McDonaldization of Society*, New Century edition. Thousand Oaks, California: Pine Forge Press, 2000.

Roberts, Sam. "Carol Doda, Pioneer of Topless Entertainment, Dies at 78." *New York Times*, November 11, 1985, at: https://www.nytimes.com/2015/11/12/arts/dance/carol-doda-pioneer-of-topless-entertainment-dies-at-78.html.

Roberts, Tomi-Ann, Rachel M. Calogero, and Sarah J. Gervais. "Objectification Theory: Continuing Contributions to Feminist Psychology." In *APA Handbook of the Psychology of Women: History, Theory, and Battlegrounds*, edited by Cheryl B. Travis, Jacquelyn W. White, Alexandra Rutherford, Wendi S. Williams, Sarah L. Cook, and Karen Fraser Whyche, 249–71. Washington, DC: American Psychological Association, 2018.

Robinson, Dwight. "The Rules of Fashion Cycles." *Harvard Business Review* 1, no. 4 (1958): 62.

Robinson, James O. "The Barber-Surgeons of London." *Archives of Surgery* 119, no. 10 (1984): 1171–5.

Robinson, Thomas N., Dina L.G. Borzekowski, Donna M. Matheson, and Helena C. Kraemer. "Effects of Fast Food Branding on Young Children's Taste Preferences." *Archives of Pediatric Adolescent Medicine* 161, no. 8 (2007): 792–7.

Robson, Stephani K.A. "Turning the Tables: The Psychology of Design for High-volume Restaurants." *Cornell Hotel and Restaurant Administration Quarterly* 40, no. 3 (1999): 56–63.

Rogers, Everett M. *Diffusion of Innovations.* New York: The Free Press, 1962.

Rogers, Nate. "'So Elegant, So Sensual': Chris Farley Should Be Remembered for His Grace, Not His Falls." *The Ringer,* March 31, 2020, at: https://www.theringer.com/tv/2020/3/31/21200801/chris-farley-chippendales-patrick-swayze-skating-snl-sketch.

Rogers, Nicole. "Law and the Fool." *Law Text Culture* 14, no. 1 (2010): 286–309.

Romero, Mary. *Maid in the U.S.A.* New York: Routledge, 1992.

Root, Stephen C. "The Meaning of Franchise Under the California Franchise Investment Law: A Definition in Search of a Concept." *McGeorge Law Review* 30, no. 4 (1999): 1163–220.

Ross, Andrew. "No-Collar Labour in America's 'New Economy'." *Socialist Register* 37 (2001): 77–87.

Roth, Julius A. "Ritual and Magic in the Control of Contagion." *American Sociological Review* 22, no. 3 (1957): 310–14.

Rotramel, Ariella, Megan Tracy, and Emma Coles. "Weighing the Value of Femininity: Casino Cocktail Personal Appearance Standards." *Fat Studies* (2021). Doi: 10.1080/21604851.2021.2009682.

Ryan, Kathleen M. "Uniform Matters: Fashion Design in World War II Women's Recruitment." *Journal of American Culture* 37, no. 4 (2014): 419–29.

Sachdeva, Ishita and Suhsma Goel. "Retail Store Environment and Customer Experience: A Paradigm." *Journal of Fashion Marketing and Management* 19, no. 3 (2015): 290–8.

Saelinger, Tracy. "Out with the Red, in with the Gray: See McDonald's New Uniforms." *Today,* April 24, 2017, at: https://www.today.com/food/mcdonald-s-unveils-new-uniforms-t110736.

Salti, Rasha. "Do Not Go Gentle into That Good Night: Film Festivals, Pandemic, Aftermath." *Film Quarterly* 74, no. 1 (2020): 88–96.

San Francisco Airport Commission. "Fashion in Flight: A History of Airline Uniform Design." SFO Museum, 2016, at: https://www.sfomuseum.org/exhibitions/fashion-flight-history-airline-uniform-design.

Sandell, Scott. "L.A.'s Answer to the Doorman." *Los Angeles Times,* October 16, 2003, at: https://www.latimes.com/local/la-hm-concierge16oct16203418-story.html.

Sandy, Larissa, ed. *Women and Sex Work in Cambodia: Blood, Sweat and Tears.* London: Routledge, 2014.

Sanna, Piera, Alfonso Sollami, Giuseppina Nicosia, Rita Bruna Dicembrino, Rebecca Gandolfi, Flavia Primosa, Rachele La Sala, and Giuseppe Marletta. "The Nurses' Uniform in Pediatrics, The Opinion of Children and Nurses." *Acta Biomedica* 91, supplement 2 (2020): 67–76.

Santino, Jack. *Miles of Smiles, Years of Struggle: Stories of Black Pullman Porters.* Champaign, Illinois: University of Illinois Press, 1991.

Saturday Night Live. "Chippendales Audition." YouTube, 2019, at: https://www.youtube.com/watch?v=stqG2ihMvP0.

Savikas, Victor and Fred Shandling. "Credit Cards: A Survey of the Bank Card Revolution and Applicability of the Uniform Commercial Code." *DePaul Law Review* 16, no. 2 (1967): 389–408.

Scaturro, Sarah. "From Combat to Couture: Camouflage in Fashion." MA thesis, Fashion Institute of Technology, New York.

Scott, Erin Elizabeth. "Mississippi Motoring: Mom and Pops and Entrepreneurs." MA thesis, University of Mississippi, 2014.

Scott III, Robert. "Fill 'er Up: A Study of Statewide Self-Service Gasoline Station Bans." *Challenge* 50, no. 5 (2007): 103–14.

Scripps Howard News Service. "Scrub Suit Dispensers Stop Thefts." *The Salina Journal* (Salina, Kansas), December 24, 1987.

Scull, Maren T. "Reinforcing Gender Roles at the Male Strip Show: A Qualitative Analysis of Men Who Dance for Women." *Deviant Behavior* 34, no. 7 (2013): 557–78.

Segrave, Kerry. *Policewomen: A History*. Jefferson, North Carolina: McFarland & Company, Inc., 2014.

Segrave, Kerry. *Vending Machines: An American Social History*. Jefferson, North Carolina: McFarland & Company, 2003.

SFO Museum. *Fashion in Flight: A History of Airline Uniform Design*. San Francisco, California: San Francisco Airports Commission, 2020.

Shannon, Bill. "Sheetz Pulls Controversial 'Smile Policy' From Handbook." *The Hill*, February 2, 2023, at: https://thehill.com/homenews/3840323-sheetz-pulls-controversial-smile-policy-from-handbook/.

Shapiro, Sidney A. and Randy Rabinowitz. "Voluntary Regulatory Compliance in Theory and Practice: The Case of OSHA." *Administrative Law Review* 52, no. 1 (2000): 97–156.

Sherman, Erik. "How Wal-Mart's 'Dress Code' Costs Employees." *Forbes*, September 8, 2014, at: https://www.forbes.com/sites/eriksherman/2014/09/08/how-walmarts-dress-code-costs-employees/?sh=1db6aea07e00.

Sherman, Harry M. "The Green Operating Room at St. Luke's Hospital." *California State Journal of Medicine* 12, no. 5 (1914): 181–3.

Sides, Pat. "Shane Uniform Company." *The City-County Observer* (Evansville, Indiana), December 10, 2018, at: https://city-countyobserver.com/shane-uniform-company/.

Simmel, Georg. "Fashion." *International Quarterly* 10 (1904): 130–55.

Simon, Joshua and Michael Mamp. "'Nostalgic Elegance': The Enduring Style of the Gibson Girl." *Dress* 47, no. 1 (2021): 61–77.

Smith, Christian. "Second Hooters Restaurant Approved for UK Despite Backlash." *The Drinks Business*, February 16, 2022, at: https://www.thedrinksbusiness.com/2022/02/second-hooters-restaurant-approved-for-uk-despite-backlash/.

Smith, Clarissa. "Shiny Chests and Heaving G-Strings: A Night Out with the Chippendales," *Sexualities* 5, no. 1 (2022): 67–89.

Smith, Nicole. "Truly Integrating Volunteers and Interns into Your Organization." Tessitura Network, July 31, 2019, at: https://www.tessituranetwork.com/Items/Articles/Innovator-Series/2019/Nicole-Smith. See also: https://web.archive.org/web/20230807154411/https://www.tessituranetwork.com/Items/Articles/Innovator-Series/2019/Nicole-Smith.

Smith, Robert Emmett. "The Development and Impact of the Parking Meter Before World War II." MA thesis, Oklahoma State University, 1960.

Smoot, Cynthia. "Terra Saunders brings Waitressville to CNBC's Crowd Rules." *Oh So Cynthia*, May 28, 2013, at: https://www.ohsocynthia.com/2013/05/terra-saunders-brings-waitressville-to.html. See also: https://web.archive.org/web/20230807184801/https://www.ohsocynthia.com/2013/05/terra-saunders-brings-waitressville-to.html.

Snavely, Timothy N. "A Brief Economic Analysis of the Looming Nursing Shortage in the United States." *Nursing Economics* 34, no. 2 (2016): 98–100.

Snow, Robert L. *Policewomen Who Made History: Breaking Through the Ranks.* Lanham, Maryland: Rowman & Littlefield, 2010.

Splint, Sarah Field. *The Art of Cooking and Serving.* Cincinnati, Ohio: Proctor & Gamble, 1929.

Sprague, Karisa "Express Yourself: Walmart Introduces Relaxed Dress Guidelines in Stores," Walmart, May 30, 2018, https://corporate.walmart.com/newsroom/business/20180530/express-yourself-walmart-introduces-relaxed-dress-guidelines-in-stores. See also: https://web.archive.org/web/20230807185433/https://corporate.walmart.com/newsroom/business/20180530/express-yourself-walmart-introduces-relaxed-dress-guidelines-in-storesStallard, Dan. "Esprit de Corps: Moral and Force Preservation." *Marine Corps Gazette* (2018): 78–82, at: https://www.hqmc.marines.mil/Portals/61/Users/254/50/4350/Esprit%20de%20Corps_Morale_Force%20Preservation_Stallard_Gazzette_April%2018.pdf.

Stanton, Robert. "Director's Order #43: Uniform Program." US National Park Service, October 2000, at: https://www.nps.gov/policy/DOrders/DOrder43.htm.

Starbucks Corporation. "Starbucks Creative Expression: Color," starbucks.com, 2020, at: https://creative.starbucks.com/color/. See also: https://web.archive.org/web/20230807182840/https://creative.starbucks.com/color/.

Starbucks Corporation. "Starbucks Dress Code Lookbook." starbucks.com, 2019, 2, at: https://stories.starbucks.com/wp-content/uploads/2019/01/Dress_Code_Look_Book_-_US_English.pdf.

Stark, Evan. *Coercive Control: The Entrapment of Women in Personal Life.* Oxford: Oxford University Press, 2009.

State Board of Barber Examiners. "Amendment to Rule 023.00.92-001," State of Arkansas, 2018, at: http://170.94.37.152/REGS/023.00.18-002P-18172.pdf.

State of Texas. "Title 16, Part 4, Chapter 82, Rule §82.70." Texas Administrative Code, 2020, at: https://texreg.sos.state.tx.us/public/readtac$ext.TacPage?sl=R&app=9&p_dir=&p_rloc=&p_tloc=&p_ploc=&pg=1&p_tac=&ti=16&pt=4&ch=82&rl=70.

Stearns, David L. *Electronic Value Exchange: Origins of the Visa Electronic Payment System*. London: Springer, 2011.

Steele, Valerie. "Dressing for Work." In *Men and Women: Dressing the Part*, edited by Claudia Kidwell and Valerie Steele, 64–91. Washington, DC: Smithsonian Institution Press, 1989.

Steele, Valerie. *Fetish: Fashion, Sex, and Power*. New York: Oxford University Press, 1996.

Steil, Tim. *Fantastic Filling Stations*. Saint Paul, Minnesota: MBI Publishing Company, 2002.

Stephenson, Kate. "Uniform Adoption in English Public Schools, 1830–1930." In *Uniform: Clothing and Discipline in the Modern World*, edited by Jane Tynan and Lisa Godson, 67–86. London: Bloomsbury Visual Arts, 2019.

Sterling, Greg. "Report: Nike's Sales Jump 31% in Wake of Kaepernick Ad Campaign." MarTech, September 11, 2018, at: https://martech.org/report-nikes-sales-jump-31-in-wake-of-kaepernick-ad-campaign/. See also: https://web.archive.org/web/20230807185550/https://martech.org/report-nikes-sales-jump-31-in-wake-of-kaepernick-ad-campaign/.

Stewart, Jude. *Patternalia: An Unconventional History of Polka Dots, Stripes, Plaid, Camouflage, & Other Graphic Patterns*. London: Bloomsbury Academic, 2015.

Strawn, Susan, Jane Farrell-Beck, and Ann R. Hemken. "Bib Overalls: Function and Fashion." *Dress* 32, no. 1 (2005): 43–55.

Student Conservation Association. "Everything You Wanted to Know about Park Rangers… But Were Afraid to Ask." thesca.org, 2021, at: https://www.thesca.org/connect/blog/everything-you-wanted-know-about-park-rangers…-were-afraid-ask. See also: https://web.archive.org/web/20230807180604/https://www.thesca.org/connect/blog/everything-you-wanted-to-know-about-park-rangers-but-were-afraid-to-ask/.

Styles, John. "Involuntary Consumers? Servants and Their Clothes in Eighteenth-Century England." *Textile History* 33, no. 1 (2002): 9–21.

Summers, Clyde W. "Employment at Will in the United States: The Divine Right of Employers." *University of Pennsylvania Journal of Labor and Employment Law* 3, no. 1 (2000): 65–86.

Summers, Sandy. *Saving Lives: Why the Media's Portrayal of Nurses Puts All of Us At Risk*. New York: Kaplan Publications, 2010.

Szasz, Shermalayne Southard. "The Tyranny of Uniforms." In *Socialization, Sexism, and Stereotyping: Women's Issues in Nursing*, edited by Janet Muff, 397–401. St. Louis, Missouri: Mosby, 1982.

Taco John's International. "Join our Team!" tacojohns.com, 2022, at: https://careers.tacojohns.com. See also: https://web.archive.org/web/20230807183532/https://careers.tacojohns.com/.

Target Corporation. "Let's Hear It For the Stores! Target Store Team Members Can Now Rock Denim All Week Long." target.com, February 14, 2019, at: https://corporate.target.com/article/2019/02/employee-dress-code-policy See also: https://web.

archive.org/web/20230807150612/https://corporate.target.com/article/2019/02/
    employee-dress-code-policy.

Tarlo, Emma and Annelies Moors, eds. *Islamic Fashion and Anti-Fashion: New
    Perspectives from Europe and North America.* London: Bloomsbury Academic, 2013.

Terra's Dancewear and Dallaswear LLC. 2011. "Breastaurant Uniforms." US Trademark
    85,273,851, filed March 22, 2011, and issued November 8, 2011.

Terra's Dancewear and Dallaswear LLC. 2015. "Dream Corset." US Trademark 86, 601,
    461, filed April 17, 2015, abandoned February 23, 2016.

Terra's Dancewear and Dallaswear LLC, 2013. "Serving Up Style." US Trademark
    85,899,897, filed April 10, 2013, and issued November 19, 2013.

Terra's Dancewear and Dallaswear LLC. 2013. "Waitressville." US Trademark 85,899,895,
    filed April 10, 2013, and issued November 19, 2013.

Thompson, Derek. "Workism is Making Americans Miserable." *The Atlantic,* February
    24, 2019, at: https://www.theatlantic.com/ideas/archive/2019/02/religion-workism-
    making-americans-miserable/583441/.

Timmons, Edward J. and Robert J. Thornton. "The Licensing of Barbers in the USA."
    British Journal of Industrial Relations 48, no. 4 (2010): 740–57.

Tirado, Linda. *Hand to Mouth: Living in Bootstrap America.* New York: Berkley Books, 2015.

Tonchi, Stefano. "Military Style." In *The Berg Companion to Fashion,* edited by Valerie
    Steele, 507–8. Oxford: Bloomsbury Academic, 2010.

Toolan, Maria. "Say No to Hooters Liverpool." Change.org, 2022, at: https://www.change.
    org/p/liverpool-city-council-say-no-to-hooters-liverpool?utm_source=share_
    petition&utm_medium=custom_url&recruited_by_id=1c6078d0-d5ed-11e8-b7c0-
    352bdcade225.

Toon, Elizabeth A. "Managing the Conduct of Individual Life: Public Health Education and
    American Public Health, 1910 to 1940." PhD diss., University of Pennsylvania, 1998.

Top Hat Imagewear. "Front Desk Collection: Style ID FD358." tophatimagewear.com,
    2022, at: https://tophatimagewear.com/collections/front-desk. See also: https://web.
    archive.org/web/20230807181958/https://tophatimagewear.com/collections/
    front-desk.

Toscani, Oliviero and Olivier Saillard. *Workwear: Work Fashion Seduction.* Milan:
    Rizzoli International, 2009.

Tye, Larry. *Rising From the Rails: Pullman Porters and the Making of the Black Middle
    Class.* New York: Henry Holt, 2004.

Tynan, Jane. *Trench Coat.* London: Bloomsbury Academic, 2022.

Tynan, Jane and Suzannah Biernoff. "Making and Remaking the Civilian Soldier: The
    World War I Photographs of Horace Nicholls." *Journal of War & Culture Studies* 5,
    no. 3 (2013): 277–93.

Uniform Retailers Association. "Homepage." uniformretailers.org, 2021, at: https://
    uniformretailers.org/aws/URA/pt/sp/home_page. See also: https://web.archive.org/
    web/20230807151749/https://www.uniformretailers.org/aws/URA/pt/sp/home_
    page.

Upton, Charles L. "Los Angeles Pullman Porters Should Have Locker Space for Uniforms." *California Eagle* (Los Angeles), September 5, 1930.

US Bureau of Labor Statistics. "Employment, Hours, and Earnings from the Current Employment Statistics." bls.gov, July 2, 2021, at: https://data.bls.gov/timeseries/CES0700000001?amp%253bdata_tool=XGtable&output_view=data&include_graphs=true.

US Bureau of Labor Statistics. "Food and Beverage Serving and Related Workers." bls.gov, September 8, 2021, at: https://www.bls.gov/ooh/food-preparation-and-serving/food-and-beverage-serving-and-related-workers.htm#tab-1.

US Bureau of Labor Statistics. "Occupational Outlook Handbook: Tellers." bls.gov, 2021, at: https://www.bls.gov/ooh/office-and-administrative-support/tellers.htm.

US Bureau of Labor Statistics. "The De-Licensing of Occupations in the United States." *Monthly Labor Review*, 2015, at: https://www.bls.gov/opub/mlr/2015/article/the-de-licensing-of-occupations-in-the-united-states.htm.

US Census Bureau. "The Number of Firms and Establishments, Employment, and Annual Payroll by State, Industry, and Enterprise Employment Size." census.gov, 2018, at: https://www.census.gov/data/tables/2018/econ/susb/2018-susb-annual.html.

US Food and Drug Administration. "N95 Respirators, Surgical Masks, Face Masks, and Barrier Face Coverings," Medical Devices, September 15, 2021, at: https://www.fda.gov/medical-devices/personal-protective-equipment-infection-control/n95-respirators-surgical-masks-face-masks-and-barrier-face-coverings.

US Government Accountability Office. "Federal Prison Industries: Actions Needed to Evaluate Program Effectiveness." gao.gov, July 2020, at: https://www.gao.gov/assets/gao-20-505.pdf.

US Government Accountability Office. "The Role of the GAO in Assisting Congressional Oversight." gao.gov, 2002, at: https://www.gao.gov/products/gao-02-816t.

US General Accountability Office. "US Postal Service: Information on Centralized Procurement of Uniforms, Report #B-279075." gao.gov, January 28, 1998, at: https://www.gao.gov/assets/ggd-98-58r.pdf.

US Internal Revenue Service. "Identifying Full-time Employees." irs.gov, 2021, at: https://www.irs.gov/affordable-care-act/employers/identifying-full-time-employees#:~:text=Definition%20of%20Full%2DTime%20Employee,hours%20of%20service%20per%20month.

US Office of Personnel Management. "Classification & Qualifications: Park Ranger Series, 0025." opm.gov, 2022, at: https://www.opm.gov/policy-data-oversight/classification-qualifications/general-schedule-qualification-standards/0000/park-ranger-series-0025/.

US Postal Service. "930: Work Clothes and Uniforms." *Employee and Labor Relations Manual*, 2022, at: https://about.usps.com/manuals/elm/html/elmc9_009.htm#ep96853.

US Postal Service. "Letter Carriers' Uniform: Overview." usps.com, 2002, at: https://about.usps.com/who-we-are/postal-history/letter-carrier-uniform-overview.pdf.

US Postal Service. "Star Routes." usps.com, 2007, at: https://about.usps.com/who-we-are/postal-history/star-routes.pdf.

US Postal Service. "Updated Uniform Allowance Vendor Listing." usps.gov, 2019, at: https://liteblue.usps.gov/humanresources/ourworkforce/uniforms/pdf/updated-uniform-allowance-vendor-listing-may2019.pdf.

Van Cleave, Kendra. "'A Style All Her Own': Fashion, Clothing Practices, and Female Community at Smith College, 1920–1929." *Dress* 32, no. 1 (2005): 56–65.

van Hoof, Joep. *Military Uniforms in the Netherlands, 1752–1800.* Vienna: Militaria, 2011.

Vanderbilt, Amy. "Amy's Etiquette: Differences Between Train, Pullman Conductors Told." *The Wichita Beacon* (Wichita, Kansas), November 14, 1956.

Vantoch, Victoria. *The Jet Sex: Airline Stewardesses and the Making of an American Icon.* Philadelphia, Pennsylvania: University of Pennsylvania Press, 2013.

Veblen, Thorstein. *The Theory of the Leisure Class: An Economic Study of Institutions.* New York: The Macmillan Company, 1899.

Vera Bradley. "About Us." verabradley.com, 2022, at: https://verabradley.com/pages/about-us. See also: https://web.archive.org/web/20230807173016/https://verabradley.com/pages/about-us

Verma, Santosh K., Wen-Ruey Chang, Theodore K. Courtney, David A. Lombardi, Yueng-Hsiang Huang, Melanye J. Brennan, Murray A. Mittleman, and Melissa J. Perry. "Workers' Experience of Slipping in US Limited-Service Restaurants." *Journal of Occupational and Environmental Hygiene* 7, no. 9 (2010): 491–500.

VF Imagewear. "LMA Online Uniform System." vfimagewear.com, 2022, at: https://uniforms.vfimagewear.com/vfweb/rwdprogram/coms/index_lma.htm.

von Rauch, Elsa. "The Servant Girl for the Well-to-Do Family." *Washington Post*, June 9, 1901.

Wage and Hour Division. "Fact Sheet #15: Tipped Employees Under the Fair Labor Standards Act (FLSA)." US Department of Labor, 2018, at: https://www.dol.gov/agencies/whd/fact-sheets/15-flsa-tipped-employees.

Walker, Rob. "Branding Operation: Reference a Fictional TV Hospital Drama in Real-Life Hospital Scrubs." *New York Times*, October 3, 2010.

Wallace, Margaret. "Queries Raised Over Uniforms for the Maids." *Washington Post*, December 6, 1936.

Walter, Brenda S. Gardenour. "Pricked, Probed and Possessed: Medical Pornography and the Birth of the Fetish Clinic." In *Pornographies: Critical Positions*, edited by Katherine Harrison and Cassandra A. Ogden, 264–86. Chester: University of Chester Press, 2018.

Ward, L. Monique. "Media and Sexualization: State of Empirical Research, 1995–2015." *Journal of Sex Research* 53, no. 4/5 (2016): 560–77.

Weatherford, Doris. *American Women During World War II: An Encyclopedia.* New York: Routledge, 2010.

Wedemeyer, Dee. "In Fashion for Doormen: Few Frills, Some Fray." *New York Times*, June 25, 1978.

Weinberg, Charles B., Cord Otten, Barak Orbach, Jordi McKenzie, Ricard Gil, Darlene C. Chisholm, and Suman Basuroy. "Technological Change and Managerial Challenges in the Movie Theater Industry." *Journal of Cultural Economics* 45 (2021): 239–62.

Weissinger, Sandra E. and Dwayne A. Mack, eds. *Law Enforcement in the Age of Black Lives Matter: Policing Black and Brown Bodies.* Lanham, Maryland: Lexington Books, 2021.

Wendy's. "Crew Member." wendys.com, 2021, at: https://wendys-careers.com/job-search/posting/Crew-Member/31598/, job opening in Ammon, Idaho.

Wenner, Lawrence A.. "In Search of the Sports Bar: Masculinity, Alcohol, Sports, and the Mediation of Public Space." In *Sport and Postmodern Times*, edited by Geneviève Rail, 301–32. Albany, New York: State University of New York Press, 1998.

Whang, Mikyoung and Sherry Haar. "Nelly Don's 1916 Pink Gingham Apron Frock: An Illustration of the Middle-Class American Housewife's Shifting Role from Producer to Consumer." *Fashion and Textiles* 1, no. 18 (2014). Doi: 10.1186/s40691-014-0018-1.

Wharton, Amy S. "The Sociology of Emotional Labor." *Annual Review of Sociology* 35 (2009): 146–65.

Wheeler, Claribel A. "Hospital Helpers." *The Modern Hospital* 16, no. 2 (1921): 153–4.

White, Eugene Nelson. "Before the Glass-Steagall Act: An Analysis of the Investment Banking Activities of National Banks." *Explorations in Economic History* 23, no. 1 (1986): 33–55.

White, Ryan Curran. "What's the Story of the Iconic National Park Service Ranger 'Flat Hat'?" Golden Gate National Parks Conservancy, June 21, 2019, at: https://www.parksconservancy.org/gateways-article/what-is-story-iconic-nps-ranger-flat-hat. See also: https://web.archive.org/web/20230807180926/https://www.parksconservancy.org/gateways-article/what-is-story-iconic-nps-ranger-flat-hat.

White, William J. and Lisa A. Emili. "Purification and Translation in Public Memory: 'Healing the Landscape' at the Flight 93 National Memorial." *Emotion, Space and Society* 29 (2018): 32–47.

Wietschorke, Jens. "Caretakers, Doormen, Concierges: Negotiating Intermediate Spaces." In *The Routledge History of the Domestic Sphere in Europe*, edited by Joachim Eibach and Margareth Lanzinger, 397–414. Routledge: New York, 2010.

Williams, Christine L. and Catherine Connell, "'Looking Good and Sounding Right': Aesthetic Labor and Social Inequality in the Retail Industry," *Work and Occupations* 37, no. 3 (2010): 349–77.

Wilson, Anne V. and Silvia Bellezza. "Consumer Minimalism." *Journal of Consumer Research* 48, no. 5 (2022): 796–816.

Wilson, Elizabeth. *Adorned in Dreams: Fashion and Modernity.* Berkeley, California: University of California Press, 1985.

Wilson, Kemmons. "How to Make Your Guests Happy." *Business Perspectives* 12, no. 4 (2000): 32.

Wilson, Mark R. *The Business of Civil War: Military Mobilization and the State, 1861–1865.* Baltimore, Maryland: Johns Hopkins University Press, 2006.

Witzel, Michael Karl. *The American Drive-In*. Osceola, Wisconsin: Motorbooks International, 1994.

Wolf, Tom. "Executive Order: Equal Employment Opportunity." Commonwealth of Pennsylvania Governor's Office, April 7, 2016, at: https://www.oa.pa.gov/Policies/eo/Documents/2016_04.pdf.

Workman, Jane E. and Seung-Hee Lee. "What Do We Know about Fashion Adoption Groups? A Proposal and Test of a Model of Fashion Adoption." *International Journal of Consumer Studies* 41, no. 1 (2017): 61–9.

Workman, R. Bryce. *National Park Service Uniforms: Breeches, Blouses and Skirts (1918–1991)*. Harpers Ferry, West Virginia: National Park Service, 1998.

Workman, R. Bryce. *National Park Service Uniforms: In Search of an Identity (1872–1920)*. Harpers Ferry, West Virginia: National Park Service, 1994.

Workwear Outfitters. "Who We Are." wwof.com, 2022, at: https://test.wwof.com/who-we-are. See also: https://web.archive.org/web/20230807181025/https://test.wwof.com/who-we-are.

Wyche, Steve. "Colin Kaepernick Explains Why He Sat During National Anthem." *NFL Media*, August 27, 2016, at: https://web.archive.org/web/20160827165405/http://www.nfl.com/news/story/0ap3000000691077/article/colin-kaepernick-explains-protest-of-national-anthem.

Wyndham Hotels & Resorts. "Our Brands." wyndhamhotels.com, 2022, at: https://www.wyndhamhotels.com/wyndham-rewards/our-brands.

Yap, Desmond. "Phnom Penh's Riverside District." *Retalk Asia*, April 7, 2017, at: https://www.retalkasia.com/blog/desmond-yap/phnom-penhs-riverside-district/phnom-penh/riverside. See also: https://web.archive.org/web/20230807185244/https://www.retalkasia.com/blog/desmond-yap/phnom-penhs-riverside-district/phnom-penh/riverside.

Young, Dan C. "A Card to Buyers of Stylish and Artistic Clothing," *St. Louis Post-Dispatch* (St. Louis, Missouri), March 24, 1880, 4.

Zakaras, Alex. *The Roots of American Individualism: Political Myth in the Age of Jackson*. Princeton, New Jersey: Princeton University Press, 2022.

Zemeckis, Robert, director. *Back to the Future*. Universal Pictures, 1985.

Zhang, Elissa J., Lucy P. Aitchison, Nicole Phillips, Ramon Z. Shaban, and Andrew W. Kam. "Protecting the Environment from Plastic PPE." *British Medical Journal* 372, no. 109 (2021). Doi: 10.1136/bmj.n109.

Zhang, Y., H. P. Wang, and Y. H. Chen. "Capillary Effect of Hydrophobic Polyester Fiber Bundles with Noncircular Cross Section." *Journal of Applied Polymer Science* 102 (2006): 1405–12.

Zippia. "McDonald's Dress Code." zippia.com, 2022, at: https://www.zippia.com/mcdonald-s-careers-7238/dress-code/.

Index

www.ingramcontent.com/pod-product-compliance
Lightning Source LLC
Chambersburg PA
CBHW071841270326
41929CB00013B/2064